The Land Boomers

The Land Boomers

The Complete Illustrated History

Michael Cannon

Melbourne University Press

First published 1966
First paperback edition, with corrections, 1967
Reprinted 1973, 1977, 1986
First hardback edition reprinted by Thomas Nelson 1976
Second revised edition by Heritage Publications 1972
Reprinted by Lloyd O'Neil 1986
Second paperback edition 1995

Printed in Hong Kong by
South China Printing Co. (1988) Ltd. for
Melbourne University Press, Carlton, Victoria 3053

National Library of Australia Cataloguing-in-Publication entry

Cannon, Michael, 1929–
[Land boom and bust]. The land boomers.
[Rev. ed.]
Bibliography.
Includes index.
ISBN 0 522 84663 7.
1. Real estate investment—Victoria—History. 2. Victoria —Economic conditions—1834–1900. I. Title.
332.632409945

Contents

IV THE BANKING SCANDALS

V THE MUNRO-BAILLIEU-FINK GROUP

VI THE MATTHEW DAVIES GROUP

VII FINALE

Introduction

Laissez-faire capitalism, the free interplay of economic forces, reigned in Australia for about a century. It began when the early governors found themselves unable to prevent trading for private profit, and reached its highest peak with an extravagant boom which swept the eastern colonies in the 1880s. Only when that boom collapsed, involving numberless victims in the searing depression of the 1890s, were serious attempts made at social control of individual enterprise.

The land boom tragedy was not the worst event in human history, but for reasons which unfold themselves in this book, it was one of those few social crises in which the guilt of a select group of individuals could be clearly defined. If only for this reason, the story of the land boom retains permanent significance.

Since the first publication in 1966 of *The Land Boomers*, a considerable amount of additional information and pictorial research has come to light. None of it changes the original thesis, but it seems time for a more complete analysis of the period and its people to be made available once again.

I would like to thank readers who wrote with suggestions, new information, and corrections of fact.

Younger readers who have grown accustomed to decimal currency may wish to convert the old currency as they read. There were four farthings (¼d.) to the penny (1d.), twelve pennies to the shilling (1s.), and twenty shillings to the pound (£1). Each £1 equals $2 in today's money. By comparing wages, the cost of housing, and commodity prices of the 1880s with today's levels, an inflationary factor of about fifty to one seems realistic.

Thus to take one prominent example, when B. J. Fink went bankrupt owing £1,800,000, it equalled about $180 million in today's values. This represented a vast amount of capital at that time. It was subscribed by ordinary members of the public, through various private banks which were foolish enough to lend it to Fink and his associates.

As you will see, Fink was only one case among many.

M.C.

I VICTORIAN DREAMS

THE THIRST FOR WEALTH
BUBBLE COMPANIES

AND NIGHTMARES

VICTIMS TO GREED
THE BUBBLE BURST

1

A Golden Street in Marvellous Melbourne

Visitors to the colony of Victoria in the 1880s were awed and dazzled by the astonishing progress of its capital city. They began to call it 'Marvellous Melbourne'. Everywhere they looked the humble buildings of the early colonists were being pulled down, and in their place were rising the great granite piles of a myriad financial institutions. In the suburbs, on the rolling hills of Camberwell or the level paddocks of Brighton, luxurious mansions were built by the score for the newly rich. In the nearer industrial suburbs, rows of terrace houses and cottages went up by the thousand for a suddenly prosperous and fast-breeding artisan class. Business boomed. Banking boomed. Money poured in from overseas. The frenzy grew and fed upon itself. Thousands of acres of suburban land were subdivided and resold many times, each time at a higher price. Millions of shares changed hands in a stock exchange saturnalia. Anyone, it seemed, could make a fortune in this incredible colony.

For his own amusement, a visitor might hail a horse cab and drive in leisurely fashion along the 'Golden Street', Collins Street, a street of dreams and bubble companies. On his left, before he crossed Swanston Street, he could admire Queen's Walk, with its wonderful lead-light cupolas sheltering a shopping arcade. Italianate office buildings rose magnificently on either side, and a gilt statue of Britannia reigned on the lofty cornice. This edifice was built by Sir Matthew Davies out of the lavish funds of the Freehold Investment Co. Ltd. Davies put his elder brother in charge of it. Who could dare dream that very shortly Sir Matthew Davies, leading financier and the Speaker of the Legislative Assembly, would be arrested on criminal charges? Or that his brother would go bankrupt for more than half a million pounds?

Just over Swanston Street was the elaborate five-storey Premier Building, designed in French Renaissance style. This was the home of the Premier Permanent Building Association and its guiding genius, James Mirams. A wonderful man, 'Jimmy' Mirams; a strict teetotaller (like many of his fellow company promoters of the day); a great provider of houses for the people; altogether a man to be trusted. Investors thought so, and gave millions into his keeping before his arrest and imprisonment.

Next door to the Premier Building, sandwiched between that and the *Age* office, rose a noble institution known as the Real Estate Bank. This was started

Melbourne in the 1880s . . . Cable trams, horse cabs, four-wheelers, and a lavish new portico added to the Town Hall at a cost of £10,000.

by another teetotaller, James Munro, who rose to be Premier of Victoria. He also founded the Federal Bank further down on the corner of Collins and Elizabeth Streets. Absolutely trustworthy! Depositors agreed, and their faith cost them two million pounds sterling. When the bubble was about to burst, Munro hastily had himself appointed Agent-General in London and fled the colony. He returned later to face his creditors and the Insolvency Court. There was no provision in the flimsy Companies Act of the day by which he could be charged with fraud, and he escaped without penalty.

Just on the other side of the *Age* office, at 243 Collins Street, there traded the famous partnership of Messrs Munro & Baillieu, then the city's most successful auctioneers and estate agents. Donald Munro was the son of James Munro, whose history we have just briefly scanned. W. L. Baillieu was a large, bustling young man who had pulled himself up by his own bootstraps from poverty to sudden wealth. James Munro backed the two young fellows. He arranged for his banks to lend them £180,000 to play the land market. They lost it all, and the depositors never saw the money again.

A little further down Collins Street, where Centreway Buildings now stand, were the Metropolitan Bank and the Metropolitan Permanent Building Society.

These two institutions were also highly successful in disposing of their depositors' cash. One of the directors was Henry Hayter, the widely respected Government Statist of the day. Hayter was so good at figures that he went bankrupt for £36,000 and paid his creditors 3d. in the £1.

On the other side of Collins Street was the superb new shopping arcade known simply as 'The Block'. This was the inspired creation of Benjamin Fink, another financial genius who rose from poverty to the control of millions. Shoppers who thronged The Block often saw his short, portly figure bustling from one splendid enterprise to another—to his building called Rothschild Chambers (now Collins House), or to the office block in Flinders Street called Fink's Buildings. Soon, soon, the prosperous shoppers and Fink himself were to disappear from the Melbourne scene; Fink to go bankrupt, owing £1,500,000, and to flee abroad with his family.

Further along Collins Street were the Empire Buildings, with the Dominion Bank occupying the ground floor. They were expensively erected in marble by C. H. James, a grocer from North Melbourne who temporarily became a millionaire through the buying and selling of land. Watching this frock-coated, top-hatted figure striding prosperously along Collins Street, who could have imagined that within a few years a warrant for his arrest would issue out of the Insolvency Court, that he would die in lonely and tragic circumstances, and that his estate would pay about 8d. in the £1?

Hundreds of other companies, usually short-lived, crowded the city during the hectic years of the boom. Some built whole new suburbs; pioneered telephone, electricity, gas, and tram services. Others had nothing, built nothing, and lived on borrowed time. Interspersed between these vagabond companies were the responsible banks, who usually refused to lend too high a proportion of their funds on speculative ventures. Most of these established banks weathered the hard times by one means or another—but they got such a scare that Australian banking became an extremely cautious business for many years thereafter.

All these triumphs and tragedies were based on the lust for money. Money! It made slaves of them all. Any mortal need they had, they could pay for. Here was the quintessence of the power and the possessiveness of all mankind. This, at least, would never decay into dust nor become a sourness in the mouth. Man's labour stored up. Secret atoms waiting to yield. Who among them was not a miser, an investor, and a speculator at heart?

2

The Lush 1880s

Little imagination is needed to perceive the vast changes which swept over Melbourne in the 1880s. A decade before, Melbourne was still a raw, young city, with empty spaces or humble structures dotted between the few important buildings of State, municipal, and financial activity. Then all at once there was an extraordinary efflorescence. On a time lapse camera, it would appear as if Melbourne sprang into being as one of the great cities of the world almost overnight. Everywhere there was a flurry of construction, the establishment of large companies and important new industries, the building of extravagant mansions, the golden tentacles reaching out into adjacent fields and valleys. Powered trams appeared; suddenly—whole new suburbs sprang into being; suddenly—electric light flared in the streets . . . Astonishing new applications of science; frightening new ideas of man's evolution from the jungle; colossal schemes of making fortunes from speculation; dangerous ideas of woman's place in the new society—all these things thrilled, alarmed and astonished our grandfathers and their fathers. It seemed that the huge effort which had been put into founding a new colony in the wilderness was now paying off, and that virtue was bringing its earthly reward. At few times in the world's history was it so good to be alive, and feel such faith in human progress tingling through one's veins.

Nobody had yet travelled by motor car or aeroplane. Lighter-than-air balloons were the only way that man had ever flown. Nobody had yet heard a radio or seen a television programme. People had vaguely heard of microbiology. Louis Pasteur was trying to develop an anti-rabies vaccine, but few suspected the existence of viruses. Pierre and Marie Curie were investigating a mysterious substance called radium. The word 'radioactive' had not yet been coined. But people knew that to man, arrogant man, all things were now possible. Thus Melbourne—and indeed the whole civilized world at the time—presented a chaotic picture of mankind struggling to emerge into the modern age. Much that was good, much that was evil, but all of it in turbulent motion, experiment, change, reaction, triumph, and disaster.

While men struggled to maintain their belief in the simple tenets of old-time religion, its foundations were being subtly sapped by the bold propositions of nineteenth-century science. Where nothing was static, even morality lost its old certainty. It became possible, even desirable, for Christian gentlemen to build their great houses, choking with wealth and blazing with light, alongside the racking poverty and inhuman conditions of the new industrial society which yielded that wealth. The old direct responsibility of master for servant was lost. A wider social responsibility for the unfortunate and oppressed had not yet been born.

Never was a large city built so quickly, and not often so ruthlessly, by its vigorous commercial leaders, mainly Scots, and their bewildered employees, immigrants and children of immigrants from every corner of the world. Under the strict Protectionist policy passionately supported by David Syme's *Age* and followed by nearly every Victorian government, more than 3,000 large factories had been established by 1890. The colony boasted 215 brickyards, 165 large sawmills, 128 tanneries, 93 flour mills, 68 breweries, and 6 distilleries. There was fierce and genuine competition among traders, and prices of daily commodities were kept well in check. To accommodate the artisans who worked in these new factories, 'spec.' builders ran up thousands of cottages in the inner suburbs, financing them from the bulging coffers of the building societies.

The Exhibition Building soared skywards in time for the great International Exhibition of 1880. The new Harbour Trust was busily extending the docks to handle vastly increased shipping. The face of Collins Street changed from one end to the other as companies vied with each other to raise ever-greater office blocks. The Law Courts, the General Post Office, the Railways Building, the Fish Markets, the Working Men's College, hotels and theatres, were being built or extended. David Mitchell, father of Nellie Melba, was putting up the mammoth Equitable Insurance Building at the corner of Elizabeth and Collins Streets. David Munro, another prominent contractor, was throwing great bridges across the Yarra. A Metropolitan Fire Brigades Board replaced the antiquated private fire prevention system. At the corner of Flinders and Swanston Streets, St Paul's Cathedral was being built on one of the worst sites in the lowest part of the city that could have been selected. (Bishop Moorhouse was thinking of the members of his congregation who lived in the suburbs and wished to travel to church by train, and not of traffic congestion to come.) In 1888 a syndicate of financiers offered to buy St Paul's for £300,000, knock down the partly-erected cathedral, and build an office block instead. The proposal was defeated by only one vote on the Cathedral Board of Management.

The rising price of land helped the move towards taller buildings in Melbourne, made possible by the new hydraulic lifts introduced from America. With city land costing from £1,000 to £2,000 a foot, owners found that the typical four-storey Melbourne office building did not return sufficient in rents to cover the initial outlay. But when the new Yankee 'elevators' made it possible to garner twice the revenue from the same ground area, land values soared even higher. 'It has yet to be proved that people will ascend to such heights to transact their ordinary business', said the *Australasian Sketcher* cautiously.

With few exceptions, the architecture of the period was singularly florid and ornamental. William Pitt, one of the colony's most successful architects, designed

Desire for ornate decoration even affected elevator design: velvet seats, mirrors, intricate panelling.

When St. Paul's Cathedral became a target for speculators, *Punch* suggested putting it on wheels 'to boom up property in a fresh location.'

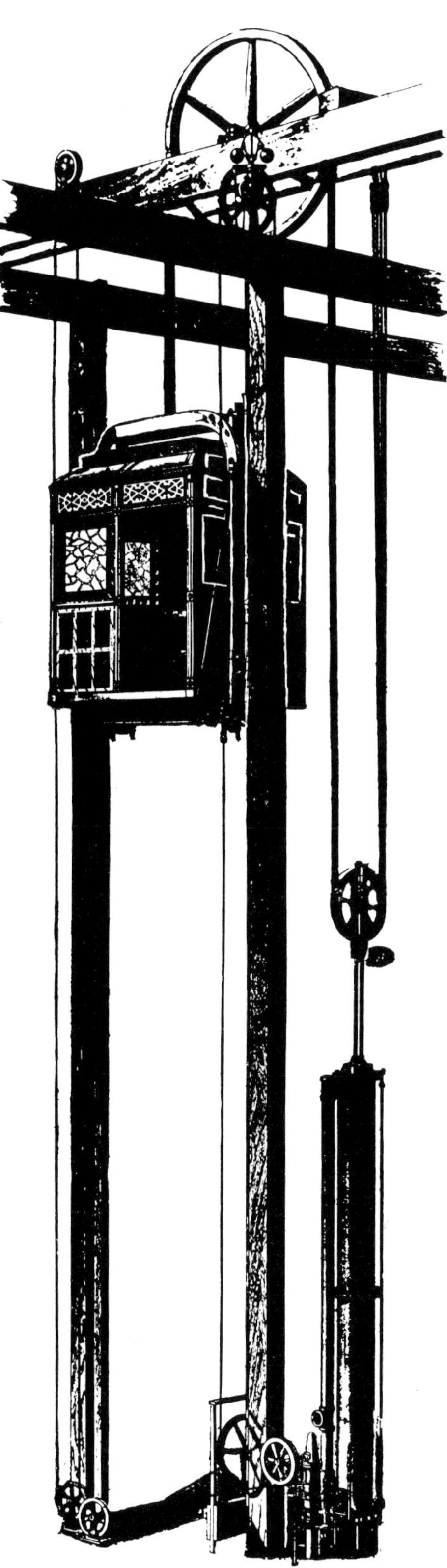

Hydraulic lifts, like this Baldwin standard elevator on huge timber uprights, enabled much taller buildings to be erected.

The new Princess Theatre in Spring Street, Melbourne, had the world's first sliding ceiling, which could be opened on hot nights.

in rapid succession the first coffee palace (the Melbourne Coffee Palace in Bourke Street), the new Falls Bridge (now called Queens Bridge), the Premier Building Association offices, Victoria Hall in Bourke Street, the Rialto, Olderfleet, and Melbourne Stock Exchange in Collins Street, and new town halls for St Kilda and Brunswick. Pitt's greatest triumph was the Princess Theatre in Spring Street, commissioned by Messrs Williamson, Garner & Musgrove. Pitt designed the world's first sliding roof and ceiling, which were rolled back on warm nights to give the effect of an open-air theatre. The mechanism failed in later years and was sealed up, but for a time Marvellous Melbourne had new glories to boast about.

On the broad acres of Brighton, Prahran, Camberwell, and Kew, successful speculators and merchants erected their stucco mansions, sometimes with good taste but more often with grotesque results. At Brighton, an eccentric Jewish money-lender, Mark Moss, built a fantastic castle called 'Norwood'. As though to represent the solidity of the Victorian tradition, Sir William Clarke built the squat, ugly pile called 'Cliveden' in East Melbourne. With more success, Albert Miller built 'Whernside' in Toorak; W. K. Thomson built 'Kamesburgh' in Brighton; and Henry Ricketson 'Glen Eira' in Caulfield. Italian craftsmen were used to build many of the mansions, and they stamped their ideas indelibly on Melbourne taste. Examples of their work were the 'Villa Maria' (Studley Park Road, Kew), the 'Villa Callantina' (Glenferrie Road, Hawthorn), and the 'Villa Alba' (Walmer Street, Kew)—all still standing but sadly diminished in lands and glory.

In the country, meanwhile, the squattocracy joined in the fun. It was not uncommon for travellers to find three houses standing on the one property. The first, thrown up by the original settlers in the 1830s, was usually a rough shack. The second, built in the gold boom of the 1850s, was a rambling, often beautiful, one-storey house with wide shady verandahs. The third, built during the boom of the 1880s, was usually an extravagant mansion aping the pretentious palaces of the city millionaires.

A growing middle class of merchants and manufacturers also copied the social leaders. Unable to afford elaborate mansions, they decorated their more modest homes with mass-produced cast-iron and stucco ornamentation. These houses, which sometimes reflected remarkably good taste, may still be seen throughout East Melbourne, Malvern, and other suburbs.

With the upsurge of building, population, and trade, it became imperative to speed up communications of all kinds. A decade before, Melbourne was not a comfortable place in which to walk about. Every shower of rain made the unpaved roads muddier and more hazardous, while great numbers of horse vehicles churned up mud and manure into an evil, greasy slime. It is difficult for us today to envisage the enormous difference which horse traffic made to the metropolis. Large open drains down the sides of the roads carried away storm water, shop and factory refuse, and excreta, depositing it either in the Yarra or in foul swamps on the outskirts of the city, such as the 'abominably malodorous' Port Melbourne lagoon. A solution was found with the use of red gum blocks or macadamizing of road surfaces, the placing underground of the main drains, and the commencement of work on a metropolitan sewerage system.

The horse-and-buggy approach to communications did not suit the late Victorian age at all. Steam trains and cable trams were more in the mood of modernization. Bicycles were more fun and less trouble than a horse. Even Supreme Court judges rode them at weekends. And, if you were one of those really advanced thinkers who owned the new-fangled device called a 'telephone',

Two leading architects who designed many ornate land boom buildings: William Pitt (left) and Lloyd Tayler.

you need not even go outdoors to communicate with other people. The electric telegraph brought news from country and interstate with astonishing speed, and after the first overseas telegraph message was received in Melbourne in 1872 the colonists no longer felt so isolated from world affairs. Soon the highlights of overseas news were being published in next morning's papers: cricket scores, London share prices, the slaughter of the Matabeles by British troops in Africa, and other great Imperial events. Newspapers expanded with the growing community. For some years during the 1880s, Melbourne had five daily newspapers, as well as numerous weekly and monthly journals of extraordinarily high literary quality. The colony's early newspapers had been set up by hand and printed on slow presses. Now they were revolutionized by the introduction of fast steam presses and mechanical typesetting. Just as important as these technical advances to the newspaper press was the rapid spread of free, compulsory, and secular education. Large schools were being built in the suburbs to cope with the increase in population. With the opening of the Teachers' College in 1891, teachers were being trained to far higher and more unified standards. At this time, the annual Victorian expenditure on primary education was not quite one million pounds, while another £50,000 was allocated to the university and technical schools. These sums seem modest by today's standards, but in those days they went much further, for many teachers were earning only £50 to £60 a year.

Until late Victorian times, woman's place remained very definitely in the home, where she was expected to rear a huge family and be prepared to see almost half die in infancy. Few women had any knowledge of birth control techniques, although copies of Charles Bradlaugh's informative pamphlet, *The Law of Population*, were surreptitiously passed from hand to hand, and women whispered behind their husbands' backs of sponge and syringe methods. Divorce was an equally sordid subject not to be openly discussed in polite circles, and to be resorted to only in extreme cases. When W. J. Shiels introduced a private bill in the 1880s to extend grounds for divorce to cases of systematic cruelty, desertion and grave felony, he was bitterly denounced by Anglican and Catholic clergy. Even after the Shiels' reforms were watered down, there was a 'remarkable' increase in divorce cases—from 35 cases in 1887 to 159 cases in 1890. What was to become of Christian marriage and morality?

However difficult their procreative role, women had an easier task in satisfying lusts of the stomach. Bread cost 4½d. per 4lb. loaf, butter averaged 1s. 5d. lb., milk 4d. a quart, beef 6d. lb., and mutton 4d. lb. Bacon averaged 1s. lb., eggs 1s. 6d. dozen, potatoes 3s. 9d. cwt., carrots 9d. per dozen bunches, lettuces 1d. each, peas 3d. lb., tea and coffee 1s. lb., and firewood 10s. ton. Whisky cost 25s. a gallon. At this time a skilled artisan could earn £8 a week, and a labourer at least £2.10s.

Servants were not easy to get. Girls preferred to work six days a week in factories with their friends than seven days a week in the comparative isolation of wealthy homes. To ease the problem, James Saunders & Co. 'imported' East Indian servants at so much a head, to the horror of those who were beginning to

Inside Victorian mansions, mother and servants were engrossed in breeding and rearing huge families. Here we see the happier side of their existence.

Part of the frontage of 'Benvenuta', an extravagant creation of the boom period in Drummond Street, Carlton. It was occupied by the widow of a small arms merchant and her four sons—Emanuel, Alfred, Edward and Louis Abrahams. In 1895 the four were found guilty of conspiracy to defraud and each sentenced to 12 months' hard labour. By the 1930s the mansion had deteriorated into a cheap lodging house. Today it is named Medley Hall, a hostel for university students.

Grotesque furniture was designed for some of the larger mansions. Here are some of Alfred Dunn's pieces built for a well-known land boomer, John Robb, for his mansion 'Coonac'.

Home-builders used hundreds of different plaster and cement ornaments, including emasculated children, urns, flowers, etc. These designs were registered by George T. Cross in Sydney in 1891.

demand a 'White Australia'. The barrier against employing women in useful occupations was slowly being lowered. Despite dire prognostications, the University of Melbourne in 1880 was the first in Australia to admit women students. Three years later Miss Bella Guerin, daughter of the Governor of Ballarat Gaol, became the university's first female Master of Arts. The medical field was more difficult ('How could one lecture on the human body in front of females?'), but in 1892 Dr Margaret White confounded the sceptics by taking higher honours than any male student in both medicine and surgery.

Hospital conditions in the 1880s were still incredibly bad. To be admitted to the maternity ward in some hospitals was almost a sentence of death. Puerperal fever and septicaemia were rife, even half a century after the discoveries and teachings of Semmelweis and Lister. Surgeons went straight from the operating theatre or dissecting room to the labour ward, their coats covered with dried blood and foetal matter—worn proudly by many as a sign of their profession. Many doctors and nurses despised the new fad of using antiseptics. Public protests against the 'insanitary conditions, the high rate of mortality, the disease impregnated walls' of Melbourne Hospital led to a parliamentary enquiry in 1886, but little effective action was taken. Under these conditions, it was not surprising that people placed more faith in patent medicines than in doctors. Journals of the day were full of extraordinary advertisements for drugs and medicines alleged to cure every ailment known to mankind, including some which have still not been conquered today. With each bottle of Eno's Fruit Salts, for instance, came a sixteen-page booklet called *Duty*, which purported to explain how to avoid indigestion, jaundice, constipation, boils, sleeplessness, colds, anaemia, gout and rheumatism; pointing out that 'Health and Longevity is Short; Time is Fleeting.' Fraudulent cures for syphilis, cancer and tuberculosis were freely advertised and sold in huge quantities.

What did the Victorian do in his leisure hours, in the days before radio, television, and motor cars? Among the well-to-do, of course, church attendance was a social necessity. The preparation and consumption of huge meals seems to have played an important and satisfying role in their lives. Home entertainments—pianoforte, singing, reciting—were far more widespread than today. Picnics on beach, river, or bushland hill were popular. Bay excursions were conducted by two competing companies. Roller skating enjoyed a sudden vogue, and board rinks sprang up in many suburbs. In Bourke Street the Cyclorama Company was showing the Battle of Waterloo, the Siege of Paris, and the Siege of Jerusalem; all scenes being hand painted and revolving before the enthralled audience. The same company proposed to build a replica of the Eiffel Tower in Victoria Parade, but the depression halted the project.

A favourite amusement was to promenade and 'window shop' in certain areas, particularly while Saturday night shopping lasted. Society promenaded on The Block. Lesser folk visited the new Eastern Market (on the site now occupied by the Southern Cross Hotel), where a variety of shopkeepers and bagmen sold their wares under electric light. Paddy's Market, meanwhile, had shifted from this site to Smith Street, Collingwood, and here, too, large crowds 'took the air' at night. But late night shopping did not last for long. W. C. Smith's Factories Act of 1874 forbade the exploitation of women and children in industrial work, although the 'advanced' conditions of the time would be regarded with astonishment today. Shop assistants were left without much protection until 1883, when a Royal Commission reported that many shops, restaurants and hotels were still forcing young women to work from ten to fifteen hours a day, six days a week, 'wherein the long hours must certainly have an injurious effect on their health'. Alfred Deakin's new Factories Act of 1886 forced shops to close at 7 p.m., except on Saturdays, when closing time was extended to 10 p.m. To many diehards, the new Act appeared to be a dictatorial attack on their freedom to shop whenever they pleased. 'The gloomy look after seven o'clock of streets that had formerly been so bright and cheery far on towards midnight imparted a feeling of resentment', said a writer in *Victoria and Its Metropolis*, published in 1888.

People of world renown came to entertain and observe Marvellous Melbourne. Rudyard Kipling, passing through in 1891, attacked the radical notion of an eight-hour working day. Sarah Bernhardt, H. M. Stanley, and other famous actors, singers, and lecturers, came to the fabled city. Many colonists made enough money to sail 'Home' to England on extended visits. In London they were able to see the theatre at its dazzling late Victorian peak—first performances of Gilbert and Sullivan operas; brilliant plays by Oscar Wilde.

For those who had to stay in Australia, there were the 'great occasions', eagerly looked forward to. On the night of Queen Victoria's Jubilee, 20 June, 1887, an enormous crowd of 200,000 people gathered in the city. They were

> quiet, orderly, good-tempered, accepting with many a joke the inevitable showers that poured from overhead while they plashed along the muddy roads, admiring the stars, the crowns, the mottoes in brilliant flame; the fine facades of public buildings picked out with electric lights; the banks and loftier shops framed in sparkling patterns of many-coloured lamps . . .

It was just fifty years since Victoria became Queen of that unique creation, the British Empire. It was just fifty years since the first land sales in Melbourne. Cheer and shout, people of Victoria! 'Health and Longevity is Short; Time is Fleeting.'

3

The Perilous Course of Events

Two great economic booms and depressions had already shaken nineteenth-century Victoria. The first occurred shortly after the early Melbourne land sales of 1837, reaching its peak about three years later. Extraordinary prices were paid. Three blocks of land which C. H. Ebden had bought for £136 were resold by auction for more than £10,000. Hundreds of people in the young colony joined in the rush to make profits from speculation. Many borrowed money from the Port Phillip Bank, which soon crashed in the first notable banking collapse. Sheep prices fell from 25s. to 1s. 6d. a head, and practically every grazier and merchant went bankrupt. The Bank of Australasia paid no dividends for five years.

The discovery of gold sparked off the second great boom, which reached a peak in the 1850s. Although there were only 200,000 people in the whole colony, about £25 million in gold was mined within a few years. The banks were so full of the precious metal that they stopped paying interest on deposits. People had money to burn, and either dissipated it in wild extravagance or bought property at inflated prices. But because of the continuous flow of gold, there was not as much suffering when the inevitable crash followed.

Then came the land boom of the 1880s. This time every type and degree of man was involved. Clergymen, labourers, widows, schoolmasters—all grasped at the chance of quick wealth and invested their savings. Many borrowed widely to invest more than their assets were worth, and later formed a pitiful kite-tail to the catalogue of insolvencies.

The land mania of the 1880s took two main forms. The first was based on a plethora of building societies, whose optimistic officials believed that every family in the colony could simultaneously build their own house, keep up the payments through good times and bad, and support an army of investors who were being paid high rates of interest for the use of their money. The second form of mania was the deeply-held belief that it was impossible to lose money by 'investing' in land—a belief which persists to the present day.

Soundly run building societies were a great asset to the growing colony, so long as they kept to their original purpose. Unfortunately, when the Victorian Parliament copied the English building society statutes in 1876, the colonial

RETURN OF THE GOLDEN AGE

Old Father Time, dressed as a land boomer, with a bottle of champagne in his hip pocket, reflects on the difference between the gold rush days and land speculation: 'This Victorian soil is rich stuff. It used to pan out hundreds . . . now it pans out millions.'

Auctioneers often gave free champagne lunches to provoke buyers into a reckless mood.

legislators added a clause which proved disastrous. Victorian building societies were permitted 'to buy and sell or mortgage freehold or leasehold estate'. The Premier Building Association, the Federal Building Society, and other leading institutions took advantage of this exceptional power. Their directors used the large deposits which had been paid into the societies to compete frantically for the best real estate. Not only did they add impetus to an already serious inflation of values; they also converted the building societies into little more than speculative operations, using public money which had been subscribed for quite different purposes. At the same time, many of the societies' directors were conducting a vast sweep of speculative dealings on their own account. In some cases, as we shall see, the temptation to use depositors' money for their own purposes proved too strong.

By 1890 the building societies held more than £5 million of the public's money on deposit, most of it from the wage-earning classes. Six years later this figure had declined to £800,000—a striking indication of the lack of public confidence in the institutions. Whole village suburbs which had been run up with building society funds were untenanted, and remained so for years afterwards.

Two of the pioneer speculators in Melbourne were C. H. James and Matthew Davies, who began operations together in the late 1870s. James sought out and sold suitable land; Davies looked after the legal and administrative side of the business. By the time the land boom reached its height, each man was worth nearly a million pounds on paper. When it crashed, they were worth nothing. At the time James and Davies began speculating, Melbourne was a comparatively small city surrounded by orchards, market gardens, and grazing paddocks. The fortunate freeholders were offered large sums for their land, which was promptly converted from richly-yielding countryside into vacant building allotments. In some cases, the land became the nucleus of important new suburbs. In others, the blocks remained covered with weeds for decades afterwards.

On the northern and eastern sides of Melbourne, the suburbs of Canterbury, Surrey Hills, Kew, Box Hill, Doncaster, Clifton Hill, Fairfield, Heidelberg, Brunswick and Northcote were pegged out or extended. On the south side, Brighton, Mentone and other bayside suburbs were 'opened up'. Even remote areas like Laverton and Ferntree Gully felt the subdivider's presence. Blocks were sold on £5 deposit at the 'charming watering place' of Frankston, 'nestling on the shore of the Bright Blue Ocean, wherein the finny denizens of the deep disport themselves lazily, and fall willing victims to the wiles of the Waltons.' Next door to Laverton, the Altona Bay Estate Company proposed to develop 'The Margate of Australia' on the wild and windy plain running down to Port Phillip Bay. Water supply, gas, and a private railway joining up with the main Geelong line were promised. The company also proposed to build a pier, to enable residents to travel to the city by fast steamer. Wonderful dreams!

The enormous expansion of the metropolis during the booming 1880s may be gauged from these population increases in particular suburbs:

	1881	1891
South Melbourne	25,000	45,000
Footscray	5,000	20,000
Brunswick	5,000	20,000
Hawthorn	5,000	20,000

Thousands of acres of suburban paddocks were floated into 'estate companies', and shares were sold to a gullible public. Some of the original owners of the land were able to store away large amounts of cash, or remit it overseas. Some were so foolish as to reinvest in other speculative companies, and lost the lot, as well as most of their personal assets. Many thought the cash would be safe with the established banks—until most of the banks were caught up in the disaster and forced to suspend business.

Usually the land was bought by a syndicate on a small deposit, and an auctioneer set to work. He advertised the land with an excess of superlatives, provided free transport and elaborate lunches for buyers, sprinkled the crowd liberally with dummy bidders, and sold perhaps half a dozen lots on deposits ranging from £1 to £10. 'The Saturday sales were a perfect carnival to many a genial fellow who never owned a foot of land in his life, and never had a pound wherewith to buy one', said *Table Talk*. Sometimes the syndicate would build one or two pretentious houses on the estate and 'sell' them at high prices to other land companies in which they held an interest. Fictitious values thus established, buyers were inveigled into paying ridiculous prices for their blocks. Another favourite device was to build a light railway line through the estate, and boldly claim that the government would operate the line once receipts equalled half the costs.

SATURDAY, 29th AUGUST.

EAST BRIGHTON VILLAGE

LOW UPSET, 10s. PER FOOT.

21 Magnificent Villa Sites, 66 x 130 Feet.

FRONTAGES TO BOUNDARY AND CENTRE ROADS, CERTAIN TO DOUBLE OR TREBLE IN VALUE VERY SHORTLY.

Are you going at once—so early?

Yes, my dear. I have to make arangements for attending the Sale of Land at EAST BRIGHTON PARK to-morrow. I have already been offered a very handsome profit on the allotments I purchased at the previous sale.

Well, I shall certainly be there too, as I want to invest £500.

£8 DEPOSIT BALANCE by INSTALMENTS.

LUNCHEON PROVIDED IN MARQUEE. RAILWAY PASSES SUPPLIED.

Admirably adapted either for Business or Residential Purposes. The People's Home Syndicate offer these 21 Splendid Allotments on their usual Liberal Terms, and Low Upset of 10s. per foot. High Lying, Well Drained, Beautiful View. Churches, Schools, and Stores close by.

LANDS UNLOCKED FOR THE PEOPLE. MONOPOLY AND HIGH PRICES NO LONGER SUPREME.

For Plans and particulars apply to

PATTERSON & SONS, 37 Collins-st. East; or, J. K. JENNINGS, 47 Queen-st.

PERTH,

Western Australia

REET

D

64 65 66

EET

39 38 37 36 35 34

1 2 3

OUTRAM STREET

Business Positions. Residence Positions.

Within the City Proper Boundary, and fronting Government Streets.

Western Australia has had a long winter of discontent, but the springtime of prosperity is now just commencing.

Those who purchase land at the present time, will occupy a similar position to those who bought land in the City of Melbourne before the advent of the Goldfields.

Fifty Pounds now invested, probably may result in a handsome independency in a few years hence.

J. H. KNIPE

Is authorised to Sell, by Auction, on MONDAY, 11th OCT., 1886, at the City Auction Mart, known as Greig & Murray's, 50 Collins Street West, commencing at 11.30 precisely,

Freehold Properties

WITHIN THE

CITY OF PERTH, THE CAPITAL OF WESTERN AUSTRALIA,

Now in its youth, but rapidly developing into the commanding importance of manhood.

Railways existing!
Railways commencing to the Interior!!
Tramways being legalised!!!
Population increasing!
Pastoral Pursuits developing!!
Agricultural Settlement developing!!!
Mining Enterprise developing!!!!
Western Australia permanently assuming the foremost of the group!
A Fifty Pound Enterprise at the above auction. A fortune secured!

Crown Title. Terms: £10 per Lot at time of Sale.

BALANCE BY SEVEN QUARTERLY PAYMENTS, WITHOUT INTEREST.

GODFREY & BULLEN, Solicitors, 23 Collins Street West.

Further particulars obtainable at KNIPE'S LAND MART, 43 COLLINS ST. WEST, MELBOURNE.

Estate agents used every conceivable device to sell city blocks and suburban paddocks, as these boom-time advertisements and posters show.

Top left: Patterson & Sons advertise 'Lands Unlocked for the people' at East Brighton by favour of the 'People's Home Syndicate'.

At right: Melbourne agents even sold blocks in Perth, where a 'springtime of prosperity' was promised.

The Railway Junction Land Association, Ltd.

OF RINGWOOD.

To be Registered under "The Companies Statute, 1864."

Capital: £14,000, in 14,000 Shares of £1 Each.

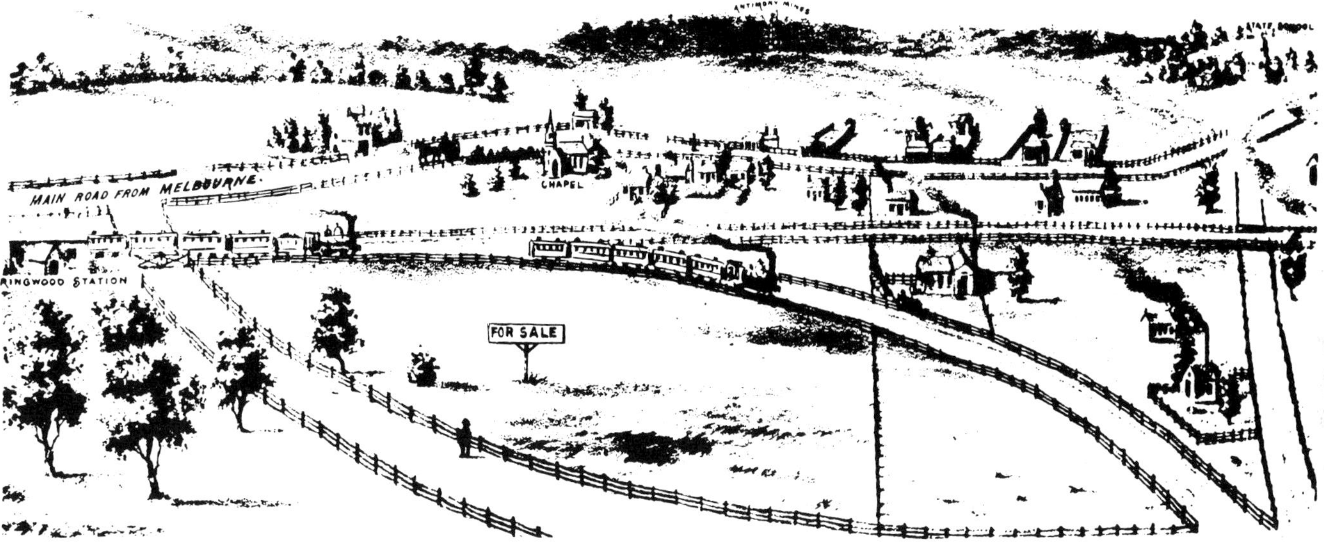

Payable:—2s. 6d. per Share on Application, 2s. 6d. on Allotment, and 5s. in Three Months. It is confidently anticipated that no further payment will be necessary.

Directors:

E. H. CAMERON, Esq., M.L.A., Evelyn
WM. PITT, Esq., Architect, Collins Street West
THOMPSON MOORE, Esq. (Chairman Australian Widows' Fund), Collins Street
N. KINGSTON, Esq., Contractor, Collins Street West
M. K. WESTCOTT, Esq. (Messrs. Westcott & Paul, Importers) Elizabeth Street

Vacant paddocks near Ringwood station were advertised by the local M.P., E. H. Cameron; architect William Pitt; and Thompson Moore, chairman of the Australian Widows Fund. Note antimony mines in the picture.

The boom continued to gather strength. In 1885 the harvest was prolific, the price of wool was high, the railways made a profit for the first time in the colony's history, and optimism reigned supreme. A few warning voices were raised overseas, but heard as from afar. In 1885 the London *Standard* pointed out that advances by Australian banks to their clients had increased from £92 million to £100 million. 'We should be terrified at "progress" of that sort in the old country for fear that the bulk of the debts might never be paid', said the journal. 'But the Australians boast of it. For them the greater the debt the greater the progress.'

In 1886 it appeared to some of the associated banks that the land boom had reached its zenith and would now plunge downwards. They became alarmed at the large withdrawals being made to meet land payments, and increased the interest rate on deposits and overdrafts by 1 per cent. Money lodged for twelve months could now earn 6 per cent. The land companies were compelled to follow suit and increase their interest rate on deposits. For a year land speculation became less profitable. Sales fell from about £12 million in 1885 to about £2¼ million in 1886. Then in 1887 there began a new wave of speculation, the land boom proper, so forceful that it over-rode all considerations of interest rates. Land selling in Surrey Hills for 15s. a foot in 1884 rose to £15 in 1887. Land at Burwood rose from £70 to £300 an acre. The Fitzroy Junction Estate was bought by members of a syndicate in November 1887 for £18,000. When the railway was extended to Heidelberg a few months later, they resold for £28,000. An extra 134 acres were provided when the Elwood swamp was filled in at a cost of £40,000.

In the city there was fantastic competition for blocks, fanned by constant reports of fortunes which had been made by holding on to the blocks for a few months and reselling. Rowland & Lewis's premises at 226 Collins Street (near Gustave Damman's tobacco shop) were bought by M. McCaughan for £25,000; then resold by him four months later for a clear profit of £30,000. Further along Collins Street, a 52-foot block next to the English, Scottish & Australian Chartered Bank was sold in September 1887 for £65,000. A few months later it was resold to the Melbourne Stock Exchange Company for £120,000—nearly double the price.

Once again the banks, dismayed by wildly fluctuating values, began calling in overdrafts. Unfortunately, some of the leading banks had encouraged speculation when money was plentiful, and ruthlessly suppressed it when the inevitable reaction set in. This 'traditional' banking policy, aimed primarily at safeguarding the banks' own interests, proved utterly ruinous to the general community.

The land promoters began looking elsewhere for easy finance. Thus the years 1888, 1889, and even 1890, saw the formation of most of the disastrous land and finance companies, and so-called 'land banks'. Under the loose banking and company laws of the time, they were able to take savings deposits, issue shares, float loans, discount promissory notes and other commercial paper, and in general perform all the functions of an established bank.

In the year ended June 1888, no fewer than 270 new companies were registered in Melbourne, with nominal capital of £50 million and paid-up capital of about £25 million. The boom soared upwards to dizzy new heights. In Swanston and Elizabeth Streets land values rose from £400 to £1,100 a foot. The Howey blocks at the corner of Swanston and Collins Streets were revalued at £890,000, and were returning £40,000 a year in rent. Scotts Hotel in Collins Street was sold to a syndicate for £92,000. At the corner of Elizabeth and Collins Streets the Equitable Life Insurance Company paid Munro's Real Estate Bank £363,000 for the site (equal to £2,700 a foot).

How could such values last? The maximum rentals which tenants were willing to pay often amounted to only $2\frac{1}{2}$ per cent return on the money spent on sites and buildings. As the boom petered out, many tenants could not pay even that. A few experienced speculators realized what would happen, and quietly began to sell off their shares and land while there was yet time. At the end of 1888 the *Illustrated Australian News* claimed that: 'The land boom has spent its force . . . There is, however, no reason to fear the terrible results which some of our neighbours with Rochefoucauldian cynicism are delighted to prophesy.'

Simultaneously, there began a series of calamitous industrial conflicts between employers and the developing unions, mainly in the maritime and pastoral industries. The trouble first started when marine officers, whose union was then affiliated with the Trades Hall, went on strike for better conditions. They were supported by other unions. The shipping companies in turn sought the aid of the Employers' Union, forerunner of the Chamber of Manufactures. For the first time in the colony, the combined power of capital and labour were brought face to face in mutual antagonism. Seamen, then stokers in gas works and railways, joined the struggle. Employers used blackleg labour to work at the gasometers, and train services were curtailed. The Mounted Rifle Corps was mobilized to prevent disorder. Deep rifts appeared in the community. While most elements of government were arrayed against the strikers, Chief Justice Higinbotham was sending £10 a week to the Trades Hall strike fund. When it seemed that only disaster could follow, the marine officers left the Trades Hall group and the strike collapsed. But business never fully picked up again.

When workers struck for higher wages, they were confronted by Colonel John Price and his mounted riflemen. 'Fire low, boys, and lay 'em out,' Price is said to have ordered. Later he denied having given the order.

John Bull.- Well, young man, you've made a pretty mess of your finance. Pay me ten shillings in the pound and I'll call it square.

Australia.- Right. Lend me the ten bob and I'll do it.

For a few months, many investors still appeared to be hypnotized by the boom. By the time they realized that the crash was indeed final, practically every land company was in liquidation and calls on their shares had gone forth. The same pressure was felt by the land banks, many of which owned shares in associated speculative companies. Some were able to use the public's cash deposits to stay open a little longer. But one after another they toppled, the pressure multiplying each day as their depositors took fright and withdrew their cash. From July 1891, when the Imperial Bank suspended payment, to March 1892, when the Australian Deposit and Mortgage Bank suspended, no fewer than 20 major financial institutions, with liabilities of nearly £20 million, closed down. In all, more than 120 public companies wound up their affairs in those eight desperate months.

English and Scottish investors, too far away to know which companies were sound and which were fraudulent, began to regard all Australian enterprises as 'unsafe'. British investments in Australia on the fixed deposit system amounted to £43 million. A large proportion fell due at this time. In the prevailing panic, most depositors refused to renew, causing new strains on the remaining banks. In November 1891 seven leading British life insurance companies announced that they would not put any more money into colonial securities 'for the present'. The colony's biggest bank, the Commercial, began to feel the pinch. Its general manager, H. G. Turner, held a private conference with Francis Grey Smith of the National Bank. Smith, who had himself followed a fairly conservative lending policy, advised Turner to make the building societies and other large borrowers bear their own financial burdens.

A few days later, the Commercial Bank began calling in many of its big overdrafts. Building societies and land banks which were dependent on its finance began toppling like wrecked chimneys. In the critical month of December 1891, four large banks suspended payment. They were the Land Credit Bank (1 December), the Metropolitan and Standard Banks (3 December), and the Real Estate Bank (15 December).

Every day brought news and rumours of fresh disasters, of another land company folding up. And when they folded, there came the inevitable calls of capital on their partly-paid shares to help pay the creditors. Men who had bought, say, 500 £5 shares paid up to £2.10s., were faced with a demand for £1,500 in cash. When they tried to borrow the money on the security of their assets, they found that the assets were suddenly worth almost nothing, and that the banks were not lending anyhow. Most speculators took the free and easy path to the Insolvency Court or private arrangements with their creditors. As they fell, they dragged others down with them. The weight of insolvencies proved too much for all manner of other under-capitalized and over-extended businesses, from timber merchants to large emporiums.

Suicide became a commonplace solution. One wealthy squatter from the Campaspe River, Tommy Robertson, had strolled down Collins Street during the boom, making a list of the building societies and the interest rates they were offering. He deposited £5,000 in each of six societies which were paying 7 per cent. When the building societies suspended, he believed he had lost the whole £30,000, and drowned himself in the Campaspe. Another prominent investor of the day was T. P. Fallon, who also happened to be Consul-General for Chile and Colombia. Fallon owned two large houses, 'Whinbank' and 'Emelton', in St Kilda. He also bought a site next to the Rialto in Collins Street and erected a large block of offices. It was completed by the end of 1891, but not a single office could be let. Fallon bought a revolver and went home to his rooms in 'Salisbury House', Carlton. Isaac Isaacs, a boarder in the same house, heard a pistol shot early one morning, and rushed into Fallon's room. There, according to the meticulous *Age* report, he saw Fallon lying with his brains spattered over the pillow. In his pocket was a letter from the Colonial Bank, asking him to call without fail that morning. Lawrence Levy, a land speculator, widely known and respected in Melbourne financial circles for nigh on forty years, left home on Boxing Day, 1891, and drowned himself in the Yarra. J. S. Rowley, the well-known cordial manufacturer, and donor of the Rowley Challenge Cup for rowing, suffered severe losses, and drowned himself in a water tank on his property at Warrnambool. Not only the speculators suffered. Alexander Lowenstein, a financier at Gresham Buildings in Elizabeth Street, lent out trust funds from the rich estate of J. C. Clauscen. The borrowers went bankrupt, the trust funds were lost, and Lowenstein shot himself.

By the end of 1891 the bottom had completely dropped out of the land market. Superb allotments could be picked up in almost any suburb for £10 to £100. When Patterson & Sons tried to auction allotments at Glen Iris, offering low deposits and ten-year terms, they could not get a single bid. 'Ah,' said the auctioneer, 'I see that you don't want these people to unload their lands and allow them for once in their later life to enjoy a little sleep and peace.' After that emotional appeal, he managed to sell four blocks out of 130 at £1 a foot. In Collins Street, sites for which £2,000 a foot had been rejected a short time before, were now being offered for £600 a foot—and could not find buyers even at that price.

As bank shares and other stocks began to slide in value, the directors of certain companies sent out dummies to buy their own shares and prop up their value temporarily while the directors sold their personal holdings. In certain cases, as we shall see, they even used the bank's funds for such purposes. Investors went to desperate lengths to rid themselves of liability on shares. Many prominent men transferred their shares to 'men of straw' who undertook to go bankrupt on their behalf.

The falsifying of balance sheets, the payment of dividends from non-existent profits, and the publication of misleadingly optimistic forecasts, were among the shocking features of the crash. Men who were widely known and trusted, who had been knighted by the Queen, who occupied the highest political and business positions, took leading parts in the manipulations. To take only three examples: At the annual meeting of the Real Estate Bank on 7 August 1891 James Munro said: 'The properties of the bank are in splendid order.' Four months later it collapsed. At the meeting of the Land Credit Bank on 31 October 1891, a 10 per cent dividend was declared, although by that date the bank had lost all its capital and reserves. On the same day, Sir Matthew Davies's Freehold Investment Co. Ltd declared an 8 per cent dividend—and went into liquic exactly three months later.

The financial scandals were not confined to Victoria. In Sydney a Mi of Mines was gaoled for fraud in connection with a banking company he controlled. In Adelaide John Nicholson, stipendiary magistrate and brother-in-law of a former Premier, Thomas Playford, was gaoled for embezzling funds from the Bowden Permanent Building Society. In Brisbane the Chief Justice, Sir Charles Lilley, decided that the State Treasurer, the President of the Legislative Council, and the General Manager of the Queensland National Bank, had dummied securities for shares on which they were liable for £66,000. His verdict was upset on appeal to the Full Court, but public confidence throughout Australia was shaken to the core.

Robert Reid, founder of the softgoods firm bearing his name, told the Athenaeum Club in December 1891: 'The disasters that have come upon us were prompted by fraud and dishonest dealing . . . A great many of our misfortunes have come about through allowing men who are not worthy of us to get into positions of trust.' Once-prosperous merchants were forced into liquidation. The George brothers, who ran George & George, drapers, in Collins Street, both made private compositions with their creditors. W. K. Thomson, who

Liquidators begin to discover some of the frauds which took place.

owned a half share in McEwan's hardware store, went bankrupt. Finney, Isles & Co., famous Brisbane store founded in the 1860s, went into liquidation with liabilities of £115,000. Said *Table Talk* on 23 September 1892:

> The shopkeepers are at their wits' end to secure sufficient trade to keep their establishments going, the theatres are half empty, and the only amusements that attract crowded houses are those where the nimble shilling affords cheap entertainment.

And just before Christmas 1892:

> Never before in the history of the colony has a Christmas holiday been shrouded in such gloom. Shop-keepers complain that their customers appeared to have forgotten that the season of good cheer was at hand, and started on being asked for the accustomed order, as if reminded of the changed condition of their purses that does not admit of luxuries or extras.

No one knew who would go to the wall next. Since the introduction of the Insolvency Act in 1871, there had been an average of 320 bankruptcies a year in Victoria. But in 1890 there were 445 schedules filed; in 1891 there were 420; and in 1892 no less than 509. That year, in addition, there were 85 private compositions and 18 liquidations by arrangement. Total private liabilities for

INSIDE THE UNION BANK.

SCENES IN COLLINS-STREET

Sir Archibald Michie said the Union Bank and the Bank of Australasia had saved the country from being known as 'hopelessly rotten'.

Dr John Madden, Victorian Chief Justice, who as Acting Governor signed the Proclamation which closed most of the banks.

1892 alone mounted to about £8 million—equivalent to, say, $240 million today.

The year 1892 may have been sombre, but the disasters to come in 1893 were quite unprecedented. Enough misuse of financial power had been revealed to make every man suspicious of the soundest institutions, and to be fearful about the safety of his own bank deposits. Quietly, then more quickly, a general run on the established banks began. Nearly £700,000 was transferred from private accounts into the supposedly more secure government savings banks, while unknown amounts were buried in backyards and under floorboards.

Public disquiet was multiplied by the suspension of the Commercial Bank on 7 April 1893, following heavy withdrawals and a slump in the value of its shares. Great secrecy was preserved on the real state of the Commercial's affairs. With extraordinary rapidity a reconstruction scheme was approved by the Chief Justice. But even the Supreme Court could not stop rumours.

On the weekend of 29–30 April, the great and powerful National Bank privately advised the Premier that because of the continuous run on its deposits, it intended to suspend business on the Monday. On Sunday, 30 April, Cabinet met secretly and decided to declare the whole week a 'banking holiday'. A

On 1 May 1893 depositors besieged the banks which remained open. At left, the frantic scene inside the Union Bank.

Proclamation was hastily drafted, and rushed by special train to Frankston for the signature of the Acting Governor, John Madden, C.J. Now an element of farce was added to tragedy. On the return trip, the locomotive driver was so excited that he ignored the signals and smashed through the closed railway gates. Without stopping, he steamed to Flinders Street, where messengers took the Proclamation to the Government Printer and the newspapers. On Monday, 1 May 1893, men picked up their morning papers to read the incredible news that the colony's entire banking system had apparently broken down.

Thousands of bewildered citizens gathered outside the suspended institutions where their money was locked up, and asked each other what to do. Collins Street was a milling sea of faces. Two banks, however, refused to obey the moratorium. The Union Bank and the Bank of Australasia remained open. Anxious crowds besieged the tellers to draw out their money. 'It looked more like the betting ring on a racecourse than anything else', said one report. 'Men literally fought with each other to get in.' Later in the day, when it became obvious that the two banks were going to keep on paying out for as long as required, the panic eased. People even started redepositing the heavy packets of gold sovereigns they had drawn out.

The government's drastic action aroused furious controversy. Some held that a complete panic had been averted; others that Victoria's credit had been deeply impaired. Sir Archibald Michie publicly thanked the Union and the Australasia for saving the country from being dubbed as 'hopelessly rotten'. The task of reconstructing the banking system occupied several months, while trade languished and men starved. Those who had ridden high on the boom now grovelled in the mud, and the whole community suffered with them.

The cumulative economic and political tides of the era almost submerged colonies whose wealth and productive capacity had never been greater. Among all depressions, that of the 1890s was the one most clearly due to individual frailty. But there were also present, working like subterranean volcanoes, a number of more general economic factors which helped to form an explosive combination of events. Some were causes, some were reflections of the boom; some that complex mixture which makes nonsense of efforts to attribute exact causes to human affairs.

A number of books and pamphlets attempted to analyse the economic causes of the boom. By far the most interesting of these was *The Australian Crisis of 1893*, written by the Hon. Arthur George Villiers Peel, then a comparatively junior official of the British Treasury. Peel's report was published by H.M. Government in 1894. Its official imprimatur enraged colonials who were already stung by Peel's scathing comments.

'The financiers of Victoria [pursued] a two-fold but continuous policy,' wrote Peel. 'They have in the first place endeavoured to create native industries by a protective tariff and in the second to borrow money in the English market. The artisans of that colony, on their side, have looked with impartial approbation on the action of their masters, being indifferent as to whether they should live by industries created at the expense of their fellow citizens or by wealth borrowed at the expense of their descendants.'

Peel had both the advantages and disadvantages of writing his report almost contemporaneously with events. He was able to see at first hand the enormous damage which had been done to the Empire's financial system by the extravagant policies of the colonials. The scandals of the day burned bright in his mind as he penned his memorable indictment. For this reason, perhaps, he was inclined to overlook the fact that unlike more settled countries, the colonies *did* need to develop, that they did need to borrow substantial funds for this purpose, and that they did need to encourage their own manufacturing industries.

A primary function of the colonial Agents-General situated in London was to ensure a steady flow of British loan money to their respective governments; while scores of private Melbourne institutions established boards of London directors to give them a head start in the competition for deposits.

English and Scottish investors were entranced by the idea of making at least double the 'Consol' rate of interest from the vigorously expanding colonies. Since these colonies were being developed by their own English and Scottish descendants, what better guarantee of success could there be? To add to their feeling of security, the names of prominent people appeared on the prospectuses of leading colonial companies.

Thus the Imperial Colonial Finance & Agency Co. Ltd., formed in 1890 with capital of £1 million, boasted the Marquis of Lorne as chairman. On the London board were Lord Eustace Cecil and Sir Hercules Robinson, a former Governor of N.S.W. The Anglo-Australian Bank, which foundered in a sea of criminal charges, had as its London directors Lord Camoys and the Honorable Ashley Ponsonby, son of Lord de Manley. The Australian Mercantile Loan & Guarantee Company had as its London figurehead Lord Ulrick Browne, a former Under-Secretary to the Government of India. The Federal Bank appointed a London

Prominent men became London directors of speculative Australian banks, helping to attract British deposits. From left: Sir Hercules Robinson, a former Governor of N.S.W., a director of the Imperial Colonial Finance Co. Ltd. Sir Henry Barkly, a former Governor of Victoria, who joined the London board of the fraudulent Federal Bank. Sir Andrew Clarke, acting Agent-General for Victoria, also a London director of the Federal Bank.

board consisting of Sir Henry Barkly; Sir Andrew Clarke, the acting Agent-General; and Howard Spensley, a leading Queen's Counsel.

Peel was horrified by the extent of Australian governmental and private borrowing. By the end of 1892, the public debt of the Australian colonies totalled £198 million, compared with only £54 million in 1875. This debt had to be supported by a population of less than four million people, whose productive power was far less than today's. Each year an £8 million interest bill had to be sent overseas to pay for the public debt, plus another £9 million interest for private loans.

During the decade from 1881 to 1890, the various Victorian governments raised no less than £30 million in London loans. Of this amount, £9 million had to be applied to paying off earlier loans. The public debt increased from £22 million to £46 million in Victoria alone. Coupled with private borrowing, about £60 million in loan money flowed into Victoria during the boom years. In one year, 1888, when Victoria's population reached one million, the circulation of money in Melbourne increased by 84 per cent.

It was impossible for the young colony to find profitable uses for this tremendous inflow of new capital in such a short period. Much of it was dissipated in the riot of mansion-building, luxurious living, and inflated development already discussed. In a moment of frankness the *Argus* admitted that: 'The wages of the Collingwood mason were paid, not by our own money, but by the English capitalists, the Government being merely the conduit pipe through which the gold flowed to us.'

As we have seen, a large proportion of government borrowing was spent on extensions of the railway system. Up to the end of 1892, nearly £40 million was spent on the Victorian railways. Of this, some £20 million was borrowed and spent in the previous decade. 'A very large proportion has been absolutely squandered and wasted on half useless lines, and on extravagant modes of construction,' said the *Argus* in 1893. 'We must build cheap railways like sensible men, and not equip them with station palaces to sell lollies in.'

Other funds were spent on a great variety of imports, encompassing everything from rolling stock for the railways to gorgeous decorations for the palaces of the new millionaires. During the lush years, 1885 to 1890, Victoria imported £54 million worth more goods than she exported. No-one in power seemed capable of halting or even openly recognising the huge drain on her financial strength which these figures disclosed. Thus the true criticism of Victoria's protective tariff policy was not that it stifled trade, but that it was not applied vigorously enough to help stem this huge flood of imported goods.

Much of the new money from Britain was kept on call in the banks, rather than on fixed deposit. Despite this, the banks began to lend on mortgage, often on poor security, far larger amounts than they were receiving in deposits. In 1888, the sixteen Banks of Issue trading in Melbourne loaned £7,750,000 more than they received the same year on deposit. In 1889, they loaned £10 million more. As late as 1892, the twenty-five established Australian banks received £155 million on deposit and loaned out the same total amount!

Even the fixed deposits were unsafe. 'Fixed deposits held in Australia are fixed only in name,' wrote Peel. 'A pernicious habit has grown up of allowing the customer to withdraw his fixed deposit at any time . . . The complicated evils entailed upon the Banks by their deposit system were thus both obvious and pressing. This money was too gigantic in amount; it was only gathered in at the expense of a high rate of interest payable by the Banks; it was easily withdrawable; it was of necessity invested in assets whose value could not easily be realised in cash in the hour of need.'

The safe rule in 19th century banking was to only accept deposits roughly equal to the bank's paid-up capital and reserves. In this way, no matter what sort of panic occurred, the bank could keep its doors open and pay all demands. But by 1892, the Australian banks had accepted a total of £155 million in deposits, compared with their paid-up capital of only £25 million. When the run on the banks started, their capital funds were insufficient to pay their creditors. Three strong banks—the Union, the Bank of N.S.W., and the Bank of Australasia—held 44 per cent of the total cash reserves of Australia between them. These banks escaped the crash practically unscathed.

In the cases of the Mercantile Bank, the Federal Bank, and the Commercial Bank, the average of British deposits to total deposits held by them was no less than 46 per cent. Significantly enough, these three banks were among the first to close their doors.

'Conceive what a British banker would do with large deposits in the hour of commercial inflation,' wrote Peel. 'He would invest in Consols. He would invest in railway debentures. He would discount mercantile bills at short dates, and would refuse to lend at long terms. His assets would, in the jargon of banking, be liquid assets, easily realisable against the hour of collapse. But the colonial banker has no Consols in which to invest: until quite recently there has been no such stock in Australia . . . In fact the truth is that the Banks, with the exception of some few of the most careful, did advance on urban and suburban properties.' Peel continued:

> To a certain degree the Banks suffered for no fault of their own . . . But it was their fault that they had dabbled in land speculation themselves, and had encouraged others to plunge into it, that they had averted the due course of the crisis in 1889 by propping the rotten bargains of their clients, and that they had sailed so near the wind as to allow confusion to be possible between the Banks proper and the Land Banks.
>
> Bankers can find no excuses for mismanagement in the errors of Governments, the frauds of speculators, and the fall of prices; it was with justice that your shareholders were afraid of calls and your depositors of suspensions of payment; you had piled up on a slender basis of capital an immense weight of deposits, which, though easily withdrawable in time of panic, you invested in securities not easily realisable; you have been confounded with those who did bad business only because you did bad business yourselves; you abused the vast confidence of your clients, and you are failures simply because you have deserved to fail.

As a result of the expansive attitude of most colonial financiers, speculation had been encouraged beyond all bounds of prudence. By 1888 more allotments had been subdivided for suburban houses in Melbourne than would have been sufficient for the entire population of London. In 1880 the total investments in Melbourne land and mortgages was £5 million; in 1886 nearly £12 million; and in 1890 nearly £16 million.

If most of these transactions had been settled in cash, the bubble could never have expanded so greatly nor burst so explosively. But land prices were pushed up to even more abnormal levels by the common practice among owners and estate agents of offering extended terms to purchasers. When the purchasers could not continue their payments, the vendors in turn could not meet their obligations to the banks.

Another primary cause of the disaster was the belief that the State should interfere as little as possible with the free operations of private capital. Thus the Banking Act was so weak that almost anyone could start a bank and accept deposits. The Companies Act was so weak that directors could mislead their shareholders and escape most of the consequences. As part of the prevailing philosophy that businessmen could do no wrong, the government was slow to investigate allegations of financial roguery. In a land where sinister rumour held sway, who could blame British and Australian depositors from trying to withdraw their savings from all suspected institutions?

'Let the facts speak for themselves,' Peel concluded tartly. 'It would be beyond the proportions of official modesty to criticise any statesmen, even those of the Antipodes.'

4

The Hungry 1890s

The Angel of Death came early and stayed late in the Melbourne of 1892 and 1893. The collapse of the boom economy was sudden and dramatic. As each company closed its doors, it dragged others down with it. Clerks, surveyors, accountants, builders—every kind of employee was thrown out of work, on to a labour market which was harsh enough in good times but almost non-existent in bad times. Their savings ran out, and still there was no work to be had. Nor was there any form of help, beyond private charity which usually came too little and too late.

To working-class unemployment there was added a new and possibly worse kind of suffering—the destitution of formerly well-to-do people who had no conception of how to survive hard times. Some of them were given food and shelter by relatives whose assets had survived the calling-up of shares. The sufferings of others were immortalized by the *Bulletin* in October 1892:

THE GHOSTS OF THE BOOM

> It is a heart-rending job in these times to be a liquidator in one of the many companies which were financed by MATTHEW DAVIES and his 'pals.' All day long the pitiable procession keeps coming—the old men who invested the savings of a lifetime on the strength of a lying balance-sheet and are left beggared and hopeless, and who will presently be homeless as well if the calls are enforced; the servant girls whose few pounds have been grabbed by the 'tentacles'; the widows who invested their little all in shares, and who come to weep piteously and pray that they may not be sold up and thrown out into the gutter to help pay the liabilities of the lying institution; the haggard, joyless spinsters who had a small competence till the saints in shiny hats devoured it; the cripples; the despairing semi-maniacs whose wits are fast going after their lost savings; the red-eyed shareholders who are trying to drown their miseries in drink; the paralytic old shareholders who are fast dying of MATTHEW DAVIES; the pious shareholders who want to know in their rage and agony if GOD will really allow such things as these to be, and will not launch a thunderbolt at the board . . .

The nightmare of unemployment was accentuated by epidemics of influenza, typhoid, and measles, which swept the badly-drained slums and killed thousands. In the winter of 1891, and again in 1892, there was a terrible influenza epidemic, which even laid low the Governor and his wife, M.P.s, doctors, lawyers, and police, and killed many thousands of people. There was such an enormous rise

JOY.
1st Evicted Family. – Cheer up old man, the *Argus* says wool has gone up ten per cent and added £2 million to the wealth of the country.
2nd Evicted Family. – Hooray!

in the number of typhoid cases that thirteen emergency tents had to be erected in the grounds of the Alfred Hospital to hold the patients. Two major sources of typhoid infection were found. Auguste de Bavay, the head brewer of Foster's Brewery in Collingwood, found that water from the Yan Yean reservoir was heavily polluted with typhoid germs. He corresponded with Louis Pasteur, and tried to develop a typhoid vaccine in his laboratory at the brewery, but was unsuccessful. Then in 1892, Dr Gresswell of the Board of Health reported that the excreta of typhoid patients from the Melbourne Hospital was being dumped on a market garden at Oakleigh; that from the Alfred Hospital on a dairy farm at Balwyn; and that from the Children's Hospital was fertilizing several market gardens at Moorabbin. Said he scornfully: 'If you desire to be affected with typhoid fever by all means drink the water and the milk raw as it is delivered at your homes.'

Among the daily newspapers, only the *Age*, still a mighty radical force under the firm hand of the uncrowned 'King of Victoria', David Syme ('Ananias' to his enemies), displayed much real interest in the sufferings of the unemployed. In June 1892 the *Age* published a grimly realistic series of articles entitled 'Among The Workless', which may still serve as a model of down-to-earth journalism. We cannot do better than borrow a few paragraphs from that long-forgotten reporter, who had seen enough 'to make the heart of the least susceptible and sentimental ache'. His articles were written, one may add, some years before Jack London's famous exposé of English poverty, *The People of the Abyss*.

> Privation, want and semi-starvation stand gaunt and inflexible as the prospects to be gloomily faced by hundreds of sturdy fellows, who cannot, try as they may, get a day's work; whilst faintly, but with sharp meaning, may be heard the cry of children and the wailing of women . . .
>
> Whilst the Block is crowded with its well-dressed throng, or the play-houses

Strikes, unemployment, suicide and disease added to the suffering caused by the breaking of the land boom. Melbourne lost 50,000 of its population within three years.

> receiving their thousands of satisfied patrons, the forlorn and destitute workers are herding in alleys and lanes, or cowering in garret and cellar like hunted animals; and side by side, almost rubbing shoulders with the children of the rich, can be found the emaciated and wasted faces of the women and their little ones . . .
>
> In hundreds of houses men have sold furniture article by article and stick by stick in order to ward off the desperate day that has been creeping on them steadily for weeks past, when there should be neither the wherewithal nor any prospect of providing expectant mouths with bread . . . There are cases where widows have had to dispose of their clothing even, in order to provide their children with sustenance.

The man from the *Age* donned old rags and spent a night at the Salvation Refuge in Lonsdale Street. There he learned from an old hand the methods by which some people, evicted for failure to pay their rent, had found shelter.

> Out in the suburbs there's scores and scores of empty houses, and not a soul comes near them from morning till night. Well, I'd get some old papers and perhaps some straw now and then, and in I'd go, make myself as comfortable as possible, and put in the time that way.

The fate of a man who chose to sleep in the open air in a freezing Melbourne winter was worse.

> He has been used, when he has been earning regular wages, if not to luxury, at any rate to substantial comfort, and the exposure to the night air, and the damp, unhealthy surroundings of his resting place, make the trial a terribly exacting one to a man's self-respect and pluck.

A year later, when conditions had grown much worse, the *Age* published another remarkable series of articles under the title 'Poorer Than The Poor', which surveyed each industrial suburb in turn. In South Melbourne the reporter told of house after house, 'the kitchen with its empty shelves, the fireless grate, the solitary crust on a plate placed high up on the dresser to be out of the reach of the children until the time comes for its use'. In another, a local clergyman found 'the baby lying dead on the boards of the garret, the mother sinking fast, and the rest of the household drooping under their long denial.'

In another trenchant series of articles, the *Age* exposed the evil of 'sweating' which went hand in hand with depressed times. 'Sweating' was the practice of farming out work, mainly the making of clothing, to families at home. In turn, of course, this practice led to even lower demand for factory labour. As conditions worsened, there was a continual tendency to reduce the rates paid to out-workers. One sweating den visited by the *Age* reporters was 'indescribably dirty and malodorous'. Here a man employed his own family and several other women from 8 a.m. to 8 p.m. Each earned about 15s. for a 72-hour week—one-third of official factory rates. In another den, some of the girls were employed as 'improvers' at 2s. 6d. a week. They were given a cup of tea and slice of bread twice throughout the working day of twelve hours. The effect upon the girls was apparent—most were 'pale, emaciated and depraved in appearance'.

The *Illustrated Australian News* (a monthly periodical published by the *Age*) pointed out on I July 1890 that

> the work turned out . . . is mostly worn by well-to-do and professional men,

Handouts for the unemployed: a piece of bread and a billy of soup or tea.

> including doctors and ministers. If the latter could only see how their clothing is produced it would scarcely sit so well upon them . . .
>
> Rich people, who live in roomy, well ventilated houses in breezy suburbs, wonder often how their wives and children die of fever, or how they themselves are attacked. Where the sweaters ply their trade, unclean operatives, wearied of their task, cast themselves upon the floor from time to time to snatch a sleep, covered with the half finished clothes which the wealthy have to wear. Thus the contamination of the sweating room is conveyed to the homes of the rich.

Sweating was not only the province of the more ruthless type of private employer. Government also had a hand in the slavery. For example, men who worked on the construction of the Natimuk to Goroke railway line in 1893 earned 9s. clear a week. After their personal expenses, there was scarcely anything left to send to their families in Melbourne. A deputation protested to the Minister of Works, William T. Webb, about the starvation wages being offered. Webb replied that they should think of themselves and their wives and families,

HOW IT IS DONE.

The Victorian Minister for Works said he would have to reduce labourers' wages to 5s. a day: 'It is all nonsense to say they cannot live on the smaller sum.' *The Ant*, a short-lived Melbourne journal, gave this 'practical illustration of How to keep a Family on thirty shillings a week'.

and not worry about observing the rates of wages demanded by their unions. When the Metropolitan Board built a new sewerage pumping station on the Yarra bank in 1893, the men received an average of 9s. 9d. for eight days' labour. Even at that, hundreds of men besieged the site, having walked there to beg for the right to dig out the clay and shift it at 9d. a yard. This rate was about half the amount quoted by the successful tenderer for the job.

Thus it may be seen that some of our present amenities—railways, sewerage works, private buildings—were made for us by the protesting muscles of underfed men, and washed by the tears of their suffering wives and children. Of the monstrous extortions, the blind follies, the arrant humbug of our grandfathers, only the *Age, Table Talk,* and the *Bulletin* ever had much to say. The results were soon buried and forgotten—usually six feet deep in neglected graveyards.

In the absence of trustworthy statistics, it is difficult for us today to form a complete picture of the extent of unemployment and the human suffering it produced. Some contemporary observers claimed that every second man was out of work, but these estimates could only be guesswork. Thousands of people were privately supported by others. Thousands left Melbourne. Thousands lived on scraps and municipal handouts. All we can say for certain is that this was the worst depression in Australian history, before or since.

Shocking individual cases of suffering could be cited by the hundred. The Rev. J. Dawborn, of St Matthias, Richmond, described two cases which he claimed were typical of his parish:

> A man who is an expert tradesman earning in good times from £7 to £10 per week came to me at half-past 6 p.m. begging me to accompany him to his 'home,' for, said he, 'I want you to see with your eyes what a landlord will do to a tenant, and which you would never believe unless you were a witness of it.' I went with him. His story was as follows:—'I am three weeks back in my rent, 42/–. I got notice of distraint yesterday. I left my five little children and housekeeper this morning, hoping to get work or borrow the whole or part of the overdue rent, but failing, returned at 5 o'clock in the evening to find my house as you see it.' And what did I see? Four absolutely bare rooms; not a mattress nor scrap of blanket or covering of any kind; not a cooking utensil, not even a cup wherewith to take a drink of water; and even the boxes which contained a little spare clothing belonging to the seven inmates—all gone. It appears that during the temporary absence of the man's children and housekeeper the bailiff had entered the house and made an absolute clearance . . . Thus, for 42/– rent, a comparatively tidy and comfortable home was wrecked, and the man and family demoralised and pauperised. And yet the landlord lives in really good style!

In another case:

> A woman, haggard and worn, with baby in arms, knocked at my door and asked for relief. Questioning her, she stated that her husband (a mason) was out of work, that she had six children, and that they had scarcely tasted bread for three days. What had they lived on? The woman said—'The children pick up the stalks of cauliflowers and cabbages and bring them home, and I boil and mash them and we eat them with a little fat.'

At the next stage of desperation were the tragic police cases which filled the newspaper columns of the day. Here is one from the *Age* of 4 April 1893:

> Between 10 and 11 p.m. on Sunday night Constable Scholes, on duty in Victoria Street, Brunswick, on examining an outhouse at the rear of an unoccupied house, was surprised to find an old man and two little boys huddled up together, not having as much as an old bag to cover them, and he at once removed them to the police station, where the man gave the name of Charles Costan, 50, and the boys Albert and Henry Costan, age 8 and 10 years. The man was yesterday charged before Mr D. V. Hennessy, J.P., with having no lawful visible means of support, and the children with being neglected. The father, in answer to the bench, said he had come down from the country, but could get no work to do, and his relations would have nothing to do with him. The children were remanded to the schools for 7 days, and the father sent to gaol. The trio presented a pitiful spectacle.

The first reaction of the politicians to the widespread suffering was to deny that it existed, then to say that it had been exaggerated. The colony was always 'about to turn the corner' and the policies of 'restraint and patience' would be proved correct. Meanwhile, deputations of unionists protesting against wage cuts were 'practically asking the Government to crush private enterprise'.

Occasionally a mother did not agree with the politicians that conditions were good and were going to get even better. One woman, Mary Newman, deserted by a husband who could not support her, was living in 'a miserable hovel' with her three children. She was observed by a neighbour, Mrs Burton, piling bushes on a fire in the back yard. Mrs Burton smelled something which resembled the burning of meat, and asked Mrs Newman what was being burnt. When an evasive answer was returned, Mrs Burton picked up a stick, and turning over the fire, exposed the body of a newly-born infant. The distraught mother told the police that she had no food for the rest of the family, let alone a new baby. She herself was too weak to be brought before the court, and was left in the gaol hospital.

Those women who were fortunate enough to obtain positions were forced to hand their families over to the care of a fatly prospering race of 'baby farmers'. Sometimes the children were fed and cared for; sometimes they were not. Newspapers constantly reported that babies' bodies were being found in gutters, sewers, or vacant allotments. Not a typical case, but still not so extraordinary, was that of Mrs Knorr, a baby farmer who pocketed the money for 'looking after' several children but murdered them instead. The Executive Council refused to commute the death sentence passed on her, feeling it was 'absolutely necessary that an example should be made in order to act as a deterrent.' It was the first hanging of a woman in Victoria for twenty-five years. The hangman at Pentridge declared he could never hang a woman, not even Mrs Knorr. He got drunk, and cut his throat. However, another hangman was found, and in January 1894 Mrs Knorr was finally executed.

Many women took to the streets and brothels in order to survive, or earn enough to feed their families. Most contemporary estimates agree that there were about 10,000 prostitutes in the Melbourne of the 1890s, and this figure does not appear to have been seriously questioned by the police. Statistics compiled in England by the Rev. Mr Merrick, a prison chaplain, probably applied just as much in Melbourne. Mr Merrick interviewed 14,000 London prostitutes who had been sent to his prison. Most of them had previously been domestic servants or factory workers. They had borne 6,365 children, of whom 2,400 had died. A total of 540 women had taken to the streets to maintain their families or unemployed husbands. The average time which they lived after becoming prostitutes was three years and six weeks.

In most country areas, there was food and security of a sort, although some storekeepers were giving mortgages on farms in return for food, and foreclosing rapidly when payments became overdue. William Bruce, a mallee farmer at Lah, a few miles from Warracknabeal, gave telling evidence to the 1895 Royal Commission on State Banking:

> Had you any capital when you went on the land?—Not of money.
>
> How did you get the capital?—Robert Smith, the storekeeper, got me a bag of flour.
>
> What else did you have?—We lived on rabbits.

> That constituted the whole advance you had—a bag of flour?—Yes. At that time I had two old horses and a few tools, and I made a plough, because I could not raise one. I made the first stump-jumper in Victoria, that was made on a mallee farm . . .
>
> How did you manage the first year?—I went out working as a labourer . . . cracking stones and so on . . . But in the meantime it killed my poor wife.
>
> What is your experience in regard to dealing with storekeepers?—Robert Smith is a decent fellow, but the others, as a rule, are very hard . . .
>
> What is the average interest rate?—They pretend to charge 10 per cent, and the unfortunate man finds they charged 2½ per cent for a renewal, and that comes about three times a year.
>
> That is 17½ per cent per annum.—Yes.

As with the metropolitan area, it is difficult today to assess the real extent of suffering in the country. There are occasional flashes of information which light up areas of struggle and despair, but how typical are they? Mr Ingram, a Beechworth magistrate, told a charity meeting in Melbourne that he had to send people to gaol to keep them alive. One old man had walked twenty-six miles to his court to ask for a place in the local benevolent asylum. Since it was full, the only thing he could do was to send him to gaol. 'To gaol!' echoed the old man. 'I winna gang tae gaol. I never was in gaol in my life, and rather than gang there noo I'll die in the bush.'

At Springhurst, a farmer named Dobson, oppressed by financial difficulties, killed himself and his three children. At Ballarat, the bank withdrew the £6,000 overdraft of James Johnson, a prominent stock and station agent. Johnson shot his wife, chloroformed his four children as they lay asleep, and poisoned himself. He recovered, but remained paralysed from the waist down. So they took him to the gallows in a wheelchair, and hanged him.

When there was no work to be had in country districts, many families flocked to the city, possessed of the illusion that where people herded together, there must be gainful employment. Most of them clung to this illusion through every form of privation and distress.

Protest meetings and processions of ragged, hungry men and women became a common feature of Melbourne, but were ruthlessly broken up by the police at the first sign of riotous behaviour. One such torchlight procession was announced for the night of 9 June 1892. A large crowd gathered on a vacant block at the corner of Madeline and Queensberry Streets, Carlton. Sixty foot constables and three mounted troopers were summoned to control them. The hour for the march came and went, but no torches, banners or marchers appeared. Then the police realized they had been fooled. Another large crowd of unemployed had assembled at the Trades Hall, and marched through the city with their fiery banners of protest. Many of the women demonstrators carried small children in their arms. Another sixty police were called out, but the march concluded with little violence.

A week later, a more serious incident occurred. A muttering crowd gathered at the premises of an auctioneer, Robert Wilson, of Station Street, Carlton. Wilson had evicted one Clarissa Stringer and her family into the street and seized their furniture for non-payment of rent. At about 5 p.m. the crowd rushed

Wilson's premises, and proceeded to tear away the iron bars guarding his windows. One iron bar had been torn loose, and most of the windows smashed, when a large squad of police arrived. They quickly dispersed the crowd by means of a baton charge. That was not the end of the incident. As the early winter darkness fell, large numbers of slum dwellers poured into the street, to be harangued by hot-tongued orators. One advised the crowd to obtain firearms. Another shouted that the police 'should have holes put through them'. But when a large detachment of foot police and mounted troopers arrived from the Russell Street barracks, the crowd was once again broken up. The troopers galloped up and down the road forcibly dispersing groups of agitators, 'amid groans and yells and curses, and cries of "Go in, Carlton," from larrikins in full retreat.'

Different tactics were now applied. Five hundred unemployed men and women marched without notice into Scots Church. They barracked the Rev. Marshall's sermon 'much to the horror of smug and scented Toorakia', sniggered the *Bulletin*.

Then in April 1893 a deputation of the unemployed waylaid the Premier, Mr Patterson, on the steps of the old Treasury building. They told him they were starving. One ragged figure told the Premier he had a wife and seven children who were near to death. If his protests failed, he said, the men would have to resort to violence. Mr Patterson replied that the government was doing what it could, and escaped into his office. That night a mass meeting at Richmond formed an Unemployed Workers' Association to continue the battle. Four days later, 2,000 of them marched in their rags through the city to the government buildings. A deputation was admitted to the Premier's office. Mr Patterson castigated them for their 'wild remarks' but said he would do what he could to find them employment.

What of the Trades Hall during this turbulent period? As always, it was divided between extremists who saw in mass suffering a reason and an opportunity to initiate a social revolution, and moderates who wished merely to alleviate the immediate distress. Their parliamentary representative, William Trenwith, M.L.A. for Richmond, helped to organize the unemployed into processions and protests. But, he warned them, 'As for using force, even if 30,000 men rioted in a body, they would fall before the onslaught of the police and military like corn before the wind.'

For a time the T.H.C. tried to maintain union rates of pay. But as conditions grew worse, it became a question of 'Work at the bosses' rate of pay—or starve.' Soon the T.H.C. was even forced to cut its own secretary's salary by 75 per cent—from £4 to £1 a week—and after that its bargaining position was hopeless. In the end, however, the sufferings of the unemployed provided much of the emotional mainspring for the rising Labor movement. Much of its militancy, surviving even down to the present day, can be traced back to the Great Depression of the 1890s.

While some worked, some starved, and some made speeches, others were

THE OLD MAN OF THE SEASON.

'Put me down on the land, or I'll bring the both of us down together with a crash,' the unemployed warned the Premier, J. B. Patterson.

fleeing for their very lives from the ruined city. During the summer of 1892 there began a significant exodus to other colonies. The discovery of rich gold deposits at Coolgardie, Western Australia, caused a sensation in the East. Soon hundreds of men were hurrying by ship to Perth and along the 370-mile track to the new El Dorado. Others headed for South Africa and New Zealand. In both countries they met a fairly chilly reception and found work nearly as difficult to get.

In three dreadful years, 1891, 1892, and 1893, Melbourne lost nearly 50,000 of her population. Typical population decreases in those years were:

Melbourne City	8,158
South Melbourne	7,874
Richmond	7,085
Collingwood	5,182
Fitzroy	4,183

The number of empty houses in city and suburbs grew from month to month. In 1891 J. H. Knipe, a real estate authority, estimated there were 7,000 empty houses in Melbourne. In November 1892 it was estimated that there were at least 12,000 houses standing empty in Melbourne, and average rents had dropped by half. Even wealthy suburbs like Kew had 132 houses standing empty by the end of 1893. Population of the suburb had dropped by 550.

'General' William Booth, the Salvation Army leader, visited Australia in 1891 in an endeavour to raise funds for his 'Darkest England' scheme—an attempt to show wealthy Britons that their charity was needed at home rather than among the natives of Africa. His first tour of Victoria raised only £400, but by the time he had toured the whole of Australia and New Zealand, £10,000 was in hand. Then Booth spoke out. While in the outback he had seen rich land on the Darling Downs going to waste. He proposed that three million paupers from London should be settled on small farms in the area. 'Where do these Australians get the land from that they should sit down like dogs in the manger and neither use the land themselves nor let anyone else do so?' he demanded. The scheme came to nothing. James Munro wrote to his fellow premiers: 'I should be prepared to take effectual measures to frustrate such a proceeding in relation to Victoria.' The other Premiers heartily concurred. What Booth had overlooked was that this was a self-righteous society which could cheerfully gaol an unemployed labourer who stole bread to feed his starving family, and yet tolerate shameful jobbery by its politicians and financiers operating under the cloak of respectable commerce.

5

Victorian Politics, 1875-1895

To understand how the Victorian dream of eternal prosperity was converted into nightmare, it is necessary to examine closely the political structure and events of the period.

The Australian States had arrived at that stage of evolution under the British flag where they had the power to make laws on practically every question that mattered. But because members of Parliament were poorly paid, if at all, it was almost essential for them to be 'men of property' in one form or another before they could afford to stand for election. One could be a self-made man like James Munro, M.L.A.; or the owner of great estates like Sir William Clarke, M.L.C.; or a tortured visionary like Alfred Deakin, M.L.A., who could make a living at the Bar during the day and fulfil his parliamentary duties in his free time. The principle was the same in each case: that before one could be elected to Parliament, it was almost essential to be a supporter of the general aims and outlook of the propertied class. The artisan and the labourer had a vote, but little effective choice between candidates. The final result was that the privileges and powers of Parliament were captured by men who, with a few notable exceptions, had risen by self-seeking methods and who were able to continue the process of self-aggrandizement backed by the machinery of State.

During the land boom the easiest way for an ambitious man to join this power elite was to put his spare cash into land speculation and trust in its rapid increase. If he had no cash, he could borrow it only too easily. For some years, especially in the 1880s, he could be practically certain of making his fortune. Few realized the curious economic osmosis which was taking place: much of the money being borrowed by the State was finally flowing into the pockets of the land profiteers, many of them actually being members of the governments which were floating the huge loans. Thus, as year followed greedy year, a group of men emerged who practically took over the functions of State and used them for private gain. Parliament became a sort of land speculators' club, where the most blatant 'log-rolling'—the use of political power for private gain—became commonplace. Fantastic sums were borrowed and spent on extending the railway network; and when the rails reached any particular point, it was often found that syndicates of M.P.s and their associates had bought up the land in advance for subdivision and resale. A rich State was plundered by the very men who had been elected to advance its interests; and many a perverted commercial and religious principle was advanced to support their activities.

There was no check from a truly radical party. Combinations in Parliament were erratic and liable to swift change, with only a vague general division at times between 'liberals' and 'conservatives'. Artisans in many trades were still trying to organize themselves into unions, often against the bitter and successful opposition of employers. It was too early for a Labor Party to be formed—although New South Wales was much nearer to it than Victoria.

When the land boom burst, many politicians who had been lent great sums by various financial institutions suddenly found themselves faced with cancellation of their overdrafts, as well as demands for large additional sums in payment of calls on shares. Their friends were suddenly penniless too. Many took advantage of a peculiar provision in Victorian law at the time, which enabled them to make a secret 'Composition by Arrangement' with their creditors, pay small amounts like 1d. in the £1 on their debts, and be completely discharged from insolvency without the knowledge of anyone beyond their creditors. The scandal of these 'secret compositions', or 'compotes' as they were often called, festered inside the body politic. Few people knew for certain who was solvent and who was not. Bank managers and moneylenders kept their own lists of these secret insolvencies, to guard against granting further credit. Public confidence and credit was severely shaken by the mysterious bankruptcies, and took years to recover.

The story of these extraordinary years may well start with Sir Graham Berry, liberal leader or demagogue according to taste. Berry was hated by the conservative element: to H. G. Turner his appointment as Premier in 1875 'marked the commencement of an era of political intrigue, Parliamentary degradation and shameless self-seeking'. Berry carried on an unrelenting war against the Upper House for its opposition to his radical measures, and even tried to reform the Council itself before the 1880 elections. In this ambitious endeavour he failed, and his followers were decimated at the polls. During his years in political eclipse, Berry became closely associated with a succession of bubble companies formed by Sir Matthew Davies. He was a director of Davies's Freehold Investment Co. Ltd, which took over a million of depositors' money with it when it crashed. He was London director of Davies's Mercantile Bank while holding the official post of Agent-General. On his return to Victoria to become State Treasurer in 1893, he joined the Mercantile's Melbourne board during the last dark days of that crumbling institution. And he defended Davies when nearly every other hand outside Parliament was turned against him.

After many complex manoeuvres, Sir Bryan O'Loghlen, an impecunious Irish baronet, succeeded to the Premiership in 1881. O'Loghlen's reign lasted less than two years, 1881 to 1883, during which time, in the words of H. G. Turner, the State finances 'drifted into a somewhat chaotic condition, involving the constant borrowing of trust funds, and the incurring of heavy obligations in anticipation of the floating of loans'. O'Loghlen was personally defeated in

GRAHAM BERRY ACCEPTS A KNIGHTHOOD

The Labour Party. – I made him what he is, and now he won't even look at me!
Sir Graham Berry. – Paw fellah! He weally doesn't seem to wealise that times 'as changed since I used to 'arangue him from a cart in Paddy's Market.

Duncan Gillies and Alfred Deakin subdivide the electoral paddock.

the 1883 elections, and did not regain a seat until 1888. He was Attorney-General in 1893, and became involved in a notable battle with his Solicitor-General, Isaac Isaacs, who insisted on prosecuting leading financiers. After that episode the electors again turned O'Loghlen out.

James Service was Premier of Victoria in the early days of the land boom, from 1883 to 1885. He was founder of James Service & Co., importers and wholesalers, and had been in Parliament intermittently since 1857. Probably his wisest parliamentary move was the introduction of a new Railway Management Act in 1883, which tried to abolish political influence over railway appointments. To a contemporary observer, Francis Adams, Service was a 'canny, senile Scotchman, listened to with respect as a preacher of monetary moderation, but more and more disregarded by a community which will bear neither whip nor rein on the financial road to (let us say) embarrassment'. But Service was by no means uninvolved in the land boom. He was a large shareholder and director of the Commercial Bank, which crashed largely because of its lavish advances to speculators. Service was also a director of the City Road Property Co. Ltd, whose curious methods of business were brought before the courts more than once.

Service retired through ill-health in 1886, and was succeeded by his Minister of Railways, Duncan Gillies, an old hand who had been in Parliament since 1860. Gillies kept on the Railways portfolio, took over the Treasury, and in a burst of political elephantiasis became Minister of Mines as well. He remained Premier throughout what H. G. Turner aptly described as 'The Era of Extravagance'. His greatest achievement was to raise Victoria's public debt from £19 million to £43 million in little more than six years, a record difficult to equal in any era of peace.

Gillies was described by his closest associate, Alfred Deakin, as

> short, stout, sturdy, florid, with clean-shaven face and close thin hair; an excellent constitutional authority and man of ripe experience in parliamentary affairs, a master both of the motives and dialect characteristic of the Victorian Chamber, clear-headed, and cold in temperament . . . without intimate friends but loyal to his associates and enjoying the confidence even of his opponents in his judgment and fairness.

But it was this model of political rectitude who, along with Alfred Deakin, was to give free rein to the land boomers and borrowers. No extravagance was too absurd for it to obtain Cabinet's tacit or open approval. Huge government and private loans were floated in Britain; enormous railway projects were undertaken; lavish exhibitions were planned; and the boom was merrily set upon its way.

Fairly typical of the companies formed by M.P.s during Gillies's reign was the Country Estates Co. Ltd, which proposed to subdivide land covered by thick scrub near the railway line at Neerim, Gippsland. The major shareholders were four members of the Legislative Assembly—J. F. Levien, A. C. Groom, Matthew Davies, and J. H. McColl—and two members of the Legislative Council—Sir Benjamin Benjamin, and Henry Gore. The government was persuaded that it was essential to build a station in the area, so the Railways Department bought six acres from the company at thirty times the original price. The government was also persuaded to build a metalled road through the scrub. The blocks were sold by A. C. Groom, M.L.A., an auctioneer who represented the district in Parliament. For years the area remained as weed-covered paddocks, but eventually became the township of Neerim South.

One of the key events of Gillies's reign as Premier was the appointment in 1887 of a Royal Commission on Banking. Its purpose was to examine the effect of the Companies Act upon banking business in Victoria. Under this Act 'banks of issue' were theoretically prohibited from making advances on the security of land. As chairman, Gillies appointed the colony's newest and most ambitious banker—Matthew Davies, M.L.A., who was making a great display with his new banks and land companies. Evidence was gravely taken from thirteen leading bankers, and the Royal Commission closed in record time. The only witness who spoke against the notion of allowing banks to speculate in land was Robert Dyce Reid, a squatter who had invested in some of the new companies. 'The charters which were given in old England, which restricted these powers, should not be rent and torn asunder very lightly', he told the Commissioners. They took no notice whatever. The new powers were granted to the banks, in time to exaggerate the effects of the land boom.

Alfred Deakin as a Victorian M.L.A. and Minister was deeply involved in land-booming activities. He later prayed in his diaries for forgiveness.

Offices of the City of Melbourne Building Society, still standing on the corner of Elizabeth and Little Collins Streets. Alfred Deakin was chairman.

The seriousness of coming events was little understood by the time of the 1889 elections, and Gillies was returned to power. Conditions were still quite prosperous, there was little unemployment so far, and Gillies's policies of extravagant borrowing seemed to work. Few realized how deeply the future was being mortgaged. Businessmen and land speculators were still popular figures: they packed the Gillies Cabinet and the Parliament.

As his Chief Secretary and Acting Premier during his absences, Gillies appointed the brilliant barrister and journalist, the ambitious and practised politician, Alfred Deakin. In Francis Adams's view, Deakin was 'the Victorian native of ability, tempted by the Anglomania of the rich Melbournians to schemes of Imperial Federation, but at heart undecided, waiting his hour and chance.' Deakin's part in the land boom remains an enigma. Adept at describing other people and their motives, he did not describe his own—a characteristic which we may perhaps attribute to his early journalistic training. Deakin was a leading Cabinet Minister during almost the entire period of the 1880s, yet does not seem to have brought his keen intelligence to bear on the State's headlong rush to disaster. Radical yet not radical, Deakin soon showed that as a Cabinet Minister he was not the man to prosecute the authors of financial disaster with any vigour. The reasons are not hard to find. Deakin was too closely involved with several of the biggest land boomers to be very interested in checking their meteoric careers. For instance, Deakin became chairman of the City of Melbourne Building Society when Sir Matthew Davies retired from that position. Its over-decorated building still stands on the southeastern corner of Elizabeth Street and Little Collins Street. Deakin was also a director of James Munro's Australian Property & Investment Co. Ltd when it crashed. Ambition, if not desire for a quick fortune, makes strange bedfellows. Thus in 1888 we see Deakin becoming foundation chairman of the Australian City & Suburban Investment & Banking Co. Ltd. This company with its grandiloquent title floated on the stock market and asked the public to subscribe no less than £5 million for its shares. Its purpose was to take over the properties of G. W. Taylor, a land-booming Mayor of Prahran, who had engorged 35,000 acres of land and was suffering serious financial indigestion as a result. How Deakin came to be so closely associated with Taylor and his crew remains one of the mysteries which the future Prime Minister never revealed. The best guess is that it was through his close friend, Theodore Fink. The firm of Fink, Best & Phillips acted as legal advisers to Taylor's great boom company, which ruined thousands of people when it crashed.

As Minister of Defence, Gillies had James Bell, M.L.C., a Melbourne businessman who had been a Minister without Portfolio from 1886 onwards. Bell was a director of the Mercantile Bank. He was to be charged (but not committed) for agreeing to issue a false balance sheet to shareholders of the bank.

Gillies appointed an *Age* journalist, John Lamont Dow, as his Minister of Lands. Dow became a director of the notorious Premier Building Association, and borrowed heavily here and there for personal land transactions. His creditors were held off until 1893, when he went bankrupt for £26,000, with assets worth precisely twelve shillings. Cross-examined in court, he claimed he had been 'induced' into land deals. 'The next man that comes to you with a good thing, hit him with a club', he advised Judge Molesworth. 'From 1886 to 1890 I was Minister of Lands and was paying all I could out of my salary of £1,500 a year to my creditors', Dow told the court. (It was supposed to be illegal for an insolvent to remain a Member of Parliament.) Dow's cross-examination revealed other scandalous facts. He had made early application for the release of his estate, because he 'wanted to regain his seat in Parliament'. His creditors had agreed in advance to release him if he impounded his parliamentary salary for their benefit. Among these creditors were George Chaffey and Stephen Cureton, two directors of Chaffey Bros Ltd. Dow had been Minister of Lands at the time that independent Mallee settlers were battling against the Chaffey interests. He had helped put through the Act which in effect gave control of the Murray waters to the Chaffeys, while at the same time borrowing money from them for his personal expenses.

Gillies appointed a biscuit manufacturer, F. T. Derham, M.L.A. for Port Melbourne, as his Postmaster-General. Derham had married Frances Swallow, and become managing director of her father's biscuit manufactory, Swallow & Ariell Ltd. But Frederick Derham's world was not circumscribed by biscuits, or even politics. In a colossal, outrageous series of land boom transactions, he went bankrupt for £550,000, made a secret composition with his creditors, paid 1d. in the £1, and gracefully retired from Cabinet—nonetheless remaining in Parliament until defeated at the general election in 1892.

As Commissioner of Public Works, Gillies appointed John Nimmo, who was M.L.A. for South Melbourne, and chairman of the Premier Building Association. Nimmo was an engineer by profession, who had become municipal surveyor for South Melbourne when it was known as Emerald Hill. He was more famous for being Melbourne's leading exponent of the poetry of his countryman, Robert Burns. Nimmo was first elected to the Assembly in 1877, was tried (but found not guilty) in connection with the building society frauds, and departed from the colony never to return. Nimmo was followed as Minister of Public Works by William Anderson, M.L.A. for Heytesbury, a Western District builder and farmer, an elder of the Presbyterian Church, and a director of the Mercantile Bank. He was later tried (but acquitted) in connection with the Mercantile Bank conspiracy charges.

Outside Cabinet, both the Lower and Upper Houses were full of financiers, speculators, and entrepreneurs of high and low degree. Some went bankrupt during the crash, some escaped insolvency by a narrow margin.

Sir Matthew Davies, M.L.A. for Toorak, and Speaker during the Munro government's period of office, was not the greatest of speculators on his own account. His personal debts totalled a mere £280,000 when he went bankrupt. His chief claim to fame was that he built up a fantastic network of more than thirty interlocking companies, which borrowed millions from the public and lent it to each other for land speculation. Theodore Fink's and Frank Gavan Duffy's brilliant court-room defence saved Davies from almost certain imprison-

THE PERSONIFICATION OF VICTORIAN STATESMANSHIP.

A contemporary view of the ethics of mixing business with politics.

PROSPECTUS

OF

THE "FREEHOLD FARMS" COMPANY

(LIMITED.)

To be Registered under the "Companies Statute 1864."

CAPITAL, £1,000,000 IN 200,000 SHARES OF £5 EAC[H]

The first issue, now offered to the public, will be limited to 100,000 shares, of which 35,000 have been take[n] privately, leaving 65,000 to be subscribed for.

Two pounds per share only to be called up, in the following manner: 5s. per share on application, 10s. per shar[e on] allotment, 5s. per share at intervals of two months until the £2 per share is paid up.

It is not anticipated that any further calls will be required, but should any be made, they will not exceed 5s. per share, nor be at intervals of less than three months. No PREFERENTIAL [or] PROMOTERS' shares will be issued. The share list will remain open until Monday, July 30th, but shares will be allotted according to priority of application.

THE COMPANY WILL BE REGISTERED WHEN 70,000 SHARES ARE APPLIED [FOR]

OFFICE OF THE COMPANY:

Premier Buildings, 54 Collins Street East.

Provisional Directors:—

Hon. GEO. YOUNG, M.L.C.
Hon. JAMES MUNRO, M.L.A.
Hon. JOHN DOW, M.L.A.
Hon. JOHN NIMMO, M.L.A.
Hon. JAMES WILLIAMSON, M.L.C.
J. H. WHEELER, ESQ., M.L.A.
C. YOUNG, ESQ., M.L.A.
WM. ANDERSON, ESQ., M.L.A.
J. HARRIS, ESQ., (St. Kilda), M.L.A.
JOSEPH BOSISTO, ESQ., C.M.G., M.L.A.
CHAS. SMITH, ESQ., M.L.A.
THOS. HUNT, ESQ., M.L.A.
E. H. CAMERON, ESQ., M.L.A.
JAMES SHACKELL, ESQ., M.L.A.
GEO. GODFREY, ESQ.
JOSEPH TROTMAN, ESQ., Wangaratta, J.P.
J. H. CHRYSTAL, ESQ., Yea.
T. K. DOW, ESQ.

Bankers:—

CITY OF MELBOURNE BANK.

Surveyors:—

Messrs. MUNTZ & BAGE, Collins-street West.
Messrs. ANDERSON & BROWN, Collins-street East.

Solicitors:—

Messrs. MADDOCK & JOHNSTON, Queen street.
(Another Firm to be appointed.)

Brokers:—

Messrs. WILLDER & GRIFFITHS, 22 Collins street West.
Messrs. JAMES DONALDSON & CO., Collins street West.
Messrs. ROBERTS & EVANS, 104 Elizabeth-street.
Mr. H. F. RICHARDSON, Geelong.
Messrs. D. & H. M'LEAN, Geelong.
Messrs. LAMBERT & WALKER, Ballarat.
Messrs. A. PORRITT & CO., Beechworth.
Messrs. A. M'LEAN & CO., Maffra.

Auctioneers & Agents:—

Messrs. GREIG & MURRAY, Limited, Queen-street.
Messrs. GEMMELL & TUCKETT, Collins-street West.
Messrs. SHACKELL & WHITE, Echuca.
Messrs. MUNRO & BAILLIEU, Collins-street East.

Secretary:—

JAMES H. MIRAMS, ESQ., 54 Collins-street East.

This company is being formed for the purpose of purchasing the following country properties, with the object of subdividing them into farm, orchard, garden, and vineyard lots, to be re-sold upon easy and extended terms, thereby giving to country residents and investors the same and even greater opportunities for securing freehold properties as town residents have long enjoyed through the medium of building societies. The properties referred to are the Glenmore Estate, near Ballan; the Ballark Estate, near Mount Wallace; the Killingworth Estate, on the Goulbourn, near Yea; Bushby park, on the Avon, Gippsland; and the far-famed Barwon park Estate, near Geelong. These properties have all been selected on account of the special facilities they afford for subdivision, and also on account of their suitableness for every variety of cultivation.

The provisional directors are assured that, as no more Crown lands are available for agricultural settlement, the demand for farms, orchards, vineyards and gardens can only be supplied by the subdivision of the immense areas now held by private owners; and that the operations, therefore, of this company must, while meeting a great and growing public want, also provide large and continuous profits for its shareholders.

It is evident also, from the present state of opinion upon agricultural questions, that the time has come when wheat growing must be abandoned to a large extent in favour of the cultivation of other products which are suitable to our soils and climate, and for the production of which smaller areas and greater attention are required. To meet this phase of this industry every encouragement will be afforded by this company, while the easy terms upon which it will be prepared to treat with its customers will place the land required within the reach of all.

The following is the scale of repayments upon which it is proposed to offer the various subdivisions to intending purchasers.—

TABLES of REPAYMENTS.

To be made on £100 of Purchase Money for Allotments in—

	Monthly.			Quarterly.			Half-yearly.		
	£	s.	d.	£	s.	d.	£	s.	d.
For 2 years	4	10	0	13	12	0	27	7	6
For 4 years	2	8	0	7	6	0	14	18	9
For 6 years	1	14	6	5	4	6	10	11	0
For 8 years	1	7	6	4	3	3	8	8	0

If the purchaser elects to buy upon the above terms, he must pay 20 per cent. of his purchase money in cash, and for the balance pay according to this table for every £100, or fraction of £100, for the number of years he chooses.

While these extended terms will be availab[le to] all who choose to make use of them, it wi[ll be] optional for any purchaser to buy upon the [illegible] terms of one fourth cash, and the balance in [illegible] 18, and 24 months.

There can be no question but that, with [illegible] terms available, the demand for land on the [illegible] of the public must be large and increasing, [illegible] young men in the country districts find it [illegible]sary to strike out for themselves and make [illegible] of their own. So long, therefore, as this [illegible] continues, this company must reap the [illegible] arising from its operations in finding the [illegible] the manner and upon the terms specified.

Applications for shares can be made [illegible] or by letter, not later than July 28, to [illegible] the brokers or agents; or to the secretary, [illegible] Jas. H. Mirams, at the office of the company, Premier-buildings, 54 Collins-street east.

Part of the prospectus of the Freehold Farms Co. Ltd, which included 14 members of Parliament as provisional directors.

ment. Sir Matthew Davies retired from Parliament during his time of troubles, and after one abortive attempt to re-establish himself, never entered politics again.

His successor as member for the wealthy area of Toorak was Alexander McKinley, President of the Malvern Shire Council, proprietor of the weekly comic paper, *Melbourne Punch*, and manager (with his brother James) of the ill-fated *Daily Telegraph*. McKinley bought the Austral Buildings at 115 Collins Street, and a printery in Alfred Place nearby. He used the columns of *Punch* and the *Daily Telegraph* to attack his enemies inside and outside Parliament. He even berated one of the Justices of the Peace who was hearing the committal proceedings against Sir Matthew Davies. (At the time, Davies's banks were financing both *Punch* and the *Telegraph*.) In 1895, however, the depression finally caught up with McKinley. He made a secret composition with his creditors for debts of £45,000, paying them 3d. in the £1.

B. J. Fink, M.L.A. for Maryborough, was undoubtedly the greatest suburban and city land boomer in Australian history. His private composition with creditors in 1892 was so vast and involved so many people that it could not be kept quiet. Fink listed £1,520,000 in debts, and paid ½d. in the £1 before departing to London for ever.

Joseph Harris, M.L.A. for South Yarra, was a nurseryman who got himself involved in land deals to the extent of £40,000. His secret composition was made in 1895, when he paid 7d. in the £1. Harris's continued occupation of his parliamentary seat when undoubtedly insolvent was a hidden scandal of no mean order.

Thomas Langdon, M.L.A. for Korong, was a farmer and produce dealer in the Boort district when he first persuaded his fellows to elect him. He soon became involved in the land boom as director of Thomas Bent's marvellous Heights of Maribyrnong Estate Co. Ltd. Langdon went bankrupt in 1889. He became a Minister in Bent's Cabinets early in the twentieth century.

Richard Bulmer Stamp was a financial agent and manager of the Commercial Financial Property Co. Ltd of 229 Collins Street. He borrowed heavily from Sir Matthew Davies's institutions, lost the lot, and quietly paid 6d. in the £1. Then he got Cabinet's backing to stand for Parliament in 1892, but withdrew when exposed as a secret insolvent by *Table Talk*.

Captain Charles Frederick Taylor, M.L.A. for Hawthorn, was a barrister who accumulated £96,000 in debts on land transactions. Taylor made a secret composition in 1892, paying his creditors 2s. 6d. in the £1. More than £20,000 of the money came from Davies's Australian Deposit & Mortgage Bank. Captain Taylor continued to occupy his seat in Parliament both before and after the election of 20 April 1892, even though his secret composition had been made sixteen days before that date.

Joseph Winter, M.L.A. for Melbourne South, was a paper ruler, journalist, and former president of the Trades Hall Council. Winter was undoubtedly in a state of insolvency while still holding his seat in Parliament, but managed to stave off his creditors until just before his premature death in 1896. A relative,

THE MINISTER AND THE INVENTOR.

Minister.—"TAKE A SEAT, MR. WOODS. YOU GOT MY LETTER; GOOD. YOU ARE AWARE THAT THE DEPARTMENT IS VERY ANXIOUS TO PURCHASE THE PATENT OF YOUR EXCELLENT CONTINUOUS BREAK. WOULD YOU KINDLY NAME A SUM?"

Mr. Woods.—"OH, REALLY YOU'RE TOO KIND. I HARDLY KNOW—THAT IS, I WOULD MUCH SOONER YOU PUT A VALUE ON IT FOR ME—*(pause)*—SUPPOSE I SAY—AHEM--£6000."

Minister.—"NONSENSE; YOU'RE TOO MODEST, DOUBLE IT—SAY £12,000."

Mr. Woods.—"VERY WELL, MY DEAR SIR, JUST AS *you* WISH."

Minister.—"RIGHT, MY DEAR BOY."

An early railways scandal: John Woods, MLA, pays himself twice as much for his patent braking system as it is worth.

Sam Winter, owner of the *Herald*, gave him good advice and small loans, but when the day of reckoning came it was found that Joseph had accumulated £50,000 in debts and could pay only 3d. in the £1. Most of the debts dated back to the land boom. After the 1894 elections which swept the conservatives from power, Joseph Winter became deputy leader of the embryonic Parliamentary Labor Party. He was appointed chairman of a Royal Commission on State Banking, which reported adversely on the private banks' policies during the boom and led to the establishment of a State-guaranteed credit foncier system. The report was only just completed in 1896 when Winter died at the age of forty-three.

John Woods, M.L.A. for Stawell, was a fiery character, a Liverpool-born locomotive engineer, who had played a leading part in the goldminers' agitations at the Ovens, Goulburn and Ararat diggings. He was elected almost continuously to Parliament until his death, except for a period from 1865–6, when he was employed by the government to supervise works at the Malmesbury reservoir. He was summarily dismissed from this post for conniving with the contractors to break down the standards of construction, but was soon returned to Parliament again by the miners' votes. Woods became Minister of Railways in the Berry government of 1875, and again from 1877–80. He became involved with James Munro in certain curious land boom deals to be specified later. He died in 1892, just as the financial manoeuvres were emerging into the light of day.

While the Legislative Assembly was permeated with the activities of the speculator, the Legislative Council was just as entranced by the land boom. Of its forty-eight members, no fewer than thirty were directors of public companies inviting deposits from or selling their shares to the public. Committed to *laissez-faire* capitalism, rationalizing others' misfortunes as 'survival of the fittest', the Victorian Upper House fought for years to maintain the privileges of its class and to emasculate desperately needed measures of reform.

James Balfour, M.L.C. for South-Eastern Province, was a leading Melbourne merchant who became deeply involved in the boom through his association with Sir Matthew Davies and E. C. Elliott, a stockbroker. He narrowly escaped sequestration, and painfully built up his business again after the crash.

Sir Benjamin Benjamin, sometime Lord Mayor, and M.L.C. for Melbourne Province, was a director of both the Colonial Bank and the Imperial Bank. His dealings with those collapsed institutions drove him into bankruptcy and out of public life.

James Stewart Butters, M.L.C. for North-Eastern Province, was a broker, a founder of the Caledonian Society in 1859, Mayor of Melbourne in 1867, and a great charity worker. Unfortunately he dabbled too deeply in shares on his own account. He made a secret composition for £27,000 in 1892, paying ½d. in the £1, but at least had the grace to resign his seat beforehand for 'private reasons'.

J. M. Davies, M.L.C. for South Yarra, was not as deeply involved in the land boom as his brother Sir Matthew, but suffered nearly as hard a fall. James Munro appointed him Minister of Justice in his 1890 Cabinet. At this time he was also a director of the Commercial Bank and the Trustees, Executors & Agency Co. Ltd, but was forced to resign these positions when the Davies scandals emerged in 1892. He stopped work on his 'gorgeous, palace-like' £70,000 house opposite the Malvern Convent, and resumed practice as a solicitor.

Henry Gore, M.L.C. for Wellington electorate, a civil engineer by profession, was enticed into several strange deals. He bought Yawong Station near St Arnaud (Vic.) for £7,000, but had to sell for £2,000 'owing to incursion of rabbits'. He sank another £12,000 into shares in the Zeehan & Dundas Railway, the Country Estates Co. Ltd, and the British Broken Hill Co.—'all of which collapsed and the said amounts absolutely lost'. Then, he told the Ballarat Supreme Court, 'I was induced by misrepresentations to buy £5,000 worth of shares in the North Shore Tramway Co. of Sydney'—which was nothing but a line on the map drawn through impenetrable scrub on the north side of Sydney Harbour.

An estate agent, Frederick Illingworth, M.L.C. for Northern Province, helped form the Centennial Land Bank in 1888. He used the bank's funds and floated huge overdrafts on his own account for a series of disastrous speculations which lost his creditors nearly a quarter of a million pounds, and drove him out of the colony.

C. H. James, M.L.C. for Southern Province, was one of the earliest land boomers, whose techniques were borrowed by his young solicitor, Matthew Davies. James became a millionaire on paper, a leading banker and entrepreneur, and a large-scale grazier. After the crash his debts were proved at £850,000, on which his deceased estate paid about 8d. in the £1.

Dr George LeFevre, M.L.C. for North Yarra, was a Collins Street specialist who had studied in Edinburgh under Lister. For many years he extracted diseased organs from his patients and a fortune from land deals with equal dexterity; while helping to make the State's laws in his spare time. He was associated with the temperance movement from its inception; and was a chairman of the Freehold Investment Co. Ltd. LeFevre died in Edinburgh during the crash, and according to his will left an estate valued at £100,000. But within a few months of his death, most of the companies in which he owned shares had failed. Practically his entire fortune disappeared into the maw of the land crash. In 1913 LeFevre's estate paid a first and final dividend of ½d. in the £1. The Bank of Victoria, to which he owed £20,000, got £40. The Mercantile Bank liquidators got back £20; and the Federal Bank liquidators £14. Such sums were typical of the meagre repayments made to their creditors by many of the speculating politicians and businessmen of the land boom era.

The Gillies-Deakin government, engorged, bloated and rotten, fell in October 1890. Its remarkably long reign of eight years was attributed by the *Illustrated Australian News* to the fact that 'the carrots were always ready and the asses were willing to nibble'. But when the Treasury had been emptied, when the trust funds had been drained of more than one million pounds, when the public was at last beginning to doubt the wisdom of extravagance as a method of government, a large group of members rebelled and voted Gillies and Deakin out of office. Ironically enough, the rebellion was led by James Munro, an excitable Scot who enjoyed an extraordinary rise from obscurity to fame, thence to notoriety, thence back to obscurity. Munro was head of the Federal Bank and Real Estate Bank, whose collapse was to disclose wholesale milking of depositors' funds by Munro and his family. Munro's cabinet may be considered as somewhat an improvement on that of Gillies, but the basic nature of Parliament remained practically the same. The major accomplishment of Munro's short reign was to rush through the Voluntary Liquidation Act 1891, by means of which the boom companies (including Munro's own) were protected from compulsory liquidation and subsequent court examination. A few weeks later, Munro appointed himself Agent-General in London, and fled the colony.

After Munro's hasty departure, William Shiels, M.L.A. for Normanby, who had consistently opposed Gillies's extravagant policies, became Premier and Treasurer early in 1892. Shiels did what he could to retrench and save the

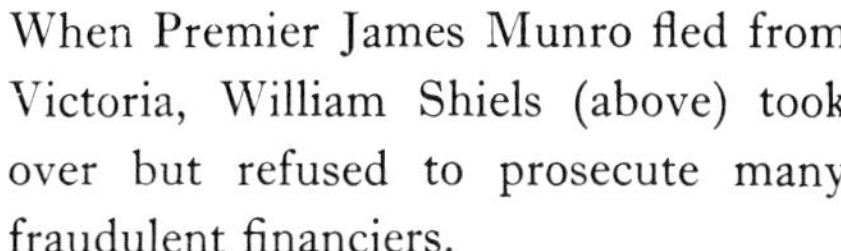

When Premier James Munro fled from Victoria, William Shiels (above) took over but refused to prosecute many fraudulent financiers.

J. B. Patterson, who followed William Shiels as Premier, also refused to prosecute many bank directors and others who had caused the depression.

colony's credit, but later complained (in an apologia called *The World's Depression*) that 'if all our bankers, our statesmen, our merchants, and our private investors had been a combination of the wisdom of Solomon and Solon, we could not have escaped a time of severe depression.' In brief, Shiels believed that the crash in Victoria was only a symptom of world-wide depression. This convenient excuse was used to avoid official prosecutions on the financial scandals which were then sweeping the city.

Shiels' reluctance to act was echoed by his successor, J. B. Patterson, who forced the Solicitor-General, Isaac Isaacs, out of his Cabinet when Isaacs insisted on prosecutions being launched. Patterson himself, it must be noted, was not entirely free of the taint of speculation. He was an estate agent by profession, and one of the foundation subscribers in the Heights of Maribyrnong Estate Co. Ltd, along with Thomas Bent, B. J. Fink, and other M.P.s.

When the banks reached a point of no return in 1893, Patterson proved himself an incompetent fumbler. 'We are all floundering', was his helpless comment when told that the National Bank intended to suspend business. In New South Wales the government quickly guaranteed the payment of bank notes in gold, and public alarm in that State was quelled. In Victoria the government proclaimed a week's 'banking holiday', adding panic to depression. Patterson's excuse did not help matters: 'I do not think it would be profitable to employ Sands & McDougall's to print off bank notes and let everyone have thousands of them.'

Thus the whole of the State's political power was riddled through and through by the activities and offshoots of the land speculators. Only a rare voice in Parliament, that of a Robert Reid or an Isaac Isaacs, was raised against the scandals of the day. Newspaper criticism caused the fall of government after government at the polls, yet the position did not really improve until after the grim lessons of 1893, when half of Melbourne was out of work and starving.

Before the 1894 elections, the *Age* thundered: 'The very political depravity of the Premier has raised up a revulsion of feeling.' After the elections:

> The country has spoken, and its voice is a rout for Toryism . . . The Patterson Government, bad as it was, was a sort of blessing in disguise. The very monstrousness of its sins made the populace revolt, and Parliament is swept as with a broom by the fiery breath of public indignation.

Three of Patterson's Ministers were rejected by the aroused electorate, and Patterson himself was humiliated by being elected 'second candidate' in his constituency. The Liberal-Protectionist Party—whose candidates were supported by the *Age*—won a sweeping victory. Conservatives and land boomers were toppled from power. Sir Bryan O'Loghlen was crushingly defeated at Port Fairy. Brighton rejected the Speaker, Thomas Bent, for the first time in nearly twenty-five years. Even Toorak threw out McKinley and Langdon in favour of Robert Reid. G. D. Carter narrowly escaped defeat. Joseph Harris lost South Yarra. And so it went.

George Turner, a cautious but liberal-minded solicitor, headed the cleansed Parliament, with a triumphantly vindicated Isaac Isaacs as his Attorney-General. They instituted a far-reaching legislative programme—reform of the insolvency laws, reform of the company laws, reform of the banking system. Every bill was attacked, deferred, and watered down by the aristocrats of the Legislative Council, sitting sullenly behind their ramparts while the radical phase lasted. But some useful measures were pushed through in amended form.

The events of earlier years cried aloud for a Royal Commission, but part of the price of political power was that no vindictiveness should be shown towards the leaders of the boom. Besides, the Turner government was too busy with the work of clearing up the wreckage and rigging a jury mast to enable the tattered ship of State to sail on. Only two specialized investigations were made. One was a Royal Commission into events at Mildura, where the Chaffey brothers' enterprise had crashed. The second was a Royal Commission on State Banking, appointed mainly to enquire into the feasibility of establishing a State Bank. The majority report was caustic enough:

> The recommendation of the Royal Commission on Banking Laws of 1887, subsequently passed into law, providing that all banks should come under the Companies Act and loan their deposits on landed security without restriction, gave legal sanction to a practice which has been fraught with serious consequences to the community . . . The recommendations of that Commission were evidently made in the spirit of speculation which dominated the community during the 'boom' period . . .

Robert Murray-Smith and F. S. Grimwade put in a dissenting minority report: 'The permanent prosperity and progress of the country will be best

SCHEDULE D.; OR PREPARING TO GO THROUGH THE COURT.
(A VERY DISTRESSING CASE).

Loopholes in the insolvency laws made fraud easy.

secured by leaving to free and unchecked development the forces of individual energy and enterprise which have always distinguished British communities.'

Meanwhile, behind the smoke of battle and the work of reconstruction, a powerful new political force, the Labor Party, was emerging. Led by two survivors from the old Parliament, W. A. Trenwith and Joseph Winter, the party was now reckoned to number sixteen members of the Legislative Assembly, give or take one or two wavering liberals. Henceforth, until the emergence of the Country Party, no Victorian government could make a move without taking the attitude of the Labor bloc into consideration. It was a startling change from the time when the land boomers ran Parliament as they pleased, not so many years before.

6

F. T. Derham, Postmaster-General and Speculator

In the wildest reaches of fiction, it would be hard to imagine a Postmaster-General of Her Majesty's Government who could accumulate more than half a million pounds in debts on land and share deals, who could make a secret composition with his creditors, and who could satisfy them by paying a penny in the pound. Yet that is what happened in the 1880s, to Federick Thomas Derham, Postmaster-General in the Gillies-Deakin Government, managing director of Swallow & Ariell Ltd, and land-boomer extraordinary. As in the case of B. J. Fink and other large speculators, it is necessary to multiply his debts by at least fifteen times to simulate present-day values. Today the equivalent of Derham's debts would be nearer $17 million.

Derham was the son of Thomas Plumley Derham, a solicitor of Bristol, England, who migrated to Victoria in 1856, bringing his wife Sarah and family. Young Frederick was twelve at the time. T. P. Derham went into partnership with J. W. Eggleston at Imperial Chambers, Bank Place, Melbourne, and conducted a thriving legal business until entwined with his son Frederick in certain land transactions.

In 1864, at the age of twenty, Frederick Derham married Ada M. Anderson, who died at an early age. During this period Derham was working as a wheat broker for Callender, Caldwell & Co. of King Street. In 1878, he married Frances D. Swallow, daughter of a prosperous Welsh-born biscuit manufacturer, Thomas Swallow of Port Melbourne. Following the death of his partner T. H. Ariell (the other half of 'Swallow & Ariell'), Swallow took his son-in-law into the business in 1879 and changed the firm's name to Swallow & Derham. The firm progressed rapidly, extending its business from biscuits to plum puddings (introduced in 1882) and hermetically sealed 'Canterbury Cakes' (1885).

But Frederick Derham had political ambitions, which were to bring him into early contact with the parliamentary land-boomers and cause his financial downfall. In 1883, at the age of thirty-nine, Derham was elected as M.L.A. for Sandridge (now Port Melbourne), and in 1886 was appointed Postmaster-General by Duncan Gillies.

It was a time when a firm hand was needed in the Post Office. The colony's

F. T. Derham, Postmaster-General and managing director of Swallow & Ariell Ltd.

Thomas Swallow, founder of the biscuit firm, who put son-in-law Derham in charge.

DERHAM NATIONALISES THE TELEPHONE SERVICE

Henry Byron Moore (right) demands £77,000 compensation for his private phone exchange. Derham cannot hear him at that price.

Already unscrupulous persons are taking advantage of the helplessness of the victims in the late banking disasters by buying up banking deposits at a tithe of their real value.—Vide Daily Paper.

The *Illustrated Sydney News* foresaw how some people would profit from the smash.

telephone services, run by private companies, were in complete chaos. No-one knew how to sort out the mess until Derham came along and nationalised them, much to their unspoken relief. In 1888 he reduced the inland postage rate from 2d. to 1d. a letter, and post office business doubled almost overnight. Deposits in the Post Office Savings Bank increased enormously—and helped many thrifty folk to cushion the blow of the coming smash.

At George Meudell's suggestion, Derham copied the Berlin *rohrpost* system of sending letters and telegrams across the city by pneumatic tube. The first tube was opened in 1889 between the Stock Exchange and Elizabeth Street Post Office, later being extended to newspaper offices and other centres of activity. Derham also established a rapid direct mail service between Adelaide and Melbourne. Special express trains brought the mails to Melbourne in a few hours instead of the day or more taken by ships.

With his substantial private fortune and business operations behind him, and a successful record as government minister, Derham rushed headlong into the land boom. His reputation was sufficient to get him overdrafts, mortgages, whatever he wanted, from the colony's leading financial institutions. His first move was to set up the Queensland Investment Company to purchase sugar and fruit plantations in that State. The company borrowed heavily from the banks, and Derham in turn borrowed £33,000 from it for his other enterprises. In 1883, the company established the Hambledon Sugar Plantations, acquired sixty years later by the CSR Co. Ltd.

In 1888, Swallow and Derham floated the biscuit factory as a public company, using the old name Swallow & Ariell Ltd. One of the new directors was James Bell, Minister of Defence in the Gillies Government, and director of Matthew Davies's Mercantile Bank. Derham received £140,000 in ready cash from the flotation. But it all went down the gurgling sink of the crash. When Swallow & Ariell Ltd went into liquidation and called up the balance of its capital, Derham himself could not pay nearly £30,000 due in calls on his own company's shares.

During the same year as the flotation, Derham bought the site of a former E.S. & A. Bank on the north-western corner of Elizabeth Street and Flinders Lane, paying £65,000 for the 80-foot x 53-foot block. He demolished it and started building a new office block before arranging the finance to finish the job—'one of the maddest things done in the mad boom era,' wrote Meudell. But Derham's imagination was soaring high. He planned to erect Melbourne's tallest building—no less than fifteen storeys, almost a skyscraper! In honour of his adopted country, Derham called it the Australian Building. It still stands today as the Australian Provincial Assurance Building. To raise the money to complete the structure, Derham floated the Australian Property & Investment Co. Ltd and sent George Meudell to London, where he succeeded in borrowing £400,000 from the Home & Colonial Assets & Debenture Corporation Ltd. 'Most reluctantly one had to agree to cut four stories off the top of the fifteen-story building, plans of which I carried in a golf bag,' wrote Meudell.

And so the wondrous building soared skywards under the inspiration of its young architect, Henry Kemp, and its builder, James Anderson. To support its 150-foot height, the granite walls were more than three feet thick at the base, tapering as they rose. Even at its reduced height, it was still the tallest office building in the world at that time—and remained Melbourne's highest building for more than sixty years. On the ground floor was a row of shops. Two hydraulic lifts took visitors up to the 220 offices, each of which was connected by a speaking tube with the entrance hall, with an electric indicator showing whether a tenant was in or out. Cost of the building was £80,000, making the total value of building and site £145,000. But when it was finished and opened for business towards the end of 1889, the boom had already begun to burst and office space proved almost impossible to let.

Derham now operated an ingenious *blague* on the shareholders of the Real Estate Bank. It must be remembered that Derham owned a large proportion of the Australian Property Co.'s 20,000 £10 shares, which had been paid up to only £5. (Another large parcel was held by David Beath, the Flinders Lane softgoods trader, and a fellow director with Derham of the Royal Bank). If the Australian Property Co. failed and was forced to call up its remaining capital, this event alone would have sent Derham bankrupt. So, with the connivance of the Real Estate Bank's chairman, James Munro, the bank bought out the company's assets in November, 1889. That is why, in Derham's subsequent insolvency in 1892, not a mention appeared of his losses on the Australian Building.

Table Talk picked up the matter from the Real Estate Bank's next balance sheet, and pointedly said on 14 August 1891: 'It is very difficult to understand why the keen-witted directors, of which Mr. Munro is the chairman, saddled themselves with these enormous additional liabilities.' The whole horrific story was finally disclosed in the report of the liquidators of the Real Estate Bank early in 1893. It was shown that the bank's purchases for the year ended 30 June 1891 were £633,000, which 'comprised chiefly the assets of the Australian Property Co . . . the sales for the same period being £3,490.' The liquidators submitted a case for the opinion of counsel, but were advised that 'no criminal action would lie against the directors.' The shareholders just had to grin and bear it.

Meanwhile, F. T. Derham was in serious trouble on other fronts. As companies fell right and left, constant callsa nd demands for mortgage payments came in. In 1890 Derham made a final desperate effort to avoid the Insolvency Court. One of his creditors held a £20,000 mortgage over a large area of land which Derham had bought at Preston, and was pressing for repayment. Derham floated a mirage called the Balmoral Land Company, with a nominal capital of £45,000, to subdivide and resell the land—an almost impossible task in that year.

At the same time (it was later revealed in the Supreme Court), Derham's colleagues in Cabinet and certain other associates agreed to contribute £500 each towards his assistance. One of these was William Irving Winter, M.L.C., who sent a cheque for £125 and promissory notes for the balance. But when Winter's cheque arrived, it was paid into the Balmoral Land Company, and he

While their employer engaged in his extraordinary speculative activities, girls worked long hours in the Swallow & Ariell factory for low wages -- and considered themselves lucky to have a job at all.

was allotted a number of partly-paid shares without being informed of the transaction. More than a year later, Winter was stunned to receive a demand for calls of nearly £1,000 on his shares in the Balmoral Land Company! Winter stormed with rage. He applied to Mr Justice Hood for his name to be struck from the list of Balmoral shareholders, and won the case. Derham had the audacity to appeal to the Full Court, where Winter won again.

Derham resigned as Postmaster-General in 1890, giving as his reason the 'over-pressure of private business.' At a retirement dinner at Port Melbourne Town Hall, Alfred Deakin jocularly remarked that 'the main reason Mr Derham had given for retiring was one connected with sex. Mr Derham had stated that he wished to give up his portfolio because his wife and daughters had ordered him to do so. (Laughter).'

To add to his troubles, Thomas Swallow died, leaving Derham to make the biscuits as best he could. That was not easy, as sales had dropped seriously during the slump. In 1892, Derham cut the wages of his factory workers, making a saving of £1,000 a year. The move enabled the company to show a profit of £272 3s for the year.

Derham's final solution to his difficulties was a private composition with his creditors. He met them in October 1892, and presented a balance sheet showing debts of £548,000. His deficit would have been much greater, probably another £200,000, if he had not been able to transfer his responsibilities in the Australian Property Co. to the unfortunate shareholders of the Real Estate Bank. His other transactions involved many of the leading boom institutions of Melbourne. As the statutory requirement of 75 per cent of his creditors agreed to accept the composition of 1d. in the £1, Derham was released from insolvency and was able to carry on the biscuit business without that being sold up too.

Somehow the secret was kept from Swallow & Ariell's shareholders, so that in June 1893 Derham was proudly able to tell the company's annual meeting, 'The directors have nothing to hide.' This, from a speculator who had made a secret composition for more than half a million pounds! But it worked. The company struggled back to solvency, sales being greatly assisted by its introduction of vegetable canning in 1894.

The Derhams left their fine house in Queens Road, Melbourne, and shifted to a cottage in Rouse Street, Port Melbourne, near the factory. Before the century was out they were able to buy 'St. Ive's,' in Barry Street, Kew, and shift to that more salubrious suburb. Derham became president of the Chamber of Manufactures from 1897 to 1902, a founder and first president of the Victorian Employers' Federation, a director of the Patriotic Insurance Co., and so on. But he never became reconciled to the laws which tried to lead capitalism out of the jungle. When he was re-elected President of the Victorian Chamber of Manufactures in 1901, members tendered him a special banquet. After being presented with an illuminated address, Derham said: 'In the initiation of factory legislation, it was merely desired that sweating should be abolished, but a number of reckless radicals and weak-kneed liberals encouraged and tolerated a policy which was neither more nor less than pure socialism. The spirit of enterprise is being crushed out of the men who have spent their whole lives in building up large industries. (Prolonged cheering).'

Derham's father, Thomas Plumley Derham, a solicitor, got into serious difficulties in 1890 when trying to keep his son solvent. The father mortgaged his beautiful house 'Astolat' in Riversdale Road, Camberwell, three times over—the worthless third mortgage being accepted by his solicitor-partner J. W. Eggleston. He also borrowed during this period several thousand pounds from the Bank of Victoria and the Commercial Bank. But the amounts involved in his son's schemes were finally too enormous, and in 1893 T. P. Derham himself was forced into a private composition for £22,000. He undertook to pay 1s. 6d. in the £1, at the rate of 3d. a year.

T. P. Derham had the grace to resign as legal adviser to the Melbourne Permanent Building Society after thirteen years in that position. His resignation led to unfounded rumours that he was involved in the notorious defalcations of James Johnson, the society's secretary. T. P. Derham publicly denied the rumours at a meeting of the society in 1894, and eventually won the account back again, thus re-establishing himself in the legal world.

In the final chapter of the Derham saga, we come to the brother, Charles Walter Derham, a grain broker of Flinders Lane. Charles was forced to make his private composition in 1892, with debts of £36,000, paying 1s. in the £1. He had plunged heavily on shares in his brother's Balmoral Land Company. Most of his money came from the Land Mortgage Bank; plus another £2,000 from the Melbourne Permanent Building Society, of which his father had been legal adviser.

The two Derham brothers, Frederick and Charles, went into the flour milling business soon afterwards, and made excellent profits from this activity as conditions improved. Another grain merchant, Edward William Lightfoot, gave considerable financial assistance to the Derhams and went bankrupt partly as a result, paying ¼d. in the £1 on nearly £100,000 debts. Most of his cash came from the Commercial Bank.

7

The Curious Case of the City Road Property Co.

Lust for profit brought together the strangest bedfellows. One of the oddest combinations was the syndicate known as the City Road Property Co. Ltd, incorporated in 1888. Its purpose in life was to purchase six acres of land in City Road, South Melbourne, from William Bushby Jones; but never did any company find it more difficult to consummate its desires.

The original speculators who made up this syndicate included James Service, the canny old Scot who was to become Premier; R. J. Alcock, his business partner; Oliver Vial, a city accountant; Robert Reid, the softgoods wholesaler who later fulminated against "commercial dishonesty"; W. L. Baillieu, the city auctioneer; Stanford Chapman; and others.

The syndicate agreed to give Jones £200,000 for his land—paying a cash deposit of £10,000, and instalments starting at £20,000 a year.

Five weeks after signing this agreement, the original syndicate sold the land for £260,000 (an increase of £60,000) to Henry Butler, a director of the Centennial Land Bank, on behalf of what we shall call No. 2 company. This second company consisted of Henry Butler, James Service, R. J. Alcock, Robert Reid, B. J. Fink, J. M. Howden, W. L. Baillieu, and others. The members of No. 1 company divided up the £60,000 'profit' between themselves.

A month later, the land was again sold, this time to No. 3 company, called the 'New Melbourne Property Co. Ltd.' Directors were practically identical with No. 2 company, but the value of the land had miraculously increased to £300,000. This miracle yielded a further £40,000 'profit', which was again divided between the directors. The cash, of course, came from bankers and outside investors who were financing the ring, and who were foolish enough to agree with the speculators' estimates of increasing values.

By 1893, the original vendor (Jones) had received his first three annual payments, but No. 1 company, the City Road Property Co., was unable to pay the fourth instalment. No. 2 company was unable to pay No. 1. No. 3 was unable to pay No. 2. Then Jones, the heartless Jones, displayed bad form by suddenly departing this life. No. 1 company still owed more than £100,000 to his estate. His executors painfully checked through the various manipulations, then took

James Service, later Premier of Victoria, one of the original speculators in the City Road Property Co. Ltd.

Henry Butler, a director of the Centennial Land Bank, purported to buy land in South Melbourne from the original syndicate for an overnight increase of £60,000.

the whole imbroglio to court, claiming 'intent to defraud', and asking for all the companies to be wound up under court supervision.

The executors' affidavit claimed that between 25 May and 31 May 1893, James Service had transferred his shares and hence his further liability to one Charles Rollason, a minor clerk in his employment. Service's partner, R. J. Alcock, had transferred his shares to J. Turnbull, a storeman in his employment. Stanford Chapman had transferred his shares to C. M. Whiting, an employee of his. Robert Reid had transferred his shares to H. L. McKenzie, an employee in his firm. W. L. Baillieu still held his shares, but in the meantime had compounded with his creditors, so that he must be presumed to be penniless.

In the face of this damning affidavit, the ring of speculators broke down. They agreed to return the titles to Jones' estate, as well as paying another £25,000 in cash as full settlement. The companies were then wound up under the generous terms of the Companies Act, and the books were destroyed. There were several sadder and wiser men in Melbourne that night.

8

The Chaffey Brothers and the Mildura Crash

In the 1880s the Mallee country of northern Victoria was a sunbaked waste, redeemed only by the fat lazy snake of the Murray River crawling across the sandy plain. Settlers scratched out a living along its banks, praying for rain, cursing the floods, living off their own produce, and sending the balance interminable distances by paddle steamer to the city markets.

Abandoned homesteads and fences buried under sand drifts bore silent witness to the futility of man's efforts to fight successive droughts and invasion by rabbits in their millions. A Royal Commission in 1879 reported: 'In a journey of 100 miles from north to south, not one solitary bird or living creature was to be seen.' 'It is a Sahara of hissing hot winds,' wrote a poetic *Age* reporter.

But men never stopped trying to conquer the arid land. Hope soared anew in 1883, when the Victorian Parliament passed a Mallee Pastoral Leases Act. The Murray frontage was divided into small blocks to give access to water, with larger areas of 'back country' providing space for grazing and wheat-growing. Soon the pioneers began trickling back for another assault on nature. The 'Mallee roller,' the stump-jump plough, and McKay's stripper-harvester helped some of the settlers to succeed. Soon great loads of wheat and wool were again being taken by paddle-steamer down the Murray.

The next challenge was to use the river's abundant waters for the irrigation of small fruit-growing blocks. In 1884, Alfred Deakin, Minister of Public Works, was appointed president of a royal commission charged with investigating irrigation techniques. With an engineer and two journalists, Deakin visited Ontario, California. Here the Chaffey brothers had made a fortune by buying desert land for $1.50 an acre, irrigating it, and reselling the blocks on time payment for twenty times the price. There was plenty of water (for which the Chaffeys charged an annual fee per acre), but no alcohol, for the Chaffeys were determined to keep Ontario 'dry' in that sense. The two brothers, George and William Benjamin Chaffey, were Canadians who had studied and improved the irrigation techniques first used in California. George was also an experimental engineer of considerable talent, an innovator in hydro-electric engineering, and pioneer of the electric lighting system used in Los Angeles.

One of the Chaffeys' employees was a middle-aged journalist named Stephen Cureton, who claimed to have roamed the Murray region in earlier life. Cureton

George Chaffey (left) and William Benjamin Chaffey.

assured the Chaffeys that Deakin's glowing visions could be put into practice, and volunteered to visit Victoria again to act as the Chaffeys' agent. As a result of his enthusiastic reports, George Chaffey sailed to Melbourne in 1886.

Chaffey travelled up and down the Murray, taking soil samples and temperatures, and calculating the volume of water flowing past, until he was satisfied that the country around Mildura could become another California. Within a few weeks, Alfred Deakin arranged a Government agreement 'to secure the application of private capital to the construction of irrigation works.' Subject to the fulfillment of certain conditions, the Chaffey brothers were handed 50,000 acres of land around Mildura as an outright gift, with an option to purchase another 200,000 acres at £1 an acre. Even more important, they could pump out whatever water they needed to irrigate this huge area, and resell it to fruitgrowers who settled on their blocks. In George Chaffey's words, 'the agreement was designed to induce us to sell Mildura lands.' The brothers anticipated making between five and six million pounds profit from selling the land and supplying the necessary water.

George cabled to his brother advising him to sell up their Californian interests and come quickly to the new bonanza. Melbourne financiers moved in eagerly. The Union and National Banks gave the Chaffeys their blessing and financial accommodation. In September 1888, a £350,000 company was floated, with 35,000 shares of £10 each. Henry Byron Moore, Bernard Bradley, Kate Fink and others bought thousands of pounds worth. The company was started with three directors—J. F. Levien, M.L.C., and the two Chaffey brothers. Levien ran the office in Swanston Street, Melbourne, and looked after the company's political interests. William M. Paterson, manager of the old Mildura Station,

Thomas Bent opposed the Mildura scheme in public, but *Punch* thought he would change his mind if he could make a profit from it.

was appointed general manager. The company's legal adviser was Theodore Fink.

Chaffey Bros Ltd also opened offices in Adelaide and London to sell its lands and shares. The Government had limited the size of individual blocks to a maximum of 80 acres for fruit-growing and 160 acres for general crops. The company sold these blocks, which had been handed over to it as a free gift, for £20 an acre, on ten-year terms. The site of Mildura was marked out near the old Mildura Homestead, with a five-mile Deakin Avenue running down the middle, named after Alfred Deakin in gratitude to the Chaffeys' political friend and benefactor. Residential blocks in the town were sold for £100 each. Like the Californian enterprise, this too was a prohibition town while the Chaffeys ran it—the only 'dry' area in Australia at the time.

To help sell their blocks of land, Chaffey Bros Ltd organised cheap river excursions once a week. For £7 all found, tourists left Melbourne by train on Saturday morning, boarded the paddle steamer at Swan Hill, sailed to Mildura and Renmark, and were sent back by train to Melbourne to sing the irrigation company's praises.

In another endeavour to publicise the scheme, the Chaffeys engaged J.E.M. Vincent, FRGS, to write a book about their plans. The result, entitled *The Australian Irrigation Colonies, Illustrated*, sold all over the world for 3s. 6d. a copy. With its striking red and gold embossed cover, the work became famed as 'The Red Book', helping to lure hundreds of settlers to the project. In its pages the Bishop of Ballarat was induced to write of Mildura's 'Bosky slopes spotted with picturesque white tents . . . Cheery whistles echoing through the forest.' Sons of the nobility, remittance men, unfrocked clergymen, restless souls of all types came from all parts of the world to settle where the desert bloomed anew.

In partial fulfillment of their agreement, the Chaffeys built several huge pumping plants to raise the water from the river. A further 150 miles of mains were dug to take the water to each property, and 300 miles of secondary distribution channels. To pay the cost of delivering sufficient water to each block, the Chaffeys levied 6s. per acre per year on all land-owners.

Now Melbourne's frenzy of speculation spread to Mildura. Blocks for which £20 an acre had been paid were resold for three times the price—and often remained objects for speculation instead of fruitful production. The Chaffeys held on to many of the best blocks near the township, and seemed to be sitting on a fortune.

By 1891, it appeared that the settlement would justify all their expectations. Mildura had grown to a town of 4,000 people, about half of whom were actually engaged in working the soil. The Chaffeys had sold 17,000 acres, of which 10,000 acres had been planted with fruit trees or crops. Raisins, wine grapes, apricots, oranges, lemons, peaches and olives were thriving where once the desert sands had blown.

But under the superficial appearance of prosperity, there were signs of approaching difficulties. Many of the settlers were suspicious of the Chaffeys' real motives and long-term interests, and complained bitterly of 'broken promises' through their own organisation, the Mildura Irrigation Co. Ltd. George H. Tolley, secretary of the company, wrote in a letter to the Premier in 1892: 'Messrs. Chaffey covenanted to do certain specific acts in return for the magnificent concessions granted to them, and we maintain that Mr. [George] Chaffey has entirely failed to meet the complaints as to breaches of those covenants, the allegations remaining unanswered, that Messrs. Chaffey have *not* constructed proper irrigation works, have *not* used and distributed through them the water diverted from the Murray, have *not* established a cannery, and have *not* erected an agricultural college.'

The most urgent ground of complaint was the question of 'proper irrigation works.' The Chaffey company had simply dug earthen channels and built earthen

The 1896 inquiry found that the Chaffeys and J.F. Levien, MLC, were deeply involved in what one journal called an 'abominable stagnant pool, with stenches so strong and dreadful in its muddy mysterious depths, that one almost recoils from disturbing it further.'

The Mildura inquiry found that British investors had been 'milked dry'. J. F. Levien, MLC, had received £36,000 in fees and commissions.

banks—even this being a major undertaking in the days before the general use of powered excavators. The practice served well enough in other parts of the world, given a reasonable amount of maintenance. But in Mildura, a settler could be standing on his property watching the water flowing past, when suddenly he would be horrified to see a whole section of the bank collapse into the channel. What had happened was that the ubiquitous Murray crayfish—the 'yabbie'—bred in its millions in the shallow warm water of the channels, dug tunnels into the earthen banks, and brought them tumbling down.

However brilliant his engineering record in California, George Chaffey had also failed to allow for another peculiarity of Mildura—the saltiness of the subsoil, which rose to the surface when irrigated and killed thousands of fruit trees.

Simultaneously with these technical troubles, the general collapse of the land boom began to affect the enterprise. Nearly £300,000 cash invested in Chaffey Bros Ltd had been spent on capital works. So far, however, almost no fruit had been put on the market, and there was no income. At the same time, the money markets of Melbourne and London completely dried up. In order to raise fresh funds for repair work to the undermined channels, the Chaffeys decided to raise the water rates to £1 per acre per year.

There was an agonised outcry from the settlers. How could they pay higher water rates when they had no income? Alfred Deakin made a hurried trip to the north, and by unsparing eloquence persuaded both the Chaffeys and the settlers to accept a compromise figure of 15s. an acre. It seemed that the venture might yet be saved.

Late in 1892 there was a superb harvest of fruit. Apricots yielded 3 cwt to the tree. Peaches weighed up to 11 oz each. Just as the fruit was being harvested, nature struck her final blow. The river became too shallow for the paddle-steamers, which were forced to suspend operations. All the fruit had to be taken overland, by dray to Swan Hill and then by rail to Melbourne. By the time it arrived at the markets, it was bruised, rotten, and unsaleable.

A few consignments of raisins were sold at low prices, and some of the fruit was used for jam making. But what really saved the Mildura settlement was its new harvest of wine grapes. Bowing to the laws of economic survival, the Chaffeys' articles of prohibition were repealed, and wine cellars and distilleries were set up. At the same time a new Workingmen's Club was opened, which eventually boasted thousands of members and built itself the largest bar in the Southern Hemisphere. So much for prohibition.

Meanwhile, the settlers had fallen £40,000 in arrears in payments to the Chaffeys for their blocks. W.B. Chaffey left for London to float a new £100,000 loan. He might as well have asked for the moon. Too many English settlers had written home with tales of hardship and despair. In the eyes of the world, Mildura was a ghastly failure, another rotten product of colonial wishful thinking and land booming.

Soon Mildura became almost a ghost town, where houses could be rented for 2s. a week. On the blocks, the irrigation channels collapsed and were not repaired. The rabbits burrowed under the fences and were not stopped. The National Bank at Mildura closed its doors. The irrigation pumps were turned off. Orchards were sold up for a pound note, or simply deserted, as gaunt, stony-faced men and women left for the Coolgardie goldfields to try their luck in that next stop on the road to Hades.

On Christmas Eve, 1895, Chaffey Bros Ltd closed its offices and George Chaffey began preparing his insolvency papers. The Chaffey assets were sold up for almost nothing. George Chaffey had to borrow his fare to return to America. W. B. Chaffey stayed on, worked as a laborer, and eventually restored some of the family fortunes.

George Chaffey filed his petition in liquidation in May 1896. His total liabilities were £402,000; his assets only £5,800. Some of the people to whom he owed money were the National Bank (£39,000), CML Assurance Co. (£32,000), Union Bank (£31,000), Glyn, Mills & Currie (£22,000), Federal Bank (£3,600), and Mercantile Bank (£3,600).

Two months later a Royal Commission began inquiring into the reasons for the Mildura failure. The commissioners found against the Chaffeys on practically every point at issue. For example, the brothers had advertised that the channels would be concreted where necessary to prevent leakage. In fact this had only been done for three miles, and more than half the water was lost in the remaining channels.

William Paterson, the Chaffeys' general manager, gave sensational evidence. In 1886, he said, George Chaffey had told him that he and his brother had £900,000 cash to invest. He had 'put things so flowery to him' that Paterson invested his own savings of £5,000 in the scheme. He was also appointed manager, and for the next eighteen months supervised the construction of irrigation channels, about which he knew very little. During that time the Chaffeys were 'very seldom there.' Another great cause of the failure, said Paterson, was the way that young settlers with perhaps £500 were induced to buy more land than they could afford. As no return could be obtained for three to four years, 'they were on their beam ends after twelve months.'

Paterson alleged that vouchers for some contracts were put through the company's books two or three times, in order to build up the amount apparently spent on improvements. When he challenged George Chaffey with fraud, Chaffey 'threatened to put a bullet through me.' Then 'I chased him round the room because he had no revolver,' Paterson said. There was no evidence in reply from George Chaffey. He had already left the country and returned to California.

Later that year, Isaac Isaacs introduced a Bill which abolished the rights granted to the Chaffeys, and established a Mildura Irrigation Trust charged with restoring the irrigation works. Every landholder was to be a shareholder, and all directors were to be elected by the landholders. Working under this unique blend of capitalism, communism, and democracy, the land recovered most of its former productivity. George Chaffey's vision in time became reality. By that time George didn't care a fig. He was busy in America, planning the diversion of the Colorado River into the Colorado desert, followed by the more successful Imperial Valley irrigation project in California.

9

The Railway and Tramway Boom

Improved transport was an essential prelude to the land boom. Without rapid, cheap, and efficient methods of travelling to and from the new suburbs, so many thousands of building blocks could never have been sold and resold in the speculative mania which burst upon Melbourne. While the city was still fairly small, and without an extensive suburban transport system, most of the population was concentrated in the inner suburbs—Carlton, Richmond, and so on. The poor walked to work, while the rich drove horse-drawn vehicles from their more salubrious suburbs slightly further out. Gradually the population crept to the outer limits of horse-drawn traffic. If railways and tramways had not already existed, it would have been necessary to invent them.

So vital was transport to the growing metropolis that the story of Victorian politics in the 1880s was largely the story of the building of railways. Hundreds of miles of track, some of it quite useless, pushed out from the egocentric city to the rampant suburbs and the far countryside. Hardly a member of Parliament whose vote could be bought went without his bribe in the form of a new railway, a spur line, or advance information on governmental plans to enable him to buy choice land in advance—the value of which was enormously enhanced when the line went through. It was a dispiriting chapter in Victorian political morality.

The Berry government opened the boom decade in 1880 with a Railways Act authorizing the construction of 475 miles of new line. But even as the building of these lines began, curious influences got to work within the Railways Department. J. B. Patterson, Berry's Minister of Railways, was so plagued by fellow politicians trying to get jobs for their friends in the railways that he handed the whole power of appointments and promotions over to the departmental heads. In 1881, when Thomas Bent came in as new Minister of Railways in the O'Loghlen government, he immediately resumed the power of making appointments. If you wanted a position or promotion in the railways, you had to see Tommy Bent and arrange it with him personally. Rumours of patronage were whispered all over Melbourne. An even graver scandal involving Bent, known as 'The Kensington Hill Job', became public knowledge. As Minister, Bent arranged that the Railways Department should pay Messrs J. Straker and J. S. Vickery £20,000 for the right of removing a gravel hill on their land at Kensington. Two years later, the vendors transferred to Bent personally 101 acres of the land. When James Service became Premier, he examined the files and confessed: 'I must say that to me the transaction as a whole is an incomprehensible one . . . the material [i.e., the gravel] is not required for present purposes at all.'

While still Minister, Bent arranged a huge railway building programme, far greater than anything Berry had envisaged. To pay for it the O'Loghlen government used up all the cash balances in the State Treasury, borrowed nearly £1 million from trust funds, and incurred a further £1 million indebtedness by ordering enough rails for 800 miles of line, the construction of which had not been authorized by Parliament. As a result of such eccentricities, the O'Loghlen-Bent government suffered a crushing defeat at the 1883 elections. James Service's new 'housecleaning' government introduced a Railway Management Act, which removed practically all planning and administration powers from the Minister and vested them in a Board of three technical experts, appointed for a seven-year term to give them reasonable security from interference. As chairman, the government appointed an English railways expert, Richard Speight. They paid him £3,000 a year salary—a considerable figure for those days.

Speight started well. Inferior staff, the inevitable result of nepotism, was gradually weeded out. Administration was improved, and uneconomic lines were closed down. But then a deplorable process began. Instead of taking a firm stand against political interference, Speight was courted and flattered into becoming a creature of the parliamentary land boomers. In the cautious words of H. G. Turner, 'he became a pliant instrument in the hands of cliques and schemers'.

Unfortunately neither the Service government, nor its successor, the Gillies-Deakin government, was immune from the railway building mania. In 1884, on Speight's recommendation, Parliament passed the so-called 'Octopus Act', authorizing the construction of a further 65 lines, totalling 1,170 miles, at an estimated cost of £44 million. The 'Octopus Act' authorized two major extensions to the suburban system—the connection of Flinders Street and Spencer Street stations, and the building of a ludicrous enterprise known as the Outer

Thomas Bent arranged the building of many railway lines, running the State heavily into debt. At left, Bent seeks a salaried position on the Railways Committee as a Christmas treat.

Enormous railway building programmes were undertaken in the 1880s. To this *Punch* artist it seemed that the lines might reach the moon.

Circle Railway. The Outer Circle, built at a cost of £292,000, was opened in 1890 and closed three years later. It meandered for nineteen miles around Melbourne's northern suburbs, from North Melbourne through to Brunswick, across empty paddocks to Fairfield, thence to East Kew, then to Hartwell, finally joining the main Gippsland line near Oakleigh. The land boomers inside and outside Parliament saw it as a speculators' paradise and invested heavily in broad acres along the route. They were caught with their signals down. No sane passenger would use the line, when it took him 4 hours 20 minutes to travel from Oakleigh to the city by this route. Nor was there much intermediate traffic. For decades later, the rusting rails and abandoned stations of the Outer Circle route remained as a silent reminder of the boom years.

In 1890, when the London loan market still seemed favourable to Australian investments, the Gillies-Deakin government introduced yet another extravagant Railways Bill. This proposed to build no less than 1,116 more miles of suburban and country lines. Such extraordinary projects as a line from the tiny hamlet of Bittern to the tiny fishing village of Flinders were included in the Bill. 'Mad extravagance!' cried the *Age*. Instead of pushing on with the Bill, Gillies appointed a Parliamentary Committee, with none other than Thomas Bent as chairman, to examine the plans. All proposals for new lines, including those from private members, had to be submitted to this committee. Its responsible members blithely approved schemes for 4,630 miles of new line to cost £40 million without stations or rolling stock! As though to climax the 'Era of Extravagance', a brand-new edifice for railway officials was erected in Spencer Street in 1890 at a cost of £130,000. This remarkably ugly building, the creation of one James Moore, still houses civil servants of the Railways Department within its dun-coloured walls.

Meanwhile, the building of lines previously authorized was proceeding apace. By the middle of 1891 a total of 2,764 miles of line was open for traffic, 278 miles being double tracks. They had cost the State about £37 million since it first took over the railways. Within two years, practically the entire Melbourne suburban railway system which exists today had been completed. In the south, trains went to Sandringham and Frankston; in the north, to Coburg and Whittlesea.

The full provisions of the last great Railway Bill of 1890 were not carried out, however. Many of the lines then proposed have not been built even today, and probably never will be. The Gillies government fell, the Munro government began its brief hour of glory, and William Shiels became Minister of Railways. On 23 July 1891 Shiels startled Parliament by launching a bitter attack on the 'incapacity and extravagance, the despotism and disloyalty' of his Railways Commissioners. The railways accounts, said the new Minister, were 'literally cooked', and the results would prove 'financially disastrous' to the colony. So another Railway Management Bill was introduced to strip the Commissioners of their 'despotic' powers. Instead of passing it, the Legislative Council called Commissioner Speight to the Bar of the House, examined him, and accepted his view that the Victorian railways were 'the best managed in the world'.

Unfortunately for Speight, David Syme had assigned some of his most pains-

Richard Speight, chairman of the Victorian Railways Commissioners, 'pliant instrument' of land boomers.

David Syme, whose *Age* newspaper vigorously exposed corruption in the Railways Department.

James Liddle Purves, Q.C., who fought the historic *Speight* v. *Syme* libel case on David Syme's behalf.

taking journalists to investigate the railways. Their explosive series of articles led to one of the classic libel trials of the nineteenth century: *Speight* v. *Syme*. Speight claimed £25,000 damages for allegations contained in the articles; Syme pleaded 'justification as a public journalist'. The case occupied the courts for the second half of 1893 and nearly all of 1894. It ended in almost complete victory for Syme and the *Age*. The newspaper started its investigations at the time of the Railway Construction Bill of 1890. It sent reporters out to visit many of the districts through which the proposed lines were to run, and proved that the reasons given for their construction were 'a tissue of misrepresentations and absurdities'. Other articles attacked Speight as being 'politically profligate', and the last of the series alleged incompetence, lying and deceit. It was strong meat, in the great tradition of muck-raking journalism.

One article in particular related how Speight had received a deputation consisting of Sir Matthew Davies and Messrs Harper and Staughton, all M.P.s, asking for increased train services to their subdivisions at Broadmeadows. Speight had given way, costing the railways thousands a year for the benefit of these powerful politicians. In yet another instance proven in court, Dr George LeFevre, M.L.C., agreed to pay half the cost of building a station near his land at St Albans, provided the Braybrook trains would stop there. Speight agreed, the station was built, and Dr LeFevre was able to sell his land. The station at Laverton was built, largely at public expense, on what was then a 'miserable, desolate wind-swept plain'. A. T. Clark, M.L.A., as head of a land syndicate, visited the place with Speight. Although only one house had been built there, the station was established, and a train service provided at a loss of £1,000 a year.

The *Age* also published in full, column after column, a list of names which showed that since 1884 about 10,000 free rail passes a year had been issued to 'distinguished visitors', while another 45,000 departmental free passes had been issued! About 400 free passes had been issued to members of Speight's own household, and thousands more to relatives of M.P.s.

Premier Shiels offered Speight £6,000 to resign and return to England. Speight stayed to fight the *Age*, but succeeded in winning only ¼d. damages.

The libel case commenced before Mr Justice Hodges and a special jury in the Supreme Court on 1 June 1893, and occupied seven weary months. On 28 December, after being locked up for fifty-four hours, the jury announced that there was no hope of reaching a verdict. The judge declined to discharge, and told them he would accept a three-fourths verdict. They then awarded Speight a general verdict of £100 damages. His Honour said that he must have a specific verdict on each count, and locked them up again over the whole New Year period. When the jury emerged for the last time, they announced disagreement on the first ten counts, but awarded Speight £100 damages on the eleventh count, on a three-fourths majority. Syme thereupon appealed to the Full Court.

The second tortuous case, *Speight* v. *Syme*, commenced before Sir Hartley Williams and a jury of twelve in April 1894, and dragged on for five more months. One of the jurymen died during the trial. The survivors found in favour of the *Age* on almost every count. On one small point, apparently a technical error by a reporter, the jury awarded Speight the magnificent sum of one farthing in damages. Speight resigned as Railways Commissioner after this contemptuous verdict, and was glad to shake the dust of the squabbling colony from his heels.

He returned to England to manage successfully a large private railway company, where he was comparatively free from political interference.

In 1895 Mr Purves, Q.C., arranged a great banquet to celebrate Syme's victory over Speight. It was attended by many government and civic leaders, but land boomers were noticeably absent. In a long speech surveying the history of the court cases, Purves said of the *Age* articles that 'no such series . . . has ever been published in any daily publication within my knowledge, since the great series which was published in regard to the Reform Bill.' Regarding Syme himself, Purves forecast that 'the work accomplished by this man will at least live in the hearts of our children when we probably have passed away.'[5]

What was the final cost to the State and its people of the great railway building spree? The average loss in operating the railways throughout the 1890s was £1,000 a day. By the turn of the century, a total deficiency of £9 million had been reached. The interest on this figure, and on the capital costs, crippled Victorian budgets for decades. During the 1950s, interest payments alone on the Victorian railways were costing up to £4 million a year. By 1955 many of the lines built seventy years before were literally falling to pieces. In the ten-year period 1955–64, there were 558 derailments on Victorian lines, and the number was increasing each year. The State Public Accounts Committee reported in 1964 that nearly 70 per cent of Victoria's rails, and 35 per cent of its rolling stock, were more than fifty years old. Huge expenditure would be needed to make good the errors of the past. Even today the incubus of the railway boom of the 1880s lies heavily on the taxpayer.

Since tramways were more suitable for carrying smaller numbers of people over shorter distances, their effect on the land boom was not as profound as that of the railways. Nevertheless, the spread of tramway systems had a considerable influence on city and suburban land values. As distinct from the railways, the tramway companies were all privately owned. In the outer suburbs almost anyone could start his own tramway system, given the formality of municipal approval, and he could float its shares on the various stock exchanges. The consequent boom and bust in tramway shares forms one of the less happy chapters of the boom era.

The history of Melbourne tramways may be traced back to the early 1860s, when Francis Boardman Clapp and other businessmen approached the City Council and requested a permit to build and operate a horse-drawn tram service in Bourke Street. The council procrastinated, so Clapp went overseas, returning in 1869 with a new type of horse tram called the 'Broadway Stage'. He and Andrew Rowan formed the Melbourne Omnibus Company, which was licensed to operate in the city area with the new coaches. In 1881 a man named Henry Hoyt floated the Victorian Tramway Company, his idea being to introduce the new cable trams to Melbourne. Hoyt worked quietly behind the scenes to secure the agreement of several inner municipalities to his scheme. The following year Duncan Gillies undertook to arrange the necessary Act of Parliament, but there were protests against 'the gigantic nature of the monopoly' envisaged by Henry

Hoyt. The Bill was thrown out, and Melbourne continued to travel in its now-dilapidated horse buses.

In 1883 the Service government was elected to power. A compromise Bill was presented to Parliament, and the Tramways Trust Act became law in October of that year. Clapp's company now bought out Hoyt's company, the consideration being the issue of nearly 100,000 shares to Hoyt in a new amalgamation called the Melbourne Tramway and Omnibus Co. Ltd. On 1 July 1884 the Tramways Trust granted the company a thirty-two-year lease of the right to operate cable trams to thirteen municipalities. The company had to pay interest on overseas loans raised to build the cable tracks, provide a sinking fund, buy its own tram cars, and finally hand back the tracks to the government in good order in July 1916. In addition, the Trust reserved the right to fix fares to be charged. Threepence within a three-mile radius was the initial fare laid down.

On this basis, Melbourne's first cable tramway, running from the city to Richmond, commenced operations on 11 November 1885. Other lines were opened to Fitzroy and Victoria Street (1886), Clifton Hill, Nicholson Street, Brunswick, and Carlton (1887), Brighton Road (1888), North Melbourne, West Melbourne, South Melbourne, and Port Melbourne (1890), Windsor and St Kilda (1891). By the end of 1891 the company was operating forty-seven miles of cable tramway and four miles of horse tramway. It was the largest such system in the world. Lines were also started to Kew, Hawthorn, and Toorak, but were abandoned when the economic collapse caused a heavy drop in the number of people using trams.

Stock exchange speculation in Melbourne Tramway Co. Ltd shares began about 1885, when the land boom was already under way. Shares paid up to 10s. were selling at 25s. each. The following year they went up to 36s. During 1888 they sold for up to 56s. Then in 1889 the Melbourne Tramway Co. Ltd declared a 20 per cent dividend, as well as giving a bonus of three new shares to every five held. The price of shares soared again, changing hands for up to £9 each. By this time, a total of 960,000 shares had been issued, so that in theory the Melbourne tramway system was valued by the stock market at more than £8,500,000. It was too ridiculous to last. When the slump started, people walked rather than pay tram fares. By mid-1892, four million fewer passengers a year were being carried than in the previous year. The company's shares were unloaded in the stock exchange panic, and dropped as low as 8s. each. Thousands of people were ruined—including the company's secretary, William Gardiner Sprigg. Sprigg made a secret composition in 1894, with debts totalling £150,000. His schedule showed that he had gambled heavily in land and share deals, using money supplied by the Union Bank (£22,000), James Grice (£16,000), the London Chartered Bank (£9,000), and the Australian Mutual Provident Society (£9,000). Sprigg paid his creditors 4d. in the £1 as full settlement. (When he died in 1926 he left a fortune of £100,000.)

In a vain attempt to prop up the price of their shares on the falling market, the directors of the Melbourne Tramway Co. Ltd began buying tramway shares whenever they became available. A private syndicate consisting of F. B. Clapp,

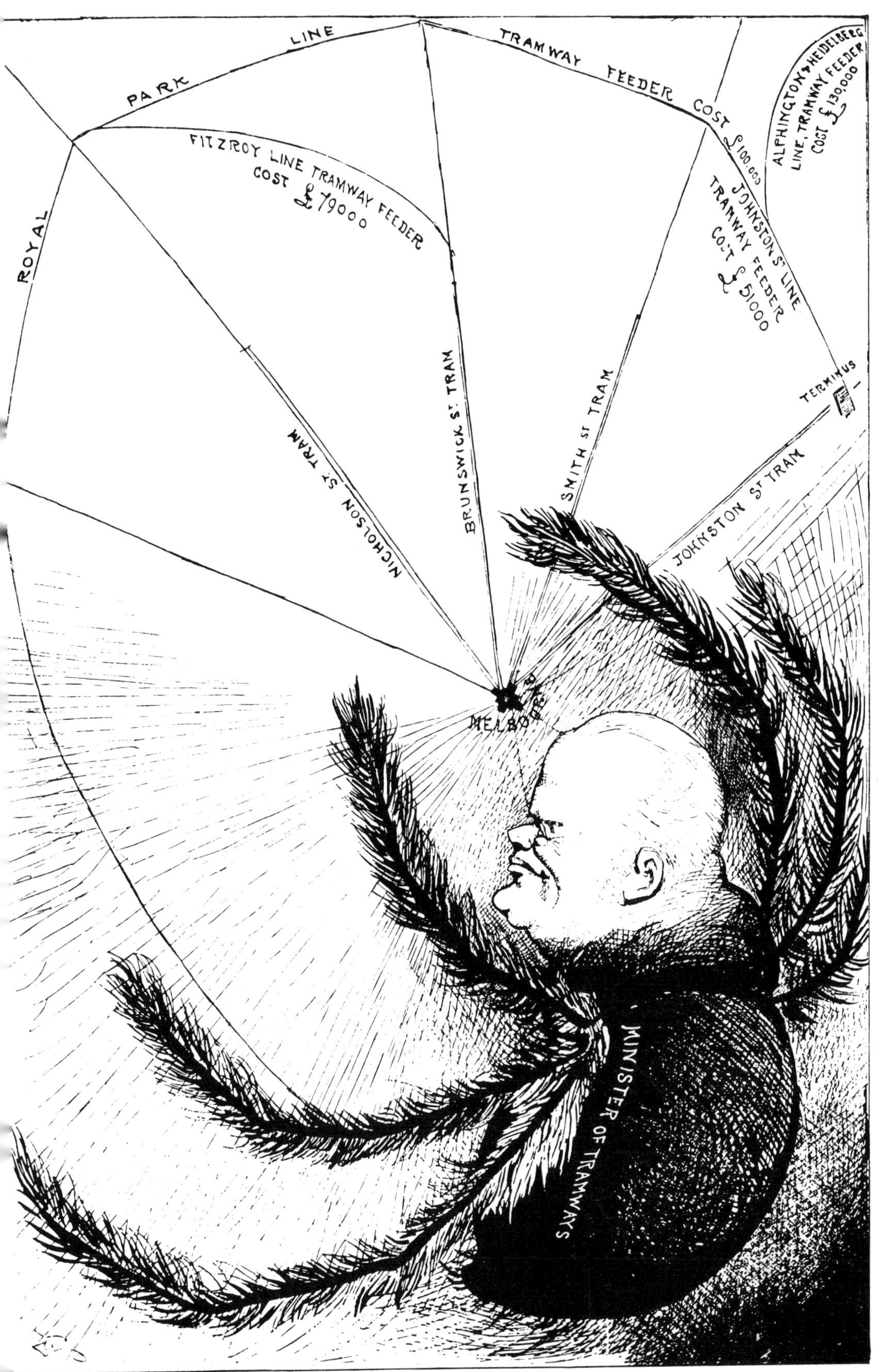

THE ARTFUL SPIDER.

Duncan Gillies proposed to Parliament that a private monopoly should operate Melbourne's suburban tramways, but his Bill was rejected. *Punch* saw him as an artful spider weaving a profitable web.

W. G. Sprigg, William McCulloch, and Andrew Rowan, was formed for this purpose. Andrew Rowan's confidential manager, Joseph Flanagan, claimed in court that when an investigation was threatened he was told to be ready to obliterate all trace of these share dealings from the books.

As its profits started to drop, the company tried to save money by cutting employees' wages. By February 1893 wages had been reduced by one-third, and the end was not yet in sight. To fight the reductions, eighteen employees tried to form a union of tram workers. F. B. Clapp, the managing director, sacked them all on the spot, then graciously reinstated them when they agreed to disband the union. Clapp then cut his own £3,000 salary by £1,000 a year. But the bitter memories remained. For many years thereafter, the Tramways Union was among the most militant of all trades unions in Victoria.

Those municipalities which had not agreed to participate in the Tramways Trust were still able to license smaller private companies to run tramway services within their own suburbs. The promoters started with good intentions, but the usual result was that their tramway company floatations became simply another siphon draining away the spare cash of trusting investors.

One such company was the Clifton Hill to Northcote & Preston Tram Co. Ltd. This was formed in 1888 by a syndicate of notable speculators, among them being B. J. Fink, J. Macmeikan, A. Kozminsky, and G. C. Clauscen. This company actually built a line from Preston, through Northcote, to Clifton Hill, at a cost of £90,000. At Clifton Hill the line connected with the metropolitan system, so that one could continue to Spencer Street station for a total fare of sixpence. But the Preston brickworks closed, population in the area dwindled, the tramway closed down in 1892, and the English, Scottish & Australian Chartered Bank foreclosed on the company's assets.

Another famous line was started at Essendon in 1889 by the Essendon Land & Tramway Co. Ltd. The chief promoter of this enterprise was James Mirams, manager of the Premier Building Association. As we will see, Mirams sold his own land to the tramway company for more than £200,000. The City of Melbourne Bank foreclosed on most of the company's other assets. These smaller lines were later incorporated in a unified metropolitan system.

The next great surge in tramway building in Melbourne did not come for more than twenty years. A Royal Commission on Railways and Tramways in 1911 recommended immediate nationalization of the private and municipal tramway operations, electrification of all cable and horse tramways (horses still pulled trams in Hawthorn and Kew), and extension of the whole system. The reforms took many years, but gave Melbourne a suburban transport system which worked reasonably well until the population explosion after World War II.

10

The Run on Goldsbrough Mort

The story of how the great woolbroking firm of Goldsbrough Mort fell into the hands of speculators, was forced to suspend business, and was successfully reincarnated, forms another of the untold epics of the land boom era.

The founder of the company was Richard Goldsbrough, a Yorkshire-born woolstapler who became popularly known as 'father of the Victorian wool trade.' Goldsbrough, born in 1821, came to Melbourne in 1848. He bought a weatherboard building on the corner of William Street and Flinders Lane, went into business as a wool buyer, and prospered so well that he was soon able to erect a substantial bluestone warehouse.

During the tumultuous years of the gold rush, Goldsbrough persistently championed his industry, one of slow but certain growth, against the allure of quick fortunes to be made from mining. He became known as an enemy of speculation and a spokesman for the cautious, steady progress of permanently productive industries in the young colony.

In 1857, Goldsbrough took in his brother-in-law, Hugh Parker, as a partner. Five years later they began building their second block of bluestone warehouses, which still stand at the corner of Bourke and William Streets, occupied by the PMGs Department. The area of the floors exceeded five acres, making it one of the greatest wool stores in the world. In 1873, an old employee named John Sutcliffe Horsfall was admitted to the partnership. After the death of Hugh Parker, his son Arthur and nephew David Parker were also admitted.

This strong partnership of four experienced woolmen entered the dangerous world of high finance in 1881 by amalgamating with the Australasian Agency & Banking Corporation. They floated Goldsbrough & Co. Ltd as a public company with £3 million capital in shares of £10 each, issuing a parcel of them in exchange for the assets of the bank. These shares were paid up to only £1 each—one-tenth of face value—and herein lay one basic cause of the tragedy to come.

Richard Goldsbrough died in 1886 without leaving any children. The surviving directors conferred, and decided to appoint one Francis Edward Stewart as director and general manager to supervise the company's affairs. Stewart had two apparent qualifications: he was manager of Younghusband & Co., and thus experienced in pastoral affairs. He was also chairman of the Equity

Trustees, Executors & Agency Co. Ltd, then a company with £125,000 capital, and thus was experienced in financial operations. Or so it seemed.

Stewart's first move was to stack the board of Goldsbrough & Co. Ltd by arranging the appointment of a new director, Andrew Rowan. Rowan was a well-known entrepreneur who had helped F. B. Clapp to form the Melbourne Omnibus Company, which operated horse-drawn buses, but now spent most of his time on land and share speculations. Stewart and Rowan arranged to take over the Sydney woolbroking firm of Mort & Co., increased their total capital to £3½ million, and changed the company's name to Goldsbrough, Mort & Co. Ltd. At this stage they had the support of the *Age*: David Syme used to lunch at Scott's Hotel every day with Andrew Rowan; William Sprigg, the tramway company secretary; and William Henry Croker, a leading maritime solicitor who built the mansion 'Maritimo' which still stands in The Strand in Williamstown.

Stewart and Rowan now began a remarkable career of self-aggrandisement through speculations in land and tramway shares. According to unchallenged evidence given later in court, the pair used at least £30,000 of Goldsbrough Mort's funds for various share dealings of their own. At one stage Rowan held 100,000 Melbourne Tramway shares, but managed to divest himself of the holdings before the stock exchange crash.

One of the older directors, J. S. Horsfall, became aware of what was going on, and protested strenuously at board meetings. Rowan's reply was to circulate a pamphlet to all Goldsbrough Mort shareholders, accusing Horsfall of being the one who was a 'wild, reckless speculator.' In return, Horsfall circulated his *Reply to Andrew Rowan.* The two pamphlets contain endless accusations and counter-charges, the unravelling of which could occupy several volumes.

In 1891, Rowan sued Horsfall for £25,000 damages for alleged libel, and

Richard Goldsbrough, founder of the great woolbroking firm, was 'a little fleshy', noted *Punch*, but went 'like a steam-engine'.

J. S. Horsfall, the old director of Goldsbrough & Co. Ltd forced out by the 'new blood' of speculative interests.

Andrew Rowan, the tramway share speculator who helped to arrange amalgamation of the Goldsbrough and Mort companies.

Joseph Flanagan, Rowan's 'confidential man', later exposed the conspiracy to milk Goldsbrough Mort's funds.

Horsfall counter-sued for £30,000. The case was settled without a court hearing. It appears that Rowan and Stewart won the battle behind the scenes, for Horsfall was forced to resign from the board of Goldsbrough Mort. Said Rowan in a published statement: 'It is a good thing the company is rid of him.' But by the end of 1892, when calls on shares were being widely made, the other directors found that Horsfall's charges contained more substance than they had believed. An internal investigation was held, the results of which were never disclosed. Rowan and Stewart were forced to resign from the company, and a new general manager, A. McDonald Cooper, was appointed.

Rumour now took a hand in the company's affairs. At that time Goldsbrough Mort was still acting as a banking company, and was accepting deposits from the public. The Melbourne deposits totalled £300,000. Alarmed by whispers from the boardroom, the depositors withdrew no less than two-thirds of their funds in a steady run lasting some weeks. With little cash left for trading, the great company was brought to its knees. It suspended payment on 26 June 1893, less than three months after declaring an 8 per cent dividended, and closed its doors to reorganise its affairs.

A scheme was offered to creditors along familiar lines—reconstruction and conversion of liabilities into debenture stock. A call of £2 per share was made on the company's 450,000 issued shares— and many large shareholders immediately tumbled into bankruptcy, despite the fact that they could have had five years to pay the call.

A protest meeting against the scheme was summoned by the ex-director, Andrew Rowan. As a large shareholder, he said, he did not know where the money was going to come from. 'It is becoming a fashion of the day to look upon shareholders as a kind of criminal who should be punished,' he complained. He had no desire to 'avoid any manly obligation,' but creditors would have to exercise greater consideration to escape 'universal bankruptcy.' Rowan's protest meeting went unheeded, and the company followed the normal course and made the calls.

F. E. Stewart, Rowan's associate in speculation, was caught with many shares still registered in his name. He made a private composition with his creditors, showing debts of nearly £40,000, and paid 1½d. in the £1 as settlement.

The market price of Goldsbrough Mort shares had meanwhile fallen to about 2s. A few farsighted speculators, those who still had cash to invest, bought up the shares by the thousand, and made considerable fortunes in later years as the company recovered its position.

All might now have been forgotten, had not a further extraordinary series of events occurred. During the boom years, Andrew Rowan had employed as his 'confidential manager' a man named Joseph Flanagan. As the boom petered out, Flanagan began to feel that he was running too many risks in conducting his master's dubious dealings. He therefore wrote his own colorful version of events, and published it as a pamphlet entitled *A Sample of the Commercial and Financial Morality (?) of Melbourne.* Once again it would be wearisome and unrewarding to disinter the detailed charges and counter-charges.

Rowan, however, determined to have his revenge. He had Flanagan arrested for allegedly defrauding him over share deals. A jury found Flanagan not guilty. Rowan had him arrested again on a somewhat similar charge. Again a jury discharged Flanagan. Rowan now cooked up a stronger charge. He had Flanagan arrested and charged a third time, on this occasion charging him with selling £365 worth of Rowan's wire netting to F. E. Stewart and pocketing the proceeds for his own use.

In his defence, Flanagan described what he alleged was a conspiracy between Rowan and Stewart to use Goldsbrough Mort's funds for their own purposes. He was able to name six separate instances where a total of £32,000 of the company's funds had been used for share manipulations and speculations, some of them through the Mercantile Bank. Neither Stewart nor Rowan answered the accusations.

Judge Gaunt called it 'a most extraordinary thing' that Rowan had not checked his books at the time of Flanagan's alleged offence, instead of waiting nearly seven years to lay a charge against him. After twenty minutes' retirement the jury found Flanagan not guilty. The verdict was greeted with warm applause and cheering in the court, a display of popular feeling sternly repressed by the judge.

Next morning the *Age* called the applause 'The echo of a sentiment which is almost general in the city.' All three verdicts fell 'with a crushing weight of censure on Rowan' for having used the process of the criminal courts 'to vent his hatred on a man with whom he was in private quarrel.'

The warriors departed from the scene, and took good care to stay away from the glare of publicity after that. Their curious pamphlets, which have been preserved for posterity, survive as another reminder of days when matters of finance aroused the angriest passions in the hearts of men.

11

Wild Days on the Stock Exchange

The stock exchange was the barometer of the boom—but a most peculiar instrument, for it seemed to be always on the rise. The further its readings of share values departed from reality, the more anxious investors were to get in on the rising market. Companies whose assets were worth a few thousands found investors anxious to buy their shares at ten times their real value. As an example of mass delusion, the Melbourne share market of the 1880s has few parallels.

The history of joint stock companies in Victoria only went back as far as the gold-rush days of the early 1850s. With the rapid growth of population, men banded together in joint enterprises to supply the colony's needs for land, gas, water, insurance, transport, and similar services. A means of trafficking in their shares soon followed. A small group of share dealers used to congregate under a verandah in Collins Street outside a building owned by 'Money' Miller. Here business was conducted in all kinds of weather. Melbourne's first regular stock exchange was established in 1859 under the chairmanship of J. B. Were, a wily financier who had mortgaged and finally taken over nearly one-half of 'Dendy's Special Survey'—eight square miles of land at Brighton. Were was probably the first man to import whisky and was first president of the British & Foreign Bible Society in Melbourne. His stock exchange met daily in the Hall of Commerce, later the site of Capel Court, Collins Street. J. B. Were may have operated with a bottle of whisky in one hand and a Bible in the other, with a mortgage tucked in his coat pocket, but he had very clear and advanced ideas on the ethical standard required of stockbrokers. All his life he fought against the idea that brokers should be allowed to speculate for the sake of personal profit. They were, he insisted, merely agents for investors, and their advice would never be trusted fully unless it was known to be impartial.

Relations between the early stockbrokers soon worsened—on this very question of whether brokers should themselves be allowed to speculate in shares. J. B. Were advertised in the *Argus* in 1860: 'Mr Were acts solely as Broker and Agent.' When the other members of the Brokers' Association refused to make his policy a condition of membership, Were resigned in 1861 and formed a second group known as the Associated Brokers. This cleavage between the two types of brokers continued for many years—with extraordinary results in the share boom of the

'Under the Verandah': Melbourne's first stock exchange was this infor

hering in Collins Street, where business continued in all weathers.

1880s. Practically no broker who followed Were's policy became insolvent. Dozens who speculated on their own account went to the wall, often for large sums, at the expense of various creditors. Rare indeed was the broker who resisted the temptation to plunge, even if he did it secretly through a relation or trusted friend. And before it was all over, M. J. Keane, whom Were had appointed secretary of *his* exchange, had become insolvent too. He even borrowed £50 from Were himself and poured it down the bottomless drain of speculation.

In 1882 the rival brokers were organized into two groups known as the Victorian Stock Exchange and the Melbourne Stock Exchange, the latter being Were's group. In 1885 an attempt was made to unite all brokers in a new organization called the Stock Exchange of Melbourne. This new group decided in 1886 to limit its membership to a maximum of one hundred brokers, and increase its entrance fee from £200 to £1,000. For a time, its seats became valuable property. William Knox, for instance, lent £2,000 to George Meudell in 1889 to buy a place on the Exchange. (After the crash the price dropped to £250, and took many years to recover.)

Brokers waxed fat on the large commissions made from each successive day's buying and selling. Not unnaturally, many were tempted to start other stock exchanges to break the profitable monopoly held by the existing group. By 1888 there were three major exchanges operating. One group was called the Stock Exchange of Melbourne. The 'No. 2 Exchange' was called the Melbourne Stock Exchange, and met in the same premises. A third exchange, floated in May 1888, was the Federal Stock Exchange Co. Ltd, situated at 375 Collins Street. Its 100,000 shares were over-subscribed three times. These £1 shares, paid up to 10s., reached a top price of £9. Chairman was John Woods, M.L.A.—acting on behalf of James Munro. The Federal Exchange crashed with the other

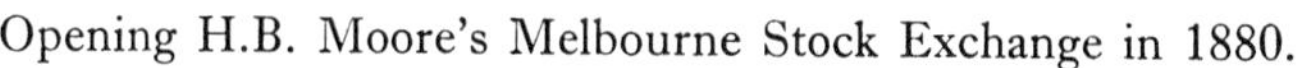
Opening H.B. Moore's Melbourne Stock Exchange in 1880.

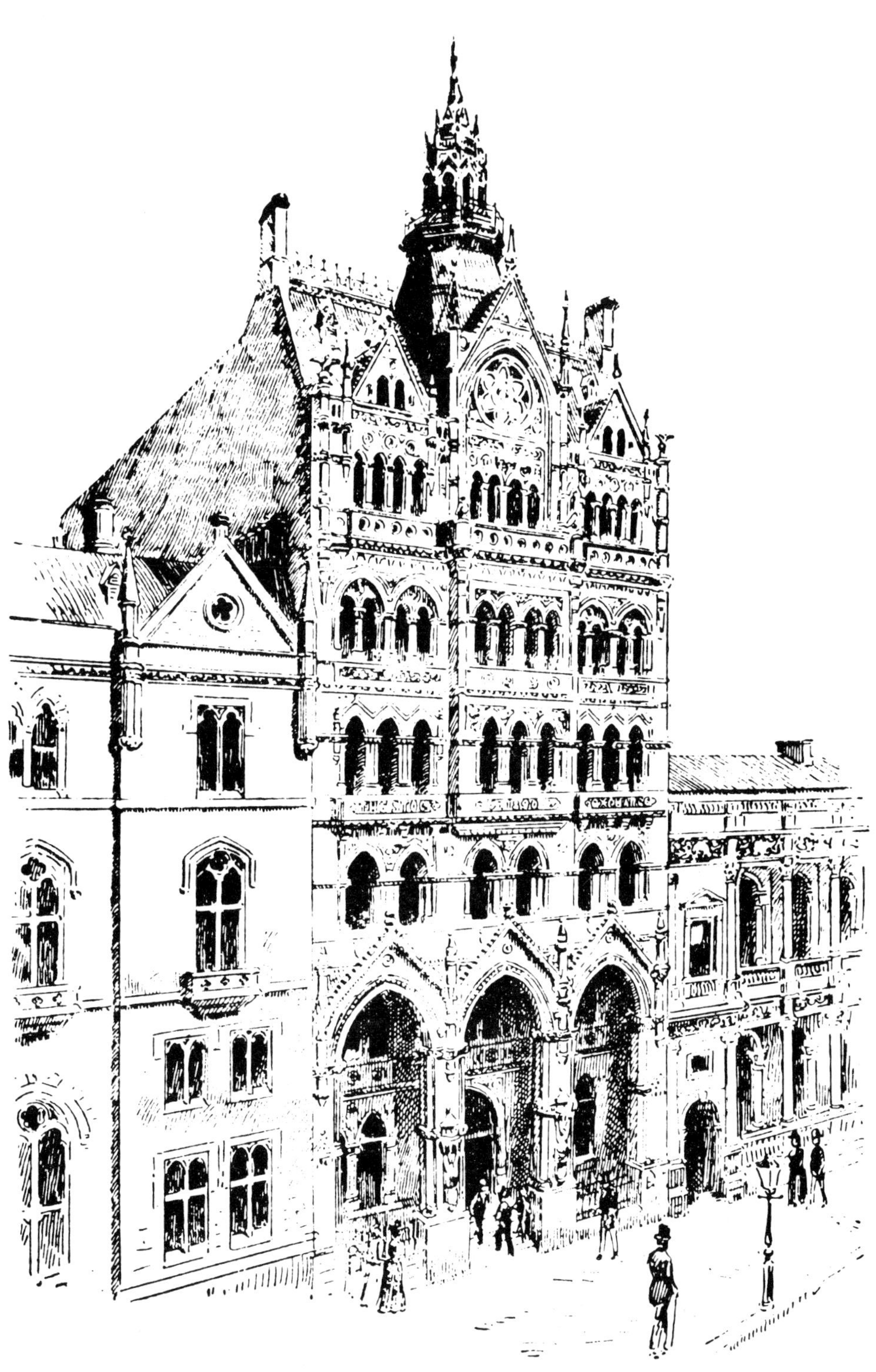

The new Melbourne stock exchange, which opened in 1891 just as the boom burst.

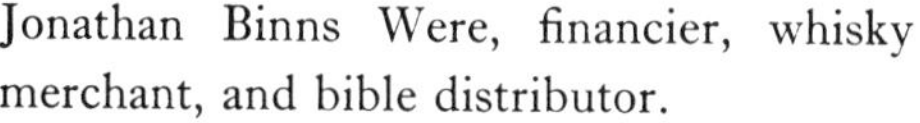

Jonathan Binns Were, financier, whisky merchant, and bible distributor.

Henry Byron Moore, who crashed on Beaum land deals and paid 3d. in the £1.

enterprises of its directors and never opened its doors again. Several other stock exchanges were also started with high hopes but failed to survive for more than a few months. At one stage during the boom there were no less than six separate exchanges conducting operations.

Until 1889 the business of the two major exchanges was conducted in 'The Exchange'. This was a £20,000 building erected by R. J. Jeffray in Collins Street near the south-eastern corner of Queen Street. (Today it is a branch of the Commonwealth Bank.) The building was leased by Henry Byron Moore, a broker who also ran a financial newspaper and sub-let the rest of the premises for share trading. All sorts of facilities were provided for brokers—even an hourly law report from the courts giving latest news on major cases. There was a press table, a hairdresser, a billiards room, telegraph office, and so on.

Moore was one of the most picturesque characters of the boom era. He had been a lithographer and surveyor, and was secretary of the Victoria Racing Club from 1881 onwards. Moore gave Melbourne a telephone service long before London had one. He bought the Melbourne rights to the invention and established a primitive telephone exchange on the roof of 'The Exchange' building. Moore was also an accomplished composer and author, and a fervent supporter of charitable works. His compositions, *Twelve Double Chants*, were sold in the streets in aid of St Paul's Cathedral building fund. Then he wrote a fairy tale called *How the Cruel Imp Became A Good Fairy*, copies of which raised £200 for charity.

Henry Byron Moore was, however, no match for the impish B. J. Fink, who convinced his fellow members of the Stock Exchange committee that they should buy a block of land across the road and build their own exchange. Fink's coup helped to send Henry Byron Moore into the Insolvency Court.

J. S. Butters, MLC, whose composition of ½d. in the £1 was disallowed by the court.

Henry Ricketson, who lost his Caulfield mansion 'Glen Eira' after plunging on shares.

Moore had plunged into the land boom as one of the sponsors of the Beaumaris Park Estate Co. Ltd, and had given his personal guarantee for more than £20,000 to the London Chartered Bank of Australia for money borrowed by that unsuccessful land company. Moore crashed for a total of £66,000, paying his creditors 3d. in the £1. But he stayed in Melbourne and fought his way back to commercial success, unlike his enemy B. J. Fink. He remained secretary of the Victoria Racing Club until 1925.

The site of the new exchange, next door to the English, Scottish & Australian Chartered Bank, had been owned by the wealthy Miller family. B. J. Fink had quietly bought it from the Millers for £65,000. Three months later the Stock Exchange of Melbourne paid £120,000—yielding Fink a tidy profit of £55,000. The incredibly ornate building, which still survives as a post office, cost £100,000 to build. George Meudell called the erection 'a fool of a building' which kept the Stock Exchange 'dog-poor for about 40 years', and was 'a pure act of treason to the members'. Its erection after the boom had practically burst sent its company into liquidation and reconstruction—but it was still the only stock exchange to survive, although it has long since shifted to different premises. Today the membership is limited to 166, and seats sell for high prices.

Meanwhile, the share boom which supported all these activities continued without pause. Shares in gold mines had been the mainstay of speculators for many years, but annual production of gold had been steadily decreasing ever since the peak year of 1856, when £12 million worth was won. By 1890 Victoria was producing only £250,000 worth of gold a year.

To replace the gold shares came a remarkable boom in silver shares. Whoever could sell his gold shares did so and put the proceeds into silver. The great mining successes of the 1880s were the discovery of the Mount Morgan mine in 1882, and the formation of the Broken Hill Proprietary Co. Ltd in 1885. By Christmas 1887 B.H.P. shares (sold originally for £9) had risen to £176 each; by January 1888, to £223. It was hysterical, fantastic, and crazy. Investors besieged their brokers; share clerks worked through the night transacting the deals. It was difficult for members to get into their offices each morning through the milling crowds of speculators. On 20 January 1888 more than £2 million worth of shares were sold at the Stock Exchange of Melbourne alone.

A vivid first-hand picture of the operations was given by the *Illustrated Australian News*:

> You only had to iusse a prospectus which contained the magic words Broken Hill, and draw some lines on a piece of paper and say it was a plan showing the lode to run 'right through the centre of this valuable property,' and that certain wonderful assays had been made, and an eager frantic public was ready to subscribe £50,000 or £100,000 in half an hour; and next morning the stock was launched upon the market and snapped up at 100, or even 500, per cent premium. And this was continued for many days—during the best part of January, throughout the whole of February . . .

The share boom of the 1880s may have started with mining stock, but it

Collins Street speculators in action during the silver boom of 1887–8.

rapidly developed into speculation in shares of hundreds of new land companies and 'land banks'. As these new companies started to 'open up' the suburbs, tramway shares also became a favourite form of speculation. If the railways had not been government-owned, no doubt there would have been a boom in railway shares too. Of the new companies incorporated in 1888, only a small number were intended to add anything to the colony's manufacturing resources. The remainder were purely speculative enterprises. Their total nominal capital was about £50 million, falling into the following categories:

	£ million
Land and finance	33
Trading companies	9.5
Mining companies	3.5
Breweries	3
Manufacturing	1

But the depression left no man untouched. As the effects of the crash began to spread to all sections of the community, brokers desperate to earn a commission began speculating in bank shares. The practice had been banned by the London Stock Exchange, due to fears of the public panic which could follow and accelerate any sudden decline in bank shares. In Melbourne at least a portion of the blame for the crash can be traced to the unchecked practice of dealing in bank shares. As prices dropped, more and more shares flooded on to the market. Some of the banks secretly bought them up through dummies to try and strengthen their value. All in vain!

During the terrible year of 1892, share prices in Melbourne dropped by a total of £36 million, in the following groups:

	£ million
Financial institutions	8.5
Tramway companies	8.5
Six major banks	4.5
Building societies	4
Davies companies	3.5
Broken Hill silver companies	3
Metropolitan Gas Co.	1
Breweries	1
Miscellaneous	2.5

No less than thirty-five members of the two main stock exchanges became officially insolvent as a result of their personal land and share dealings during the boom. Others were able to conceal the true state of their affairs, or were helped by friends to stay out of the Insolvency Court. Others liquidated their assets to pay their debts, such as Henry Ricketson, who was forced to sell his glorious mansion 'Glen Eira' to F. G. Sargood after losing heavily on the stock market. (The home later became Caulfield Military Hospital, and was demolished in 1964.)

Bulls and bears on the stock market.

Other brokers took a shorter cut to the solution of their worldly problems. Charles E. Broome, insolvent stockbroker, of Elwood, poisoned himself with prussic acid. Another, George Ford, stabbed himself fifteen times in a room at Scotts Hotel and bled to death. A bankrupt mining speculator, William James Irwin, walked in broad daylight to the Yarra near Princes Bridge, deliberately took off his hat, coat and vest, waded in, and was drowned.

However, most of the irrepressible members of the stock exchanges found it hard to stay downhearted. According to their annual report of October 1893: 'The depression has brought with it much that will have a lasting and beneficial effect on the future of the colony . . . We are sanguine that the dark days are over.'

12

James Balfour Floats Away

Some of the leading figures of the boom period were obvious villains, some operated in the shadowy area between legality and malpractice, and many were innocently swept into the maelstrom of events. James Balfour, M.L.C., may, with the exercise of a certain amount of charity, be included in the latter group.

Balfour was born in Edinburgh in 1830 and migrated to Victoria at the age of twenty-two. In 1859 he married Frances, eldest daughter of James Henty, M.L.C. Henty took his new son-in-law into his merchants' business as a partner. As a prosperous importer, Balfour quickly became a respected pillar of the business community. Wherever there was a worthy institution to support, Balfour could be found. He was elected president of the Melbourne Chamber of Commerce, and helped to keep the Protectionist agitators at bay. He joined the Y.M.C.A. committee to assist Matthew Davies, John Kitchen and other members to inculcate sound principles in the young. He became a member of the Legislative Assembly in 1866, and the Legislative Council in 1874, voting to bring about the downfall of the Berry Government when that alliance of radicals tried to force through a Bill for the payment of members of Parliament. Nowhere in Melbourne could there be found a sounder man than James Balfour, M.L.C.

In 1874, Balfour formed the Australian Deposit & Mortgage Bank Ltd, remaining chairman of directors until the smash. His fellow directors, staunch conservatives all, were Cornelius Job Ham, M.L.C.; Samuel Thomas Staughton, M.L.A.; Edward Waters; John Thompson; and Robert Harper, M.L.A.

When the Equitable Life Insurance Society of New York opened a Melbourne branch, Balfour was the natural choice to be appointed as its local chairman. At the height of the land boom, Balfour purchased for the Equitable the site at the north-west corner of Collins and Elizabeth Streets, paying James Munro £363,000 for the property—equivalent to £2,700 per foot. Despite the ensuing depression, the Equitable proceeded with its plans, and succeeded in getting its massive building erected by David Mitchell for little more than £40,000. Seventy years later, the wreckers charged nearly as much to pull it down.

As his major personal investment, Balfour acquired 'Round Hill' property, near Culcairn in the Riverina, prospering greatly as its leasehold land was gradually converted to freehold. Balfour's sons ran the property on modern lines, and 'Round Hill' merino wool became world-famous for its remarkable

James Balfour,
MLC, in 1888.

quality. Later a portion of the property was converted to wheat growing. The income from this enterprise was to save Balfour from complete bankruptcy a decade later.

In 1878 Balfour left the Henty firm and formed his own importing business under the style of James Balfour & Co. Then he made the mistake of taking into partnership a close associate of Matthew Davies named Edwin Charles Elliott. Elliott, a speculating stockbroker who crashed for £270,000, persuaded Balfour to float the firm on the stock market under the name of Balfour, Elliott & Co. Ltd.

Balfour was also one of the original promoters and directors of the Trustees, Executors & Agency Co. Ltd. This company lost heavily on its advances to land boomers—not least of all on its loans to E. C. Elliott.

One version of Balfour's subsequent history was given in a book called *The Honourable James Balfour, M.L.C.—A Memoir*, published in 1918. The author was the Rev. Andrew Harper, principal of St. Andrews College, Sydney—a son of the Robert Harper who was a director of some of Balfour's companies. The Rev. Harper wrote:

> When the great financial crisis of 1891–3 occurred, several of the institutions with which Balfour was connected as a Director were among the large number affected . . . Unfortunately he had been for nearly a year just prior to the collapse absent in Europe, and he did not see, as he might have done, had he been on the spot, the peril of the situation which was developing . . . The consequences to thousands of people were disastrous; and, amongst others, Balfour suffered greatly . . . He found himself, no longer a young man, saddled with liabilities which it would take him years under favourable circumstances to liquidate. The position would have appalled many a younger man . . .
>
> With indomitable courage, he set himself to the task of meeting his liabilities—and not only his own liabilities, but those of others—and of repairing his broken fortunes. Characteristically, he started by pruning his own personal comforts and those of his family. He gave up his beautiful residence in Toorak, and retired to a less pretentious dwelling. Anything that he or his family could do without they scrupulously denied themselves. But he did not become engrossed with his own troubles. He grieved for others who had sustained losses like himself, and he did what he could to help them. Instances could be multiplied of assistance rendered, even in the dark days following the collapse, to persons whose fortunes had been wrecked in the storm. He re-established his old business of James Balfour &

Entrance to the massive stone building erected by David Mitchell in 1893 for the Equitable Assurance Society. James Balfour was chairman of the Australian branch.

> Company, although there was no inducement at that time to embark on any fresh enterprise, in order that his employees might not be forced to swell the ranks of the unemployed . . .

Unfortunately this fine example of literary booming was merely another of the guilt-ridden attempts to rewrite history which occupied some of the leading figures of the land boom for years after its calamitous breakdown. The facts were much less flattering to Balfour and his associates.

Who, for example, comprised the board of Balfour, Elliott & Co. Ltd in 1889? Apart from Messrs Balfour and Elliott themselves, none other than Matthew Davies, J.B. Davies, and John Moodie. The same five directors also made up the board of the Freehold Investment Co. Ltd. And when the liquidators dug into the books of the latter company, they found that the Freehold had loaned

Balfour, Elliott & Co. Ltd the sum of £60,000—on the sole security of land at Elsternwick bought the previous year for £25,000. Profits from the sale of the Elsternwick land had been paid out to the directors themselves.

The liquidators demanded the return of the money, whereupon Balfour submitted the following written proposal of compromise:

> I beg to inform you that while I dispute the justice of your claim and any liability in connection therewith, yet in view of the expense, delay and annoyance attending litigation, I am willing to agree to the following proposal, but without prejudice, viz:- "That I pay you £5,000, extending over 10 years in equal instalments without interest on condition that you accept it in full satisfaction of all claims you have or believe you have on me, and that you undertake to give me a full legal discharge and release from all claims against me by the company, and any action whatsoever for which I am or may be liable in respect to 146 shares standing in my name in the company's register."

When the committee of advice met, Messrs. Mason and Balderson moved that the liquidators should decline the compromise and take legal steps without delay against Balfour and the other directors for recovery of the money. H.G. Turner dissented, considering that the proposed compromise should be accepted. The liquidators reported that they had inquired into Balfour's financial position and believed his estate would not pay more than the proposed compromise, and if the estate was sequestrated Balfour would be unable to pay calls on his shares, amounting to £2,718.

The majority liquidators took the whole story to the Supreme Court and asked for a ruling. James Mason, a member of the committee of advice, claimed in evidence that each of the directors, including Balfour, had put £6,500 profit from the Elsternwick deal 'out of the funds of the company into their own pockets.'

> *Mr Justice Holroyd*: Were these four gentlemen you have named members of the firm of Balfour, Elliott & Company?
>
> *Mason*: They were.
>
> *His Honour*: And at the same time directors of the company that made the loan?—Yes.
>
> *His Honour*: Then they were lending to themselves?—Yes.

In his decision, the judge pointed out that the depositors were the persons whose interests must be paramount. He ordered a meeting of the creditors be held to consider Balfour's proposed compromise. Rather than lose the £5,000 offered, this meeting accepted the proposition, thus saving Balfour from immediate bankruptcy and possible criminal action. The final result was that Balfour's firm lost £60,000 of the Freehold depositors' money, in return for which Balfour had to repay only £500 a year for ten years, interest free. So much for the Rev. Harper's description of the 'indomitable courage' with which Balfour met his liabilities.

Then in September 1891, Mr Justice Hood awarded substantial damages, totalling £1,125 plus costs, against James Balfour for selling to W. H. Roberts, a fellow M.L.C., a block of land in Melbourne Road, North Williamstown, to which he did not hold a valid title. What other curious deals might have been uncovered if Balfour had been forced into the Insolvency Court?

Some indication of the full truth was disclosed in the affairs of his partner, E.C. Elliott, who went bankrupt in 1892 for £270,000. Elliott's debts included £40,000 loaned to him by Balfour's own companies—the Australian Deposit & Mortgage Bank; the Trustees, Executors & Agency Co.; and Balfour, Elliott & Co. Ltd. The fact that Elliott was loaned more than £27,000 by the last-named company, controlled by himself and Balfour, shortly before the company crashed, cried aloud foı explanation. None was ever given. Nor was there any investigation of the fate of the £200,000 loaned to Elliott by Matthew Davies's companies.

Lucky as he was to escape personal insolvency, Balfour was just as fortunate in the circumstances which surrounded the closure of his Australian Deposit & Mortgage Bank in Collins Street. At its half-yearly meeting on 2 February 1892, Balfour declared a 12½ per cent dividend. He told shareholders that £370,000 had been sent from Edinburgh for investment in the company, the money being obtained from the best houses in Edinburgh and some of the insurance companies. Many people in Scotland had been frightened by the Australian land boom, but their bank 'could not be a loser by the boom'; indeed, he thought it would benefit by it, as money had been brought to the bank by the difficulties of other companies. Seven weeks after this sanguine pronouncement, the bank suddenly suspended payment and closed its doors, creating an enormous sensation among depositors who had trusted to Balfour's reputation.

Shares in the bank were held mainly by clergymen, widows, and civil servants. Balfour called a shareholders' meeting, and persuaded the members to agree to voluntary liquidation under a director of the bank, John Thompson. When Thompson resigned and left for England, the bank's manager, William Reid, was appointed liquidator. Thus no comprehensive investigation into the bank's affairs was ever made public. Most of the depositors quietly accepted 5 per cent preference shares in a reconstructed company called the Australian Mortgage & Deposit Bank, managed by the same directors.

Only a muffled bleat was heard when the 5 per cent rate was subsequently reduced to 2 per cent. 'A painful situation,' commented *The Economist*. Ultimately the new bank also went into liquidation, its head office at 267 Collins Street becoming the present-day site of the Bank of Adelaide.

After the crash, Balfour did indeed 'give up his beautiful residence in Toorak.' This was the mansion known as 'Tyalla,' in Heyington Place. In 1895 the family moved to 'Illapa,' in Princess Street, Kew; then, when conditions improved, to 'Windella,' in Studley Park Road, Kew (now Studley Park Hospital). 'Amid all the storm he never lost the poise and balance of his spirit,' wrote the Rev. Harper. With this statement at least we are forced to agree.

13

When McEwan's Floated and Fell

The beautiful colonnaded mansion called 'Kamesburgh' survives from the land boom era by a freak of fate. It slumbers in spacious grounds in North Road, Brighton, displaying cool indifference to the closely-packed suburban villas which cluster upon its borders. On a bright moonlit evening, when the sea breeze rustles the trees and moves their shadows on the broad lawns, and lights blaze from every room, it is not too fanciful to imagine the carriages even now pulling up to the main doors, the horses stamping and steaming in the night air, the charming ladies and gentlemen of the boom times bustling and bantering their way into the main ballroom. What you will really see at 'Kamesburgh' today, especially if you return in the daylight, are a few disabled men, some of them confined to wheelchairs, some of them restricted to stretchers, each of them surveying the wonders of the past with that peculiarly Australian patience which seems to know everything and admit nothing. These ageing men were not placed in 'Kamesburgh' by some wildly ironical jester for purposes of *grand guignol*, or even for some moralistic lesson about the vanity of human hopes and ambitions. The old mansion has simply become an Anzac Hostel, and the presence of its occupants (forgotten men now, except briefly on Anzac Day) is the only reason why the suburban villas have so far been held at bay from this corner of Brighton.

The origins of 'Kamesburgh' lie far in the past, probably a century ago, when a young immigrant named William Kerr Thomson first saw an illustration of a Southern-style mansion derived from Georgian architecture, and determined that one day *he* would build a house like that. In 1852 Thomson was merely an obscure 18-year-old employee in James McEwan's hardware store—first at the Bendigo goldfields, then in Elizabeth Street, Melbourne. The dour old Scottish chandler died in 1868. Thomson and another employee, Samuel Renwick, took over the business as a partnership, retaining the former name of James McEwan & Co. Profits flowed in during the expansive years which followed, and soon Thomson was in sight of achieving his dream.

In 1872, Thomson bought his twelve acres of land at Brighton from a syndicate, and engaged the leading architect Lloyd Tayler to design 'Kamesburgh'—a name derived from the Scottish seaside resort on the Island of Bute. Built by David Mitchell at a cost of £17,000, the huge but beautiful structure

'Kamesburgh', the beautiful Brighton mansion today known as 'Anzac Hostel'.

consisted of forty rooms, including nineteen bedrooms. The mansion was almost entirely free of the fussy ornamentation which marred most of the later architecture of the boom. Its noble entrance hall, 35 feet long, led to an intersecting hall and broad staircase. Downstairs rooms included a drawing room, dining room, breakfast room, conservatory, billiards room, and glass and china room. There was a large library, fitted with what has been described as 'surely the first known room divider'—a steel-framed counterweighted wall measuring 18 feet long by 14 feet high. This wall could be wound up and down, sliding neatly between two walls on the next floor. When 'down,' the wall divided off one-third of the library.

Underneath most of the house were cellars and a huge underground room fitted with a fireplace, but there remains no indication of the use to which this room was put. On the first floor, a 50-foot hallway led to the main bedrooms, which in turn opened on to the west verandah. The boudoir ceilings were painted in floral designs by Charles Stewart Paterson, but only one faded example of his work remains.

The spacious grounds were laid out by George Kenner, head gardener, and included a sunken rose garden, summer houses, a pigeon loft, stables, and hothouses. Thomson entered the gardens for a Cup presented by Thomas Bent in 1875 for 'the best kept gentleman's garden'—but missed winning by one point. Three years later, however, his entries made practically a clean sweep of the prizes at the Camellia Show.

Thomson made several overseas trips to select furnishings for the house. In Paris, for instance, he bought a marvellous instrument called 'le piano melodieux'

—a combination of piano and organ—which was later used to play the Wedding March at the marriage at 'Kamesburgh' of his 'remarkably handsome' daughter Maggie. On another trip to Paris, Thomson bought two cast iron figures which supported lamps on either side of the main entrance, and which can still be seen there today.

Each August a grand ball was held at 'Kamesburgh' for hundreds of guests, when 'dancing was continued to a late hour to the music of Herr Plock's Band, which rendered a charming selection of the newest music most effectively.' The following day a children's party was always held, at which Thomson's three sons and two daughters presumably practised the social graces appropriate to their station.

Alas, that gracious position in life was soon to be shattered. In 1887, Thomson and Renwick decided to float McEwan's as a public company on the booming stock exchanges. At first McEwan's Ltd paid substantial dividends from its £800,000 a year turnover. Thomson put most of his proceeds from the flotation into the Fiji Trading Company, which owned several sugar plantations in the islands. It was his first serious miscalculation, for the company failed and Thomson lost £55,000. He became a foundation director of David Munro & Co. Ltd, and again lost heavily when that enterprise collapsed.

In 1888, Thomson began borrowing large sums of money all over Melbourne. He was given nearly £17,000 by the Colonial Bank; £8,000 by the New Oriental Bank; and £4,000 by the City of Melbourne Bank. The same year, his co-director Samuel Renwick died, and Thomson decided to try and buy up his shares in McEwan's Ltd. A complex series of negotiations took place with B. J. Fink and his Mercantile Finance Co. Ltd, which resulted in loans of £160,000 being given to Thomson. Exactly twelve months later, when his other debts had reached £100,000, Thomson was forced to file his schedule in insolvency. His sworn statement showed only £12,600 as owing to the Mercantile Finance Co. Years later, the liquidators of Fink's companies reported a total loss of £140,000 on Thomson's account. The balance had been 'written off' to conceal his huge indebtedness to the Mercantile.

Thomson dismissed all his servants and broke the news to his family that they must leave 'Kamesburgh'. They must leave their carriages and the sunken rose garden, and 'le piano melodieux' too. There would be no more parties and balls, and never more would Thomson be able to demonstrate to his astonished guests the false wall which glided down from his library ceiling. Gone—all gone: the servants to the slums, no doubt; the crushed Thomson family to a humble cottage in Malvern.

In December 1892, Thomson offered a composition of ¼d. in the £1 to his creditors, which they accepted and freed him from sequestration. Business friends rallied to his assistance, and through James Service presented him with a sum which provided a small income for the remainder of his life. During this period Thomson appears to have been still working at McEwan's. After that the family seems to have disappeared from Melbourne. Thomson finally died in North Kensington, London, in 1906.

W. K. Thomson, who built and occupied 'Kamesburgh' until the crash.

D. E. McBryde, the BHP director who occupied 'Kamesburgh' after the Thomson family went bankrupt.

Thomas Luxton, MLC, who took over McEwan's hardware business after the crash.

The original James McEwan and Company store at Elizabeth and Little Collins Streets, Melbourne – rebuilt recently as Elizabeth Arcade.

'Kamesburgh' remained vacant for some time after Thomson's bankruptcy. It was listed for sale for £25,000 in C. J. & T. Ham's *Register of Properties for Sale* issued in 1892. Along came a 40-year-old Scot named Duncan Elphinstone McBryde, who offered a laughable £10,000 for the property and found his offer snapped up.

McBryde was a N.S.W. squatter who dabbled in finance and politics. One-time owner of Mt. Poole Station, 150 miles north of Broken Hill, he became a foundation director of the Broken Hill Proprietary in 1885 and later vice-chairman, making a fortune as the mine's output increased. McBryde then spent most of his time in Melbourne, becoming a president of the Caledonian Society, and a member of the Legislative Council in 1891. McBryde lived quietly enough at 'Kamesburgh' with his family during the succeeding decades when the face of Australian industry was being changed by the emergence of W. L. Baillieu's Collins House group. McBryde also became Minister of Public Health and Commissioner of Public Works in Thomas Bent's last Ministry.

Meanwhile the other half of W. K. Thomson's interests—McEwan's Ltd—was undergoing several changes of control. In the complex shaking-down process which continued for many years after the boom, the hardware store fell into the hands of the London Bank of Australia, which in turn fell into the hands of W. L. Baillieu, who later amalgamated it with the E.S. & A. Bank.

In 1910, Baillieu (by then Minister of Public Health and Commissioner of Public Works in succession to McBryde), offered McEwan's as a going concern to his fellow member of the Legislative Council, the Honorable Thomas Luxton. Luxton, a sharebroker and financier, had participated in the wild days of the Stock Exchange boom. He was a rollicking speculator who once laid wagers with his fellow brokers that he would sing a song in the call room of the Stock Exchange. One day when the room was at its most crowded, he broke into a jaunty ballad which sounded 'like five hundred rusty nails shaken in an empty kerosene tin.' But when he was not skylarking, Luxton was a keen horse-trader. He had already bought the depression-wrecked business of McLean Bros. & Rigg further up Elizabeth Street. Baillieu sold him McEwan's on no deposit and gave him ten years to pay off the balance. Luxton died the following year, but his sons Harold and T. J. Luxton continued the business with great success.

In the closing years of the first World War, Duncan McBryde, now nearing the end of his life, decided that he wanted to sell 'Kamesburgh' and move to a smaller house. The mansion was offered to the Repatriation Department for use as a hostel on 8 April 1918, the very day on which the department commenced operations. The price asked was £18,000.

The Baillieu family now came directly into the 'Kamesburgh' story, by donating £25,000 to the Federal Government for repatriation purposes. Of the six Baillieu brothers who lived until World War I, only one, Maurice Howard Baillieu, had been able to serve abroad. The remaining five brothers of the original family decided to donate £5,000 each to the government. This donation, called 'The Baillieu Gift', and consisting largely of Harbour Trust debentures, was placed under the administration of the new Repatriation Department.

The Minister for Repatriation, Senator E. D. Millen, toured Melbourne to examine vacant boom-time mansions which would be suitable for use as a convalescent hostel. The list was finally narrowed down to 'Brommerton' and 'Crotonhurst' in Caulfield, and 'Kamesburgh' in Brighton. By the happiest of coincidences, Senator Millen decided to accept the offer of W. L. Baillieu's fellow-director of B.H.P., Duncan McBryde. McBryde shifted to Toorak, nostalgically called his new home 'Kamesburgh', and died there two years later.

The Brighton mansion was taken over and officially opened as Anzac Hostel in July 1919. Guests at the ceremony were entertained by the band of the Brighton Rifles, and a tablet was unveiled in the main hall:–

IN HONOUR OF THE BRAVE MEN WHO FOUGHT
IN THE GREAT WAR OF 1914–18
This property was provided by the
Commonwealth of Australia from the
donation of William Lawrence Baillieu
and his brothers for the use of
incapacitated soldiers.

The public's reaction to the gift was not quite as enthusiastic as might have been expected. Those with longish memories recalled the Commonwealth

Solicitor-General's police raid on Collins House early in the war, in an attempt to find documents proving war-time trading with the enemy. (The documents seized all related to pre-war trading, showing that the only Australian metal which could have been used in shells fired by the Germans on Allied troops must have been sold to Germany before the war).

Some more effective gesture than the mere presentation of £25,000 for wounded soldiers was, under the circumstances, felt to be necessary. The opportunity came when Edward, Prince of Wales, visited Melbourne in 1920. Every conceivable pressure was brought to bear on the Prince's advisers to persuade him to visit the crippled men in Anzac Hostel. 'For weeks before, amid much wrangling, it had seemed that Anzac Hostel was far too low on the list of priorities to earn such an overwhelming honour,' wrote Weston Bate in his *History of Brighton*. On his visit, the Prince was 'a little nervous perhaps, even slightly sour; immaculate . . . but not fully at ease.' Nevertheless, the precedent had been set, and in later years the Dukes of York and Gloucester also visited the home.

In 1927, the hostel's grounds were divided in half, 6¼ acres being sold as building blocks to realise a total of £23,000. This amount was paid into the Baillieu Gift. It remained idle for some years in the Treasury accounts, until its existence was discovered almost simultaneously by the University of Melbourne and Legacy, the latter being an organisation which cares for the children of deceased ex-servicemen. The University and Legacy both applied for use of the cash. Eventually a bargain was struck. Legacy was given use of the interest for fifteen years, and with it managed to educate 1,400 children of men who had died in the war. After that, universities in various States were given the interest money for post-graduate 'Baillieu Research Scholarships', with preference to former Legacy children. In addition the Baillieu family gave £10,000 to Melbourne University to help build the Baillieu Library.

The ultimate fate of old 'Kamesburgh' remains uncertain. As the years pass, the number of permanently invalid soldiers being nursed there steadily decreases, and it becomes probably the most expensive public hospital per patient known anywhere in the world. Just before World War II, when most of the First A.I.F. veterans had died, the Commonwealth tried to close down the hostel. Members of the Baillieu family fought the move tooth and nail, and privately donated several thousand pounds more to keep the hostel going—a fortunate development in view of the new wars and their inevitable toll of shattered men.

It now appears that Anzac Hostel will be kept in operation until the last patient dies. The property will probably then be sold and the money paid into the Baillieu Gift, thus in one way or another continuing to aid Legacy children and other students. Whether 'Kamesburgh' itself will survive this change of ownership, or whether the subdividers will be allowed to snap it up, seems an open question.

14

The Boom and Crash in Sydney

(i) A Taste of the Boom

To the gleeful writers of the *Bulletin*, Melbourne was always 'Smellboom,' and the long procession of financial scandals in the southern city was simply proof of the 'cronk' state of its affairs. The *Bulletin* could perhaps afford to be critical, for its own city of Sydney was comparatively free from the malign influence of land boomers in control of the State's political and economic machinery.

N.S.W. had already had a foretaste of what could happen when a boom burst. The State had gone through an inflationary period from 1876 to 1880, when British investors poured in £8 million capital; and the N.S.W. Treasury gained another £12 million through sales of Crown land. But in 1884–5 a two-year drought decimated millions of sheep and bankrupted many graziers. At the same time the export price of greasy wool dropped from 12¼d. to 9¼d. a pound. E. O. G. Shann calls these misfortunes 'inoculations against boom fever.' Certainly they had the effect of sparing N.S.W. from the worst excesses of the land boom. Overseas investors became more anxious to sink their funds into Victoria, which had escaped the worst effects of the drought.

Not that N.S.W. got off scot-free. There was a similar development to Victoria in the efflorescence of building societies and land banks. The suburbs of Sydney were carved up and offered for sale on long terms. The established banks displayed the same ambivalent attitude as in Melbourne: anxious to make a profit from the boom but determined to withdraw their financial accommodation at the first sign of danger. And when the collapse did come, the same financial cancers were revealed in the commercial framework, even though they had not eaten so deeply as in the south.

The number of building societies in N.S.W. grew quickly from seventeen in 1864 to ninety-four in 1880—about one-third in Sydney and the rest in country centres. Fortunately, however, most of the N.S.W. societies were strictly run and supervised, and only three collapsed in the smash. Sydney thus escaped the terrible assault on public morale which occurred in Melbourne when its trusted religious and commercial leaders were shown to be involved in the building society scandals.

"SHOWING THE LAND."

'One day soon there will be rows of houses here,' promised the auctioneer, showing prospective buyers around the rocky outcrops of Sydney.

Meanwhile, however, the land banks of Sydney were offering interest rates ranging from seven to ten per cent in order to obtain deposits, which were in turn expended on acres for subdivision. Forty Sydney land companies went into liquidation during the smash, losing the greater part of their shareholders' and depositors' assets.

Frantic competition existed between the established banks, which opened hundreds of unprofitable branches to take deposits and grant overdrafts. (In five years after the smash, 464 bank branches in N.S.W. were closed down). In 1891, the banks of issue allowed their reserves to fall to only 12.8 per cent of their liabilities. As the crisis deepened, they started calling in overdrafts in order to strengthen their own position, thus precipitating the insolvency of many of their customers.

One of the most interesting of the many Sydney land companies was known as the North Sydney Investment & Tramway Co. Ltd. This institution was formed in 1888 to purchase 1,000 acres of land at North Sydney for £512,000; to build a bridge over Long Bay to give access to the land; to build a four-mile private tramway from the terminus of the Government cable tramway from Sydney; and to subdivide and resell the land.

Directors of the company included John Grice (chairman of the National Bank); William Smith (deputy chairman of the Colonial Bank); J.P. Abbott (chairman of the A.M.P. Society); and R.J. Alcock (partner in James Service

One Sydney
oom palace was
equal to
anything
lelbourne could
produce: The
ustral Banking
& Land
Proprietary,
ilt in Elizabeth
reet, Sydney, in
1889.

Two directors of the consortium which tried to open up North Sydney to housing and tramways: J. P. Abbott, chairman of the A.M.P. Society (left) and R. J. Alcock, partner of the Victorian merchant-politician James Service.

& Co., Melbourne merchants). The project was largely underwritten by the National Bank, which accepted £300,000 in debentures from British investors. The company produced a glowing prospectus, extolling the estate as 'admirably situated for the formation of a high class suburb . . . being the most elevated land in the neighbourhood, and having six miles frontage to the beautiful waters of Middle Harbour . . . The roads on the estate are being rapidly formed . . . ' and so on.

In 1891 a writer for the London *Financial News*, in Sydney on a tour, visited the area with a professional surveyor. Both were aghast, and reported:

> The land is rocky—hilly spurs between crests—inaccessible on horseback over a large portion. The crest above the suspension bridge is 200 ft. . . . with an incline of 1 in 9 to it. The company does not own the land by which an easier descent could be made . . . The land is such that it is impossible to subdivide it into small allotments, as the boulders are some of them 40 ft. high . . . The man who owned it tried hard to borrow £100 an acre, and could not do so. The land is rocky, sparsely covered by low scrub, and bleak-looking—only fit for a rabbit warren, and with too little earth for many rabbits.

The company rapidly went into liquidation.

Bad luck rather than bad management destroyed another famous company—the Anglo-Australian Land Co., which built the Australia Hotel in Sydney. This company had no connection with the notorious Anglo-Australian Bank of Melbourne. Unfortunately, when the promoters of the Melbourne bank were gaoled for fraud, the public confused the two enterprises. Depositors besieged the Sydney company and demanded their money back, forcing it into premature liquidation and reconstruction.

Liquidation of three building societies and dozens of land companies bore most heavily on the working class seeking to buy land and establish their own homes. Said the *Bulletin* in May 1893: 'During the last two years nearly 40 land banks have suspended payment in New South Wales; their depositors, who number tens of thousands, were almost exclusively working men and women, and these depositors lost on an average three-fourths of their savings.'

There was widespread distress, intensified by falling Government revenue and cutting of public works. Income from land sales, the State's chief source of revenue, dropped from £2 6s. per head of population in 1887 to £1 14s. per head in 1892. The Government's Casual Labour Board and its soup kitchens had to cope with an army of more than 50,000 unemployed.

(ii) The Banking Frauds

The first and worst of the Sydney banking scandals was that of the Australian Banking Company of Sydney, which suspended payment on 2 November 1891. Its chairman was Francis Abigail, Minister for Mines in the Parkes Government. Abigail was originally a bootmaker, who for many years carried on business in George Street, Sydney. He was elected member for West Sydney and appointed to the Parkes Ministry in 1885.

During the Sydney land boom, Abigail formed the Australian Banking Co., his avowed object being 'to assist and encourage small traders.' Prominent men were induced to buy shares or deposit their cash with the bank, thus attesting to its soundness. The other directors were S. G. Davidson, a suburban butcher; R. Cunningham; Mr Hurley, M.L.A.; T. H. Hassall, M.L.A.; and William Bull. The bank's paid-up capital was £100,000 and its deposits about the same amount—another proof to the public of its sound financial principles.

But before long Abigail and some of his fellow directors had succeeded in milking the bank of most of its ready cash. Rumours doubting the bank's soundness spread through Parliament and eventually reached the public, culminating in a run on its remaining funds. The bank was forced to close its doors, but Abigail managed to get himself appointed liquidator 'in the interests of the shareholders' and because of his 'past good services.'

However, some shareholders were suspicious enough to insist on the appointment of a committee of inquiry. In July 1892, this committee announced that all the bank's directors, nine of its employees, and its solicitor, were indebted to the bank for £62,000; the security for these loans being almost worthless. Abigail owed £4,000; Davidson £10,000; Nathan £11,000; Roderick McNamara (the manager) £3,000; and so on. Hurley, M.L.A., a former chairman, owed nearly £8,000. As security he had handed over 750 shares in the bank for which he had paid nothing.

A new liquidator was appointed, who reported on 'the awful consequences of this way of doing business.' He discovered that 'A heavy loss was sustained during the bank's first half-year, and this loss, like a rolling snowball, has continued until the closing up of the concern . . . As regularly as the half-year closed a large net profit was reported . . . '

Abigail was arrested on a charge of 'concurring in the making of a false entry in the bank's return book with intent to defraud.' At the police court hearing, Abigail claimed that his connection with the bank was 'a purely ornamental one.' The other villainous directors, he claimed, attended to all the business.

McNamara, the manager, was committed separately for 'fraudulent appropriation of moneys and false entries.' The information was laid by Richard Neville, an elderly gentleman of Phillip Street who was a shareholder and depositor in the bank. 'Until the bank went smash,' Neville deposed, 'I lived on my means, but the smash has made me almost a pauper.'

At this preliminary hearing, it was revealed that McNamara had written to Abigail some months before: 'Perhaps it would not be out of place to mention just now the fact that £35,421 was taken out of the bank's coffers by former directors, and £17,736 by the present board . . . The details are sufficiently sickening to make even the most hardened ruffian blush. My advice to you at present is this, "Do not allow the drama to become too ludicrous before my return to the bank".' The letter was used to help prove that Abigail knew and concealed the rotten state of the bank.

After their trial before Sir William Windeyer, Abigail was sentenced to five years hard labour and McNamara to seven years. Sentencing Abigail, Windeyer said: 'A good man, a man of high character, might sometimes commit some act of indiscretion and crime, but good men more often drift into them.' The stern old judge was quite overcome and wept when sentencing Abigail to gaol, leading the *Bulletin* to a scarifying verse:–

WINDEYER WEPT

Windeyer wept salt, bitter tears,
   His voice began to fail;
The pain of giving five long years
   To Francis Abigail
Was more than gentle judge could stand
   Without betraying grief—
He hid his face behind his hand
   In tears to find relief.

Windeyer wept (a note of that—
   Aye, make a little note!)
For crime that wears a shiny hat
   And pious-looking coat.
The hypocrite whose life has been
   A bold, unblushing lie—
For him the party in the gown
   Can pipe his learned eye.

Another serious scandal evolved out of the dealings of the Australian Mercantile Loan & Guarantee Company. This institution was floated in 1888 to purchase a financial agency belonging to Alexander Hastings Malcolm, an

Two members of Parliament were among those charged over the Australian Banking Company frauds in Sydney. Francis Abigail, MLA, was sentenced to five years' hard labour.

uncertificated insolvent. Its paid-up capital was only £4,000, yet Malcolm was given 50,000 fully-paid £1 shares for his business.

Directors of the company were two Sydney warehousemen, Charles Bell and Samuel Davies; James Peter Howe, M.L.A. for Redfern; James Miller; A.W. Miller; Thomas Jones; and F.J. Smith. Another director, E.H. Buchanan, went to England and formed a London office to tout for deposits. He persuaded Lord Ulrich Browne and other prominent Englishmen to join a 'London Board of Advice,' then used their names to attract more deposits.

The parliamentary member of the Sydney board, J. P. Howe, was originally a blacksmith. He had been a mayor of Redfern, and was elected as M.L.A. for that district in 1888. He was defeated in 1891, but with the help of W. N. Willis, one of the proprietors of *Truth*, was elected to the seat of Bourke.

In July 1891, two directors, Bell and Davies, neatly defrauded the company of its spare cash—£30,000 in gold sovereigns. The company was forced to suspend business. Bell and Davies made off to Melbourne with their loot, which weighed more than 500 pounds. They changed their names to Bloom and Douglas, shaved off their beards, and, according to one Melbourne report, led 'the lives of veritable lotus eaters in our midst.'

The pair then bought a schooner called the *Beagle*, and commissioned a Captain J. H. Gill to take them on a South Seas trading cruise. An iron safe full of gold sovereigns and boxes of stores were loaded aboard at Williamstown. Conspicuous among these were several cases of rare champagne. After assorted adventures, Captain Gill was put ashore in the Hawaiian Islands with a steamship ticket to Hong Kong, where at last he learned the true identity of his companions. They meanwhile had disappeared, the captain's Conradian opinion being that they were 'still cruising the islands, taking life leisurely, and purchasing with their stolen sovereigns as much happiness as is accessible to men of their stamp in such remote latitudes.' They were never heard of again.

Meanwhile, shareholders of the insolvent company appointed a committee of investigation. A meeting was called in August 1891, to hear its report. Proceedings opened with a stormy discussion on the appointment of a chairman, in the course of which one of the directors, A. W. Miller, and a depositor engaged in 'a vigorous scuffle.' The investigators' report showed that the company had only been kept going and 'profits' paid regularly by using depositors' money and cooking the books. Five directors had been loaned more than £25,000 of the company's funds, on no security whatever. In all, more than £80,000 in depositors' funds had disappeared.

In November, prosecutions were launched against two of the directors for helping to defraud the depositors. J. P. Howe, M.L.A. for Bourke, and James Miller, were each sentenced to seven years' hard labour.

Meanwhile, the official liquidator, Augustus Morris, was conducting a fuller investigation. In July 1892, he reported:

> Had the true position of the company been set forth in its first balance sheet . . . it would have been shown to have been hopelessly insolvent. The balance sheet was unquestionably a false one, and designedly so . . . The dividend which it will be possible to pay is so wretchedly small that there can be no hope of allaying the bitter indignation of the numerous depositors who have been tricked out of their hard earned savings.'

The lax state of the colony's banking laws was again illustrated by the closure of the Sydney Deposit Bank in January 1892. The founder and manager of this bank was T. S. Richardson. The bank was Mr Richardson, and Mr Richardson was the bank. There were no other shareholders. Under N.S.W. law, he was even able to make his own note issue. Fooled by its title, and its status as 'a bank of issue,' credulous investors deposited £75,000 with the Sydney Deposit Bank. Richardson appropriated most of the money and spent it on land purchases. When depositors started withdrawing their cash, he could no longer meet the payments on his land deals. He simply closed the bank's doors, went insolvent, and calmly waited for the storm to blow over.

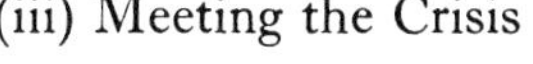

(iii) Meeting the Crisis

Events such as these, and rumours of further disasters to come, caused a serious run to begin on the government Savings Bank in Barrack Street on 10 February 1892. The Premier, Sir George Dibbs, issued a proclamation stating that the Government would guarantee the bank's deposits. The notice was posted at the doors of the bank and the *Sydney Morning Herald* office, and the run was halted.

Early in 1893 the big banks in Melbourne began to fall, dragging their Sydney connections down with them. In April, five major Sydney banks closed their doors: the Commercial, the E.S. & A., the Australian Joint Stock Bank, the London Chartered Bank, and the Standard Bank. In May, another four suspended: the National, the Queensland National, the Commercial Banking Co. of Sydney, and the Bank of North Queensland. 'It seemed as if something substantial and dependable in life had suddenly crumbled, and there could be no security or freedom from anxiety any more,' wrote H. L. Harris in *The Financial Crisis of 1893 in New South Wales*.

Suspension of the Australian Joint Stock Bank on 20 April was the worst blow for N.S.W. It boasted of 30,000 accounts and a larger amount of deposits than all the other banks combined. Rumours swept the city that the eccentric millionaire James Tyson had withdrawn £300,000 from the bank in a lump sum. By the time this rumour was scotched, the damage had been done.

Another shock to public opinion was the suspension of the Commercial Banking Co. of Sydney on 15 May. This bank had been regarded almost as an integral part of N.S.W. Its £25 shares had been quoted at up to £115 each. But as depositors grew more and more anxious, they started withdrawing their funds, forcing this bank too to close its doors.

Sir George Dibbs, 59-year-old leader of the Protectionist Party, attempted

Sir George Dibbs, Premier of N.S.W., whose prompt action stopped the run on Sydney banks.

to meet the banking crisis with an Act enabling the banks to apply 'to make bank notes a first charge upon bank assets . . . and to declare bank notes to be legal tender.' But only one bank asked to have its notes guaranteed in this way. By 15 May, when most of the banks had suspended business, Dibbs rushed through the Bank Issue Act making their notes legal tender regardless of the banks' own wishes. Instantly the panic eased. With notes guaranteed by the State, and hence 'as good as gold,' commercial dealings resumed and the banks were given a breathing space for reconstruction.

Dibbs himself was a controversial figure of the period, who had gone bankrupt on a debt for £90 only a few weeks before the crisis. He resigned the Premiership, but was immediately re-elected unopposed for Murrumbidgee, leading 'Oriel' to comment in the *Argus*:

> And the only weapon left him,
> When of cash they have bereft him,
> Is a list of all the debts in his estate . . .
> Then without undue dejection
> He submits to re-election,
> And he governs all the better for the 'job'.

Dibbs had alienated his earliest supporters in the strong Sydney labor movement. Previously he proclaimed himself a fervent Republican, but in 1892 he spent £1,000 of public money on a trip to London, where he was knighted by Queen Victoria. Dowell O'Reilly wrote savagely in the *Worker*:

> Ladies to right of him,
> Ladies to left of him,
> Ladies in front of him,
> Curtsied and wondered.
> Charmed with their subtle spell,
> Boldly he strode, and well
> He, the Republican—
> Up to the Royal Throne:
> "Arise, sir, happy one!"
> Noble ten hundred!

Yet this turncoat radical, this Premier who could not pay a debt of £90, showed himself competent and resolute in the hour of crisis. The passage of the Bank Issue Act 1893 restored confidence like magic. It was reinforced on 26 May by the Current Account Depositors Act 1893, by which Treasury notes could be issued to depositors whose money had been locked up in the suspended banks. A total of £358,490 in Treasury notes was issued, and by the following October all but £24,000 had been repaid.

Soon the *Sydney Morning Herald* was able to report that 'Banking affairs in New South Wales are continuing to move towards their normal conditions, if not quickly, yet steadily.' Most citizens realised their great good fortune, in comparison with the unhappy state of affairs in the neighbouring colony of Victoria. A testimonial fund was opened for Dibbs to acknowledge his prompt action in meeting the crisis. £2,500 was quickly subscribed for the insolvent Premier who had saved the State's commercial and banking system almost against its will.

II THE MUCKRAKERS

THE CITY OF DREADFUL STINKS.

15

Maurice Brodzky, Editor of *Table Talk*

'The Press lives by disclosures', thundered *The Times* in 1852 in a memorable rebuke to Lord John Russell's government. 'The first duty of the Press is to obtain the earliest and most correct intelligence of the events of the time, and instantly, by disclosing them, to make them the common property of the nation.' This dictum, simple, forthright, and compelling, appeared to override all other considerations. But did it? What was the function of a newspaper in a time of financial depression? Should it risk intensifying the depression by printing all it knew? Did the exposure of financial corruption justify the entire destruction of public confidence and the probable prolongation of suffering?

This terrible dilemma for any editor was at first answered unanimously by the Melbourne daily press of the 1890s. Every newspaper ignored the crisis for as long as possible. When the obvious could no longer be ignored, every newspaper insisted, and kept on insisting, that the depression would be short-lived. Naturally they were compelled to report the early company crashes and court cases as they occurred. The *Age*, as we have seen, went further and published well-documented articles on the shocking state of distress into which the industrial suburbs were drifting. But no daily newspaper thought fit to make a full investigation of the land banks or the financial manipulations of the leading men of the day. That thankless task was left to an almost-forgotten man called Maurice Brodzky, who published an almost-forgotten weekly journal called *Table Talk*.

Little is known of Brodzky's antecedents. One may surmise that his racial origin was with the Jewish Brodskys who migrated into southern Russia from the Balkans hundreds of years before, taking their name from the locality of Brod. The Brodzkys became prominent landowners and bankers as far north as Poland, where the name was spelt with a 'z' as 'Brodzki'. Brodzky's parents settled temporarily in Markowitz, Poland, where Maurice was born on 25 November 1847. Further wanderings took the family to Vienna, London, and Paris, giving Brodzky a cosmopolitan outlook and remarkable linguistic ability in lieu of a settled background.

Brodzky was still a student in Paris when the Franco-Prussian war broke out. He enlisted in the French army as an *engagé volontaire*, and was awarded a medal by the French government for his services. Shortly afterwards Brodzky

What is a newspaper's duty in times of financial crisis? Even David Syme, proprietor of the *Age*, was not always sure.

emigrated to Australia in the 960-ton *Sussex*. On New Year's Eve 1871, when the vessel was sailing in moderate seas off the Victorian coast, the master mistook a light on shore for Cape Schanck lighthouse. He altered course for the entrance to Port Phillip Bay, and ran his ship hard aground in the breakers at Barwon Heads. Maurice Brodzky was rowed ashore in his undershirt and trousers, with only a few shillings in his pocket. The survivors arrived at Queen's Wharf, Melbourne, on New Year's Day 'in a sorry condition'.

Brodzky, however, was soon able to find employment teaching Hebrew, French and German at Melbourne schools. Later he went to Rockhampton, Queensland, to teach; then became a journalist with the local newspaper. From there he went to Sydney as a reporter on the *Evening News*, which sent him to Melbourne to cover the Exhibition of 1880. Here he met Florence Leon, sister of a prominent barrister, Samuel Leon, who had married his own cousin Theodora Fink. The meeting led to a job on the Melbourne *Herald* and Brodzky's first acquaintance with Theodore Fink. Brodzky settled in quickly at the *Herald*. By 1881 Sam Winter, the tight-fisted old proprietor of the paper, was paying him a reasonable salary of £3 a week. In addition, Brodzky was acting as Australian correspondent for the London *Daily Telegraph*, and making enough money to marry Florence Leon; they lived modestly at No. 1 Princess Terrace, Fitzroy, and began their family of five boys and two girls.

To make life ever busier, Brodzky wrote a book about Judaism in Melbourne, which he published under the title, *The History of the Two Synagogues*. After its publication, according to Brodzky, the Rev. Elias Blaubaum of St Kilda spread slanderous rumours about him. Brodzky sued the minister in the Supreme Court, but lost the case. Faced with the problem of paying £55 in costs to the other side, Brodzky went to his wife's cousin, Theodore Fink, who arranged a voluntary petition in bankruptcy for him. His sole assets: 900 unsold copies of *The Two Synagogues*, valued at £29. Brodzky stayed in this state of undischarged bankruptcy until June 1885, when Theodore Fink again appeared in the Insolvency Court on his behalf and petitioned for a discharge. Brodzky deposed that the Rev. Blaubaum (who still had not received his £55) had no objection to his release. He could not pay 7s. in the £1 as required by the Insolvency Act, because his salary was 'barely sufficient to keep his wife and family'. The discharge was granted.

In the same month, June 1885, Brodzky resigned from the *Herald* and began publication of his own paper, *Table Talk*, the first issue being dated 26 June 1885. How a £3-a-week journalist, who could not pay 7s. in the £1 on a debt of £55, was immediately able to start a substantial weekly journal, remains an unsolved mystery. It seems possible that his friend, Theodore Fink, provided the capital, as well as some of its light and learned articles, but these possibilities are little more than conjecture.

Table Talk was an immediate success. Its main ingredients were brilliant political and financial pages, obviously written with deep inside knowledge of Victorian politics and commerce; a keen eye for scandal; a wide appreciation of the arts; and a detailed social gazette which enabled readers to discover, for instance, exactly what Mrs Rupert Clarke wore to the Bachelors of Melbourne Club ball on 10 March 1893. (It was a yellow brocade gown and diamond coronet.) M. Oscar Comettant, French representative at the Melbourne Centennial Exhibition in 1888, described *Table Talk* as the Australian equivalent of Labouchère's *Truth*: 'With *The Bulletin* of Sydney it is the raciest paper—that is to say the most characteristic of the colonial spirit, and the most daring.' '*Table Talk* for many years was a highly profitable venture', Brodzky said later in court. 'During the year 1888, commonly known as the Boom Year, I made a profit of over £4,000.' Among those who worked for the journal at different times were Victor J. Daley, Will Dyson, E. A. Vidler, C. H. Chomley, and Eugenia Stone, all of whom became prominent in other literary and artistic fields. Florence Brodzky helped by interviewing visiting celebrities.

In 1889 Brodzky bought his own premises at 112 Little Bourke Street, mortgaging them to Montague Cohen. He also borrowed £2,250 cash from

Cohen and others to keep him going during the comparatively lean year which followed. In an attempt to cut costs, he bought his own printing plant from Alex. Cowan Pty Ltd for £800, giving them a lien on the purchase—a fatal move, as it happened.

In common with the rest of the Melbourne press, *Table Talk* at first paid little attention to the long-term consequences of the boom, although it did express occasional misgivings. In 1890, when the depression was already under way, though few would admit it, Brodzky began devoting a good deal of space to investigations of land companies and mushroom banks. The hand of Theodore Fink showed through now and again, as in the occasional phrase: 'Information in the hands of Fink, Best and Phillips is understood to show . . . '

Soon there was plenty for Brodzky to get his teeth into, and from 1891 onwards the columns of *Table Talk* were increasingly filled with the most detailed and sensational evidence of company manipulations. The space given to society gossip and culture shrank. Some of the information obviously came from the early court cases, some from company liquidators, some from angry shareholders. Some of it could only have come from bank officials who must have taken copies of overdraft lists and unlawfully passed them on to Brodzky. Some of the facts may have come from J. S. Horsfall, a wealthy director of Goldsbrough Mort, who was well disposed towards Brodzky and possibly helped him with cash as well as information. Whatever the sources were, there is no question that most of the frauds of the boom period would have been successfully covered up had it not been for Brodzky's work.

Table Talk's circulation increased rapidly, although advertising revenue fell away almost to nothing. Its publication was awaited impatiently each week by thousands of small shareholders who suspected they were being defrauded; and with trepidation by company directors who were just as likely to find themselves named in the next issue as partners in some audacious conspiracy. The astonishing thing was that not once during those years was Brodzky sued for libel; although a parliamentary committee once angrily summoned him to explain an article stating that the Speaker's mace was being kept in a Melbourne brothel. Every damning fact that Brodzky published on company affairs was proven twice over by the spate of official and quasi-official investigations which followed his financial articles. The need for reform of the Companies Act and Insolvency Act became obvious to all. In comparing the old *Table Talk* files with official documents which later became available, one is constantly amazed by the depth and thoroughness of Brodzky's investigations. His work forms a record of individual public service which, it is safe to say, has never been surpassed anywhere in the world.

From all this it may be thought that Brodzky published a radical journal, but that was certainly not the case. The rising force of labour got scant notice or sympathy from *Table Talk*. Brodzky was more concerned that the capitalist class, the new aristocracy, should cleanse itself in order to be worthy leaders of a constitutional democracy. His attacks were not on commerce or Parliament, but on the cancerous elements in the colony's institutions.

The hand of Theodore Fink became less and less evident as events moved on, and more and more of Fink's friends, clients, and business associates became involved in the *Table Talk* exposures. To this day, nobody knows how Brodzky discovered the truth about the Mercantile Bank machinations, which led to the lengthy prosecutions of its directors. Then followed the Federal Bank revelations, 'most shamefully depleted of its cash', said Brodzky, by its directors and their relatives—the Munros, the Baillieus, and the Finks. 'An unclean business', wrote Brodzky.

Family friendships could not long survive such home truths. Little evidence remains of the breach between the two men, but it is obvious that there came a time when Fink decided to stick by his land-booming associates, and Brodzky decided to stand by his editorial policy. The only public hint of the breach was a biographical study of Theodore Fink published in *Table Talk* on 12 May 1893 under the title 'Coming Men'. Of Fink's legal reputation, Brodzky wrote ironically:

> Mr. Fink is a leading authority on company and insolvency law, and during his extensive practice in this direction re-discovered certain procedure now extensively adopted [i.e. the process of secret composition] . . . An expert in his own department, he is the one lawyer who is consulted by most lawyers themselves as to their own difficulties.

(Theodore Fink had made two secret compositions with his own creditors the year before.)

From that point on, the paths of the two men diverged widely. One son, Horace Brodzky of London, recalled a dramatic scene when Samuel Leon (brother-in-law to both Fink and Brodzky) visited the *Table Talk* office. There was a heated discussion between Leon, Brodzky, and his wife. Leon emerged from Brodzky's office with tears running down his face. Young Horace gathered that relations with the Finks were under discussion, but was never told the details. 'Leon was only weeping crocodile tears', his father told him scornfully. However, another brother says that there was no permanent disruption between the Brodzkys and the Finks, and in later years all was forgiven and forgotten.

As the State slowly recovered from the depression, *Table Talk's* advertising columns began to yield more revenue. Brodzky was again making a profit from the paper, sometimes as much as £8 a week. But most of it went on family expenses for his wife and seven children, the oldest of whom were now able to help him in the business. Leon Herbert Spencer Brodzky was writing theatre criticism and other articles for him; Selina Brodzky was reading proofs; and Horace Brodzky was working in the circulation department. Despite these economies, Maurice Brodzky never accumulated enough spare cash to pay off Montague Cohen's mortgage, nor to discharge the lien on his plant. The colony had little surplus money to support publishing ventures during the 1890s.

Then, in 1902, Brodzky published a damaging article involving Frederick H. Bromley, M.L.A. for Carlton since 1893, and leader of the Labor Party in Parliament. *Table Talk* alleged that Bromley had tried to 'whitewash' a criminal;

Maurice Brodzky, editor of *Table Talk*, was the only man courageous enough to expose the worst financial scandals.

Judge Hickman Molesworth, insolvency judge of the land boom period, before whom Brodzky was forced to appear.

and that he had falsely reported to the police the theft of £150 from his home. Bromley sued for £1,000 damages, winning a verdict for £500. With costs, Brodzky had to find £924, and could not. 'I immediately instructed my solicitors to appeal, but before the application could be heard the plaintiff proceeded to compulsorily sequestrate my estate', Brodzky claimed in an affidavit. He also claimed that when Cowan's heard of the proceedings, they entered the building and seized the plant while he was absent and seriously ill. Without plant, credit, or the presence of its owner, *Table Talk* ground to a halt.

Brodzky escaped his creditors for a short time. When Bromley's solicitors (Joseph Woolf's firm) tried to serve bankruptcy papers at his office in April 1903, they were told he was gravely ill at home. When they visited his last address in Nicholson Street, Fitzroy, they found that the family had shifted a few days before, leaving no forwarding address. Back at the *Table Talk* office, Mrs Brodzky refused to give them the new address (later revealed as the Queens Coffee Palace, 1 Rathdowne Street, Carlton—which became St Anne's Hall, a Catholic girls' hostel, and was demolished in 1971). Ultimately Joseph Woolf was granted an order for substituted service and forced the issue.

It was, one may surmise, a poignant scene when Brodzky was eventually brought into the Insolvency Court. On the bench was the same Judge Hickman Molesworth who had attempted to halt the insolvency scandals of the 1890s, and whose efforts had been vigorously supported by Brodzky in *Table Talk*. Now the courageous editor himself was appearing penniless before the tribunal where so many of Brodzky's enemies had pleaded justification for their actions. Brodzky told the judge the story of his fortunes and misfortunes, and the reasons why *Table Talk* had ceased publication. 'Since then', Brodzky deposed, 'I have endeavoured to maintain myself, my wife and my family of seven by sundry contributions to newspapers, but have been unable to obtain regular employment'. Judge Molesworth ordered a payment of £8 from the estate to help support Brodzky's family, who by then had been forced to shift into the silent printing office in order to have a roof over their heads. In August 1904 Molesworth gave Brodzky an unconditional discharge from bankruptcy.

In his insolvency papers, Brodzky valued the goodwill of *Table Talk* at £3,330. William Denham, the official assignee, sold it for £15. The last issue of *Table Talk* bearing Maurice Brodzky's imprint was dated 30 April 1903. A month passed without a further issue. On 29 May 1903, it appeared again as 'No. 1, New Series', published by Edgerton & Moore, printers and publishers of 241 Flinders Lane, with the price reduced from 6d. to 3d. The redesigned journal contained flattering references to leading men, but left any muckraking to John Norton's *Melbourne Truth*. Later, by a final irony of history, the title *Table Talk* found its way into the possession of the Herald & Standard Newspaper Co. Ltd: Theodore Fink, managing director. The Herald toned down *Table Talk*'s aggressiveness still further and continued its publication as a polite society journal. *Table Talk* ceased publication a fortnight after the outbreak of World War II—3,723 issues after Brodzky's first venture into independent journalism.

For a few months after his bankruptcy, Brodzky eked out a miserable existence writing for John Norton. He was then given a loan from an unidentified source to take his family abroad. They went to San Francisco, where he worked on the *Examiner*, and later became editor of a weekly paper called the *Wasp*. This new career was cut short by the San Francisco earthquake of 1906, which practically destroyed the whole city. The indestructible Brodzkys made their way to New York, thence to London, then back to New York, where Maurice Brodzky died in 1919. Hardly anyone in Melbourne remembered the gadfly of the boom era: his death raised not a ripple in the city where his greatest years were spent.

16

The Meudell Mystery

Maurice Brodzky wrote and published contemporaneously with events, successfully confronting the risks of legal action and the reprisals of some of Melbourne's most prominent men. His was the great courage and achievement. Another man of the time, George Meudell, kept notes and records of events for a book which was not published for another forty years, but which even then had some of the same explosive effect on Melbourne as the old *Table Talk*. That alone was a fair measure of the scarifying results of the land boom, and the long memories of men.

George Dick Meudell, author of *The Pleasant Career of a Spendthrift*, was another of the unique characters thrown up by the Victorian age. Company promoter, stockbroker, the intimate of millionaires, charity worker, oil searcher, and colourful writer, he remained until his death shortly before World War II almost a comic opera character, a short rotund figure in frock coat bustling about his affairs, eternally seeking wealth and fame, and finding only a belated portion of the latter through his scandalous book.

Meudell, the son of a bank manager, was born at Bendigo in 1860. He was educated at the local schools, passing his matriculation examination at Bendigo High School at the age of fourteen. George started to study for the Bar, but weak eyesight compelled him to give up consistent reading. About this time his father was appointed general manager of 'Money' Miller's Bank of Victoria, a position which involved supervising £10 million worth of assets on a salary of £14 a week. The parents—with George, his brother Grant, and their six sisters—moved to a flat on top of the bank's headquarters in Collins Street.

Henry Miller advised George to be a good honest banker like his father, but was alleged to have added jokingly, 'If you ever feel a desire to go wrong, don't prig petty cash or enter threepenny letters as sixpences. Collar £10,000 and be sure to burn the bally books.' This note of jocular cynicism stayed with Meudell for the rest of his life. His father took him into the bank, but George was obviously unfitted for the usually unimaginative toil of a bank clerk. He was possessed of the typically Victorian passion to be 'first' in new fields of endeavour. After a few weeks' concentrated effort, he became the first Victorian to win Isaac Pitman's shorthand certificate. Impressed by the achievement, John Alsop, actuary of the Melbourne Savings Bank, made the young man his

George Dick Meudell, the former employee of B. J. Fink who wrote *The Pleasant Career of a Spendthrift* – suppressed by land boomers.

William Knox loaned Meudell £2,000 to buy a stock exchange seat and help handle share business for the Broken Hill Proprietary.

personal assistant. Meudell was on the way up. He started business as a public accountant and built up a good connection among the hundreds of new companies in Melbourne. Then, in 1888, Andrew Lyell resigned as assistant manager of the Mercantile Finance Co. Ltd in order to start his own accountancy firm. Melbourne's 'King of Finance', in the person of B. J. Fink, offered the vacant position to Meudell.

Meudell accepted the opportunity and began to see the inner workings of Victorian commercial morality. One of his tasks was to write 'a good many prospectuses' under Fink's tutelage. 'The most splendid specimen of the art of imagining the basis of a prospectus ever perpetrated in Australia was my draft of the Australian Assets Purchase Company', said Meudell. This company was floated with £5½ million authorized capital 'to take over and liquidate the landed properties in houses, cottages, farms, suburban subdivisions, city lots, blank broad acres held by the late G. W. Taylor, of Prahran, one of the most notorious land boomers. It was a rare farrago of high-priced rubbish'.

Meudell began trading heavily on the stock exchanges on his own account. 'I learned high finance all right and lost £20,000 buying the blessed or cursed shares of the [Mercantile Finance] Company', he confessed. Meanwhile, Meudell's father had protested to his directors about the large bank loans being given to B. J. Fink, G. W. Taylor, Thomas Bent, W. L. Baillieu, and other speculators. His reward was to be dismissed as general manager in 1889 and transferred to London. George Meudell stayed behind to take up a seat on the

Stock Exchange of Melbourne. William Knox lent him £2,000 to buy the seat, and to carry out the share business of the Broken Hill Proprietary in partnership with F. M. Dickenson. With silver shares booming, Meudell paid back the loan within three months. However, said Meudell, he was writing regularly on banking for the press and saw portents of a financial crisis. He 'rented a box in the Safe Deposit and when the last bank had failed, and the forty-seventh building society had gone into liquidation', he had saved another 1,000 sovereigns. During the crash Meudell lived largely on his savings. With ample leisure (for there was little profit to be had on the Stock Exchange) he organized a 'Legion of Relief', which collected £1,500 in one-shilling subscriptions and spent it on food and clothing for the unemployed.

Early in the new century Meudell contracted tuberculosis, and doctors predicted his early death. He spent twelve months living on 'milk, eggs, and fresh air', made a complete recovery, travelled the world looking at oil fields, and returned to Australia determined to start a petroleum industry. He held public meetings all over the country, sold thousands of 2s. shares, drilled a few wells, and never found a drop of oil. Even the boom of the 1920s showed little profit for Meudell's proliferating schemes. He did, however, warn of the danger of plunging the country into another depression. In a paper read to the Historical Society of Victoria in 1927, Meudell said: 'No ordinary man can see prices of building allotments jumping without itching to have some. It's more catching than mumps, measles or influenza.'

There were not many years left to the little man. More and more his thoughts began to turn back—back to the colourful, roaring days of the eighties and nineties. With the aid of his memories, notes, and a few old copies of *Table Talk*, Meudell wrote his reminiscences, *The Pleasant Career of a Spendthrift*. It was a rambling work, quite disorganized and jumping from one subject to another, but on the whole an accurate and often vivid account of 'the ancient land boom'. 'This book has been written because the buttons tore from the pants of my patience', Meudell wrote. 'Australia is a good country badly managed.'

In view of what happened next, it is important to consider Meudell's real motives. One school of thought held that Meudell wrote the book almost as a blackmailing enterprise, hoping that he would be paid to keep quiet. The only apparent support for this idea was that Meudell had cards printed and mailed to survivors of the land boom and certain of their descendants, advising them that they were mentioned in the book. The opposing theory was that Meudell wanted to tell the truth as he knew it about the land boom, before he died. The present writer has made extensive enquiries among people who knew Meudell well, and supports the latter view. The unanimous verdict was that Meudell was honest—too honest for his own good.

Meudell's book was published in London in 1929 by George Routledge & Sons Ltd (now Routledge & Kegan Paul Ltd). The first man in Melbourne to see it was Frank Campbell, manager of the Book Department of Robertson & Mullens Ltd, who was sent an advance copy by the publishers. Campbell knew Meudell well, and showed him the copy before even Meudell had seen one.

Robertson & Mullens then ordered another 260 copies, which were dispatched from London on 17 March 1929. The book was put on sale during the latter half of the year. It caused a profound sensation and was widely reviewed. By December 1929 Robertson & Mullens alone had ordered a further 714 copies. Together with orders from other booksellers, this practically bought out the publishers' stocks. But just as Robertson & Mullens's new supplies arrived from London, instructions came down from the boardroom to withdraw the book from sale. The copies were crated up again and put back into store. The man who instructed its withdrawal was J. M. Gillespie, chairman of Robertson & Mullens. —and Gillespie was named in the book as one of the land boomers of the 1880s Although Meudell did not say so, Gillespie had made a secret composition in 1893 for £47,000, paying his creditors 1d. in the £1. Most of this money had come from Sir Matthew Davies's Mercantile Bank, and had been spent on land speculation. After the boom Gillespie was closely associated with the Baillieu interests for many years. Other booksellers were warned that they ran the risk of legal action by stocking the book, and most of them withdrew it from open sale.

When he heard of the withdrawal, Meudell pointed to the prophetic finale to his book: 'I have committed the immorality of being too far in front of my own age, and in other times gone by I might probably have been tortured and hung.' His immediate reaction was to retail the book himself. Somehow he got hold of a few hundred copies, and advertised them for sale from his office in St James's Building, 135 William Street, Melbourne. No record survives of the number of copies finally sold, but the book is exceedingly scarce today and commands a high secondhand value. In his unpublished MS., 'Unofficial History of Victoria', Meudell wrote: 'My story of the last land boom and bank smash in 1886 to 1893 was boycotted, banned, suppressed by the Booksellers' Association, at the behest of several senile land-boomers who were named in *The Pleasant Career.*'

With the sale or disappearance of all copies of the first edition, it might be expected that a man of Meudell's outlook would have promptly arranged publication of a second edition. But time was moving on. The ubiquitous figure of Theodore Fink, chairman of the *Herald*, now appeared on the scene. Fink, as it happened, had been lightly dealt with in the book, Meudell writing about him: 'Theodore Fink is rapidly approaching the six figure boundary [i.e., becoming a millionaire] but he's a brainy little man with a kind word and a smile for everybody except those he hates.' There were some old associations between the two men, too. In the 1890s Fink had chaired meetings for Meudell while the latter expounded his views on how the State finances should be organized. Meudell had also lent Fink £150 when the latter was stone broke in 1892.

What took place between the two men in the 1930s will probably never be known. Did Fink try to blame Meudell for Baillieu's mental collapse? Did a sum of money change hands? Whatever happened, Theodore Fink persuaded Meudell to revise his book. Meudell, probably in conjunction with Fink, sub-edited the book so cleverly and neatly that not a hint of shame remained. The services of Wilke & Co. Pty Ltd, law stationers and printers of 241 William Street, Melbourne, were called upon to publish the expurgated work in 1935 under the ingenious title, *The Pleasant Career of a Spendthrift and His Later Reflections.* This edition was misleadingly labelled 'Second Impression'.

To give a few examples of the purging of the original edition, all mention of Theodore's brother, B. J. Fink, was omitted from pages 20, 23, 27, 32, 60, 66, and 82. A long list of insolvent land boomers on page 28 was omitted. The fact that Maurice Brodzky married a relation of the Finks was carefully struck out. All criticism of W. L. Baillieu was omitted, and Meudell's few flattering remarks were retained, to give a completely opposite version to his original intention. The fact that the stockbrokers, Lionel Robinson and William Clark, 'left Melbourne stone-broke' owing £25 each to their grocer, butcher and milkman, was omitted; but the revised edition credited them with paying their creditors 20s. in the £1. S. M. Bruce, 'more celebrated than cerebrated' in the first edition, was endowed with 'tact, brains and ability' in the revised edition.

Towards the end of the new edition, several extra sections were written in, with curious results. On page 208, W. L. Baillieu's death was mourned as 'a serious blow'. Thirteen pages later, the same edition had him miraculously restored to 'health and a pleasant existence'. Another new section claimed that B. J. Fink 'retained throughout the confidence of all the important people with whom he dealt'. Other sections gave quite tendentious accounts of the law cases concerning the Mercantile Bank and Premier Building Society, both defended by the young solicitor, Theodore Fink. Thus was history rewritten.

The tale of wonders is not yet quite complete. Among Meudell's notes and letters, one might expect, would be found some explanation of the events of these later years. Grant Meudell, his executor, gave some trivial documents to public libraries. But all the rest he destroyed, together with remaining copies of the first edition. Grant Meudell, one year younger than his forthright brother, was certainly a man of very different character. He had been secretary of J. Kitchen & Sons Ltd during the boom years, when several of the Kitchen boys were making disastrous ventures into land speculation. No doubt Grant Meudell felt that his brother's first-hand records of those adventures should be destroyed for ever. 'The rest of the family didn't quite approve of George', one friend told the present writer. 'They regarded him as a trouble-maker.'

In such ways as these, the psychoses of the land boom jangled on in the tortured cerebella of its survivors. Beneath the surface of a Melbourne in which respectability had become all-important, there lurked a thousand half-suppressed devils. What temptations had existed, and what results followed, we must now examine in further detail.

III THE BUILDIN

SOCIETY SCANDALS

17

John Bellin and the General Mutual Building Society

The building societies of Victoria had done invaluable work in the construction of houses for honest artisans. True, their red-brick designs looked as though they had been pressed out of standardized moulds; for the most part they were solidly built, and usually lasted far longer than the ramshackle constructions of the jerry-builders employed by speculators seeking quick profits. Most of the building societies charged moderate interest rates, enabling buyers to pay off their homes that much sooner and become the outright owners. And when the crash came, the trustworthy societies hung on to the last extremity before foreclosing on slow payers; whereas the private capitalist was compelled to foreclose immediately he needed cash for his personal commitments.

Thus the building societies enjoyed and usually deserved a high reputation. Men of apparent probity, often with long records of service in religious organizations, were sought after to manage their affairs. The result was that people with spare money to invest, who were seeking a safe home for their cash and higher interest rates than the banks would allow, had no hesitation in depositing it with the building society of their choice. Their capital helped to build houses, it yielded good interest rates, and it seemed perfectly safe. God was in his heaven and virtue was in his building societies.

So it was, until the land boom, when even the best reputation was not always a sufficient defence against the manifold snares and temptations of speculation. For our first demonstration of this melancholy fact, we may turn to the story of John Bellin, an auctioneer of Frankston, who at the age of fifty-four was appointed manager of the General Mutual Building Society. Bellin had been in business for thirty years without a breath of scandal ever fogging his name. The directors had no hesitation in bringing him to Collins Street in 1881 to run the building society's affairs. These directors included the Rev. Henry Plow Kane, a prominent Anglican minister; F. E. Beaver, the society's chairman; and John McDonald, an auditor of Munro's Federal Bank.

Very soon, however, the virus of land fever began to circulate in their new manager's veins. Perhaps Bellin was not entirely to blame, for in 1883 he was asked to lend £3,000 of the building society's money to the chairman, F. E.

John Bellin was assisted by Messrs Munro & Baillieu to sell suburban blocks, including the Edcarleigh Estate at Elsternwick.

Beaver, who used the money for speculative ventures. Shortly afterwards, Bellin quietly began using the funds for his own purposes. Affairs proceeded smoothly and secretly enough until 1888, the year in which the land boom reached its peak. During that year, Bellin fell in with John Turner and James Hobson Turner, two auctioneers and warehousemen of Flinders Lane who were engaged in many speculative ventures with B. J. Fink. Bellin and the Turner brothers formed a new financial institution, called the Fourth Industrial Building Society. With Bellin's reputation behind it, the public willingly placed their faith and their deposits in its hands. Bellin, as manager, proceeded to borrow heavily from the funds of this second 'building society', and to open its coffers to his friends.

By mid-1890 Bellin had accumulated more than £70,000 in personal debts, mostly representing loans which he had spent in buying land in different suburbs. Nearly £13,000 consisted of loans which he had given himself from the two building societies, on practically no security. Bellin took nearly £10,000 from the General Mutual Building Society, and more than £3,000 from the short-lived Fourth Industrial Building Society. The Standard Banking Co. Ltd, which failed in December 1891, lent him more than £15,000. J. A. Bevan lent him nearly £13,000. Two other building societies run by his friends lent him more than £7,000. In addition, Bellin borrowed at least £2,500 from widows who did business with the building societies, promising them that he could invest their money wisely. Even the Rev. W. C. Bunning gave him £500 to 'invest'. All of it went in pursuit of the phantom El Dorado of the land boom.

By September 1890 Bellin could hold off his creditors no longer, and a petition in bankruptcy was filed against him. The affairs of the two building societies were immediately investigated. Bellin, it was found, had been so desperate for cash that he had misappropriated thousands of pounds from clients who had given the money directly to him in the belief that it would be paid into their accounts. Bellin was charged with two of the latter offences. Overcome by shame, his eldest daughter committed suicide the day after he was arrested.

At the committal proceedings, it was disclosed that the directors were aware of the large loans to Bellin. They claimed, however, that they thought he was using the money to buy land on behalf of the building societies. The Rev. Henry Kane deposed that although he was a director, he had never really looked into the General Mutual Building Society's affairs. He had trusted in his friend Beaver, and also had perfect confidence in the other directors and auditors. The first time he became aware that Bellin had embezzled nearly all the funds was shortly before Bellin's arrest. The knowledge 'had nearly killed him'. He had signed the balance sheets without knowing the true position, and could not explain why the last balance sheet showed that the society had £24,000 assets, when in fact there were none.

At the Criminal Court proceedings, Bellin pleaded guilty, so little evidence was called. His counsel, Dr Madden, asked for a merciful sentence. 'Like many others, Bellin gave way to temptation during the speculative mania, and is exceedingly sorry for his fault', said Dr Madden. Then Bellin himself addressed the court in a broken voice. He was deeply grieved by what he had done, which had caused the death of his daughter, but wanted a chance to redeem his character. Here Bellin was overcome by emotion and burst into tears.

Mr Justice Williams took a stern view of the case. 'It is unfortunately now public knowledge that crimes of this description have of late been committed by men holding high positions of trust with alarming frequency', His Honour said. 'Many blameless, honest and industrious persons have been ruined or have lost the result of years of toil by your criminal appropriations.' Whereupon he sent the sixty-three-year-old speculator to gaol for five years. It was a terrible example of crime and punishment—but not, as we shall see, sufficient to deter other would-be titans of the Melbourne financial world.

18

James Mirams and the Premier Building Association

Melbourne had no sooner recovered from the shock and shame of the Bellin frauds than another building society scandal burst upon bewildered investors. This time the revelations were of deeper significance, involving one of the city's biggest societies, the Premier Permanent Building Association; and one of its leading financiers, James Mirams.

Like his close friend, the politician James Munro, 'Jimmy' Mirams was a self-made man, a staunch teetotaller, an indefatigable floater of financial institutions, and an expert extractor of their funds. There is considerable evidence that the two men of God operated together on the heart, pulse, and purse of the investing public. Like Munro, Mirams remained convinced to the end that he was innocent of any wrongdoing. When he emerged from twelve months in gaol, he wrote two books to prove it.

James Mirams was born in Lambeth, London, in 1839. He came to Melbourne with his parents at the age of eighteen when his father, the Rev. James Mirams, was appointed minister of the Congregational Church in Collins Street. For a few years James Jnr tried dairy farming at Braybrook. After all his cattle died, he took up school teaching in Fitzroy, then opened a newsagency in Smith Street, Collingwood. The brisk young man soon became a deacon of the Collingwood Congregational Church, a trustee of the Church's Building Association, and a fervent member of the 'Undaunted Tent' of the Order of Rechabites. He stood for the Collingwood seat in Parliament as a protectionist and land reformer, and was elected in 1876 by a record majority. A year later his temperance friend, James Munro, won the new seat of Carlton and began his climb to the Premiership. Ironically enough, the thirty-seven-year-old Mirams had the more imaginative political ideas. Perhaps they were too positive, too uncompromising, to win him high political honours. He told the voters that he wanted the State to retain permanent ownership of all land and merely lease it to holders. Then in 1880 he campaigned for a National Bank of Issue—held to be a dangerously radical idea at the time, but one which could, nevertheless, have mitigated the evils of the bank smash. In 1882 Mirams was appointed chairman of a Royal Commission on the Customs Tariff, and for the three years of its sittings gave conscientious service.

Mirams's success in raising finance for the church, and his widening circle of highly placed friends, gave wings to his own ambitions. He sold his Collingwood newsagency and started an institution called the Premier Permanent Building Association. Mirams brought together a strong board of seven directors. Among them was that keen student of Robert Burns's works, John Nimmo, Commissioner of Public Works in the Gillies-Deakin government. There was J. L. Dow, the journalist who became President of the Board of Works and Minister of Agriculture. There was Thomas Ferguson, Secretary of the Temperance Hall. There was Donald Munro, the son of James Munro and partner of W. L. Baillieu. (Munro resigned in 1887, before the scandal burst, but was subsequently included in the original summons of conspiring to defraud.) There was John E. Gourlay, brother-in-law of David Syme and cashier of the *Age*. The remaining director was John Stewart.

In the March 1886 elections Mirams lost the Collingwood seat, and decided to concentrate on his land and building enterprises. The former radical politician, now forty-seven, began to use his theories of land value not for social reform, but for personal gain. Money was pouring into the financial arteries of Melbourne. Mirams used a bucketful of it to buy a site near the *Age* office in Collins Street and build new premises for the thriving Premier Building Association. A contemporary description in *The Picturesque Atlas of Australasia* showed that behind his Rechabite vest there dwelt a sensual love of decoration:

> It is a five-story edifice, the architect of which has adopted the style of the French Renaissance, as exemplified by the colony of Italians who settled at Amboise in the middle of the sixteenth century, and left their impress on many of the chateaux in the valley of the Loire. A somewhat narrow front—consisting of three divisions, the centre one recessed, so as to admit of the introduction of an effective bay, enriched with polished columns and pilasters of red granite—is ornate with carvings in freestone, embracing caryatides, foliated ornaments on panels, and a certain elegance of detail such as the architects of the period substituted for the grander forms and more massive features of the Gothic and Classic styles which the Renaissance had superseded. The leading characteristic of the building before us is what would be described, if feminine beauty were being spoken of, as 'a distracting prettiness' . . .

The offices were lit by Hayward's new patent prismatic lights. The Otis elevator was worked by a gas engine, and each office had its own gas heater fitted into the wall. The building was demolished in 1964, but investors and hopeful home owners of the 1880s loved it. In 1887 they placed £300,000 on deposit with the Premier Building Association. In 1888 they more than doubled this amount—nearly £660,000 in new deposits in the one year.

What of Mirams's personal affairs? In his last book, he wrote: 'I was personally, and entirely, apart from any connection with the [Premier Building] Association, very largely concerned in land purchases, the aggregate amount involved being close on £1 million.' There is no reason to doubt this statement, for his personal dealings embraced every facet of the land boom.

James Mirams, founder, and the Premier Building Association's offices which stood at 229 Collins Street until demolished in 1964.

Mirams and James Munro planned and financed the Federal Coffee Palace together—Mirams as secretary and Munro as chairman. Both had access to ample supplies of finance through their various banks and building societies. The site, sold originally by the Crown for £500, was bought by Mirams and Munro in 1886 for £48,000. The ornate building cost £90,000 to erect and another £20,000 to furnish. Land and building were mortgaged to the Melbourne Savings Bank for £70,000. In this way Melbourne's newest coffee palace came into being. To make up for the lack of alcohol, it had five hundred bedrooms and 'the largest and handsomest dining room on this side of the world'. The plans also provided for the erection of shops along the whole street frontage, 'which will produce a large income'. (During the lean years they produced almost no income. The Federal had to apply for a liquor licence in order to stay afloat, and in March 1897 became the Federal Palace Hotel Ltd.)

While the new coffee palace was still being built, Mirams turned his attention to the countryside. He paid William Winter £50,000 for the Mount Scobie Estate, 9,000 acres of irrigable land in the Goulburn Valley. Mirams carved up the land into small orchards and sold them on extended terms.

Meanwhile, Mirams was also holding on to more than 1,000 acres of land on Keilor Road, Essendon. In July 1888 he formed a peculiar enterprise called the Essendon Land & Tramway Co. Ltd, with authorized capital of £1 million. Mirams appointed himself secretary of this company. As directors he had most of the committee of the Premier Building Association. Altogether there were four M.L.A.s and two M.L.C.s on the board, along with Frank Stuart of Lincoln, Stuart & Co., and other prominent merchants. The public was warmly invited to buy shares, the advertisements boldly stating that there would be 'NO PREFERENTIAL OR PROMOTERS' SHARES'. Later, however, it was shown that with part of the money subscribed, the company had paid Mirams more than £200,000 for his otherwise useless land. Eighteen months later, a new company called the Essendon Land & Finance Association was formed to purchase the assets of the first company. This piece of legalized trickery enabled the original promoters to escape their liability for calls of £2. 10s. a share on the 75,000 shares involved. The M.P.s concerned in this stratagem were James J. Williamson, W. H. Roberts, John Nimmo, J. L. Dow, J. E. Peirce, and A. R. Outtrim.

Another marvellous enterprise started by Mirams was called the Freehold Farms Co. Ltd. This time he appointed no fewer than fourteen M.P.s to the board. The company floated for a million pounds, and with the money purchased the Glenmore Estate, near Ballan; the Allanvale Estate, near Ararat; the Englefield Estate, on the Glenelg River; the Ballark Estate, near Mt Wallace; the Killingworth Estate, near Yea; the Bushby Park Estate, on the Avon River; and the Barwon Park Estate, near Geelong. The company's idea was to divide these estates into smaller blocks suitable for growing various products—figs, nuts, prunes 'and all kindred products grown in semi-tropical climates'. With unbounded optimism, Mirams advertised that 'no one with any enterprise and a little money need be left in the lurch'. Many hopeful people took up the blocks

Federal Coffee Palace, demolished in 197

THE FEDERAL COFFEE-(ROYAL) PALACE SONG.

"It is proposed to obtain a Hotel Licence for the Federal Coffee Palace."—NEWS ITEM.

AIR: "TAKE IT, BOB."

We're strictly blue ribbon, and coffee's our lay;
Which we sought to dispense in the usual way,
By raising a glorious edifice up
Where the coffee and tea should be sold at per cup.
The palace was built and sculptured in stone
At the entrance the head of Jim Mirams was shown.
To the tea and the coffee it motioned the way,
And seemed to the thirsty beholder to say—
Take it, Bob, take it, Bob,
Take it, Bob, take it, Bob,
There's never a headache in coffee or tea;
Take it, Bob, take it, Bob,
Take it, Bob, take it, Bob,
Take it, Bob, take it, it beats all P. B.

But somehow the public did not seem to be
Devoured by a thirst for the coffee and tea.
That stone head of Mirams could not tempt them in
To take tea and not beer, and coffee not gin.
The shares will not boom, so we cannot but choose,
If coffee won't pay, we must try them with booze,
And henceforth that stone head of Mirams will be
Forced to pitch the old chorus in quite a new key.
Take it, Bob, take it, Bob,
Take it, Bob, take it, Bob,
Say what you fancy, beer, rum or P. B.;
Take it, Bob, take it, Bob,
Take it, Bob, take it, Bob,
Take it, Bob, take it, it's better than tea.

on low deposits and £1 a week repayments. Their degree of success in growing 'figs, nuts and prunes' in the cool temperate climate of Gippsland and the Western District of Victoria is not on record.

Until about 1888 Mirams lived at 'Royston' in Caulfield. Then, with his increasing profits, he built himself a substantial town house (since demolished) next to the Parade Hotel in Wellington Parade, East Melbourne. It is little wonder that a chronicler in Leavitt's book, *Australian Representative Men*, was able to describe Mirams as 'active, energetic, irrepressible, with a marvellous aptitude for figures, a keen perspicacity, a power of lucid expression, and a far-reaching grasp of circumstances and conditions.'

Soon, however, the irrepressible Mirams began to see storm clouds on the economic horizon. Just before the boom burst, he managed to unload a huge city block on the western side of Russell Street, running from Bourke Street right back to Little Collins Street. The estate agency he employed for the deal was the firm of Munro & Baillieu, and the unlucky purchaser was the Bourke Street Freehold & Investment Co. Ltd, a company formed by the Munro-Baillieu-Fink group.

A succession of disasters quickly overwhelmed Mirams. He was one of the first boomsters to fall. In March 1890 he filed his application for Liquidation by Arrangement—a very similar process to the secret compositions already discussed. Mirams later claimed that he followed this secretive procedure in an attempt to prevent a run on his building society. Whatever the truth, his schedule showed debts amounting to more than £370,000—mainly unpaid balances owing on land purchases. The 'assets' largely comprised Mirams's interests in various properties, few of which realized anything like the claimed value.

It was shown that Mirams had borrowed from banks and companies all over Melbourne. The City of Melbourne Bank had given him £20,000 to finance one land deal. Other institutions run by James Munro and B. J. Fink had advanced him large amounts. Mirams had 'borrowed' more than £2,000 from his own building society. And in the very month of his insolvency, James Munro had come to the aid of his old friend and lent him £5,000 of the Real Estate Bank's cash—none of which was ever recovered.

Mirams's estate finally paid 2d. in the £1 on his huge total of debts. This was a tale to be repeated over and over again during the crash, when first-mortgage assets were repossessed by the original owners, and the balance of an insolvent's assets realized pitifully low amounts for the remaining creditors.

Liquidation of the Premier Building Association followed rapidly. It disclosed an incredible financial policy followed by Mirams and the society's major creditors. New money was borrowed on the security of the building society's own loans to its borrowers. Thus, if the Association lent £1 million to its customers, those mortgages were used as security to borrow another million. This spiralling technique was used by Mirams and his fellow directors to borrow such amounts as £85,000 from the London Trust Co. Ltd; £60,000 from the Trust & Agency Co. of Australasia Ltd; and £87,000 from the City of Melbourne Bank. The extreme danger of this method of financing was that a

immo applies for a liquor licence to keep the Federal afloat.

failure anywhere along the line could bring about the collapse of all involved.

So far Mirams, although shown to be extremely reckless, had not been proved a criminal under the laws of the day. The proceedings which finally gaoled him were to take their place as one of the most hotly debated trials of the nineteenth century, second only in our story to the trial of Sir Matthew Davies and his associates.

After the building society's collapse, the depositors appointed as liquidator Colonel John Montgomery Templeton, who had founded the National Mutual Life Association and was a former chairman of the Public Service Board. Colonel Templeton quickly discovered misfeasance and embezzlement on the part of William Doherty, the society's accountant and secretary. Doherty was immediately charged, tried and convicted.

During his investigations, Templeton also became convinced that most of the directors were involved in a separate series of brazen frauds. He reported the facts to the Crown Law authorities, but the Premier, Duncan Gillies, refused to allow criminal proceedings to be taken against his two Ministers (Nimmo and Dow) and their friends. Colonel Templeton courageously laid the charges himself. Mirams and his associates were brought into court on summons. The first count was that they did

> Conspire together by means of artful devices to grant loans to Patrick John Murphy, or to Robert Murphy and Philip Corkhill, on the pretended security of certain lands, and in excess of the value of the said lands, which were passed by defendant Gourlay to them by means of a pretended sale.

The second count accused Mirams, Nimmo, Dow, Gourlay, Stewart and Ferguson of conspiring to defraud the shareholders of the association by issuing shares of the nominal value of £5 at a premium of £1, and splitting up the proceeds between them.

All the directors except Dow were committed for trial, thus forcing the Crown to take over the conduct of the case. After a thirty-day trial, all defendants were found innocent of the two charges brought against them, and were discharged 'without a stain on their character'. Most of them remained in Melbourne, but John Nimmo left the colony for Catrine, Scotland, where he resumed his former occupation as a civil engineer. Mirams himself had been charged with a third offence, that of issuing a false balance sheet with intent to defraud. The substance of the complaint was that as manager he had permitted a balance sheet to be issued which claimed that the building society was making larger profits than it actually was. After another lengthy trial, Mirams was found guilty and sentenced to twelve months' imprisonment. To ameliorate the punishment, the Chief Justice, George Higinbotham, ordered that his beard should not be shaven off, and that he should be imprisoned at Sale instead of Pentridge.

For years after his trial Mirams hotly disputed the verdict, the principle of 'responsibility' for balance sheets, and everything else about the case. A fierce controversy over the verdict raged in the press between barristers, solicitors, and onlookers. Shortly after Mirams was imprisoned, a number of prominent

With the collapse of the Premier balloon, directors throw their assets to safety. At lower right, J. L. Dow escapes on a parachute marked *Age*.

P.C. Punch thought the commodious premises of Pentridge Gaol would suit Mirams, Dow and Nimmo.

Justice, blindfolded and decrepit, refuses to act against the Premier directors. J. M. Templeton, at left, laid the charges himself.

land boomers and their associates unsuccessfully petitioned the Governor for his release. They included Sir Bryan O'Loghlen, J. B. Lawrence, James Campbell, E. C. Elliott, John Robb, F. G. Wood, Thomas Bent, J. L. Dow, James Balfour, and Rev. W. H. Fitchett. John Mark Davies, appointed Solicitor-General in 1891, wrote to Mirams: 'If I had been one of the jury to try the case, I should have brought in a verdict of not guilty.' James Munro, the new Premier, and William Shiels, the new Attorney-General, claimed there was 'not a tittle of evidence to support the charge'. However, they refused to pardon Mirams on the ground that 'the Chief Justice evidently regarded the verdict as correct'.

After his release from prison, Mirams applied for the vacant position of secretary to the Agent-General in London—which would have made him secretary to James Munro when the Premier resigned and hurriedly left the colony. But by this time Munro was more intent on looking after himself. Mirams was left behind in Melbourne, where he divided his time between making a meagre living as a milkman, petitioning Parliament for redress for his 'wrongful imprisonment', and writing a book called *The Present Depression—Its Cause and Cure*. Publication of this work was supported by advertisements paid for by land boomers and former associates such as G. C. Clauscen (furniture), F. G. Wood (finance) and J. Kitchen (soap). In May 1893 Mirams tried to call a meeting of his former friends to consider his case. James Service, M.L.C., wrote to say that he could not attend. Charles Young, M.L.A., regretted that he was detained elsewhere. Rev. W. H. Fitchett wrote: 'I am so engaged that I cannot possibly attend.'

Throughout these years, the newspapers maintained a rather cool attitude to Mirams's continued protestations of innocence. In 1895 the *Argus* sent a reporter to look at some of the houses which Mirams's building society had erected. The newspaper claimed that the houses were falling to pieces and that Mirams and his associates had 'played ducks and drakes with the Association's money'. Mirams sued for defamation, but the jury decided that the above allegations were true and fair comment. However, the *Argus* also alleged that:

> After these men had got rid of the depositors' money, with the aid of Mr Run-em-up, they calmly proceeded to pawn every asset and every deed so as to obtain more money for illegitimate transactions, with the result that when the inevitable liquidator appeared upon the scene, all the money that could be raised had gone to take assets and deeds out of pawn.

The jury thought that this was a little strong, and awarded Mirams £5 damages against the *Argus*.

Mirams kept on battling. In 1900, when the Commonwealth of Australia was gestating, he decided to stand for Federal Parliament and bring his case to national attention. He produced a turgid apologia once again canvassing all aspects of his conviction, called *A Generation of Victorian Politics*. In the foreword Mirams claimed: 'I have been most grievously wronged . . . my case is the case of Dreyfus on a narrower theatre . . . Justice has been denied me.' The electors were not impressed. Mirams, by now suffering from a deep-seated persecution complex, went to his reward without society's acknowledgment of the terrible sin it had committed.

Colonel Templeton's fee for liquidating the affairs of the Premier Building Association was £24,290, equivalent to £10 a day. In 1903, on the application of the creditors, Mr Justice Holroyd made an order reducing his fee to £17,000. 'The last groan of the depleted shareholders is the loudest groan of all', said John Norton's new paper, *Melbourne Truth*.

19

Matthias Larkin and the South Melbourne Building Society

Public anguish over these building society peculations had hardly died down when yet another series of brazen frauds was discovered. This time they involved the respected secretary of the South Melbourne Building Society, one Matthias Larkin. Larkin's parents were among the teeming multitude of immigrants who came to Victoria during the gold-rush days of the early 1850s. Disappointed in their search for a fortune, the Larkins took up dairy farming near Melbourne. Young Matthias, born in 1853, was apprenticed to a saddler in Emerald Hill, later renamed South Melbourne.

Matthias soon proceeded to work his way up through the loosely formed ranks of raw suburban society. At all times he carried a miniature edition of the New Testament in his vest pocket. Often he could be seen wandering down the main street, deep in thought. one hand holding the Testament open at an inspiring chapter, the other pressed gravely against his young forehead. Such devout behaviour could not escape notice. When a number of South Melbourne businessmen decided in 1877 to form a building society to erect cottages for artisans in the rapidly developing suburb, they asked the twenty-four-year-old saddler to become its secretary. Larkin accepted the position with enthusiasm, and began canvassing depositors and investors. Everyone trusted the modest, vigorous young worker whose only aim was, as he said, to settle every family into its own home. As the area became steadily more industrialized, the South Melbourne Building Society became one of the largest in the suburbs. Larkin's success was so great and his judgment considered so sound that whatever he advised was acted upon without question by the committee.

Larkin was soon elected to the local council, became president of the Albert Park Bowling Club, continued his earnest work for the Hibernian Society, and became president of the Rowing Club. Then, in 1881, came a crowning honour. At the age of twenty-eight, Larkin was appointed a magistrate—the youngest in Victoria. 'I always put men away in a scientific and gentlemanly manner', Larkin said proudly in a speech delivered shortly before his own imprisonment.

Early in the 1880s, as the boom gathered strength, Larkin became dissatisfied

Front of *The Book of Matthias*, published by the *South Melbourne Citizen*.

W. J. Mountain, liquidator, evicted families who could not meet their payments.

with his building society salary of £600 a year. Up to this point he appears to have managed the society's affairs honestly enough. His downfall dates from the time when the land boom held out her bejewelled fingers and beckoned him on with her lures of fame and fortune.

Larkin's first method of capitalizing on the boom was to start his own estate agency. To assist him he appointed one Patrick Cleary as his 'private accountant'. The pair began to operate the building society and their own private business almost as one unit. Investors in the building society who also wanted rents collected or properties sold were referred to 'the only reliable people'—Larkin and Cleary. At this time Cleary was described as 'a young man of good appearance, about 20 years of age'. Because of his position with Larkin, he was appointed auditor of a number of firms, including the Albert Park Coffee Palace Company. He bought the *Kyneton Observer*; married, had children, and lived happily in Howe Crescent, South Melbourne.

As his profits grew, and with them his taste for gracious living, Larkin decided to imitate the Collins Street 'speckers' by building his own mansion. Up to this time he had lived modestly enough above his offices at 242 Clarendon Street, South Melbourne (today a row of small shops with flaking stucco cornices). Larkin set up a lavish new household in Canterbury Road, Albert Park, which he called 'Lake View' because Albert Park Lake could be seen from the upper storey.

Larkin was careful to keep in favour with the building society's directors, while just as carefully denying them any real knowledge of his affairs. Thomas Stead, the president of the building society, later confessed that he had entered into several private speculations in partnership with Larkin, in which 'both made handsome profits'. The confession came hard, for Stead was president of the local Band of Hope, and had started the first 'Penny Bank' in South Melbourne. In a separate deal, Larkin, George Gray (another director of the building society), and other speculators bought Aitken's Flour Mill in Elizabeth Street. They paid £20,000 for it in May 1888, then sold it a few days later for more than £6,000 profit. Later the same syndicate bought a property on the Yarra bank for £35,000; reselling it to Thomas Bent, George Swinburne, and others for £10,000 profit.

These profits could not satisfy what by now had apparently become an insatiable lust for money. Larkin and Cleary began operating an ingenious series of frauds on clients who used the services of their estate agency. Any such clients who had surplus capital from rents or sale of property were advised to invest it in the building society. Larkin took charge of the money, and either failed to record it in the society's books, or made fictitious entries. 'He exploited the whole suburb of South Melbourne', said the *Age*. 'Everyone who came to Larkin's office seems to have been considered fair game by him, and clients . . . were robbed with equal audacity, equal heartlessness.'

In the end, the very complexity of Larkin's misdemeanours brought about his downfall. An unusually persistent auditor who was puzzled by the state of the society's books asked him to explain certain anomalies. Larkin quickly broke down, and admitted that the funds were short. But, said he with virtuous indignation, he had only used the money for a few months to tide him over temporary difficulties. He offered to repay it with interest. Some of the directors were shocked. The following day, 11 November 1891, they applied for a warrant for Larkin's arrest on a preliminary charge of embezzling £400. The move caused 'profound surprise to a great number of people by whom he had been greatly respected'. The warrant was duly issued and Larkin was formally charged and freed on bail. The next day, 12 December, Larkin transferred to George Gray, a fellow director, all his land in Young Street, South Melbourne. On the same day he transferred a ten-acre property to another director, W. Marshall. These transactions, an obvious attempt to hoodwink the Insolvency Court, were disclosed the following February by an alert suburban newspaper, the *South Melbourne Citizen*. The trustees in Larkin's estate promptly lodged a caveat against the deals, but not before the *South Melbourne Citizen* had written an amusing new chapter to its 'Book of Matthias';

> AND the king of the Grayites, one bright morning in November, 1891, rose early, and approached the king of the tribe of Larkinites, and begged him to protect his interests in the scramble that must inevitably take place shortly. The Grayite briefly said: Thou knowest, O Larkinite, that I have made myself responsible for vast sums in building up thy palace, now known to fame as 'Fraudville,' and I do beseech thee to give me some preference over others.

While Larkin was awaiting trial, the auditors made a thorough investigation of the 'formidable tissue of fraud' disclosed by the society's books. Early in December 1891 they submitted an interim report showing defalcations of about £13,000. They continued to dig. At a meeting of creditors on 10 December, they disclosed that the total amount stolen from the society was £55,000. The *Age* reported the following day:

> The announcement . . . caused the greatest consternation. It would appear that auditors have been hoodwinked, directors fooled and shareholders robbed, and through it all the principal has covered himself under the cloak of religion, and stood forward as one deserving honour for his donations to public institutions . . . An injury has been inflicted upon many hundreds of people, the effects of which will be felt by them for many years to come.

Together with the money stolen by Larkin and Cleary from their private clients, it was estimated that the total amount embezzled was nearly £100,000. The authorities of St Peter and Paul's Church in South Melbourne indignantly returned a cheque for £100 which Larkin had donated towards a new bell. But that was the only amount recovered in full. The remainder had disappeared. Larkin was rearrested on new charges shortly after midnight and lodged in the South Melbourne lockup. The auditors' report also revealed Cleary's part in the frauds. He was arrested at Bendigo and brought back to Melbourne for trial on a charge of conspiring with Larkin to defraud the shareholders. When Larkin and Cleary arrived at court to stand their trial, they were hurried by police through a threatening crowd, which according to one newspaper 'would have torn them to pieces'. The first trial finished in the fiasco of a jury disagreement. The prisoners were released on £3,000 bail and went into hiding. After their second trial, in March 1892, Larkin was sentenced to six years' gaol with hard labour, and Cleary to four years with hard labour. A highlight of the case was the appearance in court of a 'robust and irate woman, armed with a formidable umbrella'. She appealed to a constable to allow her 'just one minute with the prisoners' and she would be satisfied. The constable, according to the *Weekly Times*, 'refused to grant the modest request'.

Now the liquidators got to work on the affairs of the South Melbourne Building Society, which had been strangled beyond all hope of resuscitation. In October 1893 W. J. Mountain, chairman of the liquidators, reported to a meeting of depositors that nineteen families who had ceased their repayments had been evicted, and the houses sold. As a result he thought that in six months' time it would be possible to pay a 6d. in the £1 dividend.

W. P. Buckhurst, a prominent South Melbourne estate agent, said that shareholders did not wish Larkin to walk out of gaol and live on their money. The chairman replied that the Crown would not finance further prosecutions. Buckhurst moved that the liquidators spend £500 on new charges to keep Larkin in gaol. Thomas Stead, the former president, seconded the motion. Larkin, he said, was 'an abomination to society', and should not be allowed to revisit South Melbourne while he (Stead) was alive. In this Christian spirit the liquidators laid new charges of embezzlement from the scores of different instances available to them. On these charges, Larkin was sentenced to an extra five years—a total of eleven years' imprisonment with hard labour. 'In the evil history of an evil time, your name and conduct stand as a monument of woe to multitudes of people', said the Chief Justice, passing sentence.

Larkin enjoyed one further burst of notoriety. When he emerged from gaol in 1900 (after remissions for good conduct), two liquidators, W. J. Mountain, and John Danks the hardware merchant, were ready for him with bankruptcy proceedings. Larkin, they said, owed the building society £43,000, and nobody knew what had happened to the money. Larkin refused to answer questions, and was sent back to gaol for contempt of court. His estate was compulsorily sequestrated, and his land sold. By 1910 he had paid precisely 2d. in the £1 to the surviving creditors.

20

William McLean and the Melbourne Permanent Building Society

Men held tenaciously, even fanatically, to their religious beliefs when times were good. When the economic blizzards started to blow, not every Baptist, Methodist, Presbyterian or Anglican found his Sunday morality a sufficient cloak. For another tragic example, we may turn to the lesson of the Melbourne Permanent Building Society.

Chairman of this prosperous institution was William McLean, a leading hardware merchant, contractor and bank director. McLean, born in Dumfries, Scotland, in 1845, was also a treasurer of the Victorian Baptist Fund, and a committee member of the Young Men's Christian Association along with Sir Matthew Davies and other men of sanctity. The other directors of the building society were Law Oldfield, Stanford Chapman, W. B. Fox, R. W. Kitchen, and Hugh McKay. The society's solicitor was Thomas Plumley Derham Jnr., younger brother of the noted politician and speculator who had married into the Swallow family.

The Melbourne Permanent Building Society was formed in 1873, its first offices being at 61 Elizabeth Street. During the boom the society bought a building at 271 Collins Street and called it 'Melbourne Chambers' (now part of the National Bank premises). To finance this deal, William McLean arranged for the society to borrow £20,000 on nil security from the Federal Bank, where he was also a director.

As their trusted secretary, the directors appointed Joseph Johnson, a benign old gentleman (born in 1826) who was connected with the administration of Wesleyan Methodist church funds. With its strong board and respected officials, the building society soon became one of Melbourne's most successful institutions. Its permanent shares and reserve fund quickly climbed to nearly £200,000. In addition, nearly half a million pounds in fixed deposits was attracted to its coffers. Most of the money was loaned out on mortgage to home builders all over Melbourne.

One of these home builders was the society's own secretary, Joseph Johnson himself. Johnson built himself a fine house in Glenferrie Road, Hawthorn, for £6,000—equivalent to, say, $180,000 today. After a time, Johnson neglected to keep up the payments. To conceal this fact (it was later revealed in court), he simply omitted his own name from the list of defaulters submitted to each directors' meeting.

That elementary piece of coggery seemed to work perfectly. Johnson next decided to exercise his ageing limbs by riding the wild steed of the land boom. To get the money, he invented an artistic method of making fictitious advances through the building society. The auditor was fooled, because each loan appeared to be secured by a deposit of the scrip of the society's own permanent shares. The scrip represented shares that actually existed, but were in fact clever forgeries. Thus the auditor, James Cole, was able to report each year that he had examined all payments and securities, and found them 'correct with the books'. The solicitor, Thomas Derham, reported that all mortgages shown to the auditor had been prepared by him, and were the original mortgages.

Altogether Johnson got away with about £35,000. What did he do with the money? The harsh truth emerges that at least some of it went into financial schemes operated by the building society's own chairman, William McLean. McLean was presumably ignorant of the real source of Johnson's wealth. But, one feels, he may have been pardoned for wondering now and then how a salaried official, charged with the care of trust funds, came to have so much spare cash to invest.

Johnson associated himself closely with a group of land boomers who controlled the Melbourne *Daily Telegraph*, a somewhat sanctimonious morning newspaper which was being financed by Sir Matthew Davies's Mercantile Bank and edited by the Rev. W. H. Fitchett. When this bank crashed and the *Daily Telegraph* became financially embarrassed, Johnson was one of the prime movers in a bold attempt to amalgamate the paper with the Melbourne *Herald* and gain control of the joint company. The move was foiled by court action and the *Daily Telegraph* foundered.

Early in December 1891 the full fury of the blizzard struck. The Commercial Bank withdrew its support, and like most other building societies, the Melbourne Permanent was forced to close its doors. There had been very few signs of a run on this particular society. Its directors and officials were widely regarded as honourable men. But in the universal panic, investors did not want to risk the £100,000 of deposits which were on immediate call. Now began a painful period of reconstruction. The directors first proposed that all depositors should agree to renew their deposits for another three years. This idea was rejected, and again the society closed its doors. The directors then proposed a seven-year renewal. Another rejection; another suspension. Finally, the accountancy firm of Lyell and Butler was asked to enquire fully into the society's affairs, so that it could be placed on an acceptable foundation.

Richard Butler was given the job of examining the books. In October 1893 Butler discovered Johnson's long-standing defalcations and reported the facts to the directors. The auditor was asked to explain why he had approved the doctored accounts. It was then discovered that Johnson had kept a second ledger, which he had regularly submitted for audit. Only upon a full investigation of the society's position could his clever fraud be detected. Johnson was arrested in December 1893, and stood his trial the following February on a first charge of misappropriating £5,800. He pleaded guilty, so that little evidence was given. Mr Justice Hodges, sentencing the aged financier, said: 'There is no doubt that when the prisoner took the money he was laboring under the same excitement, the same frenzy, the same wild mad heat which was entertained by so many others.' The smallest sentence he could pass, 'with the necessity of showing the community that offences of this kind would be severely punished', was two years' imprisonment. As the prisoner had suffered from bad health, he would 'not be subjected to solitary confinement'.

The building society's chairman, William McLean, survived the immediate crisis. His hardware company, McLean Bros & Rigg Ltd, which carried on business at 107 Elizabeth Street, was still reasonably prosperous. He had worked it up from nothing after arriving in Melbourne in 1863, admitting his brother, Joseph McLean, and William Rigg as partners in 1872. The company was floated in 1887, with nominal capital of £250,000, the partners taking 60,000 shares as their equity. During the boom years, McLean became prominent in many bold new enterprises—the Real Estate Bank, Centennial Land Bank, United Property Co., Union Finance Co., and several coffee palace companies. A director of the Federal Bank, he borrowed nearly £100,000 of its assets on overdraft, later admitting in court that the balances were 'floated' in order to put directors' accounts in credit on balancing day.

By 1894 McLean could no longer hold his creditors at bay. He resigned all his directorships, along with his post as a Savings Bank Commissioner, and filed his schedule for more than £200,000 in debts—say, $6 million or so in today's values. Three widows—Mesdames Macrae, Benson, and Lennon—alone had lent him £30,000 to invest for them. Most of the balance of his debts was due to the Federal and Real Estate Banks.

McLean was allowed by the creditors to carry on his hardware business, and was realeased from sequestration in 1898. After many ups and downs, the company was finally wound up in 1903 and absorbed into McEwan's Ltd. Aged nearly sixty, McLean set about building up a modest connection as a manufacturers' agent. McLean's partner, William Rigg, who had participated in many of his boom-time speculations, died insolvent without leaving a will. He left no representative, and nobody bothered to take up the administration of his estate.

William McLean, chairman of the Melbourne Permanent Building Society, whose speculative activities sent him bankrupt and ruined his hardware firm.

21

James Hunt and the Modern Permanent Building Society

'The directors and secretaries of the building societies in Melbourne in 1886–91 were in a class by themselves,' wrote Meudell. 'All of them were earnest temperance workers, and therefore abjured alcohol, wore black broadcloth clothes, the customary suits of solemn black, drank too much water and over-ate themselves and had large families. Mostly both directors and secretaries were elders of kirks, members of chapels, bethels and churches, knew nothing, were nothing and lost nothing. Their ignorance of the ordinary rules of lending money miscalled finance was colossal.'

However vivid his picture, Meudell did not give individual instances, so perhaps it is in order for us to raise briefly the ghost of James William Hunt, secretary of the Modern Permanent Building Society and president of the Victorian Temperance Alliance.

With the best of motives, Hunt helped io start the building society in 1871 to provide homes for the rapidly increasing number of artisans in the community. His fellow directors were Orlando Fenwick, Henry Hayter, John McIlwraith, D. Black, J. E. Gourlay, J. Miller and Thomas Russell. The society's solicitor was J. M. Davies, brother of Sir Matthew.

Meudell was probably a little harsh in his judgment of these water-drinking, child-breeding type of men. They had their own vision of a nation of sober, home-owning, industrious and eternally contented workmen; which, however much at variance with the realities of human nature, at least provided some kind of moral basis for the extension of a still primitive colonial society.

Orlando Fenwick, a director of the Modern Permanent Building Society, Metropolitan Bank, and Metropolitan Building Society.

Sometimes, of course, the hedonists hit back at those who were soon to be immortalised under the name of 'wowsers.' In 1893 Dr P. B. Bennie delivered a frightening lecture in Melbourne on *The Evils of Tea-drinking*, warning his audience:

While alcohol,
Perhaps, like Saul,
His thousands slays;
The she-fiend Tea,
Like David, she,
In direr ways,
Her tens of thousands
In the cold grave lays.

The extraordinary thing about tea-drinkers like James Hunt was that they themselves were among the first to yield to the temptation of making large fortunes from speculation—fortunes which could only be gained at the expense of their fellow men. The boom was the vital catalyst needed for their moral deliquescence. As money poured into the colony and sought for profitable outlets, Hunt was among those who borrowed huge sums for personal ventures into land speculation.

We may say that at least he did not borrow from the funds of the Modern Permanent Building Society. The distinction is not so important. It was only his position as secretary of the building society, and as a pillar of the righteous elements of the community, that enabled him to be considered 'a good risk.' What did this 'good risk' do? First he built himself an elaborate mansion, 'Belmont,' on extensive grounds in Wattletree Road, Malvern.

Then he rebuilt the offices of the building society at 317 Collins Street, more in accordance with his newly inflated position. In 1888, these lavish premises soared skywards near Elizabeth Street, dwarfing everything else in the immediate vicinity. The £40,000 building consisted of eight storeys, reaching 120 feet above ground level, built of Stawell freestone, with columns of red Peterhead granite on the ground floor. Foliated caps and enriched pediments were freely inserted—in other words, it was a typical ornate palace of the boom.

Hunt continued borrowing cash, buying shares, and placing down payments on land at Malvern, South Melbourne, Prahran, and other suburbs. Finally his debts reached a total of £107,000. Then came Armageddon. Swiftly, secretly, in March 1893, Hunt made a private composition with his creditors. He had just enough cash left, he told them, to pay a penny in the pound.

All the major creditors agreed to accept the secret settlement instead of putting Hunt through the normal procedure of public insolvency, which would have disclosed their own involvement. They included the Melbourne & Suburban Property Co. Ltd (£40,000); the Caledonian & Australian Mortgage Co. Ltd (£18,000); the Commercial Bank (£8,500); Thomas Russell (£8,500); the Australian Deposit & Mortgage Bank (£7,000); the Union Trustee Co. Ltd (£4,000); and the Metropolitan Bank (£3,500).

It will be noted from this list that Hunt was favoured with loans of nearly £50,000 from various institutions where his fellow-directors were members of

Offices of the Modern Permanent Building Society were erected at 317 Collins Street, near the Federal Bank at the corner of Elizabeth Street.

the board. Fenwick and Hayter, for instance, were directors of the Metropolitan Bank; and Davies was a director of two companies which loaned large sums to Hunt. Thomas Russell was a co-director of the building society. They must have known that Hunt was using the money for speculation. Did it not occur to them that a man in a position of high trust, the manager of their building society, should be free from the taint of speculation?

To the public, Hunt remained a sober-sided pillar of the community. The creditors allowed him to keep on living in 'Belmont' for years as a 'caretaker,' until it could be sold. In this fortunate position, Hunt continued to run various fairs and functions in the grounds to raise money for the Victorian Temperance Alliance, which with extreme unction continued to tell starving workmen not to drink.

During the same month that Hunt made his secret composition, there was a slight run on the building society's deposits. Despite the ominous portent, the directors declared a 7 per cent dividend. Only two months later, the society was forced to suspend business. Half a million pounds which trusting Scottish and Australian investors had deposited were frozen for five years. A shareholders' and depositors' meeting, ignorant of Hunt's land-booming schemes and his secret composition, approved a reconstruction plan. No outside investigation of the society's affairs was ever made. It was finally wound up at a considerable loss to members, and its Collins Street building became a branch of the State Savings Bank—demolished in 1971 and the site absorbed into the new M.L.C. Building.

22

J. B. Lawrence and the Australian Widows Fund

The reader of these pages will not fail to notice that several leading land boomers got some of their gambling chips from an institution known as the Australian Widows Fund Life Assurance Co. Ltd. This generous company got *its* funds in the ordinary way of business, by canvassing prospective holders of insurance policies (particularly widows, actual or potential); and investing the resultant week-by-week payments in sound, steady and splendid enterprises, such as B. J. Fink's companies.

Founded in 1871, the Australian Widows Fund carried on business in its own two-storey building at 454 Collins Street, a site now the temporary premises of the Mutual Life & Citizens' Assurance Co. Ltd. Chairman of the Australian Widows Fund was James Black Lawrence, son of a prominent Melbourne contractor, James Lawrence, who built the E.S. & A. Bank in Elizabeth Street, Goldsbrough Mort's wool stores, and several other historic buildings.

The son, J. B. Lawrence, was a hearty but clever fellow who started trading in William Street in 1863 as a wine and spirit merchant. His partner was John Adam, a former mayor of Richmond. Their business developed into a highly prosperous partnership, with an annual turnover averaging £240,000, showing a clear profit of about £26,000 a year.

With his widows on the one hand and his wine on the other, Lawrence was generally regarded as one of the colony's soundest men. Nor did he appear to be greatly attracted by the lure of the land boom. 'I have never speculated,' he proudly told the judge when the Insolvency Court eventually caught up with him. This, as we shall see, was a vast over-simplification of the facts.

As a prominent commercial leader, Lawrence felt it his clear duty to get into the building society business, for this was providing cheap and effective housing for the growing population, thus helping to develop the colony. Early in the boom, Lawrence became chairman of an institution known as the Victoria Mutual Building Society. The workmen enrolled in large numbers and started sending in their weekly shillings for what they fondly imagined would eventually yield them a house of their own. As affairs developed, Lawrence also became a

Australian Widows' Fund advertisements assured 'an abundant harvest' – until the policy-holders' funds were invested in speculative enterprises.

founder and treasurer of the Colonial Permanent Building Society; and a director of the Victorian Estate Co. Ltd, a speculative enterprise.

Thus Lawrence had control of ample investment funds for which profitable outlets had to be found. Other building societies were lending their cash, at high interest rates, to sundry land boomers for down payments on *freehold* properties. Lawrence decided to go one better. In the most public-spirited way imaginable, he started lending out his depositors' savings on the 'security' of *leasehold* properties.

Some of the funds went to such prominent men as Captain C. F. Taylor, M.L.A. The gallant captain borrowed £17,000 of the Victoria Building Society's money, spent it all on land speculation, made a secret composition, and paid back 2s. 6d. in the £1. The transaction was kept so quiet that only J. B. Lawrence knew the truth, and *he* wasn't telling. Another £4,000 went to James Mirams's associate W. H. Roberts, M.L.C., who promptly spent it on deposits for land, and just as promptly went bankrupt.

By the second half of 1891, the industrial slump had already become so serious that many members of building societies were unable to keep up their regular payments. Simultaneously, most of the land boomers to whom large advances had been made were becoming seriously embarrassed for cash. The Victoria Mutual Building Society was forced to close its doors and call a meeting of members. A small section of depositors demanded an investigation, but the directors commanded enough votes to force through a reconstruction scheme without opening the books.

The society thereupon became known as the St. James' Building Society, and a 'fresh start' was made. A number of small mortgages were foreclosed and the properties repossessed. But when the auditors came to examine the balance sheet of the new society, they found that more than £117,000 was still owing on the 'security' of leasehold property. 'It is self-evident that the assets cannot have the value shown in the balance sheet,' they declared. It was the finish of Lawrence's reputation as a sound financier.

Captain C. F. Taylor, who speculated with the Victoria Building Society's deposits.

Meanwhile, the affairs of the Australian Widows Fund had also reached a crisis. Fewer people had the cash to pay their premiums (although many half-starved themselves in order to keep their policies going) and not even Dale Carnegie could have written new business. A large proportion of the company's funds had been loaned to such notorious speculators as Theophilus Kitchen, of the well-known soap and candle family. (Four members of the Kitchen family made secret compositions in the years 1892–5, their debts totalling £483,000). Theo was given more than £7,000 to play with—all lost when he made a secret composition for £116,000 early in the depression and paid a penny in the pound.

The Australian Widows Fund had also loaned nearly £30,000 to the West Melbourne Land Company, under the personal guarantee of B. J. Fink. Fink and the land company both burst at about the same time, paying a halfpenny in the pound. After Fink 'compoted' with his creditors, the Australian Widows Fund applied to the Supreme Court to have the composition set aside on the ground that it had been procured by fraud. But when their application came before the court in December 1892, the insurance company made no appearance. It transpired that 'a satisfactory arrangement' had been made for return of the money to the Widows Fund, thus averting open examination in court.

Now, to complete Lawrence's ruin, his partner died in 1892, and their wine and spirit business folded up. Under the partnership laws of the time, a firm had to cease trading on the death of one partner. Under normal conditions, Lawrence would undoubtedly have been able to raise enough finance to start up the business again on his own account. But, by his own admission, the firm had to write off nearly £30,000 in bad debts owed by customers who could not pay their wine and spirit bills.

Lawrence held out against the final act of insolvency until 1895. The firm then paid 9s. in the £1, and Lawrence himself paid 2s. in the £1. He told the court that he had borrowed only £250 from the Australian Widows Fund, and had 'never speculated in shares or mining or land ventures.' The judge was too kind to point out that by lending other people's savings to land boomers, through his building societies and insurance company, he had helped to intensify and prolong the speculative mania.

The Australian Widows Fund struggled on for some years longer. Alexander Dick, who in 1892 had built a huge, gloomy mansion which still stands in Canterbury Road, Albert Park (almost next door to Matthias Larkin's house), but who had managed to escape bankruptcy, took over as chairman. In 1896 the Widows Fund wrote off £125,000 capital to help cover its losses of the boom period.

By 1910 the company still had not recovered its position. The directors approached the Mutual Life Association of Australasia, which had just absorbed the Citizens' Life Company, and proposed the amalgamation which became the giant M.L.C. organization of today. There was mild surprise on the part of policy-holders, but no move to investigate the real reasons for the company's weakness. 'It is astonishing that some explanation was not demanded,' commented the *Argus*.

If the sequence of disasters had ended with the collapse of the major building societies and their associated contractors, the worst evils of the depression might yet have been averted. But on the heels of the building society scandals came a series of revelations regarding the conduct of some of the colony's leading banks. Investors were thrown into utter confusion which spelt anarchy for the economic system. Our attention must now be concentrated on the operations of these banks, the effect of their policies, and the means by which sanity was finally restored.

IV THE BANKING

CHORUS OF BANKS.– Of coursh we'll shtand shoulder t' shoulde
an' if any feller fallsh down, we'll leave him an' go on shtanding should

SCANDALS

oulder; an' if 'nother cove fallsh down, we'll go on shtanding shoulder
ulder to shoulder, etc., etc. (*Chorus continued indefinitely*).

23

C. H. James and the Dominion Bank

'I have been shamefully treated by the Government and the banks!' cried Charles Henry James in an affidavit to the Victorian Supreme Court in 1898, as he lay dying from cirrhosis of the liver at Strathfield, near Sydney. Judge Molesworth, who the year before had issued a warrant for the millionaire grazier's arrest and imprisonment, granted him a discharge from bankruptcy. A month later James died, his soul presumably tranquil at last.

Like Sir Graham Berry, C. H. James started his business life as a suburban grocer. He was one of the earliest speculators to follow up the idea of buying farm lands by the acre and reselling them by the foot. As his solicitor, he employed Matthew Davies, who quickly learned the disastrous techniques of land-booming from James.

As early as the 1870s, James was associated in various land purchases with his brother-in-law, Percy Dobson, a partner in Dobson, Watson & Co., a firm of Melbourne merchants. Their transactions were listed in a mysterious volume called the *Black Book*. The public first heard of this enigma when the bankruptcy proceedings of David Findlay Watson, Dobson's surviving partner, were called in 1891. The *Black Book*, which was alleged to show profits from land speculation amounting to £100,000, had disappeared along with James's and Dobson's share of the cash, making it difficult to elucidate their early transactions.

During the 1880s, James bought and sold land mainly among the farmlands of Fairfield, Ivanhoe, Heidelberg and Rosanna, which today are closely settled suburbs of Melbourne. In 1885 he bought one large tract of land from the Macredie family in that area, but since he still owed £10,000 on it at the time of his bankruptcy, the mortgage was foreclosed.

By the time the land boom was properly under way, James had already made huge profits. In 1888, claimed the ex-grocer, he was worth about £900,000. He owned two large sheep stations in N.S.W., 'Kentucky' and 'Bomera,' as well as his rolling acres of valuable suburban land. He maintained two large town houses—'Hazelhurst' in Waverley Road, Malvern; and 'Illawarra' in St. Georges Road, Toorak. The title to his Toorak mansion was transferred to his wife Harriette in 1887 and thus escaped sequestration.

James's major move in the financial world was the flotation of a £3 million

ST. JOHN'S

EXTENSION.

NEXT SATURDAY, JULY 25

The great demand for land in this favourite locality has induced Mr. C. H. James to place ST. JOHN'S EXTENSION thus early on the market. It is situated right on the Alphington line of railway, and directly on the junction of the Outer Circle and Alphington railway.

With the aid of atrocious verse, . H. James sells land on the Outer Circle Railway.

JUST A TOSS UP!

This is the cow with the crumpled horn,
That tossed the gentleman all forlorn,
To put him in mind that on Saturday morn,
Mr. C. H. James' St. John's Extension Sale
Takes place, right on the junction of the Outer Circle
And Alphington Railway. The toss that sends him
To purchase ensures him a small fortune.

Mr. C. H. James's Liberal Terms will be adhered to.

C. H. James, founder of the Dominion Bank, and his Empire Buildings at 418 Collins Street.

institution called the Dominion Banking & Investment Corporation Ltd. This company was formed in 1888, mainly to purchase and resell properties held by himself, and to indulge in other 'banking' practices of the day. The directors were C. H. James; George Stevenson (a leading merchant); and Henry Byron Moore (prominent stockbroker). Others among the original subscribers were S. Gardiner (stock-owner, 6,000 shares); David Ham, M.L.C. (1,000); J. W. Dixon, barrister (1,000); and William Turner, Chief Inspector of the Commercial Bank (1,000 shares).

To house the new bank, James erected the Empire Buildings in Collins Street, directly opposite Market Street. Using a public relations technique well in advance of his times, James announced a contest for the best design. He received forty entries, which were judged by his good friends H. G. Turner, manager of the Commercial Bank (with which James had a £130,000 overdraft); Mr Panton, police magistrate; and Frank Madden, then a leading barrister. They selected a design submitted by T. J. Crouch, an architect of Chancery Lane.

The building, occupying a narrow 57-foot frontage at 418 Collins Street, rose more than 100 feet above the pavement, and cost £40,000 to build. The facade was in white and pink Pacific Portland stone imported from New Zealand, and the vestibule was paved with Minton tiles. The building was the first to use fireproof terracotta timber made at Brunswick (Vic). The passenger lifts were claimed to be capable of moving at 20 feet per second, but, according to a contemporary description, 'to meet the case of the nervous visitor or tenant a noble staircase of easy ascent and occupying twenty feet square has been provided.' The lower flight was entirely of marble; the balustrade of the best Rouge Royal, elaborately carved and polished; and the remainder of best Sicilian marble.

This financier's palace accommodated in its narrow frontage no less than eighty banks, building societies, and insurance companies, besides C. H. James's own offices. In one of his affidavits, James claimed that at the height of the boom he was offered £30,000 clear profit on Empire Buildings, but refused it.

James's next project was the subdivision of a large tract of land, some 1,600 acres known as the Strathallan Estate, which started about three miles north of the suburban railway terminus at Heidelberg. The area was originally farm land owned by the late Alan McLean. McLean's Scottish trustees, James Reid and the Rev. Dr James Gibson, agreed to sell it to James for £140 an acre, a total of £224,000. The entire amount had to be remitted to Scotland in gold sovereigns within three years.

Meanwhile (according to James's affidavit of 1898), the Victorian Government had promised him that it would extend the railway line from Heidelberg to Eltham, which would enormously increase the value of his holdings. Unfortunately, James did not record the name of the Minister in the Government who made him this roseate promise. Whoever it was, James was enthusiastic enough to offer his £224,000 purchase to the directors of the Dominion Bank for a modest £500,000, which would have yielded him a cash profit of £276,000.

George Stevenson, the Melbourne softgoods merchant who became a director of C. H. James's ill-fated bank.

Harold Sparks, 'confidential man' for C. H. James, tried to save his employer from bankruptcy.

To his great surprise, the other directors rejected the offer. James later claimed that he was not perturbed by their rejection, as he knew the land must yield 'enormous profits.'

In 1889, after having made initial payments amounting to £8,000, James launched a law suit attempting to prove that the title to 'Strathallan' was bad, and that the agreement should therefore be cancelled. The trustees, Reid and Gibson, came hotfoot from Scotland, fought the case through two courts, and won it on appeal to the Full Court. James in turn appealed to the Privy Council, but before the case could be heard, a compromise was arranged. The trustees accepted a cash deposit of £50,000 and balance of £80,000 on terms—a total of £130,000 instead of £224,000. An important proviso was that if any further payments were missed, the original purchase price would again become operative.

James's version of events was that although he held more than half of the Dominion Bank's shares, he did not press the other directors to take over 'Strathallan.' He adopted this policy, he said, 'because of the large number of private and political friends who were members of the said Corporation and not desiring to jeopardise the credit of the said Corporation by a law suit.'

Soon C. H. James was treading deeper waters. As his agent in many share transactions, he used one Harold Sparks, who first came into view as the manager of a furniture store in Adelaide. In 1886, according to *Melbourne Punch*, he heard reports of the land boom, 'which were distinctly audible from the Heads to St. Vincent's Gulf,' and came to Melbourne to seek his fortune. Here he got a job as confidential secretary of C. H. James, who, again according to the sly information of *Punch*, at one time 'shed sympathetic tears in describing the varied virtues of his right-hand man and comptroller-general of the boom department.'

When the first land company crashes occurred in 1889, heavy calls were made against Sparks as apparent owner of the shares. Sparks was forced into bankruptcy in September 1889, but subsequently sued James for recompense as the real owner of the shares. A court case was averted by means of a substantial cash payment to Sparks's estate.

In 1891, when 'almost all the leading members of the Dominion Bank having become unable to lay their hands on ready cash (to meet calls on the bank's shares) . . . and being anxious not to press severely on the members, many of whom were my old friends,' James agreed to buy out their interest in the Dominion Bank. In this way he became the holder of 68,789 of the bank's 69,855 shares, and personally liable for any further calls. The shareholders of the bank whom James claimed to have saved from early insolvency in this manner included David Ham, George Stevenson, Robert Murray-Smith, Alfred Deakin, T. B. Muntz, J. M. and W. B. McCutcheon, D. F. Watson, F. C. Rowan, and John Marshall.

Thus James became practically the sole owner of the Dominion Bank. A remarkable feature of the agreement with his 'old friends' was that the money owing to them had to be used to purchase the Bundoora Park Estate from the bank. In this way James finished up with sole control of the bank and its main asset, the Heidelberg Estate. To escape from their immediate embarrassment, his friends were saddled with the Bundoora Park Estate, on which calls might be made at any time.

Meanwhile, James had built a colorful 35-roomed mansion in Toorak on a large site off St Georges Road, naming it 'Illawarra'. The main material used was bright red bricks, the roof being covered with pink Welsh slates. Around most of the exterior ran 250 feet of wide tiled verandahs and lavish cast-iron work. Downstairs were a drawing-room, dining-room, morning-room, serving-room, ballroom with orchestra gallery, billiard-room, library, etc. Upstairs were eight bedrooms, four bathrooms, nursery, servants' quarters, etc.

In September 1893, James's two bankers, the Commercial and the City of Melbourne Bank, requested James to increase the security on his overdrafts by mortgaging his station property 'Bomera' to them. James agreed, provided that they continued to meet his interest payments on 'Strathallan' and other commitments.

At this time James listed his major assets as the Empire Buildings (£120,000); Strathallan Estate (£130,000); Rosanna land, 840 acres (£168,000); Kentucky Station (£115,000); Bomera Station (£110,000); and various shares. But all these assets, and many others, were soon proved worthless or unsaleable on the open market.

Crisis after crisis sapped James's financial resources. The City of Melbourne Bank suspended payment, tried to reconstruct, and finally breathed its last. James's overdraft of £250,000 with the bank thus became due and payable. The liquidators of the City Bank visited 'Bomera' and found that the bank's 'security' consisted solely of rank ground. James's excuse was that 'unprecedentedly wet seasons caused the grass to become sour . . . and three different diseases caused enormous losses in stock.' What about the homestead and the excellent land around it, asked the liquidators. 'That has been settled on my wife,' replied James.

James's other station, 'Kentucky,' was also going through lean times. According to James, the property depreciated in value by £60,000 because the manager 'dishonoured his orders and spent too much on improvements.' To cap it all, the N.S.W. Parliament changed the Pastoral Leases Act and made his leases terminable without renewal.

In September 1896, the Dominion Bank was wound up by an official liquidator working under the supervision of the Supreme Court. Since James now owned practically all the shares, he immediately became liable for the uncalled capital of £170,000. This, he claimed, was 'unjust and unnecessary' because the bank's debts amounted to only £27,000.

In March 1897, the Commercial Bank refused to pay any further interest instalments on 'Strathallan.' The millstones of Mammon began to grind small. The vendors of 'Strathallan' could now revert to the original purchase price. When the instalment payments ceased, the creditors could sue James into bankruptcy and mortgagees could repossess their property. That is exactly what happened, in a curious and tragic manner.

The large creditors did not sue James—at least, not in their own names. Instead, one John Haines, who was a creditor for the sum of £12, pursued James with peculiar persistence. Although offered the £12 in cash by James's solicitor, J. E. Dixon, Haines filed an insolvency motion against James. According to Haines's affidavit, when he went personally to 'Illawarra' to serve the papers on James, the maid claimed she was deaf, refused to admit Haines, and refused to accept service of the summons.

James decided it was time to vanish. He left Melbourne secretly some time in September 1897. Later it was discovered that he had stayed with friends at Tinkrameanah Station—in an isolated area of N.S.W. where the postman rarely called. John Haines, the most persistent creditor who ever chased a debt of £12, filed a motion for substituted service. When James failed to file his schedule in insolvency, Haines moved to have him attached for contempt of court. Judge Molesworth agreed, and issued a warrant for James's arrest and committal to prison.

James heard the news about a fortnight later in a message from his wife. Already seriously ill, he shifted from the remote outback station to Strathfield, Sydney, and lodged an appeal with the Victorian Full Court against his sentence of imprisonment. With the appeal he sent a doctor's certificate saying that he was suffering from cirrhosis of the liver, could not travel, and had no hope of recovery. The Full Court granted the appeal in February 1898. James died eight months later, still under medical treatment in Strathfield. His estate finally paid 7d. in the £1 on debts amounting to £850,000.

James's wife retained the Toorak mansion 'Illawarra' until the early 1900s,

'Illawarra', the ornate mansion in Toorak designed by James Birtwhistle for C. H. James. Today it is maintained by the National Trust.

leasing it in turn to George Chirnside, Mrs M. Wynne, and the Paxton family. After World War I she sold the freehold to Mrs Susan Eakins. The estate was subdivided in 1925. The house with its remaining 2½ acres was bought in 1940 by William Leslie Ryan, a Melbourne wine retailer, who in 1966 presented it to the National Trust for permanent preservation.

24

Frederick Illingworth and the Centennial Bank

'The land we bought on the south side of the Yarra is a perfect white elephant', said Joseph Elam Pounds mournfully. 'We still owed £70,000 on it when the contract was cancelled.' Pounds was chairman of the once-successful Centennial Land Bank, and he was trying to explain to a meeting of angry shareholders in March 1892 why the bank had to close down. He had a difficult task. All the directors save one were deeply involved in the land boom on their own account. Pounds himself had gone bankrupt with nearly £140,000 in debts on land transactions. Another director, Frederick Illingworth, M.L.C., had plunged for nearly £300,000 and had fled to Perth, whence his creditors were vainly trying to pursue him.

Illingworth, the key to the bank's downfall, was born in Yorkshire in 1844 and brought to Australia by his father, a wool classer, at the age of four. He spent the first twenty-five years of his working life in ironmongery shops in Brighton and Melbourne city. In the late 1870s he went into business as an estate agent, in partnership with J. R. Hoskins, a former Mayor of Bendigo. Illingworth soon made enough money to buy a property near Yalook (Vic.), but was ruined by a succession of bad seasons. He returned to the hardware business, opening an electroplating establishment at 67 Swanston Street, opposite the Town Hall, in 1883. The enterprise prospered, and Illingworth soon entered politics as M.L.C. for the Northern Province.

Since most of his fellow M.L.C.s had extensive and enviable financial interests, the ambitious Illingworth decided to emulate them. He joined forces with J. E. Pounds, who was already engaged in the business of buying suburban land cheaply and trying to sell it dearly. In 1888 they floated a company called the Centennial Land Bank, with capital of £1 million in £5 shares. Also on the board were J. S. Hosie, Henry Burrows, Henry Butler, William Ellingworth, and Andrew Gilmour. As manager they appointed Frederick George Wood, who liquidated the company when it failed and destroyed its records.

Illingworth and Pounds took up large numbers of the bank's shares between them. To pay for the shares and for their personal land deals, they arranged substantial overdrafts with other leading financial houses. Illingworth, for instance, was given a £150,000 overdraft on little security by his fellow M.P., James Munro, via Munro's Real Estate Bank. So the position was that Munro was inviting bank deposits from the public, then privately lending a good portion of them to a fellow 'banker' to spend on land and share gambling.

In the Centennial Bank's first year of operations, 1888, trading had all the appearance of high prosperity. Its first issue of shares yielded a £10,000 premium. Total profits for the half year were announced as £26,000. A dividend of 10 per cent was paid, plus a bonus of 20 per cent. An easier way of making money had never been known. But the bank ran into difficulties soon afterwards. Only £52,000 of its capital was actually paid up. On the basis of this slender capital structure, plus a large overdraft from the Commercial Bank, some £330,000 was spent on land purchases in the name of the Centennial Bank.

Frederick Illingworth, director of the Centennial Land Bank, as seen by *Truth*.

The directors' fatal mistake was to buy land at high prices, on comparatively small deposits and long terms, trusting to further inflation of values to pull them out of trouble. Thus in 1888 they agreed to pay £50,000 (£1,200 a foot) for a property in Collins Street next to Scotts Hotel, but were left with £33,000 still to pay off. When land values tumbled, they had no hope of meeting the payments. In another instance, a block on the south side of the Yarra was bought from a Mr Connell in 1888 for £100,000, but on only £30,000 deposit. The vendor refused to cancel the contract until he was paid another £10,000—so he got his land back, plus £40,000 cash, plus £5,000 interest. Other land was bought at Box Hill and Whittlesea, and all contracts had to be cancelled for similar huge losses.

The bank again lost heavily when it tried to set up associated land companies and invest the depositors' money through them. In one instance, the Coburg Reserve Estate Co. Ltd was formed, with Andrew Gilmour as chairman and F. G. Wood as manager. This company paid a huge price for land at Coburg, and wound up with £100,000 worth of unsold property and houses on its books. The directors had the audacity to declare a substantial profit on the first year's trading, but next year were unable to pay calls on their own shares!

Meanwhile, both Pounds and Illingworth were plunging heavily on their own account. Pounds borrowed £23,000 from the Union Bank; £13,000 from the Kew Land Co. Ltd (of which he was a director); and many smaller amounts. In a neat piece of cross-financing, he bought land from one Davies company and borrowed money from another Davies company to pay for it. Such were the intricacies of the land boom. By the beginning of 1891 Pounds's debts had reached nearly £140,000, on which he paid a halfpenny in the pound.

Illingworth did even better. His personal commitments by this time had reached £283,000. Apart from the £150,000 loan by Munro's bank, he had borrowed more than £100,000 from the Bank of South Australia. He owed £13,000 to the Petty family, fruitgrowers of Doncaster, for land bought in that area; and other amounts. Illingworth then applied for, and was granted, leave of absence from his parliamentary duties 'for a business trip to Europe'. Without telling anyone, he left the ship at Perth and anonymously found a job to keep himself afloat. Back in Melbourne, the ravenous creditors descended on his

Sinking depositor.– Save me, save me! I've been depending on that life buoy; save me!
Shareholder.– Get away and drown, you rude fellow! Isn't *my* salvation more important than yours?

remains. The sum of £600 was realized to meet Illingworth's debts of nearly £300,000.

All was quiet for some years after that, apart from the anguished cries of creditors, until the astounding story came back from Perth that Illingworth had managed to get himself elected to the Western Australian Legislative Assembly. The story was true enough. Illingworth had opened an estate agency in the West, had done well, and in 1894 had been elected as member for East Murchison. In 1897 Judge William Gaunt issued an order that the absconder should be brought before the Perth Insolvency Court. Illingworth's new assets were rapidly stripped from him. Despite the unfortunate publicity, the Western Australian government thought so much of Illingworth that in 1901 he was appointed State Treasurer. It was one way of making history. Never before had it been known for one State to accept as its Treasurer a man who had not been released from sequestration in another State. The final act of this Gilbertian drama occurred in December 1903, when Illingworth's remaining creditors agreed to release him from sequestration.

There was never any real investigation into the affairs of the Centennial Land Bank, whose disappearance was rapidly overshadowed by the greater scandals which burst upon Melbourne.

25

G. N. Taylor and the Land Credit Bank

From all over the world came rovers and adventurers, to settle thankfully in the promising colony of Victoria. One such rover was George Nicholson Taylor, son of the Rev. Henry Taylor, a clergyman of the Church of England in Jamaica. The boy, born about 1830, rebelled against his strict religious upbringing and ran away to sea.

Another such rover was a merchant captain, William Cairncross, who married Miss Davina Dove in Melbourne. They had a daughter whom they named Jessie Pearson Dove Cairncross. George Taylor, the sailor lad from Jamaica, landed in Melbourne, met Jessie, fell in love, and married her in 1863. Under his wife's prompting, Taylor studied accountancy and other landsmen's secrets. In 1880 he succeeded in getting the post of manager of a fairly new institution, the Land Credit Bank, at a salary of £350 a year.

The Taylors enjoyed an idyllic life in boom-time Melbourne. George opened accounts for his wife and son at the Land Credit Bank, and during the next ten years they managed to siphon off more than £100,000 of the bank's money. Taylor spent it all on property speculations, with the avowed intention of making a million pounds. At his trial in 1892, when he was sentenced to eight years' hard labour, he told the judge that he had fully intended to pay back the money he had taken, 'after he had made his fortune'.

The Land Credit Bank was one of the earliest of the boom institutions, incorporated in 1876 with capital of £100,000. Its head office was at 407 Collins Street (now Aldersgate House). The main directors were C. R. Martin, J. W. Shevill, and Dr H. St John Clarke, who held most of the shares between them. Martin was a city merchant, Shevill was a large shareholder in several of the new banks, and Dr Clarke was a surgeon in Richmond. Martin and Dr Clarke invested in certain land deals with their manager, George Taylor, but claimed to be ignorant of his misappropriations over a long period.

Another early director was Matthew Davies, the bank's first solicitor, who 'floated a balance' for Taylor on at least two occasions without informing his fellow directors. The technique used was for Davies's cheque to be paid into Taylor's account on balancing day to bring it back into credit after Taylor had purchased properties. Davies resigned from the bank in 1885 after a stormy scene with the other directors, and proceeded to start his own institution, the Mercantile Bank.

As his willing tool and conspirator, Taylor used Charles Ernest Clarke, a sharebroker who had previously gone bankrupt in 1879, and now had a low overdraft limit with the bank. For several years, Taylor allowed Clarke to overdraw far beyond his means, but represented to the directors when they met each Thursday that Clarke's drawings were well within bounds. By 1888 Clarke's real indebtedness had reached £29,000, although it was only shown in the books as £6,000. Taylor covered up this discrepancy by a variety of ingenious methods, some of which were unique in the annals of financial chicanery. Each Thursday morning Taylor initialled as 'Payable' a cheque for several thousand pounds signed by Clarke. He then sent the cheque to money-lenders in the city, had it discounted, paid the cash into Clarke's account, and thus reduced his overdraft for the day. The initialled cheque held by the money-lender was not cleared until the following day, when Clarke's overdraft rose again until the following Thursday. This novel device was operated successfully for nearly three years.

In 1886 Taylor and Clarke got bolder. When Clarke's overdraft reached £9,000, Taylor simply removed the whole ledger sheet from the book shown to the directors each Thursday. Later a fresh overdraft was treated in the same way. But what of the security necessary to cover Clarke's various overdrafts? With infinite resource, Taylor informed the directors that Clarke owned a property known as Clarke's Corner, near Malvern Town Hall. In actual fact the property belonged to another Clarke altogether! In 1888 the directors instructed Taylor to call in Clarke's overdraft, which had once again risen beyond the official limit. Three months later Taylor reported to the directors that Clarke had managed to sell his Corner for a good price, and the overdraft had been paid off. Taylor had simply removed another ledger sheet.

Taylor's enormous advances to himself, his wife and his son were covered up by the same method. He omitted their names from the list of overdrafts presented to directors' meetings. After each such meeting, he negotiated extra advances in their favour by telling the bank clerks that the directors had just approved the payments. Perhaps there was more to the story than ever became known, for one dull May morning shortly after the bank closed, the body of its cashier, Joseph Cahill, was found floating in the Yarra at Richmond. No clue emerged to solve this mystery.

Taylor used £30,000 of his illegitimate gains to buy shares in the Chatsworth Estate Co. Ltd, a speculative company of which James Munro was chairman. Curiously enough, Dr St John Clarke, a director of the Land Credit Bank, was also a director of the Chatsworth enterprise. He disclaimed all knowledge of the real source of his manager's sudden wealth. Taylor himself went to considerable pains to spread the story that his wife was worth £50,000 as the result of a legacy and her share of the profits from backing the publication of Fergus Hume's popular book, *Mystery of a Hansom Cab*.

But what of the bank's accountant? What of its auditors? Surely in time they must discover the irregularities? When the bank was forced to close through Taylor's defalcations, it was discovered that Taylor had 'lent' the accountant the sum of £1,000. As for audit procedures, Taylor had called in Charles Thorpe, the same auditor who had been working for Davies's Mercantile Bank after being released from two years in gaol for fraud. In the words of the liquidator, Thomas Hills: 'Neither the directors, manager, nor accountants were properly qualified, and the book-keeping would be a disgrace to a small shopkeeper . . . The books had not been balanced for years, despite the regular half-yearly investigations of auditors.'

In March 1890 Charles Clarke became insolvent, filing debts of £27,000. His main creditors were claimed to be A. E. Clarke (£9,000), G. N. Taylor (£6,000), and Felix Kabat (£5,000), Kabat being a financier who in 1873 had been sentenced to eleven years' hard labour for forgery. In his schedule, Clarke showed nothing as owing to the Land Credit Bank, whereas he actually owed the bank £38,000. A composition of 6d. in the £1 on Clarke's debts was accepted on the motion of another creditor, James McKinley, manager of the *Daily Telegraph*, and the matter was hastily buried.

The same month, James Wotton Shevill, a leading city auctioneer and nephew of the J. W. Shevill who was a director of the Land Credit Bank, filed his schedule in insolvency. It was the same old story of heavy borrowing to support land speculations. Shevill's debts totalled £27,000, but only a few hundred pounds were shown as owing to his uncle's bank. The bulk was an overdraft of £22,000 owing to a weird and wonderful institution called the New Oriental Banking Corporation, whose Melbourne manager made large advances to land boomers while suffering from a brain disease. He was later certified as insane. Shevill's insolvency papers disclosed that a larger part of the security which he gave to the New Oriental Bank for his £22,000 overdraft consisted of a bond warrant on eighteen cases of whisky.

Towards the end of 1891 the Commercial Bank decided to call in its overdrafts from those building societies and land banks which it suspected of engaging in speculative activities. Among them was the Land Credit Bank, to which the Commercial had given financial accommodation of £50,000. The directors of the Land Credit Bank called for all the books to see how the cash could be raised. To their amazement, they discovered that the bank had been milked dry. On 1 December 1891 they closed their doors for ever.

Bank director Shevill went home to Glen Iris and gloomily surveyed his affairs. Quite obviously he, like his nephew, would have to go bankrupt. He picked up his gun, walked into the seclusion of his one-acre garden, tied a piece of string from his boot to the trigger, and shot himself dead. When his business affairs were analysed, it was found that he was £34,000 in debt—to the Land Credit Bank, the Commercial Bank, the Bank of Australasia, and the Land Mortgage Bank.

A few days later, the remaining two directors called a meeting of shareholders and depositors, at which some of Taylor's defalcations were revealed. On 15 December Taylor was arrested on two minor charges. The first was that in

SHEVILL & CO.,

General Mercantile Auctioneers,

HOUSE,

Land, Estate & Financial Agents.

Sales Held at Rooms Daily.

Outdoor Sales Conducted.

Money to Lend on all Securities.

Valuations Made.

Insurances Effected.

Estates Managed.

Advances Made on all Classes of Merchandise, and Colonial Produce for Local Sale or Shipment to London.

Corner of QUEEN STREET and FLINDERS LANE.

Branch Offices { 32 Chapel Street, South Yarra.
2 Albert Street, Windsor.

James Wootton Shevill, the city auctioneer, gave eighteen cases of whisky as security for £22,000 in land boom debts.

Shevill used much of his borrowings for this building on the corner of Queen Street and Flinders Lane, Melbourne.

1884 he had illegally converted a £1,300 promissory note of G. W. Taylor's (apparently no relation) to his own use. The second charge was that in 1885 he had illegally converted a £5,000 promissory note made by his wife, Jessie Taylor. Taylor was found guilty on both charges in February 1892, and sentenced to two years' gaol. At the trial the directors claimed they were ignorant of the state of affairs until a new ledger-keeper had given them the information. They had asked Taylor to put up security for his 'borrowings', but had taken no further action until the meeting of shareholders insisted on Taylor's arrest.

The Crown Law Department took over the investigation of Taylor's dealings, and soon uncovered his association with Clarke. The pair were charged with conspiracy to defraud, and were tried in July 1892. Alfred Deakin, who appeared for Taylor, attempted to convince the jury that Taylor had acted with the connivance of the bank's directors. J. L. Purves, Q.C., for Clarke, described his client as 'a silly, muddling old fool of a financier', and claimed he was 'an innocent tool'. Mr Walsh, Q.C., Crown prosecutor, said the bank's chairman, Charles Martin, was 'an extraordinarily stupid man', and that all the directors had been 'unutterable fools'.

In his summing-up, Mr Justice Hood castigated the bank's directors, particularly Dr Clarke, for being mixed up in 'most improper transactions' with the defendants. Dr Clarke had received 6 per cent interest on his deposits when the general public got only 4 per cent—'a most outrageous thing'. The directors had admitted taking up shares and not paying for them at the time—'another most improper thing'. With these judicial comments ringing in their ears, the jury retired. They took thirty minutes to find both Taylor and Clarke guilty. Mr Justice Hood fined Taylor £5,000 and sentenced him to eight years' hard labour. Clarke was fined £500 and sentenced to four years' hard labour—almost a sentence of death for a man of sixty. Passing sentence, the judge said:

> It is plain that you were victims of the gambling mania which seized upon many people at the time . . . Your conspiracy greatly hastened the downfall of the institution of which you, Taylor, were the manager, working ruin and misery to hundreds of innocent people . . . In offences like yours, retribution though long delayed, will surely come at last.

The following year, the liquidators paid 7s. 6d. in the £1 to the depositors who had entrusted their money to the Land Credit Bank of Melbourne. Its entire capital of £77,000 had vanished. Its reserve fund of £27,000 had vanished. The shareholders not only lost everything, but were subjected to a call to help meet the depositors' losses.

26

William Greenlaw and the Colonial Bank

'When the smash came every bank manager showed himself to be a tin man painted to look like iron', wrote George Meudell. If that were true, one of the most heavily lacquered bank managers was surely William Greenlaw of the Colonial Bank of Australasia Ltd, who speculated so wildly on his own account that he was forced to make a secret composition when his debts reached £115,000, paying his creditors 6d. in the £1. How did a great institution like the Colonial Bank, with Sir William Clarke, Baronet, as its Governor, appoint such a man as general manager? Where did the real blame lie for the bank's subsequent failure and losses to those who invested in it? The answers could only lie in the convolutions of the land boom.

The Colonial Bank, one of Victoria's oldest and most respected institutions, was incorporated in 1856. Over the years, practically all its £1 million authorized capital became paid up, so that it was anything but a fly-by-night company. It had more to lose from economic disruption than most other enterprises. In 1865 the bank had lost about £85,000 on advances to a speculator named Hugh Glass. After a special audit, the shares were written down to cover the loss. The directors dismissed the general manager and made a temporary appointment while casting around for the right man. In 1871 they decided to give the vital post to one William Greenlaw, who had entered the bank as a junior clerk in the same year in which it started business. There were no apparent traces of the boomer about this sober, respectable banker with the deep Scottish burr in his voice. Yet Greenlaw was finally revealed as one of the most profligate of speculators.

Greenlaw had arrived in the colony during the gold-rush days, and was known to have little capital. Soon after his appointment as general manager, he bought several acres of land overlooking the Yarra Valley at Kew. Here he built an extraordinary residence which he called the 'Villa Alba'. This mansion, an ugly stucco box from the outside, was entered through a large conservatory. In the spacious front hall, gilded statues of Cupid held gas burners aloft. The ceiling was decorated by more painted Cupids holding shields, on one of which was painted Greenlaw's crest—a vulture with an oak branch in its mouth. The hall was lined with black oaken boxes, behind whose glass fronts the astonished visitor could study stuffed ptarmigan, pheasant, and grouse. Later these were

New premises for the Colonial Bank at the corner of Elizabeth and Little Collins Streets, Melbourne.

removed, and scenes of Venice were painted on the walls by some long-forgotten artist. In the huge dining-room, 30 ft by 20 ft, the upper sections of the walls were painted with scenes from Rob Roy and the Waverley novels. Upstairs, the main boudoir was decorated in the style of an Oriental sultan's palace, with sky blue and russet red ceiling relieved by golden crescents and suns. Panels at intervals depicted the sacred ibis and other mystic birds. Other bedrooms were also lavishly decorated.

Greenlaw, the sober Melbourne banker, was also busily building new offices to cope with the bank's expansion policy. In 1882 he proudly led his staff into their new premises at the corner of Elizabeth and Little Collins Streets.

During this period Greenlaw began pressing the directors to take more and more speculative risks, quite outside traditional banking practice. In addition, he sought private capital to enable him to plunge headlong into the flood of speculation beginning to sweep Melbourne. In 1885 Greenlaw approached

James Munro, whose Federal Bank gave him an overdraft of £3,000. It was a modest start. In 1887 Greenlaw had dealings with B. J. Fink over certain properties. Fink arranged for him to get a £30,000 overdraft from the City of Melbourne Bank, which was already financing Fink to the tune of £90,000. Greenlaw then approached Matthew Davies, and succeeded in getting a loan of £24,000 from his Mercantile Bank. Next came the Bank of Victoria, from which he borrowed £22,000. Greenlaw had no compunction about borrowing £9,000 from Joseph Clarke, rapscallion brother of Sir William, and a former Governor of the Colonial Bank. Joseph was involved at the time in a sordid case where his mistress had allegedly attempted to defraud him of large sums over land deals, and had been spirited off to Hawaii for her pains. With these and several smaller loans from other friendly banks and land companies, Greenlaw ran up a total of £115,000 in debts. The money all disappeared into land and share purchases, and into a nickel mining venture in New Caledonia.

In 1887 we see Greenlaw in his official capacity as manager of the Colonial Bank, giving evidence before Matthew Davies's Royal Commission on Banking. The Colonial Bank was among those prohibited in theory by its Act of Incorporation from making advances directly on the security of land. Greenlaw argued that this banking tradition was outmoded and unnecessary. The honourable Commissioners agreed, and the government changed the law. Now the banks could get knee-deep into the flood of gold swirling up and down Collins Street. And they did.

In pressing for changes in the banking laws, Greenlaw had the backing of his directors, headed by Sir William Clarke. Sir William was the first Baronet in a remarkable Australian family whose fortunes were largely based on Clarke's Special Survey, a huge area of rich land around Clarkefield, bought in the colony's early days for £1 an acre. Sir William survived the land boom by only a few years, being succeeded in 1897 by Sir Rupert Clarke. Another Colonial Bank director who backed Greenlaw was Sir Benjamin Benjamin, sometime mayor of Melbourne, whose dismal fortunes are dealt with subsequently. Yet

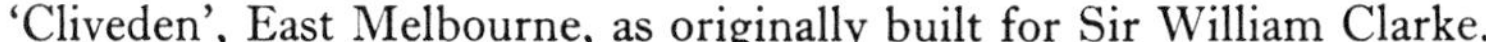

'Cliveden', East Melbourne, as originally built for Sir William Clarke.

another land-booming member of the Colonial Bank's directorate was Thomas Russell, a director of the ill-fated Modern Permanent Building Society. Russell was a stockbroker of note, as well as being owner of the freehold of Wirths Hotel in Bourke Street. Russell (who had previously become insolvent as a grazier in 1880) borrowed £20,000 from the Royal Bank. With the money he bought shares in many land companies and his seat on the Stock Exchange. By June 1892 he had amassed debts of £32,000, and went bankrupt for the second time.

After the Banking Commission, the Colonial Bank began to finance more and more speculative schemes. No precise details ever became available, and no independent investigation was ever published. But the public showed its opinion of the bank's soundness by withdrawing £400,000 in cash during one month alone, April 1893. Sir William Clarke was forced to borrow heavily from the Australian Mutual Land & Finance Co. Ltd to help make up the deficit. William Greenlaw had made his secret composition with creditors the same month. In this case, however, secrecy had the opposite effect to that intended. Rumours about Greenlaw's composition were passed around the city, and its magnitude was greatly exaggerated. Public suspicion intensified, and with it the run on the bank's deposits increased until the bank had no alternative but to close its doors.

After the crash, mass meetings of depositors and shareholders were held to decide the bank's future. Speakers unanimously supported the reconstruction scheme proposed by the directors. James Hogan expressed his sympathy with the manager and directors. James Maloney said the bank had been honourably conducted, and had 'simply come down because it was unable to stand where other banks had fallen'. J. M. Peck thought it would be 'suicidal' to take any other course but that proposed. So the meetings agreed meekly enough to the reconstruction scheme. Most of the remaining deposits were compulsorily converted into preference shares. The balance of capital was called up in stages, forcing many impecunious shareholders to forfeit their shares, and the bank was able to open again after a brief closure.

Greenlaw was later dismissed from his position and disappeared into obscurity, being succeeded as general manager by Selby Paxton. While the reconstruction scheme was being pushed through, the bank's capital losses were claimed to be only £200,000. Ultimately it was disclosed that the bank had some £3 million in overdrafts covered by doubtful securities. By prodigious efforts the new management cleaned up the mess, and paid off the entire liability by 1901. In 1918 the Colonial was merged with the National Bank, to the benefit of shareholders in both institutions.

Greenlaw's 'Villa Alba' still stands near the corner of Walmer Street and Nolan Avenue, Kew. During World War II it was taken over from the Fripp family by the Royal Women's Hospital and converted into a nurses' home. The conservatory was demolished, and the Venetian frescoes on the walls of the main hall and some bedrooms painted over. Recently the building started to subside, owing to lack of adequate foundations, and is now considered unsafe for general habitation.

27

Joseph Clarke Invests in the Kooweerup Swamp

Did Joseph Clarke, scion of the leading quasi-aristocratic Victorian family, pay to have his mistress drugged and shipped overseas? Every existing piece of evidence points directly at this reprobate younger son, the dissolute playboy of Melbourne in the 1880s. Yet no official action was ever taken to prove or disprove the matter. Only the lurid facts remain to illuminate men, morals and Mammon in the Victorian era.

Joseph Clarke, born in 1835, was a younger brother of Sir William Clarke, first Baronet of Rupertswood, Victoria (created 1882). Joseph himself was not entirely without means. He was, in fact, widely reputed to be a millionaire, owning a large station in Queensland carrying a million sheep; a property of 200,000 acres in Tasmania; and an entailed property of 75,000 acres at Mt. Schank (Vic.). His business interests included directorships of the Land Mortgage Bank and the Colonial Bank, where he served a term as Governor.

In 1860 Joseph married his own cousin Caroline, daughter of Lewis Clarke of Ararat. For his life as a respectable man of means, Joseph bought the 20-acre estate, 'St. Georges,' in Toorak. The mansion and grounds were originally planned and built in 1878 by Alfred Watson. Clarke changed the name to 'Mandeville Hall,' and added an ornate front to the rather severe lines of the original building. The rest of the estate was left as a natural bush setting, where emus, wallabies, and other native animals roamed freely. Here the Clarkes raised their two sons and acted the part of a devoted, hospitable couple, with a purse always open to the call of respectable charities. Among his benefactions, Clarke gave £5,000 towards the building of St. Paul's Cathedral, and £5,000 to the Trinity College building fund.

The mansion still stands in Mandeville Crescent, Toorak. But now it is known as Loreto Convent; and nuns may admire its beautifully carved doors and ceilings, brooding the while, perhaps, on the strange morality play acted out by its former owner.

Joseph Clarke first met the young, handsome and promiscuous Clara Amy Parker in Tasmania at the home of another brother, Thomas Clarke. Clara later came to Victoria, and was living with her husband at Cranbourne when Joseph

'Mandeville Hall', Toorak, where Joseph Clarke acted the part of a devoted family man. Later the ornate exterior was stripped off and the building became a convent.

Joseph Clarke, the millionaire implicated in 'one of the vilest conspiracies of modern times'.

Clara Amy Parker, Clarke's mistress, who speculated with him in land deals.

Clarke first endorsed bills for her in connection with properties purchased at Kooweerup. Blocks at Kooweerup, a swampy area near Westernport Bay, were not among the most popular speculations of the boom period, but apparently Clarke or Mrs Parker had heard that the Government intended to help develop the area. In 1891, the Government did in fact set 400 men to work on digging great canals to drain the swamps and reclaim the land.

Clara Parker soon left her husband, and went to live in Toorak, later shifting to North Fitzroy and Richmond. At each temporary home, she claimed, she was regularly visited by her lover, Joseph Clarke. As well as giving her bills and promissory notes, he also made progress payments for her on the Kooweerup property. Clara tried to get him interested in other land speculations in Western Australia and even in Mexico, but apparently without success.

Joseph Clarke's secret life burst upon the Melbourne public in April 1892, when Mrs Parker, then of Latrobe Street, City, sued him for £500 damages for alleged slander. She claimed that Clarke had been spreading the story that she had forged his signature to promissory notes for £5,000. Like another celebrated defamation action soon to take place on the other side of the world, that of *Wilde v. Queensberry*, the case was to rebound ruinously on the plaintiff.

At the date of her action, Mrs Parker was described by the *Age* as 'about 30, above medium height, of good physique, dark complexion, and may be fairly described as good looking.' Possibly she was older, for her good looks were said to have deteriorated quickly after her curious experiences of the next twelve months.

Mrs Parker told the court she had long wanted to invest in land speculations.

Having known Clarke 'all her life,' she met him in Collins Street one day and asked him to finance her. They went to a hotel and became 'a little merry' with drink, then proceeded to 'Martha Salter's house in Richmond,' where he signed the promissory notes for £5,000. They stayed there for some time after that: the sexual innuendo being clear to the least worldly member of the jury.

In December 1890, Mrs Parker continued, Clarke gave her another £3,000. Altogether he advanced her £11,000 on various occasions. He also paid Mr Parker (a civil servant) £1,000 to avoid being cited as a co-respondent in the Divorce Court. Mrs Parker admitted that she had since lived with three other men, temporarily assuming their name in each case.

As her cross-examination progressed, Mrs Parker refused to answer further questions about her private life, walked out of the court sobbing, and was finally non-suited. The same day, Clarke went to Mr Panton, police magistrate, laid an information charging Mrs Parker with forgery, and had her arrested. She was committed to gaol to await trial.

Panton fixed bail and bonds totalling £600. Mrs Parker was unable to raise this amount, and spent seven weeks in prison. A week before her case was due

Joseph Clarke signs a promissory note for Clara Parker. 'Was there another man under the bed?' asked Mr Purves, Q. C.

to come up, she was mysteriously bailed out by two strangers, Messrs. G. G. Morris and W. Walker. Morris was a financial agent of Toorak, and Walker was a stove manufacturer in the city. Nothing else was known about them. When Mrs Parker's case was called on 22 June 1892, she failed to appear. Frank Gavan Duffy told Mr Justice Hood that he believed she had been 'forcibly removed from the colony.' The judge estreated her bail, and the case, which attracted momentary wonder, was soon forgotten by the general public.

When the bonds were estreated, Walker could not be found, and 'was supposed to have levanted.' Morris could not pay his share, and was committed to the same gaol from which Mrs Parker had been so recently released.

Three months later, with dramatic suddenness, Mrs Parker reappeared in Melbourne. She told an extraordinary story to her solicitor, Conrad S. Scheele, of drugging and forcible abduction. 'Mrs Parker's story makes it appear that she has been the victim of one of the vilest conspiracies of modern times,' said the *Age*. The newspaper did not hesitate to name the 'friendship' between Mrs Parker and 'Mr. Joseph Clarke, the millionaire,' as the basis of 'a story as strange as many recorded in the pages of romance.'

What happened was this. Early in June 1892, Mrs Parker was visited in Melbourne Gaol by Charles Peters, a Collins Street tea merchant; and Henry Grave, a city solicitor. They told her that her own solicitor had thrown up the case, and asked her if she would like to be bailed out. She agreed. Next day, she claimed, Grave returned and told her that the case had been settled—but on one strict condition, that she must leave the colony immediately and never return. Friendless, and seeing no alternative, she agreed to this proposal.

On the next Saturday, 11 June 1892, without her own solicitor's knowledge, she was bailed out of Melbourne Gaol by G. G. Morris and W. Walker. She was taken in a hansom cab to Spencer Street station, where she, Henry Grave, and Charles Peters boarded the Sydney train. She was given a bottle of brandy to drink, and reached Albury in 'a fearful state,' leading her to conclude she had been drugged.

She managed to elude her captors during an overnight change of trains at Albury, but they searched and found her again. Changing their plans, they decided to put her on board a sailing ship at Geelong. They came back as far as North Melbourne, and stayed overnight at North Melbourne Coffee Palace. Again there was a change of plans, and a dispute between her captors. Grave told Peters, 'Take her, the she devil; I won't have the handling of her.' Grave's son and Peters took her on the Sydney train again the following day, although by this time she was very ill.

In Sydney, they stayed at the Queensland Hotel. During the night, she said, Grave Jnr. burst into her room and cried, 'My God, the detectives are after us. Mrs Parker, I will turn Queen's Evidence if you will only protect me, and I will tell where they got the money.'

When Peters came in, she said, Harry Grave was on his knees beside the bed, crying to her to protect him for the sake of his wife and children. Peters muttered to young Grave, 'You white-livered scoundrel, you are a pretty one to trust her with!' This melodramatic version of events as rendered by Mrs Parker caused a satisfying stir in the breathless courtroom.

Next, Mrs Parker continued, she was shipped on the steamer *Buninyong* to Brisbane, and held in quarantine for six weeks because of a case of smallpox aboard. All this time, she claimed, she was constantly dosed with drugs to keep her docile. Once when she tried to escape, her captors said to her, 'You've got no hope. There's three million against you.'

Finally she was booked on the *Monowai* under another name, bound for San Francisco. Her captors left her at Auckland. After the ship sailed she was given a sum of money by the purser. He had been warned that she suffered from hallucinations, and he should not take serious notice of anything she said. When the boat reached Honolulu, Mrs Parker determined to return to Melbourne at all costs, and managed to get a cheap passage back in the *Mariposa*.

In Melbourne, Mrs Parker's solicitor advised the police that she had returned voluntarily to face the forgery charge. She was arrested once again and returned to prison. Mr Panton, the elderly police magistrate, refused bail, as 'the defendant has put the court to great inconvenience.'

Mrs Parker came before Mr Justice Hood and a jury of twelve in the Criminal Court in October 1892, to face her trial. Defence witnesses identified Joseph Clarke as the man who had accompanied Mrs Parker to the house in Richmond on more than one occasion, including the date shown on the promissory notes in question.

Joseph Clarke appeared as the main prosecution witness, but cut a pathetic figure. To every question on whether he had given money or promissory notes to Mrs Parker, he replied, 'I don't remember.' When one payment of £1,500 was proved from his own books, Clarke said he could not remember whether he had taken any security for the amount. And, of course, he denied being implicated in the abduction.

When Charles Peters, the mysterious tea merchant who went under several aliases, was called as a witness, he refused to answer any questions on the ground that it might tend to incriminate him. The judge asked the Crown to note his refusal, 'whatever way this case goes.'

Thomas Charles Cooper, a Melbourne broker, apparently one of Mrs Parker's keepers on board ship, refused to answer questions for the same reason. He agreed that he knew Joseph Clarke, but would not say who had given him instructions.

Henry Grave, the solicitor, swore that he had never heard Clarke's name mentioned, and was certain Mrs Parker had left Melbourne of her own accord. After being positively identified, he admitted travelling in the same train with Mrs Parker as far as Albury, but claimed he had then brought her back at her own request.

Mr Justice Hood, in his charge to the jury, warned them strongly that they must give a verdict according to the evidence, regardless of the consequences to Joseph Clarke, Mrs Parker, or the other witnesses. After a short retirement the jury found Mrs Parker not guilty of forgery. The courtroom echoed with cheers, quickly suppressed.

Next morning the *Age* commented that 'At the first blush it appears a startling fact that a jury should have so completely discredited the testimony of a gentleman of Mr. Clarke's social standing.' The newspaper insisted that an answer must be found to the question, 'Who was the prime mover in this insolent defiance of the Supreme Court, and flagrant attempt to defeat the ends of justice?'

Henry Grave was suspended from practice as a solicitor, but there, once again, the matter rested. The Clarkes bravely tried to keep up appearances in society. When they attended the Melbourne Club Ball that year, Mrs Clarke wore 'a gown of azure satin, brocaded with shades of brown, having a petticoat of blue, draped with lovely old lace, the whole brightened by fine diamond ornaments,' while her husband stayed in close attendance.

Soon it was Mrs Parker's turn to unchain the dogs of law once again. In April 1893, she commenced an action for £10,000 damages against Joseph Clarke, alleging malicious prosecution on the forgery charge. Frank Gavan Duffy appeared for Mrs Parker; Mr Purves, Q.C., for Joseph Clarke.

Purves called handwriting experts from various banks in an attempt to prove that Mrs Parker had after all forged Clarke's signatures. He called five clerks employed by Sir William and Joseph Clarke to depose that they had never seen Joseph and Mrs Parker in company. But all in vain.

Once again Clarke ruined his defence by his demeanour in the witness box, as shown by this extract from the cross-examination:–

> *You went into land speculations to console her?*—I thought I would make money by it . . .
>
> *When the first bills were dishonoured, why did you go on giving more notes?*—I thought from what Mrs Parker told me that the swamp land would be invaluable owing to the drainage going on.
>
> *While Mrs Parker was away did you make any payments on behalf of the Kooweerup property?*—I don't know.

Then with incredible naivete, Clarke admitted having spoken to and paid Charles Peters, the tea merchant who had helped to abduct Mrs Parker.

> (Cross-examination): *You had no hand in the spiriting of the woman away?*—I never paid anyone a single sou in respect to taking her away.
>
> *Did a man named Peters tell you he had taken her away?*—He came to me and told me a story, saying that he had taken her away. I gave him a couple of pounds . . . and did not ask any questions.

Then, under Duffy's merciless examination, Clarke admitted another significant fact. He had advanced the money to a Mrs Bowes to buy the Globe Hotel at Albury, where Mrs Parker had been taken during the abduction.

> (Cross-examination): *And when Mrs Parker went away she found herself in that hotel. Is that not a curious coincidence?*—Yes, I can't account for it at all.

In his address to the jury, Duffy called Clarke 'an easy-tempered old voluptuary.' Mrs Parker had been 'a pure woman living reputably with her husband until one day she met a millionaire in the form of Joe Clarke, and that meeting marked her fall.'

Purves Q.C. retaliated by describing the whole case as 'disagreeable, prurient, and obscene.' Mrs Parker was 'a dreadful woman' who had seized upon Clarke, She was probably not the only 'harpy who followed him from public house to public house, threatening to bring false charges against him.' In short, she was 'an impudent adventuress,' and in fact that title was too good for her.

In his strongly worded charge to the jury, Mr Justice Williams said that 'If Mr Clarke knew the endorsements (on the bills) were his, and with that knowledge instituted criminal proceedings, then the act was malicious, and, in fact, could not be described in less strong terms than "diabolical" . . . For an innocent person to be placed in the criminal dock within deadly jeopardy of being convicted as a felon is enough to prostrate the mind and rack the soul with awful torture.'

The jury agreed to the extent of £1,250 damages, plus costs, against Joseph

The *Bulletin's* comment on Mrs Parker's disappearance.

Clarke. The money was not much use to Mrs Parker, because it went straight into her insolvent estate. She had, however, proved her case.

Melbourne Punch was ready with a Gilbert & Sullivan parody. The first verse ran:

JOE AND CLARA

A Disjointed Medley for Two

I have a song to sing, O!
  (Sing me your song, O!)
It's the song of a gay old clerk called Joe,
Whose smile was soft and whose laugh was low,
When Clara said—'You won't say No—
  It's all to oblige a ladye—
Heighdy—heighdy—Misere me, lack of £.s.d.'
Joe bit his lip and he sucked his thumb
  As he backed a bill for the ladye.

Two more sensations were yet to come. On 15 August 1893, Edward Parker won a decree *nisi* on the grounds of his wife's repeated adultery with Thomas Hardinge, one of her paramours. A month later, Mrs Parker caused a warrant to be issued for the arrest of Charles Peters, the tea merchant, on a charge of abduction. Peters was arrested outside the Opera House in Bourke Street, and appeared before Mr Panton, P.M., on 26 September 1893.

At these proceedings, Mrs Parker explained that she was an uncertificated insolvent, and had not been able to obtain a solicitor to conduct her case. This revealing dialogue then took place:

Mr Panton (addressing Inspector Murphy): The police can take this case up. Are you going on with it?

Murphy: Acting under instructions, I decline to take up the prosecution.

Mr Panton (with surprise): Decline!

Murphy: Well—except at your worship's direction . . .

Mr Panton (to Mrs Parker): Seeing that you are in a difficulty, and owing to the stand taken by the police, I think it would be advisable to adjourn the hearing of the case for a week . . .

The accused, stepping forward, said: Would your worship make the bail a little lighter?

Mr Panton: No.

Accused: You are unwittingly giving the people who got me into this tangle a chance of getting out of the country!

After the week's adjournment, the Crown Law Department still refused to proceed with the case, and Peters was discharged.

Nothing further was ever heard of the matter. Joseph Clarke died little more than a year later, taking the final truth with him to the grave. He was buried near where he was born, at Norton-Mandeville, Tasmania. Mrs Parker drifted into complete obscurity.

28

Sir Benjamin Benjamin and the Imperial Bank

Mayor of Melbourne during the inglorious closing years of the boom and the beginning of the depression was Sir Benjamin Benjamin, a Jewish financier of considerable rectitude. In more recent times the Lord Mayor's office has become closely associated in the public mind with charitable works. 'Bingy Bingy', as the *Bulletin* tagged him, was apparently too preoccupied in trying to make money out of his banks and land companies to be much concerned about the growing number of paupers in his municipality.

Benjamin was born in London in 1834 and brought to Melbourne at the age of nine. His early life was uneventful, and upon leaving school he went straight into his father's importing and warehouse business in Collins Street. In 1857, at the age of twenty-three, Benjamin married Fanny, daughter of Abraham Cohen of Sydney. Seven years later, he went into partnership with his uncle 'Teddy' Cohen, a tea merchant and general importer. 'Teddy' became mayor of Melbourne, and a marble tablet was erected in the old Melbourne Hospital to commemorate his work on its behalf. The alliance of Cohens and Benjamins proved a formidable one. In 1870, when only thirty-six, Benjamin was elected to the Melbourne City Council, rising slowly and surely to the mayoralty in 1887. The vigorous Jewish clan was delighted with its record of producing two Mayors of Melbourne from the one family. The Benjamins were prominent too in Jewish community affairs. Benjamin Benjamin was permanent auditor and treasurer, and several times president, of the Melbourne Hebrew Congregation.

From about 1885 onwards Benjamin began speculating in land and shares, using a £60,000 inheritance in an attempt to make a dramatic coup which would astonish the family. He operated mainly through a leading firm of auctioneers, Messrs Bradley and Curtain—who had a silent third partner named James Clarke. Clarke was an estate agent of wide and devious experience, who had already gone bankrupt once, back in 1867. In later years he took over the licence of the Talbot Hotel in Swanston Street. When the land boom developed, Clarke sought a way back into the financial world through his intermediaries, Bradley and Curtain. All the time that Benjamin Benjamin was trying to make easy money through the estate agents' firm, this crafty financier was secretly waiting to make money out of *him*. No wonder Benjamin cried out in anguished voice in the witness box, 'I was led into a trap!'

Sir Benjamin Benjamin and Lady Benjamin, Mayor and Mayoress of Melbourne in the great years of the boom.

Prompted by the Machiavellian Clarke, Bradley and Curtain advised Benjamin that he should float a banking company to raise enough money for really important land deals. What was more, they knew a brilliant financier who would manage the bank for him. This proved to be James Clarke himself, who quickly doffed his publican's checked suit and just as quickly donned the sober broadcloth of a respectable banker. Moreover, said Bradley and Curtain, a bank must have a valuator and an auditor. Who better than Messrs Bradley and Curtain? So it was arranged. The grandiloquent title selected was the Imperial Banking Co. Ltd.

This incredible company structure paddled before the bemused eyes of the investing public early in 1886, and rowed away downstream bearing with it nearly £200,000 of the public's money. This was all deposits, the paid-up capital of the bank being precisely one golden sovereign. As fellow directors in this bold enterprise, Benjamin had Thomas Hunt, M.L.A. for Kilmore; John McGee, a wine and spirit merchant; Hugh Myles Phillips, another merchant; and George Withers, Melbourne manager of the P. & O. Steam Navigation Company. Poor Withers was not long unwrung. Along with Benjamin, he gave his personal guarantee to the Bank of South Australia for £20,000, being a cash loan to start off the Imperial Bank. When both banks crashed, Withers was forced to make a secret composition, paying £1,000 in discharge of his total of £42,000 liabilities.

The Imperial Bank's professed purposes were to advance on real estate by mortgage and by the building society system. A slight digression tells the sorry story of its associated Imperial Building Society. Another member of the profligate tribe of estate agents, Louis Charles Wilkinson, was appointed secretary. Wilkinson borrowed more than £10,000 of the society's funds for his own speculations; plus £5,000 from J. Winter-Irving; £3,000 from the Mercantile Bank, and £1,300 from the City of Melbourne Building Society. When these loans, plus calls on his shares, totalled £30,000, Wilkinson called it a day and filed his schedule in the Insolvency Court.

Meanwhile, however, the Imperial Bank paddled merrily on. Its main activity was to buy at inflated prices a number of tracts of land owned by Bradley and Curtain, which they were unable to sell profitably by other means. In a typical example, James Clarke, manager of the bank and secret partner of Bradley and Curtain, cheerfully paid out £50,000 of depositors' money for a half-acre at the corner of Lonsdale and King Streets, occupied by Stephenson & Elliott's carriage works. The apparent owners: Messrs Bradley and Curtain. The real owner: James Clarke, who had bought the land for £10,000 less.

Another £20,000 was paid to a bankrupt land firm, the Royal Land Co. Ltd (liquidated by Curtain himself), for land at Mitcham and Mornington. The bank realized precisely £409 from the sale of this land, representing a loss of £19,600 on the transaction. Another £33,000 of the money which came in from a gullible public was re-loaned to Bradley, Curtain, and their relatives and children to enable them to take up shares in the bank.

In a delightfully vague manner, Benjamin Benjamin left the entire running of the Imperial Bank to Clarke, Bradley and Curtain, while concentrating on his other business interests and mayoral duties. He bought a large block of shares in the Country Estates Co. Ltd, the log-rolling enterprise of sundry politicians

Deposit form used by Bradley & Curtain for their land sales carried a picture of Queen Victoria and could be mistaken for a valuable piece of paper.

and estate agents. Then he bought into the tramway boom. Messrs Wright & Edwards, a small engineering firm of Little Bourke Street, had patented a process for shaping out of old rails the 'yokes' used by the thousand in building tramway cable tunnels. Benjamin heard about the process, and persuaded Wright & Edwards to allow him to float their little firm into a £125,000 public company. Benjamin became the first chairman of directors in 1888, and the two engineers congratulated themselves on their great good fortune. Six weeks before the 1891 general meeting, Benjamin resigned, 'deaf to all remonstrance', and the company's losses for the year were found to be in the vicinity of £40,000.

Benjamin's knighthood followed his three successive years as Lord Mayor. He was invited to grace the boardroom of Sir William Clarke's Colonial Bank, but was soon forced to resign this position when his personal financial difficulties became acute. During the heyday of the boom, Sir Benjamin had tried to ensure that other members of the family were not left out of the easy money. The young solicitor, Maurice Edward Benjamin, was put on to many good things, Sir Benjamin guaranteeing his promissory notes. Maurice Benjamin also brought his solicitor-partner, Edward Hart, into many of the speculations. In the end they showed a total deficiency of £22,000, and paid their creditors 1d. in the £1 by way of secret composition.

Meanwhile, the Imperial Bank's accountant, John Francis O'Shea, and a teller, Alfred Teale, were operating their own private swindle. O'Shea and Teale were altering figures in the day cash book—£1 being changed to £21, for instance—pocketing the difference, and using the money for speculation. Altogether they embezzled nearly £20,000 before an outside auditor reported the thefts. O'Shea and Teale were both sentenced to four years' imprisonment, some of it in solitary confinement. 'Larceny is the meanest and most dangerous of human weaknesses', said the Chief Justice. 'Those who go in for speculation without the means to pursue it are dishonest.'

The Imperial Bank suspended payment on 23 July 1891, following a run on the Geelong branch which showed signs of spreading to Melbourne. At least, that was the published reason, but stories soon began to spread that by going into voluntary liquidation, the bank was trying to hide its real position. These fears were intensified by the fact that the bank's manager, James Clarke, termed quite openly by *Table Talk* as 'belonging to the genus *oily gammon*', was one of the liquidators.

At an angry meeting of depositors, Nathaniel Levi, M.L.C., stood up and said: 'I felt just as if I had been garrotted in the street and robbed of my thousand pounds' deposit!' The bank, he claimed, had closed with precisely £30. 6s. 6d. left in its possession. Levi was too gentlemanly to add that he had personally lent Sir Benjamin several thousand pounds, and was justifiably dubious about his prospects of getting it back. Another depositor, J. Stewart, cried:

> They tell me that I am to be liable for some contributing shares. I want nothing to be done but what is honest . . . *Be merciful!* There are many women—ladies—in the bank, and they want time. I have tried to make provision for my own daughter, who has been a slave in my own family, and it is all gone, and not only that, but I have to pay more. If I had the deposit it would help me; but there, I suppose the

Thomas Hunt, M.L.A., a director of the Imperial Bank.

L. C. Wilkinson, secretary of the Imperial Building Society.

Nathaniel Levi, M.L.C., who felt as if he had been 'garrotted in the street'.

> deposit is gone, and I can get nothing of it . . . We want only mercy, justice, and temperance.

Yet another chastened depositor said:

> I came here a few years ago, having left several thousands of pounds safely invested in England. Seeing this Imperial Bank, with the mayor of your city at its head, I thought it a respectable institution, and sent for my money from England, lodged it here, and now it is gone.

So a court investigation was forced on the reluctant liquidators. Some extraordinary facts were elicited. Details of Bradley's and Curtain's accounts had been cut out of the bank's books. James Clarke did not agree that this was a 'marvellous coincidence'. Sir Benjamin admitted that he had transferred 20,000 of his shares to Bradley and Curtain. Although they were only paid up to 2s. 6d., the directors had authorized advances of 17s. 6d. on each share. Still, said Sir Benjamin, 'my word has always been my bond', and 'no deception or fraud was intended'. Such was the state of the banking laws that no further prosecutions were launched. Benjamin, Bradley, Curtain and Clarke merely went bankrupt, thus robbing the creditors of further large sums.

Bernard Bradley's schedule, filed in February 1892, showed total debts of £60,000. Of this, more than £50,000 was owing to the Imperial Bank for loans on overdraft and loans to purchase shares in the bank. Robert John Curtain's schedule, filed the same day, disclosed debts of £56,000, largely for the same reasons. James Clarke, the bank's manager, filed his schedule in September 1893. It transpired that he had advanced himself £36,000 from his own bank. In addition, he had personally borrowed more than £17,000 from the ever-willing Bank of South Australia. All these amounts had disappeared into the maw of the land boom. A year later, Clarke asked Judge Molesworth for a certificate of release from insolvency. The judge angrily refused to grant it until Clarke paid back his creditors at least 7s. in the £1. Since he owed a total of £55,000, the task was formidable.

When Sir Benjamin Benjamin filed his own sad schedule, it was shown that

"THE YOUNG MAN FROM THE COUNTRY."

Sir Benjy.– Never again. I've been had once by those shrewd financial coves, but never again!

in addition to losing the family fortune of £60,000, he had also accumulated debts of nearly £50,000 extra. Substantial institutions such as the Bank of New South Wales and the Scottish Life Assurance Society had advanced him nearly £10,000 each. The balance was for various guarantees and calls on worthless shares in such enterprises as the Mercantile Bank, Metropolitan Bank, and Real Estate Bank. Sir Benjamin's creditors agreed to accept 1s. in the £1, and he was released from sequestration within six months. The creditors allowed him to stay on in his large red brick mansion at 172 George Street, East Melbourne. (The house still stands, but is now known as 'Koorine Flats'.)

The *Bulletin*, as usual, had the last word on Sir Benjamin Benjamin:

> The cash qualification for knighthood, which enables the gaudy snob to obtain a State licence for snobbery is peculiarly hateful—hateful whilst the knight retains his qualification, and ridiculous into the bargain when he files his schedule, or is accused of having made his money by unknightly means . . . The cash and the knighthood were cause and effect. The cause has collapsed, but the miserable effect remains.

The collapse of Sir Benjamin Benjamin's Imperial Bank also brought down the Bank of South Australia. The latter bank had an old and honorable history, being connected with South Australia from its earliest pioneering days. But when the Imperial crashed, leaving £92,000 owing to the Bank of S.A., a number of peculiar rumours began to circulate about the S.A.s involvement in the land boom.

The London board had appointed Arthur Geoffrey Eagar as the bank's Melbourne manager, with full power to decide local policy. From 1888 onwards, Eagar instituted an extravagant policy of loans to speculators. Although an upper limit of £100,000 had been imposed, Eagar immediately loaned this amount to one person alone—Frederick Illingworth of the Centennial Bank. Large amounts also went to other investors.

The S.A.s Colonial Inspector, J. W. Meldrum, protested vigorously to London. When his warnings were ignored, he resigned on the ground of 'ill-health'. The London directors replaced him with James Ogilvy, Melbourne manager of the Oriental Bank, which was already in serious trouble because of its advances to land boomers. Not only that, the directors increased Eagar's limit to £750,000, authorised him to begin the issue of bank notes, and circulated a report to shareholders about the great success of their Melbourne branch.

Thus encouraged, Eagar proceeded to lend the Imperial Bank its £92,000, plus another £17,000 to its manager, James Clarke, on his personal account, plus sundry amounts to speculators like B. J. Fink, Thomas Fischer, John Harris, William Lamb Smith, and many others who made secret compositions.

The boom collapsed and the boomers ceased to make their payments. Nevertheless the London board issued a false balance sheet in April 1891, purporting to show a trading profit of £48,000 for the year, most of which was quickly paid out in 'dividends' taken from capital as a means of maintaining confidence.

With the failure of the Imperial Bank three months later, it seemed that the facts must emerge. Rumour forced the S.A.s shares down from £25 to £14. The

A. G. Eagar (right) built this weekend cottage at Kyneton, and a Malvern mansion.

directors decided to issue a further optimistic statement, claiming that the Imperial's debt was their only doubtful one, and even that was secured several times over (it wasn't).

Table Talk vigorously attacked the bank's lack of candour, but its shares crept up again to £17. A few weeks later, the shareholders were stunned to hear that Eagar had quit the bank and gone into hiding. The Adelaide directors, hastily summoned to investigate affairs in Melbourne, were faced at last with the melancholy truth: every penny had gone. The whole of the reserve fund, the whole of the current income—all had to be appropriated to meet an estimated loss of £340,000. In addition, £6 per share had to be written off the value of the subscribed capital.

Even these drastic moves could not save the bank. In 1892 all doubtful business was written off and the remaining skeleton absorbed by the Union Bank. The main benefit to the Union Bank was the additional twenty-four branches it acquired in South Australia; a disadvantage was the odium now surrounding the Bank of S.A. which no doubt helped to start the run on the Union Bank the following year.

A. G. Eagar crept back to Melbourne in 1893 to make a secret composition with his creditors. His personal debts totalled about £10,000, on which he paid only 6d. in the £1. The documents reveal that he had borrowed heavily from the Mercantile Bank. Curiously enough, the Bank of S.A., while Eagar was manager, had loaned £12,000 to J. B. Davies, brother of the Mercantile Bank's controller. This amounted to a friendly arrangement between two bankers to lend each other their depositors' money. But the procedure of secret composition saved both Eagar and Davies from that shameful revelation.

29

C. R. Staples and the Anglo-Australian Bank

While the Mayor of Melbourne was struggling in a trap of his own making, the entire board of directors of another Melbourne institution, the Anglo-Australian Bank, was engaged in a devious conspiracy to defraud its depositors. The pivotal figure in this scheme was Charles Raymond Staples, who came to Melbourne from Sydney in the 1870s with his brother, John Richard Staples. Charles first ventured into dairy farming near Melbourne, but went bankrupt in 1880. After that he got a job as a clerk in the National Bank; while John was employed as a legal accountant by an energetic young solicitor named Matthew Davies.

John Staples assiduously studied his chief's techniques of money-raising and speculation. After a time the brothers proposed to J. H. Wise, manager of the well-known Collins Street auctioneering house of Beauchamp Brothers, that they should go into business together. Thus the finance and agency firm of Staples, Wise & Co. was born. It borrowed money and bought about £150,000 worth of land on mortgage at Laverton, Mooroolbark, Mitcham, Waterloo, and elsewhere.

These broad acres, bought on terms, were then subdivided and offered for sale in the usual manner on low deposits. To help things along, C. R. Staples published in 1886 a small book called *Laverton, the New and Model Suburb*, an early exercise in public relations techniques which somehow neglected to mention that the 'suburb' consisted of exactly one house. Nevertheless, the partnership's land sales at Laverton were conducted in a spirit of extraordinary generosity. The paddocks were situated near the main line from Geelong to Melbourne, thirty minutes by train from the city, 'thus being practically as near as Caulfield, Brighton, and other favourite suburbs'. On the wide bare acres, Staples, Wise & Co. sold allotments for the full price of £10 each. The deposit was one sovereign, and payments were 10s. monthly. In addition, the partners offered to build houses free of interest, advancing 75 per cent of the total cost themselves.

Stage two came in 1888, when the business was floated into a public company under the name of the Victorian Freehold Bank Ltd. Very soon the company decided to enter the contest for London deposits, and changed its title to the British Bank of Australia Ltd. Capital was fixed at £1 million. The land for which Staples, Wise & Co. had contracted to pay about £150,000 was taken over by the new bank for £207,000. The difference went into the pockets of Wise and the Staples brothers. Wise had the uncommon foresight to take out his share and retire from the land boom. The two Staples, with greater faith in the value of property, bought shares in the bank instead.

The British Bank inveigled on to its London board Sir E. H. Galsworthy, Sir Frederick Young, and other prominent men, and soon had attracted nearly £150,000 in British deposits. Australian directors included the Staples brothers; F. H. Tuthill, M.L.A.; and Adye Douglas. Douglas later confessed in print that he had asked the British Bank's manager, W. Kelty, whether he could advise his friends to put their money in the bank. Kelty gave the enigmatic reply that 'the bank was never in a better position'. Most of the British Bank's early deposits were invested in further land purchases, including tracts at Cut Paw Paw bought from Sir William Clarke for £60,000, and other blocks bought at high prices from F. T. Derham and Dr George LeFevre. It would be pointless to list all of its innumerable and grossly inflated transactions. The big speculators were selling to the medium speculators, the medium speculators were selling to the small speculators, and madness was in the air.

As time went by, the British Bank soon found itself in difficulties. Its main assets—tracts of land in the suburbs—could no longer be sold easily by auction. To maintain an appearance of prosperity, Charles Staples suggested forming a further company to make dummy purchases of land from the bank. Fortunately for himself, John Staples refused to participate in the new company, so Charles went ahead in conjunction with a smart city auctioneer named Robert Dilly. This new company was called the Anglo-Australian Investment & Banking Co. Ltd; nominal capital £1 million. It is worth dwelling for a moment on the names of the signatories to the memorandum of association, for most of these gentlemen were sentenced to long terms of imprisonment for their part in the subsequent events. The members were: Charles Raymond Staples, banker; Robert William Dilly, auctioneer; Francis Edward Norwood, accountant; John Haraldson, accountant; and Sydney Gunn Allwright, gentleman.

John Haraldson was a youthful book-keeper who was anxious to make extra money to support his aged mother. Staples made the ambitious lad manager of the new bank, and gave him clear daily instructions on how to conceal the bank's real function. Allwright was a nephew of the Staples, little more than a boy when he first came to Melbourne from a New South Wales farm. Staples induced the young man to stay in Melbourne as a director at £150 a year. At board meetings Allwright invariably voted as Staples instructed him, and at other times earned a salary by helping in the bank.

When it opened its own London office, the Anglo-Australian Bank was able to induce Lord Camoys, and the Hon. Ashley Ponsonby, to lend the lustre of their names to its London board. Nearly forty deposit agencies were opened in the United Kingdom, and more than £100,000 had soon been removed from the open purses of British investors. The Anglo-Australian Bank now proceeded to buy from the British Bank about £90,000 worth of its unsaleable properties.

C. R. Staples, chairman of the Anglo-Australian Bank, induced titled Englishmen to join the London board.

John Haraldson, the young book-keeper whom Staples appointed Melbourne manager of the bank.

Selling up Laverton (Vic.) at £10 a block – but only a few houses were ever built there.

LAVERTON

THE

New and Model Suburb

OF MELBOURNE.

ALLOTMENTS £10 EACH.

£1 Per Lot Deposit,

BALANCE,

10s. Per Lot Per Month,

With Interest at 6 per cent.

LAVERTON

Is situate on the main Melbourne and Geelong Railway Line, within Thirty Minutes by train of the city, thus being practically as near as Caulfield, Surrey Hills, Brighton, Williamstown, and other favourite suburbs.

WONDERFUL FACILITIES

Offered to purchasers who desire to build.

75 per cent. of the money required for the erection of a house advanced for four years

Without Any Interest Whatever.

REMEMBER!

ONLY £10 Per ALLOTMENT,

PAYABLE £1 DEPOSIT,

Balance by Instalments of 10s. per Lot Monthly

TITLE, CROWN CERTIFICATE,

Which will be handed to purchasers at a cost of £2 10s. in full.

Free Deeds to Buyers of Five Allotments.

Solicitors—Messrs. PENTLAND and ROBERTS, Chancery Lane, Melbourne.

Illustrated pamphlet, with plans and all particulars, post free, on application to

STAPLES, WISE & CO.,

111 ELIZABETH STREET.

The Anglo-Australian Bank also bought up more than half the other bank's shares through dummies, thus propping up their price in the fluctuating market.

As the land and share market kept edging further downwards, Charles Staples went to his brother's former employer, Sir Matthew Davies, and asked him to help. Davies gave him £12,000 from the Mercantile Bank's funds. The security: shares in the British Bank and a mortgage on land at Footscray. But the money could not save the bank. By August 1891 deposits had fallen away and the Anglo-Australian Bank was no longer able to meet its commitments. A compulsory liquidation was ordered by Mr Justice à Beckett on the petition of a creditor, the Australian Financial Agency & Guarantee Co. Ltd.

Handing down his decision, the judge drew attention to an advertisement by the company which stated that 'The Bank is prohibited from purchasing or dealing in land, freehold property, stocks or shares of any kind whatever.' At this time, said the judge, the bank owed more than £300,000 for land it had bought and was trying to resell. 'From what has been disclosed as to the management of the company, trickery in attempting to conceal or to escape from liability may not unreasonably be expected from those who managed it', he concluded.

Taking heed of the clear warning, Charles Staples and John Haraldson promptly disappeared from Melbourne. The official liquidator, Colonel Templeton, then discovered that although the bank's paid-up capital had been publicized as £110,000, in fact only £37. 10s. had been paid up. The bank had been kept going only by the constant infusion of fresh deposits and debenture money, out of which about £40,000 in 'dividends' had been paid to Staples and his friends within three years. All told, it appeared, the directors had got away with more than £100,000 in hard cash, including an overdraft for £70,000 on which the only securities were worthless shares in the British Bank. Colonel Templeton tried to collect the uncalled capital of the British Bank, in order to help pay back the depositors. Instead of the £350,000 owing, he received less than £10,000. Depositors were repaid 3d. in the £1.

For a time it seemed that the government would try to ignore the public clamour for prosecution, and even Mr Justice à Beckett's broad hints of fraudulent practice. The Attorney-General, William Shiels, announced in Parliament that 'the Government will take no steps to initiate prosecutions against the persons implicated in the recent financial scandals in the city.' In other words, where liquidators found evidence of criminal offences, they must take the responsibility of laying the information themselves. Public and press were enraged at the government's frank abdication of its responsibility to uphold the law. The Premier, James Munro, was forced to add a rider to Shiels' statement within a few days: that 'on a complaint being made and properly authenticated,' he would look at the matter.

Munro's statement was read with great interest at Pentridge Gaol. John Hogan, an elderly warder, wrote to Shiels, stating that he had been ruined by depositing his £900 savings in the Anglo-Australian Bank after being persuaded by misleading statements in the bank's published balance sheet. True to form,

Shiels did nothing. Warder Hogan thereupon took his complaint to the *Evening Standard* office, which published his allegations. The government was at last forced to act. Charles Staples, the bank's chairman, and John Haraldson, the manager, were located in Sydney and arrested on a charge of conspiring to issue a false balance sheet.

As the liquidators and Crown Law officers dug deeper, they discovered that all the bank's directors and chief officers were involved. So they also arrested Robert Dilly and Sydney Allwright, directors; and Francis Norwood, auditor. In March 1893 all were tried on eighteen counts of issuing a false report and balance sheet with intent to defraud. Only a few witnesses were needed to prove the prosecution's case. Warder Hogan said he had spoken to the bank's manager, John Haraldson, who told him he had just returned from London, where a very strong directorate had been formed, including Lord Camoys. Asked to tell the court whether he thought Lord Camoys a substantial man because he was a lord, Hogan replied: 'I suppose lords are blackguards, the same as everybody else. I've been dealing with a good many lords the last 27 years, I can assure you, and kept them in good order too.'

In a statement to the court, Staples claimed that he had acted honestly throughout:

> After the bank went into liquidation, I tried to do business in Melbourne and Sydney, then went to San Francisco. On learning there was likely to be trouble about the bank, I took the next steamer back to Australia, although in 24 hours I could have crossed the border into Mexico and defied British law.

His protestations were in vain. Mr Justice Hood sentenced Staples to the maximum of five years' imprisonment, adding that he would have increased the sentence if Parliament had made the offence a felony instead of a misdemeanour. Norwood was given two years' imprisonment for lending his name to false purchases. John Haraldson, the youthful manager whose aged mother wept in court throughout the proceedings, was sentenced to six months' hard labour. While he had concurred in criminal practice, said the judge, he was not 'one of those fraudulent criminals who attempt to make money out of their crime'. Of the other directors, Dilly was sentenced to two years' hard labour for his part in unloading the British Bank's land on to the Anglo-Australian Bank. Allwright, the farmer lad who had played at bank directing, was fined £100. When the prisoners begged for leniency, the judge thundered: 'Against ordinary thieves the public can to some extent protect themselves, but when the robber conceals himself under a mask of respectability, trust and confidence, there can be no safeguard, and the only remedy is severe punishment following on detection.'

Charles Staples was released from gaol after serving less than three years of his sentence, and became an accountant in Sydney. He filed his schedule in insolvency in February 1896. His debts totalled £415,000 and his assets £195,000. Thus his spell in gaol probably helped his creditors somewhat. When he came out and settled his affairs, his land could be sold for considerably more than at the time he had been sentenced.

30

Henry Hayter and the Metropolitan Bank

Even in these sophisticated times, the news that a government statistician had gone bankrupt for a large sum might be expected to cause a little comment. If it were shown that he had borrowed and lost substantial amounts on share transactions, the comment might become rather sharp. If it were further shown that this important government official was also a director of a private bank which lent him most of the money, the matter might even provoke a question in Parliament.

All these things happened in Melbourne during the land boom, but there were no pointed comments and no questions in Parliament. Politicians on both sides of the House were seemingly just as anxious to conceal the scandal as the government official involved. This official was none other than Henry Heylyn Hayter, widely respected until this day as Victoria's first and most famous Government Statist. Henry Hayter, born in England and educated in Paris, emigrated to Victoria in 1852 at the age of thirty-one. At about the same period, a number of Melbourne businessmen were planning the formation of the Metropolitan Permanent Building Society, which was registered in 1854 and became the colony's most successful cottage-building enterprise. Thirty years later it was to become a fatal factor in Hayter's downfall.

First, however, Hayter had to build himself a position in the raw colonial society. In 1855 he married Susan Dodd, daughter of a London merchant, and two years later joined the Public Service as an official of the Registrar-General's Department. In 1870 he was appointed secretary of a Royal Commission which laid the foundations for reforming the public service. The following year he successfully carried out a complete census of the colony's state of development. In 1874 the Statistical Branch was separated from the Registrar-General's Office. Hayter was the natural man to put in charge of the new department. The same year Hayter published the first edition of that invaluable reference work, the *Victorian Year Book*. Soon his clear, unambiguous methods of collecting and publishing vital statistics were being copied by other colonies. In a statistical sense, the Australian colonies could now see more or less where they were going—although sometimes it seemed to be backwards instead of forwards.

Hayter's undoubted mastery of social trends makes his subsequent history all the more puzzling. Many people untrained in the analysis of banking, production

Henry Heylyn Hayter, Government Statist, founder of the *Victorian Year Book* – and secret land boomer.

NO "RUN" FOR HIM.

ALGY: "Bad time for bankers in Australia, dear boy, I wonder you don't clear out!"

ERNIE (*officer in a rocky bank*): "Cawnt, ole feller; the customers haven't left enough money."

and export-import figures could see that a major crash must inevitably follow the excesses of the boom. Hayter not only failed to see it, but allowed himself to get personally involved in boom finance to a disastrous and incredibly foolish degree.

We come now to the year 1887. The Metropolitan Building Society was doing splendid work, building hundreds of cottages for artisans in Richmond, Collingwood, and other suburbs. They were being sold on only £10 deposit and low weekly payments, the theory being that if a labourer fell ill or lost his job, the cottage could be repossessed and resold to another workman and his family. No one envisaged the position arising where every second artisan in these suburbs would be unemployed for years on end, and cottages would be selling for a fraction of their true value.

While the boom continued, the Metropolitan Building Society was doing so well out of its cottages, and earning so much interest on its money, that depositors seeking a 'safe, reliable investment' paid a total of £470,000 into its funds. Business was so brisk that the society's directors decided to capitalize on the society's reputation by forming a bank with practically the same name. In this manner, the Metropolitan Bank was incorporated in 1887. It purchased the old Athenaeum Club and adjoining premises in the heart of Collins Street for its offices (today forming the Centreway Buildings). Directors were the same in both the building society and the bank—Messrs Orlando Fenwick, James Callaghan, James Dodgshun, Alexander Gillespie, H. A. Hendren, John Manson—and Henry Hayter. It was a great victory for these businessmen to have persuaded the Government Statist to join their boards. What better guarantee could there be of the regularity of their financial methods?

There is some doubt whether Hayter made many enquiries about the bank's affairs at this stage. He was more deeply interested in his statistics, his books of mediocre verse (*My Christmas Adventure*, etc.), and such activities as the first meeting in 1888 of the Australasian Association for the Advancement of Science. Nevertheless, Hayter was also ambitious in a business sense. So the keen businessmen of Melbourne took Henry Hayter, the great statistical genius, along for the ride. The bank's chairman, Orlando Fenwick, a warehouseman who was also a director of the Modern Permanent Building Society, was a key figure in the disgraceful events which followed. Another was Robert Glover Benson, the bank's manager, who died at the height of the crisis leaving an estate of £28,000.

The *modus operandi* for the flotation of the new bank was as follows. The bank took control of the Metropolitan Building Society, thus gaining access to its huge funds. In satisfaction of this 'takeover', shares in the new bank were allotted to the building society. Even though it had an impressive board of directors, the bank found some difficulty in getting all its shares taken up when it first entered the market. To overcome this weakness, and to strengthen the price of the bank's shares, large overdrafts were given to the directors for the purpose of buying their own bank's shares through dummies on the open market. This quite illegal procedure drew caustic criticism some years later, but no criminal prosecutions were undertaken on this or other matters connected with the Metropolitan Bank and its building society.

By March 1891 the directors and manager held between them 46,000 of the bank's total of 130,000 £5 shares. In other words, they had lent themselves more than £200,000 of depositors' money in order to purchase the bank's own shares. Henry Hayter's share of this was £32,000. Benson, the manager, was due for nearly £70,000. Orlando Fenwick, the chairman, had more than £36,000 worth of the shares—practically all bought with money belonging to the bank and the building society. The arrangement paid off handsomely for a time. The Metropolitan Bank was widely regarded as 'a good investment', and the price of its shares stayed high even when other stocks had begun to fall. Trusting investors placed nearly £1 million on deposit with the bank. This amount and more was loaned out on overdraft, often on inferior security such as land valued at unreal prices. By early 1891 the bank was regarded in such favourable light that it joined the august ranks of the 'Banks of Issue', and started issuing its own bank notes.

Events far beyond the bank's control were, however, now beginning to take effect. The boom collapsed, and investors began to worry about the safety of their money. The bank and building society were forced to close their doors on 3 December 1891, following the first rumours about the bank's soundness and a run during which panic-stricken depositors withdrew more than £200,000 of their cash. Three months later, a shareholders' meeting decided to put the institutions into voluntary liquidation. Since the directors controlled a huge block of shares through their proxies, they were able to defeat a motion calling for a searching investigation. The manager, two directors, and another large shareholder were appointed liquidators. These liquidators took more than a year to 'investigate' the condition of their own bank and report back to shareholders. Then they called a meeting, but neglected to send circulars to the shareholders advising them of the time and place. Those shareholders who read about the meeting in the press were refused copies of the liquidators' report for their perusal. And those few who were able to study the figures at the meeting discovered that the balance sheet had not been audited.

Finally the long-suffering shareholders took matters into their own hands, held another meeting, and ordered the two remaining liquidators to wind up the two institutions forthwith. It was thus discovered that liabilities of both bank and building society totalled nearly £2 million. Calls on shares to meet the deficit produced very little cash. The fine Collins Street premises had to be handed over to the mortgagor, the Bank of New South Wales, and the society's 650 workmen's cottages were thrown on to an adverse market.

When the bank's troubles began, Hayter quite properly asked the government to release him from his official position. Cabinet persuaded him to stay and conduct the 1891 census. By the time that was completed, it was too late for Hayter to retire gracefully. The bank had smashed, certain revelations about its past activities began to appear, and the government was faced with the fact that one of its top civil servants was undeniably insolvent, if not worse. Here was a pretty situation! Hayter's own Royal Commission into the Public Service, and James Service's spring-cleaning Public Service Act of 1883, had been insistent that no uncertificated insolvent should be permitted to hold a permanent position in the civil service. Now a man who had given his whole life to the establishment of orderly government was to be tested. What did he do?

The shameful fact must be recorded that Henry Heylyn Hayter, with the connivance of the government and the initial liquidators of the Metropolitan Bank, managed to hold off his insolvency for three years—and then was allowed to make a secret composition so that the truth could be concealed from the public. In June 1894 this secret composition was put through by the Chief Clerk of the Insolvency Court. It showed £36,000 in debts, mostly to the Metropolitan Bank, and allowed for payment of 3d. in the £1. By this time Hayter had developed cancer. He died the following year, with many fine publications to his credit, but none telling us the true story of high finance in the 1890s.

31

Colin Longmuir and the City of Melbourne Bank

Today a branch of the Australia and New Zealand Bank stands on the south-eastern corner of Collins and Elizabeth Streets, Melbourne. Nothing but banking business of the highest respectability is ever conducted within its portals. How different it was on this corner in the 1880s, when the City of Melbourne Bank pushed its Victorian cupola skywards and backed the land boom with every penny of its depositors' money and all its shareholders' capital! Through its doors strode Benjamin Fink, C. H. James, and other mighty financiers of the day. They were lent millions to invest in speculative ventures, lost it all, and brought the bank crashing to the ground. The manager was found dead *en route* to Colombo; the directors and auditors were charged with criminal offences.

The City of Melbourne Bank was formed in 1873 to take over a finance company started by one Cunningham, a former National Bank manager. Its first directors, who stayed with it until the bitter end, were the Hon. Thomas Loader (also chairman of the Mutual Assurance Society), John Ferguson, and John Lloyd Roberts. Two years after they commenced business, the directors appointed to their staff a thirty-year-old accountant, Colin Milne Longmuir. Longmuir was a son of the Rev. John Longmuir, A.M., LL.D., of Aberdeen. He had worked in the Union Bank of Scotland and the Oriental Bank before migrating to Australia.

A serious run took place on the City of Melbourne Bank in 1879, following the exposure of frauds in connection with the Provincial & Suburban Bank. This institution kept its account at the City Bank, and depositors feared they would be liable for the Provincial's illegal note issue. The City Bank's managing director, John Young, resigned, and Colin Longmuir's chance came. He was appointed general manager at the age of thirty-five—the youngest manager of a major bank in the Australian colonies. Five years later, Longmuir brought off what was regarded as a great banking coup. He took over Benjamin Fink's Joint Stock Bank of Ballarat, amalgamating its business with the City Bank. Soon the enlarged bank was one of the biggest buyers of gold in the colony. But another part of the deal was not disclosed for some years. As well as taking over his bank, Longmuir agreed to finance Fink in a wide variety of enterprises.

In 1886 the City Bank's capital was increased to £1 million, consisting of £5 shares paid up to £2. 10s. each. The bank bought the old Clarence Hotel, a landmark of early Melbourne. On the site it built a massive four-storey headquarters, described by *The Picturesque Atlas of Australasia* as:

> a very conspicuous object, owing to the cupola of the tower, erected at the north-west angle of the structure, which rises to the height of 113 feet above the pavement. The two faces of the edifice, in Elizabeth and Collins Streets, each exhibit a Corinthian colonnade, resting upon a bluestone base or podium seven feet high, the columns themselves extending to the summit of the first storey, being thirty feet high.

Inside this impressive building, the youthful general manager planned the methods by which he could make a private fortune, help his friends, and keep the bank's shareholders in comparative ignorance of events. He succeeded only too well. In 1887 Longmuir appeared before the Royal Commission on Banking, and made a fervent plea for a change in the law which would enable banks to speculate in land. With the aid of such evidence, the banking laws were changed, and many of the leading banks leaped into an orgy of speculation. At the City Bank Longmuir lent nearly a million pounds to three borrowers alone—and this on a paid-up capital of only £500,000! David Munro & Co. Ltd got £400,000; Benjamin Fink, £310,000; M. W. Fergusson, £290,000. Longmuir himself took £75,000.

In September 1892, after B. J. Fink arranged his composition of ½d. in the £1, the London directors cabled: *Are you involved in the failure of Fink? To what extent?* Longmuir cabled back, misleadingly: *Overdrafts and discounts £57,000. We are fully covered. Three other Associated Banks heavier amounts.* By this time most of the bank's big customers were hopelessly insolvent and the bank itself was ruined. In October 1892 Longmuir presented his directors with a false balance sheet which encouraged them to declare a 10 per cent dividend. Six months later he gave them another fraudulent balance sheet which enabled them to declare an additional 8 per cent dividend—making a total of 18 per cent in one of the worst years on record.

The chairman, Thomas Loader, poured scorn on those depositors who had taken fright and were withdrawing their money. 'It is nothing short of mania for people to take a scare, the reason for which they do not know', he told the half-yearly meeting in April 1893. 'We have a profitable business, and its prosperity is dependent upon the confidence reposed in it by the shareholders and depositors.' Simon Fraser, M.L.C., told the meeting that the bank was a thoroughly sound one—(cheers)—and he asked the shareholders not to sell a single share (cheers). Fraser did not mention that Fraser & Co. Ltd had been given a £90,000 loan by the City Bank. W. A. Zeal, M.L.C., advised them not to pay attention to those 'sudden rumours' which had no foundation in fact, and which were 'perfectly baseless'. Colin Longmuir, the trusty young manager, sat there solemnly, his features composed behind his gigantic walrus moustache. Even while these directors and politicians were soothing the shareholders, his employees were down at the stock exchanges, bidding high prices for any City

An early run on the City of Melbourne Bank.

C. M. Longmuir, general manager of the City of Melbourne Bank, disappeared at sea.

Simon Fraser, M.L.C., was loaned £90,000 by the City of Melbourne Bank.

Thomas Loader, chairman of the bank, advised depositors not to 'take a scare'.

Bank shares which came on the market—and buying them with the bank's own funds. In all, nearly 10,000 shares were purchased by employees as dummies.

Three weeks later came the crash. The Scottish investors, alarmed by persistent rumours from Melbourne, refused almost to a man to renew their deposits which fell due in May. Since their deposits totalled £3,260,000, as against £1,470,000 colonial deposits, the bank was finished. On 17 May 1893 the bank closed its doors and announced that 'reconstruction' would follow. Its liquidators: Colin Longmuir himself, and William Robertson, the bank's secretary. A new company was formed with the same directors and officials. Certain ordinary shares were converted into preference shares and capital was written down.

The bank reopened its doors and resumed business. But the suspicions of the British depositors could not be allayed. They appointed Edmund W. Rouse, the bank's London manager, to investigate its affairs. Rouse asked Longmuir to visit London to explain certain matters. In May 1894 Longmuir embarked on the *Arcadia*. From Albany, W.A., he wrote to friends in Melbourne, saying that he was in the best of health and enjoying the trip very much. On 1 June, four days before reaching Colombo, he died and was buried at sea. He was forty-nine years of age. (No explanation of Longmuir's sudden death was given; nor have enquiries thrown any light on the matter.)

Rouse continued his investigations. In January 1896 he reported to the Official Receiver in London that the bank's management had been 'most reckless'. Supervision by directors had been purely perfunctory, the funds had been 'wantonly wasted', and balance sheets falsified. A total of £76,000 had been advanced to directors; another £75,000 to Longmuir himself; another £540,000 to companies in which the bank's directors were interested; and another £1,560,000 to ten 'special accounts'. Thus more than £2¼ million of the bank's funds had gone to directors and their friends.

Judge Hickman Molesworth was appointed to sit as a Special Commissioner and fully investigate the bank's affairs. Molesworth began the hearings in March 1896. Thomas Loader, chairman of the bank, was called as first witness. Loader admitted that B. J. Fink's overdraft had exceeded £300,000, on which the bank held very little security. In 1892 a company called the General Assets Co. Ltd had been formed, with two of the bank's officers as directors. This company took over some of Fink's assets as 'a device' to help satisfy his debt, and £100,000 was written off his overdraft. A few months later, a further £80,000 was transferred from the bank's reserves and written off Fink's overdraft. Thus at balance date, his indebtedness appeared far less than it actually was. In addition, Mrs Fink had been advanced £27,000 on worthless promissory notes.

David Munro & Co. Ltd owed the bank £400,000 when it suspended business, only inferior securities being held. Loader claimed that David Munro Ltd had lost nearly £70,000 on the construction of railways to Oakleigh, Whittlesea, Swan Hill, and Crib Point. 'Every penny of the loss was paid by the bank', he

The most important Land Sale ever held in the District, and occupying the **CENTRAL SPOT OF AUBURN,** comprising the Finest Sites for Business Premises outside the Metropolis. This Noble Estate has been held for years by Sir Robert Molesworth, and its subdivision has been anxiously awaited for years. It is well known that the rush of business to "Wonderfully Advancing Auburn" is simply immense, and the rise in land thereby daily increasing. This Estate is offered in

17 BUSINESS FRONTAGES

Including the PRINCELY CORNER of Auburn and Burwood Roads, by

F. L. FLINT, AUCTIONEER,
8 COLLINS STREET EAST.

Ironically, Judge Hickman Molesworth inherited gains from the land boom after his father's estate at Hawthorn was subdivided.

Two mansions built from City Bank funds: (right) Simon Fraser's 'Norla' in Irving Road, Toorak; (below) Jenkin Collier's 'Werndrew' in Toorak. Collier was acquitted on criminal charges.

said. David Munro Ltd's huge overdraft had been concealed by several ingenious methods. The day before balancing date, promissory notes for £70,000 were handed over to the bank. These were later dishonoured, but had the desired temporary effect of reducing the overdraft. On another occasion, David Munro Ltd drew orders on the State Treasury on the assumption that the government owed them money, and paid the orders into their account. There was no money owing and the orders were dishonoured in the same way. (David Munro, Esq., the bankrupt contractor, wrote a heartbroken letter to the *Age* to explain that he was not personally connected with the stratagem.)

Another of the bank's special favourites was Michael Willis Fergusson, a large wholesale stationer in Melbourne, who borrowed £290,000 from the City Bank for land speculation. With the money he started the Central City Property Co. Ltd. Its three directors were himself, his brother—and Colin Longmuir, manager of the bank. The first transaction undertaken by this remarkable partnership was to buy a building at the corner of Elizabeth and Little Collins Streets, for which they paid £82,000. Three months later they sold it for £16,000 profit. Longmuir's share of the profit was £4,500. Then the trio bought 80 acres of land at Maribyrnong, reselling it for about £10,000 profit. Longmuir's share of this profit was £3,000.

The City Bank advanced £253,000 to another well-known speculator, C. H. James. Typical securities on his overdraft were second mortgages on his sheep stations, and a *third* mortgage on his Empire Buildings in Collins Street. More than £100,000 was advanced to James Munro's two banks in a vain endeavour to keep them afloat. The sum of £80,000 was lent to the Real Estate Bank, and a further £30,000 to the Federal Bank, on practically no security. 'The chairman of those banks was Premier of the colony!' Loader told the court, apparently astonished that such men could ever make errors in financial matters. Fraser & Co. Ltd owed the City Bank £90,000. Said Loader: 'We wanted mercantile business, and we thought we were getting a good thing.' Counsel assisting the court, scornfully: 'Oh, they did well to go to you.' Finally, Colin Longmuir had advanced himself £75,000 of the bank's funds, using ten different accounts. 'He told me he was buying shares for himself and his relations', said Loader. After Longmuir's death, the bank abandoned the 'security' as worthless, and wrote off Longmuir's debts.

After the revelations of Molesworth's inquiry, prosecution of the City Bank directors was inevitable. Four directors, Thomas Loader, James Williamson, J. L. Roberts and Jenkin Collier, and the two auditors, Andrew Burns and J. B. McQuie, were charged with concurring in issuing two false balance sheets in 1892 and 1893. It was alleged that £45,000 had been paid in dividends when the bank was actually insolvent. On 24 August 1896 all defendants were committed for trial by Mr Panton, P.M. Their trial began on 21 September, and continued until 3 November. A powerful group of barristers appeared for the defence, including Alfred Deakin, James Purves, Q.C., and P. D. Phillips. Their unanimous contention was that the deceased manager, Colin Longmuir, had personally carried out all the frauds and hoodwinked the innocent directors. 'What could these poor old gentlemen do in opposition to him?' asked Mr Purves.

The prosecution had little trouble in proving that the balance sheets were completely false and misleading. However, it was more difficult to prove that the directors had 'concurred' in the issue of the documents, knowing them to be false. In the end the dead man took all the blame, and the directors and auditors were acquitted. The jury foreman attempted to add a rider accusing the directors of negligence in carrying out their duties, but was promptly ruled out of order by Mr Justice Holroyd. Said the *Age* next morning:

> Clearly the public have little or no protection against the most palpable frauds . . . The City Bank trial and its revelations will sink deep into the minds of the people and accentuate the demand everywhere made for a radical amendment of the law under which such gross doings have been possible.

32

H. G. Turner and the Commercial Bank

Behind the imposing facades of some of our better-known institutions, the sad ghosts of past years sometimes emerge from dank vaults, and the hollow rattle of skeletons may be heard by those with ears for such things. Nobody dreams for one instant that the passionate, dead events of the past have any connection with the efficient and almost foolproof way in which banking is organized today. Yet there was a time when even such respectable institutions as the Commercial Bank of Australia teetered on the brink of catastrophe. Given just a slight alteration of circumstances, the bursting of the boom might easily have swept away this great banking house.

The Commercial Bank of Australia Ltd was started in 1866 by Gideon Lang, Mars Buckley, and other leading Melbourne men. Its specific intention was 'to lend to small businessmen and farmers who are in the aggregate the great producers of capital'. The Commercial was the first bank, and for some years the only bank, to be registered under a new Victorian statute which permitted the liability of such institutions to be limited to the extent of their own assets.

The Commercial started with a strong board, but as the original directors died or retired and new men took their place, a situation gradually arose where not one director had any first-hand knowledge of banking, except as a customer. George Meares, chairman during the critical period, was a retired draper. He was perhaps better known as composer of a cantata for the Melbourne International Exhibition of 1880. Another director, George Coppin, M.L.C., was one of the most successful comedians ever to appear on the London and Australian stage, as well as being a formerly insolvent mining speculator. Nathan Thornley, M.L.C., was a building surveyor. Matthew Lang, M.L.C., was a wine and spirit merchant, and Mayor of Melbourne, who died insolvent in 1892. Thomas Mowbray was another draper and furnisher. J. M. Davies, M.L.C., was a solicitor, politician, and land speculator.

The key figure in the bank's development was undoubtedly Henry Gyles Turner, who left a position with the Bank of Australasia in 1870 to become general manager. Turner was an extraordinarily versatile and complex individual. Born in London in 1831, he was first apprenticed to a publisher but later joined the London Joint Stock Bank. He emigrated to Melbourne at the age of twenty-three, and soon rose to the top of the orthodox banking world. He became

Henry Gyles Turner, the versatile general manager of the Commercial Bank, who never admitted his liability for the results of the land boom.

The Commercial's directors were largely ignorant of good banking practice. George Meares (left) was a retired draper. George Coppin, M.L.C. (right) was a retired theatrical comedian.

100 FEET HIGH TO TOP OF PARAPET
B
COMMERCIAL
ANK OF
AUSTRALIA LIMITED

president of the Literature Society and Shakespeare Society, a prolific contributor to newspapers and magazines, a president of the Public Library trustees, and a first-class actor on the amateur stage. During these successful years, Turner lived in a delightful mansion called 'Bundalohn', situated at the corner of Tennyson and Dickens Streets, St Kilda; and notable for its glorious cast iron work and unusual tower. He built another 'Bundalohn' near Dandenong as his country residence.

Under Turner's guidance, the Commercial Bank began to build up the largest business of any bank in Australia, on the Scottish system of advancing money to farmers on the security of their future grain and wool yields. When Turner joined the bank, its deposits were only £340,000 and its advances £450,000. Within twenty years, Turner increased these figures more than twenty-fold. To his board of directors, Turner appeared the very epitome of an ideal banker. One director, George Coppin, told the *Age*: 'Mr. Turner has been wonderfully successful as a manager, and has inspired such confidence among the poorer classes of the community that there are 709 shareholders in the bank holding less than 11 shares.' It was indeed true that the bank was trusted by those who could least afford to lose their money.

Turner himself played an ambiguous part in events. As manager of the biggest bank in Melbourne throughout the boom and depression periods, he above all men was in a position to know the full story of the activities of the financiers. What later investigators had to build up slowly like a giant jigsaw puzzle, Turner knew intimately, personally, and vividly. In addition, he was able to organize his knowledge logically and write about it clearly, two capacities which George Meudell singularly lacked in writing *The Pleasant Career of a Spendthrift*. Yet when Turner came to write his two-volume *History of the Colony of Victoria* early in the twentieth century, he left large gaps in his treatment of the financial scandals. He had no hesitation in making personal and bitter attacks on radical politicians such as Sir Graham Berry. When it came to politicians and speculators on his own side of the fence, Turner remained silent. His *History* is still recommended as a standard work on Victoria in the nineteenth century. As far as the land boom was concerned, his memoirs concealed more than they revealed.

The Commercial's head office until 1893 was at 30 Collins Street. It boasted of 35,000 customers banking at more than one hundred branches throughout Australia, with outstanding overdrafts totalling nearly £13 million. The bank normally had strong reserves and a high reputation. How then could it come to be one of the weakest of the so-called Associated Banks, and one of the first to go to the wall? There were several good reasons. The bank financed too many suspect building societies. It accepted too high a ratio of deposits to capital and reserves, so that when a run occurred, a safe margin of cash was not available. It financed too many risky accounts of land speculators. And its shares were 'beared' in the market at the first rumours doubting the bank's stability.

During the building society boom, the Commercial competed keenly for

Commercial Bank opened at 335 Collins Street in 1892.

H. G. Turner's St Kilda mansion 'Bundalohn'. Turner also built a weekend 'Bundalohn' opposite the black trackers' station at Dandenong.

their accounts, and at one time had advances to eighteen societies on its books. When the building society failures began to shake public confidence, the Commercial helped them on their downward path by suddenly withdrawing their overdraft facilities. At the time of its own suspension, the Commercial carried only three such accounts. In its period of generosity, the Commercial Bank heavily financed such leading speculators as Thomas Bent, Edward Latham, J. A. Kitchen, Abraham Kozminsky, and many others. The bank's loans figured in a large proportion of debts concealed by secret compositions, as well as in many open bankruptcies.

The Commercial's huge advances to borrowers of course could not have been made without equally huge deposits, which increased from less than £2 million in 1882 to nearly £12 million in 1892. The 'complicated evils of the deposit system' were bitterly attacked by A. G. V. Peel in his contemporary report, *The Australian Crisis of 1893.* Peel devoted a special section to the Commercial Bank, whose 'hunger for deposits had been monstrous and unrivalled . . . The fact was that its rise had been too swift and gigantic to ensure confidence.'

As companies began to crash in the aftermath of the boom, the Commercial became a favourite subject for gossip. The *Age* reported:

> Up to the very time of closing the bank's doors the air was thick with suspicion and injurious rumour, the source of which no man could trace. If any two citizens met . . . and exchanged views about the institution, it was with nods of meaning, of caution and warning, as if they were the repositories of dreadful untold secrets.

At the half-yearly shareholders' meeting held in August 1892 the chairman, George Meares, tried to restore confidence by disclaiming all connection with speculation:

> In regard to the advances of this bank, during the late financial depression it was

> the policy of the management to give fair and ample accommodation to its customers in carrying out ordinary business transactions, and to encourage them in reasonable and legitimate enterprise, but it is the determination of the management to give no encouragement to undue speculation of any kind . . .

Six months later, in an emotional speech to shareholders, H. G. Turner said that the building-up of the Commercial Bank had been his life's work. 'It pains me and destroys all my energy to see the shares fall and render the stock of £300,000 less value in one week', he said. 'Our character has been whispered away'.

The fluctuations in Commercial Bank shares were, however, much more logical than the bank ever admitted. The highest price they ever reached was £12 in 1888. The first big fall, early in 1891, was due to a premonition that a building society crisis was about to occur. The shares struggled back to about £7.10s. In May 1892, when it was revealed that the Commercial had been repaid a £100,000 loan given to the Mercantile Bank shortly before the Mercantile's doors closed, the shares rose to £8. With the suspension of the Federal Bank, which had close associations with the Commercial, the latter's shares dropped to £4.4s.—only 4s. above their paid-up value. The week before the Commercial collapsed, the shares were being hastily unloaded at £2. 8s. All this time, a run was developing on the bank, starting as a trickle and swelling into a flood. During the run, more than £1,500,000, mostly in gold coin, was withdrawn from the Commercial's deposits in nine months. The rate of withdrawal was increasing all the time, for about £1 million of this figure went in the last four months before suspension. On one day alone, the Thursday before Easter, £115,000 was withdrawn. The A.M.L. & F. Co. Ltd withdrew every penny of its large deposits.

When most of their land-booming borrowers had made secret compositions with their creditors, and when depositors had withdrawn huge sums in gold to hide in their own safes or under the floorboards, the Commercial's directors decided to approach the State for assistance. They asked the Patterson government to arrange that the Commercial Bank should be publicly promised the financial backing of the State and the Associated Banks 'to such extent as might be required'. Even the friendly Patterson government could hardly undertake to guarantee a private bank with the whole resources of the State. The Treasurer, G. D. Carter, did propose raising a temporary fund of nearly £2 million to assist the Commercial through its difficulties. It seemed a generous enough offer, considering the circumstances under which the bank had lost much of its depositors' and shareholders' funds. Nevertheless, the Commercial haughtily declined the offer and decided to gamble on suspension and 'reconstruction'.

On the evening of 4 April 1893, therefore, as the Easter break came to an end, the newspapers were given the news that the great Commercial Bank had suspended payment and would not open its doors on the following morning. In their circular announcing the suspension, the directors claimed that the run on deposits was 'the direct result of the operations in the share market'. The value of the shares had been forced ever downwards as shareholders desperately tried to unload their holdings for fear that the bank's remaining capital might be called up. Why did they think this? Partly because of what the *Age* described as 'a magnetic wave of fright'. Yet there was more to it than that. The rumours that the Commercial Bank was grievously involved in the land smash proved only too true.

The reconstruction scheme, drafted by J. M. Davies, basically involved the calling-up of all outstanding capital, and the compulsory conversion of fixed deposits into preference shares. Current accounts under £100 could still be operated on, but other current obligations were postponed. It was unjust and unfair to those who had deposited large sums of cash with the bank, but at the time there seemed no alternative. The calling-up of capital was a major factor in forcing many shareholders into bankruptcy. They just did not have the cash, and could not borrow money, to pay their calls. The chairman, George Meares, was not unduly worried. 'I am the largest shareholder', he told the *Age*, 'and I will willingly pay my calls before the stipulated time.' George Coppin was a little more sympathetic. 'I am very sorry for the shareholders', he told reporters. 'Another painful recollection for me is that I recommended numerous charitable institutions in my district to invest with the Commercial. But it cannot be helped.' Coppin had troubles of his own. He had tried to develop Sorrento into a major pleasure resort by building a private tramway there at a cost of £25,000. Within a few years he was glad to sell its five carriages, tracks, and land for £700 cash.

The Premier, J. B. Patterson, said he thought the Commercial was 'quite right' to close its doors when it found its deposits drifting away. He did not share in the opinion that 'any very serious consequences' would ensue. The *Age* was able to report that 'although the collapse came as a great shock . . . it was received in a spirit of calm resignation. In fact, men talked as if the worst was now over . . . The belief is expressed on all sides that the Rubicon has been passed.' Both prophecies were wide of the mark.

The reconstruction proposals were submitted to a mass meeting of shareholders at the Athenaeum Hall on the morning of 7 April 1893. The meeting was generally sympathetic to the directors and their problems. Nobody asked any awkward questions about the bank's lending policies during the boom, and nobody suspected how deeply the bank's chief executives were personally involved. The course of the meeting was set in a speech by James Service, M.L.C., a large shareholder for many years. Service used his considerable powers of persuasion to limn 'the beauty of the reconstruction proposals', which he claimed 'conserved the interest of the shareholders'. It was 'impossible for the depositors to lose a farthing', for when their money was compulsorily converted into shares the shares would 'without doubt be easily saleable at par as soon as they were issued.' It had been suggested that a thorough investigation should be made into the bank's affairs. To do that 'would be simply to ruin the whole affair', Service continued. The object in doing everything rapidly was to save 'our magnificent business. (Cheers.) You absolutely lose nothing, and risk not one farthing. (Cheers.)' All told, it sounded as though the bank had almost done its shareholders a favour by going bankrupt. The result was that the meeting voted unanimously in favour of reconstruction. Service had been a director of the Commercial Bank before the boom period, being succeeded by the current chairman, George Meares. As a reward for his masterly performance at the Athenaeum, he was appointed chairman of the reconstructed bank.

The same afternoon, 1200 depositors met at the Athenaeum Hall to consider the proposals. This time D. R. McGregor, an original shareholder in the bank, made the rallying speech. All the depositors were 'Britons', he said. If they got a knock down, they would 'rise up more determined than ever'. He believed that the new shares would sell above par. (Loud cheers.) He was followed by Captain A. Currie, representing the Commissioners' Savings Banks, a large creditor of the Commercial. The captain told the depositors to 'be men', and have confidence in their own institution. (Cries of 'We have!') They should 'rally to the occasion'. After more speeches, they did, and voted the proposals through.

The British depositors, being far removed from the silver-tongued architects of the reconstruction scheme, were harder to convince. Although the scheme was quickly approved by the Victorian Supreme Court, they appealed to the Full Court for abolition of the clause forcing depositors to take preference shares instead of cash. Mr Justice Williams said he thought there had been 'too much rush'. Mr Justice Holroyd said, 'You give depositors only two or three days for consideration: the thing's ridiculous.' But in the end the court agreed to the general scheme, with only minor modifications.

Cheering as they sink: the Commercial Bank shareholders, ignorant of the true story, accept the reconstruction scheme enthusiastically.

James Service, M.L.C., outlines the alternatives facing the Commercial Bank after the crash.

In H. G. Turner's *History*, his exculpation for the Commercial's policies was that

> It had admittedly strained its resources by injudiciously assisting some of the financial companies banking with it, to meet the demands of their panic-stricken depositors. Viewed apart from the exciting surroundings, this policy from a bank's standpoint was indefensible; but, like the rest of the community, prior to the revelations of liquidators, the Directors of the bank believed in the temporary nature of the assistance required by their customers, and placed too optimistic a valuation on the large uncalled capital of the companies to whose aid they came.

Reluctantly, we must extend Turner's apologia. Because it believed in the 'temporary nature' of the crisis, the Commercial Bank also thought it right to conceal from its shareholders the fact that at least three of its chief executives had been indulging in land-booming activities on their own account. What would have been the mood of the reconstruction meetings had it been revealed at the time that several of the Commercial's top men were secretly insolvent land boomers? The leading politicians of the State and the directors of the bank would not have dared to bluff and bully the shareholders and depositors in the way they did. Probably the shareholders, and certainly the English depositors, would have voted for liquidation under court supervision. And there would be no Commercial Bank today.

There is no doubt that Turner knew the desperate position of his land-booming executives, and knew what a sensation such a revelation would be.

Reading between the lines of his *History*, it is obvious that he was torn between his personal honour and the necessity to save the bank. 'It was confidence, not coin, that was wanted', he wrote. Later, dealing with the reconstruction scheme he wrote that

> It was admittedly an infraction of the unwritten law and honourable traditions of the English banking system. It was fully open to the charge of being oppressive and inequitable.

Strong words! He continued:

> But the only alternative was not to be contemplated. Liquidation meant the conversion of £12 million of advances into cash. Such a proceeding would need a market, and there was none. Further, as all the other banks were rigorously restricting advances, it meant ruin to a large proportion of the Commercial Bank's borrowing customers. It meant the closing of factories, forced realization of stocks, and the eviction of hundreds of farmers, unable to transfer their mortgages. Important corporations and municipalities would have been compelled to suspend operations, and there would have been created a vast crowd of workless, hungry and angry men, thrown out of employment in all directions.

Even then, Turner could never quite bring himself to confess that his own colleagues were among the worst of the speculators. William Turner, his Chief Inspector of Branches, made a secret composition with his creditors in September 1892. His debts totalled more than £24,000, on which he was able to pay only 3d. in the £1. His chief creditors were the Federal Bank, Perpetual Executors Association, and P. W. Elliott. Cause of insolvency: speculation in land and shares. Arthur Nichols, manager of the head office of the Commercial Bank, delayed his secret composition with creditors until January 1895. By that time he had been dismissed by the bank and was out of work. He had run up nearly £26,000 in debts, and paid 3d. in the £1. His chief debt was for £7,000 to the Freehold Investment Co. Ltd. He had also borrowed £6,000 from J. M. Smith and lost it in speculation. The insolvency of John McCutcheon, assistant general manager of the Commercial Bank, and thus next in line to H. G. Turner, was concealed until his death in 1900. The researcher who turns up his official file will find the bare proof of his bankruptcy, but no schedule of his debts, so it is difficult to say with any certainty how and where he was personally involved. It is known that about 1890 he built the mansion 'Strathroy' on the south-eastern corner of Barkers and Auburn Roads, Hawthorn. In 1894 he sold it to a civil engineer named W. Thwaites, and later still it was occupied by Sir Leo Cussen. No doubt the money helped to keep his creditors at bay. The only direct evidence of McCutcheon's debts was provided by Alfred Priestley, manager of the Federal Bank, during examination in the Supreme Court in 1894. Said Priestley:

> John McCutcheon's indebtedness was transferred on October 28, 1892, to his son [and guarantor] William McCutcheon, because the directors thought he was a better mark, being in business. The indebtedness on that date according to the ledger current account was £5/2/9. His other indebtedness was on bills discounted amounting to £3,500. On March 31, 1892, William McCutcheon was overdrawn £5,480, for which he gave bills.

The Commercial Bank remained on the brink of the abyss for many years. In 1896 it showed a profit of £30,000, a sum insufficient to pay even the interest on the preference shares. The *Age* claimed that the bank's interest rates on overdrafts were too high to attract much business. It asked pointedly why the colony, which desperately needed the capital, should be 'kept in an abyss of depression to bolster up institutions which, for all we know, may be managed on the peculiar system that Mr. Rouse declares he has discovered in the City of Melbourne Bank.'

The same year, the directors called new meetings at the Athenaeum Hall to save the bank a second time. Shareholders were asked to approve what was now called a 'rearrangement scheme'. Chairman of the meeting was the President of the Legislative Council, Sir William Zeal. 'This is no time for carping, but for united effort to pull the colony out of the rut into which it has fallen', Sir William told the shareholders, who were noticeably less enthusiastic than at earlier meetings. Zeal's words were a bitter reminder of old days, old cliches. Sir William appealed to the meeting to give unanimous approval to the scheme, in order to silence the carpers:

> Everyone knows that directly an institution gets into trouble, men called 'wreckers' come forward to destroy it . . . All of us have been sufferers in the collapse, and must do what we can to put the old bank right again, as well as to put a brave face on matters and bring back prosperity to the dear old colony.

Chairman of the bank, James Service, unfolded a gloomy story of declining earnings, and the unexpectedly slow process of realizing old assets. To prevent 'a public disaster', namely, the suspension of the bank once again, the making of 'better terms with creditors' was unavoidable. J. M. Davies, as the bank's solicitor, outlined the complex rearrangement scheme by which all deposits were to be frozen, and one-thirtieth paid back at a time. The bewildered depositors and shareholders once again put their faith in promises and left their money in the bank. They approved the scheme with only two dissenting votes, one notable dissenter being W. F. Ducker, liquidator of the City of Melbourne Bank and the Mercantile Bank. Meudell's opinion was that

> When the Commercial Bank failed in 1893 it should have stayed shut. It was in a most awfully putrid state, for out of £13 million of assets only about £2 million was realizable. The bank was able to reopen because under its scheme of reconstruction the Supreme Court allowed it to annex £2 million worth of customers' deposits and turn them into preference shares at 4 per cent. The ordinary capital left from the wreck was only £95,619, and the lucky holders of ordinary shares were so protected by an unjust scheme of reconstruction that they now draw the bulk of the profits.

In March 1897 the Commercial Bank took advantage of the new Companies Act to write down its capital by £1,200,000 (equivalent to £4 a share). H. G. Turner told the Chief Justice that this amount had been lost by depreciation of its securities and the inability of its debtors to pay in full. So the Commercial Bank struggled on, with the Old Man of the Land Boom grasping its windpipe but gradually relinquishing his hold. Its shares were laughed at on the Stock

Francis Grey Smith, chief manager of the National Bank, did more than any other man to break the boom by advising H. G. Turner to call in overdrafts.

Sir William Zeal, M.L.C., persuaded Commercial Bank shareholders to accept yet another reconstruction scheme in 1896.

Exchange, and new customers were extremely loath to entrust their cash to an institution which had nearly foundered twice.

The bank formed a Special Assets Trust Co. Ltd, into which all the unrealized assets of the old bank were placed. These assets, mainly land, were gradually sold off. The sums realized were used to liquidate the bank's £12 million in liabilities. After about thirty years this enormous sum was finally extinguished, and the bank's position began to look healthier. Today it is once again one of the strongest of the Associated Banks, a position achieved at a human cost which is beyond calculation.

V THE MUNRO-BAILLIE

INK GROUP

DEBT
DEBT
DEBT
INSOLVENCY COURT
FARTHING IN THE POUND
DEBT £50.000
DEBT £100.000
DEBT

33

James Munro and His Clan

One could not imagine a less likely leader for the carefree band of adventurers who helped to launch the land boom than the Honourable James Munro. Premier of Victoria from November 1890 to February 1892, Munro not only failed to stop the onrushing financial disaster, but by his own wide speculations and intrigues over a long period did as much as any man to cause the crash. The difference between Munro and most of the other speculators was that Munro did it all with the highest moral motives. The road to Munro's private hell was paved with the good intentions of his bankrupt building societies and private banks, and the gold of thousands of naïve investors.

James Munro, who claimed descent from a baronet of the same name, was born in Scotland in 1832. He became a printer by trade. At the age of twenty-one he married Jane Macdonald in Edinburgh; and they had four sons and three daughters. One son, Donald Munro, became prominent in the Victorian land boom as partner of W. L. Baillieu in an auctioneering business. Another, Alexander Munro, was appointed manager of one of his father's companies. James Munro emigrated to Melbourne in 1858, and became a printer in the Flinders Lane factory of Fergusson & Moore. One day he was reading proofs of the regulations of a building society organized on the terminating principle. It occurred to him that a permanent building society on the lines of the Scottish Property Investment Trust might be better suited to Melbourne conditions. So in 1865, at the age of thirty-three, Munro threw in his printer's apron and started the Victorian Permanent Building Society. Of his many land and finance companies, this was the only one to survive the crash.

Meanwhile, Munro had also become a leading figure in the Victorian temperance movement and its radical offshoots. His fiery fluency on the evils of liquor, the need for a land tax, and the importance of high tariffs, made him many highly-placed friends and enemies—but more to the point, it made him widely known to the public. In 1874 he was elected to the Legislative Assembly as member for North Melbourne. Once in the House, he caused sensations on several occasions by jumping up and down in wild abandon, shaking his fist and pouring forth a stream of invective against those who opposed his ideas. He was more respected than liked. Alfred Deakin described Munro as 'a fiery Scot, a speculative plunger, at that time thought to be a sound financier, a

James Munro, the teetotal Premier of Victoria whose activities were one of the main causes of the smash.

J. B. Watson, the Bendigo mining millionaire, financed Munro in starting the notorious Federal Bank.

practised political chief, cunning, untrustworthy and unscrupulous, and an effective but sometimes injudicious debater.'

In 1877 the McCulloch government split Munro's constituency in two and created the new seat of Carlton. The hot-headed young temperance worker decided to invade the publicans' stronghold of Carlton. The only public meeting hall in the area was owned by his opponent, J. Curtain, and the local publicans combined to prevent him from obtaining any other meeting place. Munro promptly bought a vacant block, built a public hall in fourteen days at a cost of £2,000, attracted hundreds of people to his emotional meetings, and won the seat by thirty-one votes. (The publicans and the breweries never forgave him. When Munro started the Federal Bank a few years later, the breweries instructed all hotel-keepers to refuse Federal Bank notes.) After McCulloch resigned the Premiership, Munro became 'the power behind the throne' in the radical government of Graham Berry. The colony was only beginning to feel the enormous vitality of this young man with the tall, well-built figure, massive head and flowing beard. His booming voice, with its strong Gaelic accent, was heard throughout the land. He urged and nagged the government into staging the great International Exhibition of 1880, for which the present Exhibition Building was built at a cost of £250,000. Although Sir Redmond Barry resigned from the committee of management in disgust at what he considered to be senseless extravagance, the exhibition was an overwhelming success. It can be truly said to have ushered in the boom years, and sparked off the decade of gaiety, enthusiasm, and prodigality which preceded the smash.

During the booming 1880s, Munro expanded the temperance movement into a fanatical fighting force with power never known before or since. For several years he was president of the Caledonian Society, the Total Abstinence Society, and the Victorian Alliance for the Suppression of the Liquor Traffic. He was also a committee member of the Toorak Presbyterian Church, the Independent Order of Good Templars, and the Independent Order of Rechabites.

Munro used his position and influence to build and finance several of those oddly-named institutions, the 'coffee palaces'—hotels where travellers could stay without being tempted by the demon drink. Under Munro's influence, some of the best hotels in Melbourne were induced to surrender their liquor licences and become temperance houses. He was a founder and director of the Victoria Coffee Palace Co. Ltd, which maintains its original temperance principles today in the heart of Little Collins Street. Munro's direction of the Grand Coffee Palace in Spring Street was markedly less successful. He registered the Grand Coffee Palace Co. Ltd in 1886 to take over the hotel, and surrendered its liquor licence. The original subscribers were Munro, James Balfour, W. L. Baillieu, David Beath, and G. Walther. Baillieu apparently quitted the venture very shortly after its formation, by which time its Spring Street frontage had been extended from 120 ft to 212 ft. The Grand Coffee Palace suffered gravely from the depression. It was discovered that the manager, J. H. Durant, had kept up the occupancy rate by allowing his good friends to stay there for half the normal charges, and his best friends for no charge at all. Not content with that, in 1892 he absconded with about £1,000 of the Grand's funds. Later a group of shareholders led by David Syme and G. R. Murphy moved to dismiss the directors. They summoned a special meeting of shareholders, and disclosed an extraordinary state of mismanagement in the Grand's affairs, including sly-grog selling, compromising of its overdraft with the Federal Bank, and publication of balance sheets 'of a most cheerful character' at a time when the coffee palace was completely insolvent. The new controllers of the Grand applied to the Chief Justice in 1897 to be allowed to sell liquor legally, and to change the name back to the Grand Hotel. The Grand Hotel company was finally wound up in 1920, but the hotel itself continued as the Windsor—probably Melbourne's best-known hostelry.

The Federal Coffee Palace, built by Munro and James Mirams, went through a similar phase. Announcing a serious trading loss in 1893, the chairman, George Godfrey, said the directors hoped to obtain a liquor licence soon, 'and then profits are certain'. It got the licence, was renamed the Federal Hotel, and traded in its ornate building at the western end of Collins Street, until demolished in 1972.

Meanwhile, Munro's personal financial interests were expanding at a satisfying rate. In 1882 he resigned from his position as manager of the Victorian Building Society after seventeen years' untarnished service. With the help of J. B. Watson, a Bendigo gold millionaire, he started the most famous and most notorious of all boom institutions—the Federal Bank—and its associated

One of Munro's coffee palaces: the Grand Hotel (Temperance) in Spring Street – today the Windsor Hotel.

Federal Building Society. Munro managed the bank, and made his son Alexander secretary of the building society. Half a million capital was quickly subscribed. Thousands of small depositors and homeseekers opened accounts on the strength of Munro's reputation—and on the strength of its illustrious London board, which included Sir Henry Barkly, a former Governor of Victoria; and Sir Andrew Clarke, acting Agent-General.

Most of the Building Society's money, and most of Munro's personal assets, were spent in buying up paddocks and orchards on the suburban fringes. For a time it seemed as though Munro could not go wrong. With uncanny foresight, he and other politicians bought land precisely in those suburbs to which the suburban railway network was to be extended. Property values rose enormously. At the height of the boom, Munro himself would have cut up for £250,000; and his Federal Bank was able to pay huge dividends from its paper profits. In 1885 the Federal Bank was given a share of government business, as a result of Munro's growing political influence. Four years later the Associated Banks changed their rules to exclude any bank connected with the ownership of a building society. The Federal Bank thereupon sold its 130,000 Building Society shares to comply with the new rules, and in theory the two institutions were run separately for the short lease of life left to them. The Associated Banks did not have to wait long for revenge. When the slump began and the Federal Bank ran into trouble, not one bank would lift a finger to help it, nor to conceal the revelations of financial double-dealing which were to come.

It would be a thankless task to trace all of Munro's personal land dealings in the 1880s. We know that he bought and sold 13 acres at Malvern; 20 blocks at Armadale; a large property at Narbethong; 11,000 acres at Beaconsfield (S.A.); several thousand acres in Queensland; and 1¼ million acres of leasehold land in the Kimberleys (W.A.). There were countless other smaller deals.

In 1887, while still a director of the Federal Bank, Munro decided to start another more personalized institution called the Real Estate Bank. Munro never attempted to conceal his reasons for starting it. Indeed, one of the peculiarities of this righteous man's psychology was that he could always explain and defend his actions to his own satisfaction, however wayward they might seem to others. At all times, you may be sure, Munro was able to face his Maker with a clear conscience. In September 1892—five months before his bankruptcy proceedings, and when Real Estate Bank shares could be bought for 1d. each—Munro gave his reminiscences to newspaper reporters in London. 'In 1887', he said, 'the various properties which I had bought had become more than one man could manage, and acting upon the suggestion of friends I formed the Real Estate Bank to take them over.' The 'friends' were another prominent teetotaller, William McLean; an M.L.A. named John Woods; and others who had helped him to start the Federal Bank and were still large shareholders in that institution. The new bank was established at 231 Collins Street, on the other side of the *Age* office from Munro & Baillieu's estate agency.

As manager of the Real Estate Bank, Munro employed James Drysdale Purves—an accountant who soon ran into personal difficulties, lost £10,000 on share deals, and made a composition with his creditors at 2d. in the £1. Purves was

After the crash, Munro went back to his temperance activities. This 1902 photograph of the Independent Order of Rechabites shows him in the second row, second from left (No. 11). His son-in-law, Brother R. L. Balding, who had managed the insolvent Real Estate Bank, is shown in the front row, far right (No. 6).

forced to resign from the bank, whereupon Munro appointed his own son-in-law, Robert Lallam Balding, to manage its affairs. One of the earliest transactions of the new Real Estate Bank was to purchase at an inflated price 47,000 shares in the Chatsworth Estate Co. Ltd, formed by Munro to take over a large estate of 1,475 acres at Bulleen for subdivision. G. N. Taylor, manager of the Land Credit Bank, bought £30,000 worth of Chatsworth shares, and was sentenced to eight years' gaol for defrauding his bank to pay for them. An umbrella manufacturer, Robert Kingston, also bought £30,000 worth of Chatsworth shares. When they became worthless, he committed suicide.

These sensations were, however, still in the future when Munro sailed for England in 1890 to raise more cash to finance his various companies. He was completely successful, and returned buoyantly on a new wave of Scottish and English capital. Back in Parliament as leader of the Opposition, he trenchantly attacked the financial policies of the Gillies-Deakin government, toppled it from office, and in November 1890 became Premier and Treasurer of what he called a 'National Liberal' Ministry. Munro was at the top of the hill, and, from that point on, the road sloped downwards all the way.

In 1891 the first ominous portents of the financial crisis appeared. Overseas investors began to watch the Australian cables nervously. Munro himself was making new enemies, and a time would come when no prominent man would lift a finger to help him. 'He runs Parliament as though he were chairman and managing director', said one bitter observer. 'His only aim seems to be to hit home in sledge hammer style without any unnecessary flourishes', said another. As new investment money dried up, the weakest and worst-managed of the building societies began to go to the wall, and the writing on that wall was clear enough to an experienced financier like Munro.

With his own companies in grave danger, Munro consulted his Attorney-General, J. M. Davies. Together they planned an extraordinary piece of legislation called the Voluntary Liquidation Act 1891. This was rushed through both houses of Parliament on 3 December 1891, with only one dissenting voice. The Act in effect abolished the legal right of minority depositors in banks, building societies and other companies to send a business into compulsory liquidation if it could not pay its debts on demand. It was the nearest thing to legalized repudiation passed through an Australian Parliament in the nineteenth century.

During the next twelve months, this new Act enabled many a suspect land company and bank to be quietly wound up by the directors without any independent investigation—just as the process of secret composition enabled individual speculators to conceal the true state of their affairs. Munro's pretext for the legislation was that companies needed secrecy in order to avoid setting off a panic among investors. But he was the first to use the new Act. The morning after it was passed the Federal Building Society suspended payments to depositors. Instead of cash, the building society offered them deposit receipts for one year drawn on the Federal Bank. At a meeting on 11 December 1891, the frightened depositors agreed instead to renew their deposits for another three years. Ten months later the building society went into full liquidation, by which time most of its assets were almost worthless.

On 15 December, twelve days after the hasty passing of the Voluntary Liquidation Act, Munro's Real Estate Bank also suspended payment. On 19 February 1892 a meeting of creditors began the process of voluntary liquidation. J. M. Bruce, who held six hundred shares in the bank, and had a keen sense of humour, told the meeting that 'one of the reasons for the present disaster is that a number of people have made it their business to pry into the financial affairs of leading business men.' At the same meeting, Munro, as chairman, claimed that the bank would have more than £600,000 surplus assets over liabilities when its properties were sold. Four months later, the liquidators issued a circular showing not a surplus, but a deficiency of £540,000. Even that was not the final figure. In the finish the cash losses on Munro's Real Estate Bank totalled no less than £1,027,000. When the official liquidator finally unravelled its tangled affairs in 1899, he was able to pay a dividend of only 2s. 6d. in the £1.

Munro himself was not in Melbourne to supervise the liquidation. As though to produce the greatest sensation of all, in his capacity as Premier he appointed himself Victorian Agent-General in London, and quickly left the colony. Said the *Australasian*: 'It looks decidedly as if Mr Munro felt the ship to be sinking and was resolved to be in the lifeboat and off with the only water-keg before the officers and crew should be aware of their danger.' An angry meeting of 3,000 people at Melbourne Town Hall on 15 February 1892 condemned Munro's appointment. Sir Archibald Michie said that Munro was 'merely bolting'. The Governor was petitioned to disallow the appointment, but was 'laconic in his reply', and so Munro proceeded abroad. He was given an erratic farewell by the temperance movement. One speaker, the Rev. Dr D. E. Jones, took the opportunity to ask the audience, 'What is to be thought of a Government [i.e. a Munro government] that would allow its Post and Telegraph Department to supply the brothels of the city with telephones to be used as a means to minister to lust?' If Munro was glad to escape from his enemies, he must have been overjoyed to escape from his friends.

Munro left behind a dovecote of fluttering creditors. One of them, Henry Clarke, wrote plaintively to the editor of *Table Talk*:

> I was a contractor, and had saved some few thousands which I wished to invest as an income for my old age. Knowing Mr. James Munro personally for fully 30 years, about four years ago I asked his advice about the Real Estate Bank. He told me there was 'nothing equal to it.' On this I purchased 150 shares at £3/6/– . . . Later on I put the whole of my profit on completion of a contract for £18,000 on the Elwood Swamp, buying 600 shares . . . When my holding was 1,285 shares, I became so anxious that at the end of April, 1891, I went with a friend to Mr. Munro's house at Armadale . . . We had a long talk with Mr. Munro, during which he urged me to keep my shares, saying there would be no call . . . He took hold of my waistcoat in a familiar way, saying, 'Stick to your shares, they'll make a man of you' . . . After such assurances, and being reminded by him that the bank had £130,000 reserve fund, I did stick to my shares, and now I am a ruined man.

In July 1892 a solicitor named George Godfrey, who had also been personally stung by the losses, attempted to investigate the affairs of the Real Estate Bank.

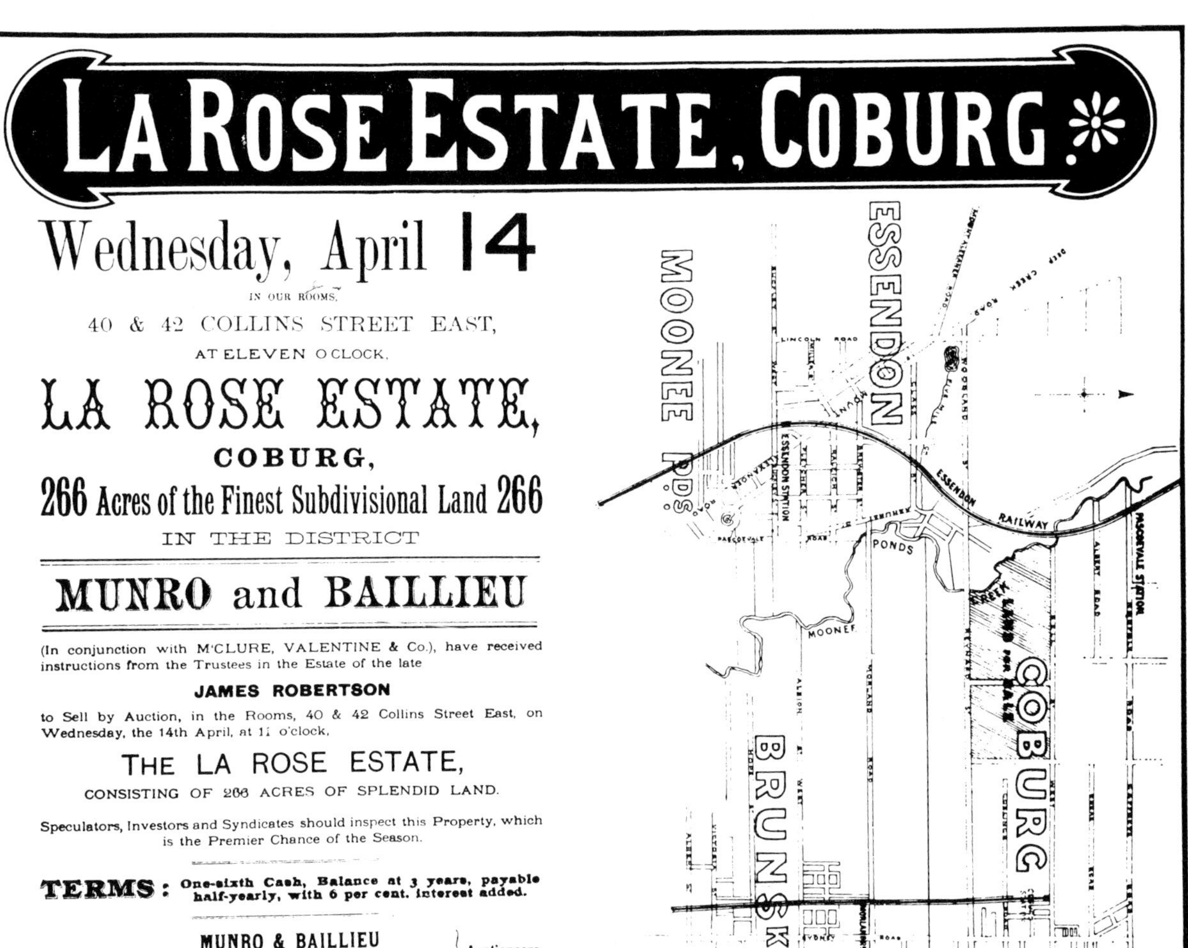

A flagrant boom scandal: the La Rose Estate, which was sold backwards and forwards whenever the Munro-Baillieu group needed money.

He discovered that in 1886 James Munro had 'sold' the La Rose Estate (near Coburg) to John Woods, M.L.A., for £28,000. The following year, the Real Estate Bank bought the property back from Woods for £55,000. Woods was well-known as a business associate of Munro's. Godfrey claimed that the £27,000 profit on the deal had disappeared, for when Woods died shortly afterwards his estate was not sufficient to pay even his funeral expenses. A few days after Godfrey's report, the liquidators stopped his investigation, on the ground that 'publication of information in the Press could not advance the interests of the liquidation'. The liquidators were Thomas Loader, director of the City of Melbourne Bank; and R. L. Balding, manager of the Real Estate Bank—both of whom had much to gain by concealment.

John Woods's widow saw Godfrey's statement in the newspapers, and made the following statutory declaration:

> I, Jessie Woods, of North Brighton, widow, do solemnly and sincerely declare—(1) That my late husband, John Woods, with whom I was acquainted for upwards of 13 years before my marriage, informed me that he had purchased the La Rose Estate for the Hon. James Munro, and that the name of the said John Woods was merely used for the convenience of the said James Munro . . .

John Woods, M.L.A., acted as dummy for James Munro in land and share deals.

George Godfrey, a Melbourne solicitor, alleged criminal offences against Munro.

and so on. In other words, Munro had used Woods as a dummy to defraud the bank. Munro replied (in the *British Australasian*) that Mrs Woods had married Mr Woods only a few months before his death, so how could she know anything about his transactions? In addition, Munro himself had arranged in April 1892 for the widow Woods to be appointed inspector of railway waiting rooms, so why was she attacking *him*? Thus did Munro coolly brush off the damning affidavit.

George Godfrey persisted with his investigation, and finally revealed that the Real Estate Bank had paid a total of £180,000 to James Munro for various properties. Their value was now practically nil. The bank was actually insolvent two years before, and the balance sheets since then, he claimed, were 'misleading' —a criminal offence even under the old Companies Act.

When the magnitude of the disaster became obvious, the Shiels government insisted on Munro's return from London. He came back to find himself completely ruined financially and as a public moralist. Yet when he went bankrupt in February 1893, Munro scorned to use the process of secret composition which by that time had been exploited by scores of other speculators, including his own son. He filed his schedule publicly, showing liabilities of £94,000. His biggest creditor was the Mercantile Bank, to which he owed £20,000 for promissory notes drawn in favour of Munro & Baillieu. The bills were discounted the morning before the Mercantile Bank closed its doors for ever. In addition, Munro had been indebted to his own Federal Bank for £125,000—but this amount had been written off only four days before that institution closed *its* doors for ever. Munro's explanation of this event was given to the Insolvency Court: 'I told Priestley [the manager] that I was going to file my schedule, and that I wanted to know my liability to the bank . . . Priestley said that the bank did not want to appear as a creditor, and that it would give me a release.' Was there ever a confession of financial roguery given in such terms of injured innocence?

In all, Munro lost £608,000 on his various land deals. He told Judge Molesworth that he had lost £112,000 on his Real Estate Bank shares; £80,000 on his drought-stricken Kimberleys property; £28,000 on his Federal Coffee Palace shares; and £9,000 on his Federal Bank shares. He was refused release from sequestration until he paid 7s. in the £1—an amount later reduced to nil, on the ground that his estate was entirely worthless. Munro had to give up his substantial mansion, 'Armadale House', in Kooyong Road, Armadale (which survives today as the Melbourne Bible Institute). Until released from sequestration, he was forced to live on the charity of relatives at North Brighton. He then started a small estate agency and auction room in High Street, Armadale, near his old home, riding around the district on a second-hand bicycle to perform his chores.

Munro's son-in-law, R. L. Balding, manager of the Real Estate Bank and secretary of the Chatsworth Estate Co. Ltd, went bankrupt at about the same time, using the rare and secret process of Liquidation by Arrangement. His debts totalled £90,000, but in respect of the two biggest amounts he claimed to be a dummy for the bank. If this claim was true (and it was never disputed), Munro's total personal debts may therefore be set down as £309,000, on which he paid nothing in the £1.

Later in 1893, a rather pathetic, grey-bearded figure of sixty-one, Munro was walking along Collins Street when he was accosted by a powerfully-built, six-foot-tall labourer of forty named George Davis. Davis shouted that he had lost all his money, there was 'nothing but the Yarra for him', so he might as well 'go to the scaffold'. Munro told Davis he would talk to him privately. Davis shouted, 'No, I will take it out of you now', and punched him savagely in the face. Munro fell unconscious to the ground, and had to be revived by spectators. Davis was immediately arrested. He told the court that he was sleeping in the public parks because he had been ruined by spending all his savings on Real Estate Bank shares. He was fined £5—a sum which was straight away paid by an anonymous sympathizer in the court. The magistrate, Mr Nicholson, said that 'considering the times the city has passed through', he thought the behaviour of the citizens in general was 'distinctly creditable'.

At this time the directors of the Federal Bank were still winding up the bank privately in order to preserve secrecy on their past dealings. Thomas Arkle, a shareholder who had been a valuer employed by the Federal Building Society and presumably knew something of its workings, asked the Supreme Court to order a compulsory winding-up. The court ruled that the liquidation should be conducted under court supervision. Then came Maurice Brodzky's revelations in *Table Talk*, confirmed by a later court enquiry. It was found that an amount equivalent to the entire paid-up capital of the bank had been lent on dubious security to James Munro; his sons Donald, Alexander, and G. M. Munro; Donald Munro's partner, W. L. Baillieu, and several other Baillieus; several directors of the bank; the Real Estate Bank's manager, R. L. Balding; and other business associates; to a grand total of more than half a million pounds. An additional £70,000 had been lent directly to the Real Estate Bank, and thus completely lost.

That was how they did things, quite legally, in the great days of Melbourne finance.

34

Munro & Baillieu, Partners in Audacity

The part played by the Baillieu family in the land boom appears to have been greatly exaggerated over the years. Certainly the auctioneering and real estate partnership of Donald Munro and William Lawrence Baillieu sold many million pounds worth of land to willing buyers during the hectic days of the boom. They were deeply involved in some of the more spectacular transactions of the period. Yet neither Donald Munro nor W. L. Baillieu were as responsible at a high political level for the disaster as, say, Thomas Bent or Sir Matthew Davies. Neither of them displayed the pietistical righteousness of James Munro. And when they made their secret compositions, the amounts involved were, on the scale of those times, comparatively small.

Why then has the legend persisted that the Baillieus were primarily responsible for the horrors of the smash? Why, as late as 1927, when the Baillieu family presented a new set of bells to St John's Church, Toorak, did the street urchins (and many of their elders) sing jeeringly, to the tune of 'Oranges and Lemons':

> What did he pay you?
> Say the bells of old Baillieu.

A variation was to sing, up and down the scale:

> He paid a farthing in the pound.

It was actually sixpence in the pound, but by that time truth and legend were inextricably mixed.

The reason for the exaggerations was, perhaps, that the Baillieus survived the lean years comparatively unscathed. W. L. Baillieu, the keystone of the family, actually seemed to revel in disaster and enjoy thrusting his broad-shouldered way through financial chaos. Where other men retired shamefacedly from business life, threw themselves in the Yarra, or simply died broken-hearted, W. L. Baillieu vigorously elbowed to the top of the political, mining, financial, and newspaper ladders. Up there, he was a sitting target for the envious, the critical, and the merely underfed sections of the population. Thus it became very simple, in the absence of factual information, to say that the Baillieus caused the land boom. Let us therefore begin to set the record straight.

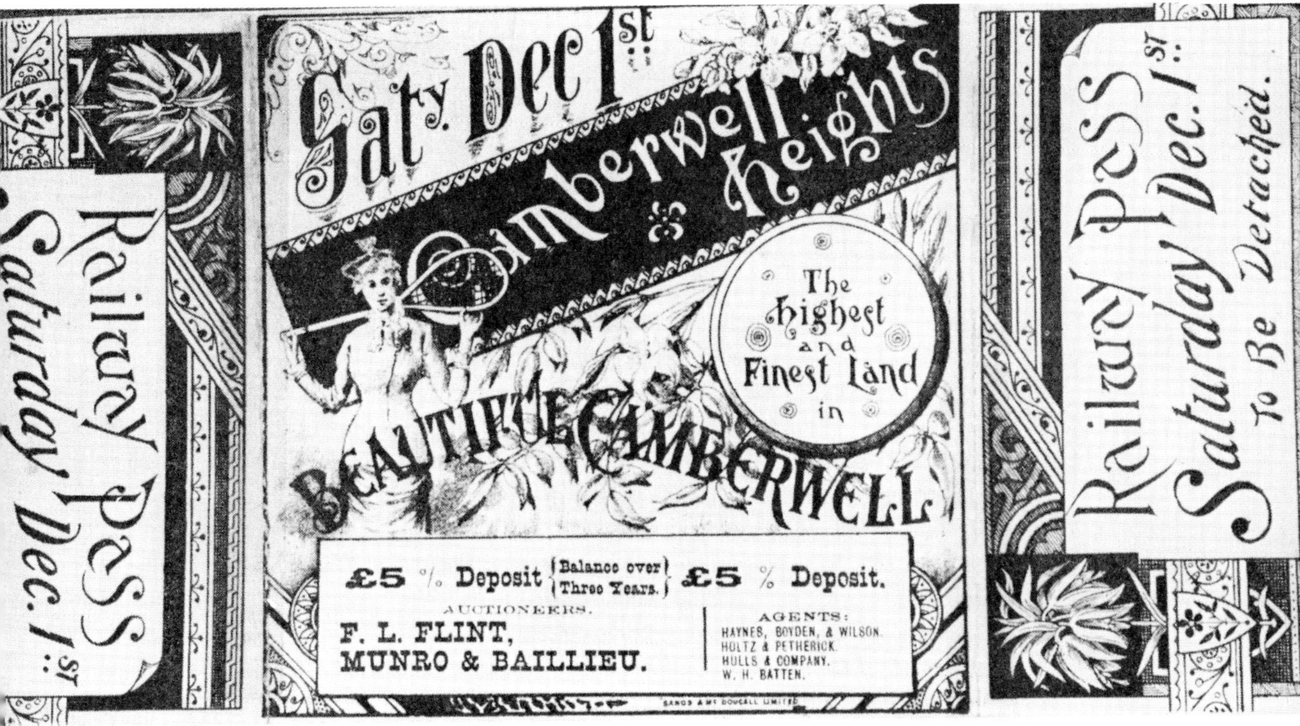

Free railway pass offered by Munro & Baillieu to the sale of Camberwell Heights.

Donald Munro, the future Premier's son, was the left arm of the partnership which set up in business in 1885 at 40 Collins Street, later shifting to No. 243. By 1887 the partners had bid their way to the top of the estate agency business. In that memorable boom year they sold more land than any other agency in Melbourne—£3,123,943. Next came B. J. Fink's Mercantile Finance Co. Ltd with £1,857,606 sales, and third was the old firm of C. J. & T. Ham, with £1,555,654 sales. So busy was the Munro & Baillieu combination that four auctioneers had to be employed to assist the two partners at Saturday sales.

Donald Munro may have been a good land salesman, but apart from that did not play a key role in events. W. L. Baillieu seems to have used him more for introductions to sources of ready finance in the lush days when his father, the Hon. James Munro, helped to rule the financial world. Baillieu also made sure that the Munros purchased large numbers of shares in his favourite land projects—the calls on which were to prove the main cause of Donald Munro's downfall.

Among the estates sold by the partners at this time was James Munro's Armadale Estate, that 'long looked for and eagerly sought after Paddock adjoining his residence', between Munro Street and High Street, Armadale. Then they subdivided Smith's Paddock opposite Camberwell Railway Station, with extensive frontages to Burwood and Burke Roads, Hawthorn—'long the envy of Investors, Speculators, and Lovers of the Beautiful'. Next to go under the hammer was the Paradise Estate, 'the envy and pride of Essendon land'—sold on £5 deposit and long terms. One of the partnership's most successful sales in 1888 was that of Mentone Heights, adjoining the new Mentone racecourse, where the race meetings 'promise to rival in splendour, fashion and popularity those of the V.R.C.' Blocks enjoying the 'salubrity of Mentone Heights' were also sold on £5 deposit.

However, two boom companies which flew the Munro & Baillieu flag lost large amounts for the partnership: The La Rose Land Co. Ltd and the Heart of Preston Land Co. Ltd. Mention either name to a 'specker' of the period and he would turn away with ashen face. La Rose was incorporated in 1888 with capital of £64,000, to buy from Barnett Hyman Altson, the well-known city tobacconist, 135 acres of land in the Parish of Jika Jika. Altson's title to the land was converted into 16,000 £1 shares in the company. After its liquidation in 1892, Altson got back precisely £18. 13s. 8d. as his first and final dividend, equivalent to approximately 2s. 9d. per acre. Donald Munro, W. L. Baillieu, and others each took up 6,000 shares in the company. Since the paid-up value was small, and unlike Altson the partners did not put any title deeds into the company, its fall did not cost them much money, but the calls on its shares presented a problem. (Altson went bankrupt in 1896, with £9,000 deficiency in his estate. In his schedule he disclosed that he had lost £13,000 in share deals connected with the Real Estate Bank, Northern Tramway Co., etc., as well as the disastrous La Rose episode.)

The Heart of Preston Land Co. Ltd was a transaction of a somewhat different colour. This company was formed in October 1888 by the Munro-Baillieu-Fink group to take over 87 acres of land at Preston owned by Edward Latham (W. L. Baillieu's father-in-law). Latham, Baillieu, and B. J. Fink each held 600 of the £10 shares, and the firm of Munro & Baillieu held another 400. By a judicious process of writing up the value of unsold blocks, the company was able to claim a £33,000 profit in 1889, and pay dividends accordingly. When it collapsed three years later, not a penny remained to pay off the creditors. A. S. Baillieu acted as liquidator.

In June 1891, when the partnership was still in existence, but when portents of the coming storm hung heavily on the horizon, Munro and Baillieu incorporated a new company through which their major assets could be siphoned off. This pipeline was called the Melbourne Joint Stock Bank Ltd, registered with nominal capital of £500,000. Its subscribers were Donald Munro and his partner W. L. Baillieu, Edward Lloyd Baillieu and his partner W. J. Malpas, with Salis Fischer as manager. Only £4,000 was subscribed in cash, but Messrs Munro and Baillieu were issued with 30,000 of the company's shares paid up to £4 each—a total of £120,000 worth—in exchange for their assets.

The registered object of the company was 'To acquire and take over certain real and personal property belonging to the said Donald Munro and William Lawrence Baillieu, and certain liabilities with such property'. The property in question comprised allotments in Carlton, North Fitzroy, East Brunswick, Armadale, Essendon, Box Hill, Balaclava, Kew, Glen Iris, Elsternwick, Malvern, Prahran, and elsewhere. This felicitous banking company was wound up in

October 1893, and the books were destroyed. A. S. Baillieu again acted as liquidator.

After the incorporation of this bank, Donald Munro began to fade out of the land boom, and may be dealt with fairly peremptorily here. The date of his secret composition was 26 July 1892. Meetings of all the creditors of Donald Munro, W. L. Baillieu, and their partnership were called for this day. Theodore Fink acted as their solicitor and trustee. He presented Donald Munro's balance sheet, showing debts of £50,000—the major creditor being James Munro with a loan of £20,000. Fink told the meeting that Donald Munro could raise £550. 15s. in ready cash. So his creditors accepted 6d. in the £1 as full satisfaction of their claims.

The meeting then proceeded to consider the affairs of the partnership, Munro & Baillieu. Their balance sheet was a little nearer the standard expected of robust land boomers, showing debts amounting to £140,000. The creditors were told that the partnership could find the sum of £1,080 in cash. Somewhat glumly, no doubt, they agreed to accept 6d. in the £1 on these debts too. Perhaps they did not look very closely at some of the transactions listed. Let us therefore divide these business arrangements into two groups—those outstanding from the early days of the boom, and those debts incurred when the slump was well under way.

1. *Long standing liabilities*

1888	Federal Bank	£5,300	Guarantee on A. G. Hall, solicitor
1888	Federal Bank	£5,800	Guarantee on Frank Stuart, warehouseman
1889	National Bank	£6,000	Guarantee on W. J. Malpas
1889	Albert Miller	£10,000	Loan
1890	G. W. Charters	£20,000	Loan

2. *Recent liabilities*

10 Aug. 1891	Real Estate Bank	£2,350	Loan

(Four months later, the Real Estate Bank, controlled by James Munro, closed its doors for ever. The above loan by Munro to his son and partner was compounded at 6d. in £1.)

10 Feb. 1892	Mercantile Bank	£20,000	Promissory note made by James Munro in favour of Munro & Baillieu and discounted by the Mercantile Bank

(This must rank as one of the strangest transactions on record. Munro & Baillieu, it would appear, repaid James Munro this £20,000 when he resigned as Premier and sailed to England: see previous chapter. Munro & Baillieu got the £20,000 cash from the Mercantile Bank, which discounted the P.N. for them on the authority of J. B. Ainslie, the new manager, and a new director, Sir Graham Berry, whom James Munro was about to replace as Agent-General in London. The only valuable security was land at Narbethong, which James Munro had bought for £2,800. The day after handing over the £20,000 cash to Munro & Baillieu, the Mercantile Bank closed its doors. The £20,000 was lost to human sight forever.)

22 Jan. 1892	Bank of Victoria	£1,500	P.N. in favour of Maurice Aron & Co. Ltd
22 Jan. 1892	Wallach's Ltd	£1,500	P.N.
21 March 1892	B. J. Fink	£1,100	P.N.
21 March 1892	R. W. Best	£1,100	P.N.

(The above four debts are apparently connected, but there was no explanation of their purpose. At this time B. J. Fink controlled both Aron's and Wallach's.)

On 15 June 1892 the partners put through their last great coup. They borrowed £3,600 from the North Union Terminating Building Society. Six weeks later Munro & Baillieu filed their schedule and repaid the building society 6d. in the £1.

However, the most extraordinary feature of the various Munro and Baillieu insolvencies was that they disclosed almost nothing of the large loans they had been given by James Munro's Federal Bank. A list of these outstanding overdrafts was published in *Table Talk* on 9 June 1893, and confirmed a year later by official investigators. (The list produced in court is given in a subsequent chapter dealing with the Federal Bank.) The question naturally arises as to how debtors could file insolvency schedules without revealing their indebtedness to the Federal Bank. The answer was that the Federal Bank arranged not to pursue them for the huge amounts involved, preferring to write them off rather than risk disclosures. It was not until the collapse of the Federal Bank, and various investigations made afterwards, that the truth became known. By that time the secret compositions of Donald Munro and W. L. Baillieu, and even the public bankruptcy proceedings of James Munro, had been buried and forgotten under a growing pile of fresh disasters.

The partnership of Munro & Baillieu did not survive beyond the date of their secret compositions. Perhaps it would not be putting matters too harshly to say that the Munro family was of no further use to the ambitious young Baillieu. As we shall see in the next chapter, Baillieu resumed business as a land agent within a few weeks—but this time without his partner. Donald Munro retired to the comparative peace of the suburbs with his shattered father, whom he helped to build up a small competency in Armadale. Donald Munro became a local councillor, and in time a member of the Board of Works. Later he enlisted to fight against the Boers in South Africa. His former partner, W. L. Baillieu, stayed in Melbourne to continue his search for the riches which the private enterprise system yields to some.

35

W. L. Baillieu, the Triumphant Survivor

William Lawrence Baillieu exerted such tremendous influence over Australian economic and political affairs for so many years, and yet remained shrouded in such mystery and legend, that it seems desirable to establish as far as possible the true facts of his extraordinary rise from poverty to wealth and power.

The Baillieu family (variously spelt Ballieux and Baillieux) originally came from the neighbourhood of Liege in Belgium. According to a romantic story told by James Baillieu, founder of the Australian family, his ancestors fled the Continent when the massacre of the Huguenots took place in 1572. But to judge from the authorized version given in *Burke's Peerage*, the family felt it desirable to leave after the French Revolution in 1789. At all events, the Baillieus settled near Bristol. James George Baillieu was born in Haverfordwest, Wales, in 1832. In 1852, at the age of twenty, we find him as a member of the crew of the migrant ship *Priscilla*, bound for Australia. Baillieu deserted from the ship when it reached Port Phillip Bay early in 1853, relating in later life how he landed in the colony by swimming ashore from the *Priscilla* to Sorrento. Thus the Baillieu dynasty and its ramifications were established in Australia by the merest combination of circumstances. James hid on shore until the *Priscilla* had transferred the sick among her passengers and crew to the hospital ship *Lysander*, a former coastal vessel which was anchored off Sorrento to take cases of smallpox and other serious diseases from incoming ships. When the *Priscilla* sailed off to Melbourne, Baillieu emerged from hiding and volunteered for the extremely dangerous work of helping to care for the sick on board the *Lysander*. No doubt his offer seemed almost a miracle to the officers of the Health Service, hard pressed for voluntary labour in that gold-rush year. So James Baillieu managed to avoid arrest for desertion, and worked on the hospital ship for several months until it was converted into a prison hulk and shifted to Williamstown. Baillieu then transferred to the Customs Department as a boatman, and later a lighthouse keeper, being posted to the small town of Queenscliff on the opposite side of Port Phillip Bay. The surviving Queenscliff records of the department show that 'J. Ballieu' was receiving 7s. 6d. a day for this work, or £11. 12s. 6d. a month, bearing out W. L. Baillieu's own recollections of his early days at Queenscliff. Once gainfully employed, James married almost immediately, on 3 November 1853, Emma Lawrence Pow, the sixteen-year-old daughter of one

James George Baillieu, founder of the Baillieu family in Australia.

The Baillieu Hotel at Queenscliff, conducted by J. G. Baillieu until the crash.

BAILLIEU HOTEL,

QUEENSCLIFF.

UNDER THE PATRONAGE OF

HIS EXCELLENCY SIR H. B. LOCH, K.C.

James Pow. They lived in a government cottage on the beach, where they had the first of their sixteen children, of whom ten boys and four girls survived.

The first son, James Lambert Baillieu, was born in 1855, married at twenty-six years of age, but died at thirty-five, after twenty years' continuous employment with Paterson, Laing & Bruce Ltd in Melbourne. The second son was William Lawrence Baillieu, of whom more presently. The third son, George Francis Baillieu, was the father of Merlyn, who married Sidney Myer in 1920 and was later created a Dame of the British Empire. The fourth son, Robert Frederick Baillieu, became a tea merchant in Melbourne with W. L.'s assistance, but went bankrupt. The fifth son was Charles Formby Baillieu, who died a bachelor. The sixth son was Edward Lloyd Baillieu, who died in 1939 at the age of seventy-two after a long career on the Melbourne and London stock exchanges. The seventh son was Arthur Sydney Baillieu, the liquidator of several of W. L.'s boom-time companies. The eighth son was Richard Percy Clive Baillieu, father of June, who married Samuel Hordern. The ninth son was Norman Horace Baillieu, who died a bachelor in 1955 at the age of seventy-seven. The tenth son was Maurice Howard Baillieu, father of John Madden Baillieu, director of Electrolytic Zinc Industries Ltd, one of the world's biggest producers of refined zinc.

James, the father, was sorely pressed to feed and clothe his brood. In later years, W. L. Baillieu was fond of recalling how he and his father earned extra money by taking sightseers rowing on the bay at weekends for sixpence an hour. There seems little doubt that the family's early struggle for pennies was a critical influence in the formative years of W. L. Baillieu's character.

The family continued to live at Queenscliff, the father becoming a councillor and mayor of the town. W. L. arranged sufficient backing from the Commerical Bank for his father to leave the Customs Department in 1880 and build the Ozone Hotel in Queenscliff. This spacious retreat was patronized during the summer by holidaying notables, including Sir Henry Loch, Governor of Victoria. That popular Victorian writer, 'The Vagabond', related how he always stayed at the Ozone when in Queenscliff.

> If this did not stand in such a magnificent position, if everything were not of the first quality, if the fish breakfasts were not things to dream of in the future, if the hot baths of mineralised water pumped up from the springs below were not so health giving, I should still be happy and satisfied at the Ozone, the proprietor of which, as an old shellback and resident, is a mine of information to me. The name of Baillieu in the stalwart sons of the house is bound up with Queenscliff.

One of the stalwarts, George Francis (the third son), managed the hotel with great success in partnership with his father. At twenty-two years of age, George became the first man born in Queenscliff to be elected to the Borough Council, subsequently becoming mayor of Queenscliff on three occasions. In 1890, when the hotel's income dropped, George went to Melbourne to become stock exchange reporter for the *Herald*. He was followed in this post in 1895 by his brother 'Prince' (E. L. Baillieu), who used the experience to start the well-known sharebroking firm of E. L. & C. Baillieu.

W. L. Baillieu completed his barefoot years at Queenscliff State School, without much distinction beyond that of growing to great height and breadth. In 1874, when 'Willie' was fourteen and a half, his father was able to get him a job with the Bank of Victoria in Queenscliff, little realizing that in doing so he was opening the first chapter of one of the most remarkable business stories that Australia has known. In 1882 the young clerk was transferred to the bank's Maryborough branch. Here he made the acquaintance of two men who first turned his thoughts to methods of making a fortune from speculative investment. The men were Alfred Outtrim, at that time mayor of Maryborough; and B. J. Fink, a young entrepreneur who took over a worked-out gold mine near Maryborough and forced it to yield him a small fortune.

In 1885, enthralled by tales of the land boom then sweeping the metropolis, W. L. Baillieu went to live in Melbourne. Probably through B. J. Fink, he met another adventurous young fellow, Donald Munro, son of the James Munro who was making such a fine show with his building societies, his temperance halls, and his Federal Bank. Baillieu suggested to Donald Munro that they go into partnership in an estate agency; and furthermore, that James Munro should finance them through the Federal Bank. Both propositions were agreed to. In 1885, when W. L. was only twenty-six, the two young men opened business as Munro & Baillieu at the eastern end of Collins Street. Later they shifted to 243 Collins Street, next door to the *Age* office—very handy for the huge amount of real estate advertising they were soon placing. With the great reputation of the Munro name behind them, and the extra business which flowed from James Munro's wide personal interests, the young firm soon took first place among all estate agencies in the city, as we have seen.

George Meudell, or perhaps Theodore Fink, gave an interesting picture of the young W. L. Baillieu, in the rewritten version of *The Pleasant Career of a Spendthrift*:

> Like his parents and brothers and sisters, he was tall and handsome, with an alluring personality . . . W. L. Baillieu, in those palmy days of rising land values, was the greatest auctioneer of all. Land Syndicates and Land Companies competed for his services . . . One such sale was memorable—Baillieu sold a subdivision called the Town Hall Estate, at Malvern, at the rate of one allotment a minute, the total purchase price being £50,000.

In 1887 James Munro invited W. L. Baillieu to become one of the foundation directors of the Real Estate Bank—which was founded largely to buy at inflated prices the unsold properties owned by Munro. The paid-up capital was £58,000. With this meagre backing the directors approved within twelve months the purchase of land to the value of £922,000. However, Baillieu was shrewd enough to buy only a few of the bank's shares. If he had followed the same policy on land company shares, he need never have been forced into insolvency.

The same year in which the Real Estate Bank was floated, W. L. made a brilliant marriage—to Bertha, the twenty-two-year-old only daughter of Edward Latham, a leading Melbourne brewer. In 1889 they began having their own sizable family, four sons and four daughters, all of whom were given the second

W. L. Baillieu at the height of his power (left) and in later life.

name 'Latham.' The first son was Clive Latham Baillieu, who was educated at Oxford, became a London barrister, fought in World War I, later became a director of many London companies and government bodies, was knighted, and was created Lord Baillieu in 1953. The second son was Harry, who was educated at Cambridge, married Margaret, daughter of W. S. Robinson (fellow director of Baillieu's mining companies), and was awarded the Military Cross in World War I. The third son was Tom, who was awarded the D.F.C. in the same war. The fourth son was James, who died unmarried in 1934.

Their mother Bertha, the brewer's daughter, was as essentially down-to-earth in her approach to life as William, the boatman's son. There were few social graces or ambitions about Bertha, and the couple rarely entertained during the boom years, unlike most other newly-rich families. Bertha seemed content to live quietly and care for her growing family, while her brilliant husband was making his first, second, and third fortunes in the city. When the young couple were first married, they did not squander money on a house of their own. They lived comfortably enough with Edward Latham in his Kew mansion called 'Knowsley.' In September 1888 Baillieu bought from W. D. Clark the house known as 'Ainslie', in Studley Park Road, Kew. In making his secret composition, Baillieu valued his own interest in this house as 'Nil', although he had certainly given Clark promissory notes for £4,360 as progress payments on the house.

Thus we must assume that Baillieu really bought the house on behalf of his father-in-law, Edward Latham, who was listed in Sands & MacDougall's directory as the occupier until 1890. (In that year, W. L. Baillieu and his family were shown as living at 89 Southey Street, St Kilda, with his bachelor brother E. L. Baillieu.) In 1890 the original 'Ainslie' was demolished to make way for the construction of Studley Park Avenue, and Edward Latham shifted to 198 Studley Park Road, alongside Wrixon's great 'Raheen' property. At the same time, W. L. and his family moved from St Kilda to the new house, living there with Latham for another four years, during which period Harry Baillieu and Vere Baillieu were born. In 1895 they shifted to their own house in Waterloo Street, Camberwell, next door to Riversdale Road Trinity Church. Later they bought a country property, 'Sefton', at Mount Macedon, with 65 acres of grounds.

The main reason for Baillieu's insolvency in 1892 was that he was not content merely to make an excellent living from commissions on the large amount of property being sold by his estate agency, but gambled on making a fortune from speculation on his own account. Thus he started the Camberwell Estate Co. Ltd with A. G. Hall (an employee and later a partner of Theodore Fink) as his fellow director. He started the Bourke Street Freehold & Investment Co. Ltd with W. J. Malpas (sharebroking partner of his brother, E. L. Baillieu) as fellow director. But the thirty-three-year-old W. L. Baillieu had not the experience, nor the foresight, nor the knowledge of economic trends, to realize when he started these companies that the land boom was over for good. In this, of course, his blinded vision was that of the whole community.

The sorry history of the Bourke Street Freehold Co. Ltd formed in itself a good illustration of the dangers of over-confidence in such matters. When James Mirams of the Premier Building Association engaged Munro & Baillieu as agents to sell a huge city block on the western side of Russell Street between Bourke Street and Little Collins Street, Baillieu thought he saw a golden opportunity for himself. In 1888 he incorporated the Bourke Street Freehold Co. Ltd with £1 million capital, sold shares to all his acquaintances, and bought the block himself from Mirams. The major shareholding in this disastrous venture was: W. L. Baillieu, 15,000 shares; E. L. Baillieu and W. J. Malpas, 12,500; Theodore Fink and R. W. Best, 10,625; B. J. Fink, 10,000; Catherine Fink, 10,000; J. M. Howden, 10,000; Donald Munro, 5,000; George Isaacs, 5,000; Wolfe Fink, 2,500; Kate Fink, 625; and Magnus Fink, 625. But when the time came to resell the individual sites in the huge block, hardly a buyer could be found. Even in 1890, when the company decided to lease the sites instead, and called up 18s. 6d. new capital on each share to meet development costs, little more than half the full amount was subscribed. Nevertheless, Baillieu proceeded to lease part of the property to the Cyclorama Company for thirty years at £2,000 a year, and rented out other sections. The Cyclorama Company and some of the other tenants dishonoured their leases during the smash, throwing the property back on Baillieu's hands and helping to send him bankrupt.

When the private meeting of W. L. Baillieu's creditors was called on 26

July 1892, only a few creditors attended, apart from the omnipresent Theodore Fink. Baillieu disclosed debts totalling £48,936. Of this amount, £26,543 was owing for calls on shares; and £22,393 for loans covered by promissory notes and the like. It is now known that Baillieu speculated in shares far beyond his means. In this, of course, he was acting in common with thousands of other Australian investors at the time, many of whom speculated far more extravagantly than he did.

From the records of Baillieu's cash debts, it may be seen that he borrowed heavily and widely. Much of the money was spent in buying shares at high premiums. Some of it was spent in buying 'Ainslie'; some, no doubt, on current expenses. It is noteworthy that in March 1892—four months before his bankruptcy—Baillieu raised a total of £7,757 in cash by means of promissory notes. Of this amount, £4,792 came from the City of Melbourne Bank; £2,372 from the Colonial Bank per Joseph Clarke; and £593 from his own Bourke Street Freehold Co. Ltd. As the time of his insolvency drew even closer, one may note how Baillieu was reduced to borrowing such insignificant amounts as £108 from Isaac Reed of the Cyclorama Company. One would hope, however, that his gardener got back the £200 which Baillieu owed him.

In his secret composition, Baillieu valued his personal assets at a total of £10,504. Since most of this consisted of shares in bankrupt land companies, his true assets were undoubtedly much less than he may have believed at the time. Among his personal property, Baillieu valued his Broken Hill shares as 'Nil'; his furniture at £450; his 500 shares in the *Herald* (£1 fully paid-up) at £200; and his buggy at £20. Included in the money owing to him was £1,286 from Robert F. Baillieu; and £106 from Marc Fink. His brother, however, was already bankrupt, and thus W. L.'s total cash assets were sworn at £771. The composition accepted by creditors was 6d. in the £1, payable within thirty days.

Baillieu's true financial position at the time of his secret composition would appear to be as follows:

Personal debts	£48,936
Half share of Munro & Baillieu debts	70,279
Indebtedness to the Federal Bank (written off)	98,828
Indebtedness to the Commercial Bank	7,555
TOTAL	£225,598

In the Insolvency Court William McLean, a director of the Federal Bank, claimed that W. L. Baillieu had helped the bank's directors to conceal the extent of his overdraft from the auditors on balancing days. On 27 September 1891, he said, Baillieu's overdraft was £26,000. On balancing date, 30 September, it was only £6,000. A few days later, it was back to £26,000. 'The effect of the entries was that Baillieu's account was about £20,000 better on balance day than it was before balance day', McLean told the court. Baillieu did not give evidence.

A succession of other tragedies hit the family. James Baillieu lost the Ozone Hotel to the Commercial Bank. Valued at £15,000, the hotel carried a first

If wealthy men could escape their debts, why couldn't ordinary people? A housewife offers her grocer ½d. in the £1.

mortgage of £10,000 to the bank, plus a second mortgage of £5,000 to the Federal Bank. Interest on the first mortgage alone amounted to £550 a year, more than the hotel's annual profits during the depression. Then Robert Frederick Baillieu (the fourth son), a tea merchant who had bought the business of F. Sandiman & Co. at 205 William Street, went bankrupt publicly, with £3,000 debts and nil assets. He had been given a £1,000 overdraft by the Federal Bank, and W. L. Baillieu had lent him £1,286 to carry on the business. Even Baillieu's first major mining venture crashed. The Broken Hill & Argenton Smelting Co. Ltd had started business on 14 March 1892, its directors being W. L. Baillicu, George Swinburne, Robert Gayer, and John Wilkinson. The company's purpose was to extract silver and lead from dumps in the Mt Zeehan district, but it lost heavily because of the low grade of the ores being treated.

Then, after the disasters, came the most extraordinary part of the Baillieu story. W. L. just carried on as though nothing had happened. He was protected from further action on his past debts by his creditors' somewhat hasty acceptance of the 6d. in the £1 settlement. His enormous indebtedness to the Federal Bank had been kindly written off the books of that wayward institution. His overdraft of £7,555. 11s. 5d. with the Commercial Bank had been guaranteed by Edward

Latham—who had made *his* secret composition two months before Baillieu's. So the way forward appeared to be clear.

Baillieu simply formed himself into 'W. L. Baillieu & Co.', auctioneer and estate agent, and blithely invited new business. Only a handful of people knew, or cared, about his secret insolvency. Thus we find in the same year—in *Table Talk* of all places—large advertisements from W. L. Baillieu & Co. announcing the auction of the contents of 'Quisisana', a mansion on the corner of Grange Road and Robertson Street, Toorak, 'lately occupied by George Fairbairn, Esq., Jun.' The sale included

> Most Magnificent and Costly ART FURNITURE, Grand Piano by Steinweg [*sic*] Paintings, Bric-a-Brac, &c., the whole forming one of the Most Superb Collections ever offered in the Southern Hemisphere . . . The Auctioneers would call the special attention of the Elite of Toorak to this Grand Sale . . . [which] presents a rare opportunity to obtain Lovely and Beautiful Furnishings at Nominal Prices.

One wonders whether Willie Baillieu, the barefoot boy from Queenscliff, took malicious secret pleasure in penning such epitaphs.

To the public, hardly any hint of Baillieu's personal affairs was ever given. With untroubled brow, he acted (and was paid) as liquidator of the Chatsworth Estate Co. Ltd, that notorious speculative enterprise of James Munro. At the wind-up meeting of the Chatsworth bubble, Baillieu said bluntly that the members of the company had been 'caught and blistered', and 'must make the best of it'. With similar feelings, no doubt, Baillieu also proceeded to liquidate the Whittingham Bros estate. But never again did he go in for big speculative land deals on his own account.

About this time, his young brother, Richard Percy Clive Baillieu, joined the firm, and helped to restore its fortunes over a period of four years. Then he left to become a partner in the sharebroking firm of E. L. Baillieu and W. J. Malpas. In 1897 W. L. Baillieu took his younger brother, Arthur, into the estate agency, and practically handed over its operations to him in time while following his own wider interests.

It is difficult to estimate W. L. Baillieu's real assets after the boom. Due to the pernicious system of secret composition, he was never examined in the Insolvency Court, nor forced to reveal the full extent of his profits and losses. All we know for certain is that he was able to buy a substantial house in Camberwell, carry on his business, and bide his time. After carefully surveying the scene, he quietly began buying certain bank shares, notably those of the London Bank of Australia, which could be picked up extremely cheaply after the bank smash of 1893. This second great gamble of Baillieu's life succeeded. As economic conditions slowly stabilized and improved in the late 1890s, bank shares and properties increased greatly from their depression values. Baillieu, who eventually owned a major interest in the bank, arranged an amalgamation with the English, Scottish & Australian Bank. The result was that Baillieu made a fortune from this deal alone.

The third great gamble of Baillieu's life, which succeeded beyond the wildest dreams, was his decision to back the De Bavay flotation process for separating zinc from Broken Hill mine tailings. The story has been fully told in Geoffrey

Blainey's book, *The Rush That Never Ended* (Melbourne, 1963). For our purposes, it was yet another illustration of Baillieu's unshaken propensity towards taking enormous risks in pursuit of fortune.

According to those who knew him, Baillieu was a man of commanding personality and vast force of character. Handicapped by his comparatively low standard of education, he found it difficult to express himself logically on paper, but more than compensated for that by his native wit and quickness of mind. 'Everyone seemed to automatically look to him for leadership', an acquaintance remarked. Most recollections of the man in his middle years bear out his spontaneous friendliness. He would talk to anyone, remembered lift drivers and clerks and generally acted like the bluff, hearty and optimistic empire-builder which he was. On one occasion the wife of the manager of one of his companies gave birth to a baby in the U.S.A., and the expenses were charged to the company. 'Don't let it happen again', Baillieu growled to his manager. 'Whenever I'm in a deal, I have to be in it right from the start.' A big man in every way, 6 ft 3 in. tall and broad in proportion, Baillieu could be brusque when necessary. At one meeting he impatiently told another director to 'pee or get off the pot'. Another director, he said, 'worried too much about doing the wrong thing'. Perhaps his best remembered epigram followed a heated dispute with two fellow directors. 'I am like a well-known historical character—I'm being crucified between Montague Cohen and Theodore Fink', he complained.

W. L. was in America at the time of the Wall Street crash, and was deeply shocked by the panic. Did the new depression take the seventy-year-old financier back, even subconsciously, to the widespread suffering of the 1890s? At all events, on his return to Australia his friends could see signs of a definite mental change. He still brooded over his wife's death in 1925. He was no longer unperturbed by small and large worries. An eye-witness related how, even in the 1930s, part of the procedure of directors' meetings at Collins House was to examine all the cheques ready to be signed. At one such meeting, Baillieu suddenly shouted, 'Why do you worry me with these things?' and flung his steel-nib pen into the boardroom table, where it remained quivering like a dagger. Such behaviour was unprecedented for W. L. Later he accused his old friend and fellow director, Montague Cohen, of being 'just another Jew'. Cohen, deeply shaken, stalked out of the boardroom. On top of all this, George Meudell's book, *The Pleasant Career of a Spendthrift*, had set Melbourne sniggering with its scandalous tales of Baillieu's financial deals of the 1880s. '*He paid a farthing in the pound*', jeered the children of a new depression.

The end came tragically, with the mind which had been so keen now clouded. On his way home from a board meeting in 1932, Baillieu, then seventy-three years of age, made an attack on his chauffeur. He was restrained, and quietly taken to London on board ship. W. L. Baillieu died in London on 6 February 1936, at the age of seventy-seven. Cause of death was certified as broncho-pneumonia and influenza. His estate, which at one time was valued in millions, went for probate at £60,000. The wily old financier had made sure long before that his hard-won fortune went to his family, not to the State.

36

Edward Latham the Brewer

For many years beer has been to Melbourne what whisky is to Edinburgh or ouzo is to Athens—one of the city's greatest recommendations. Even visitors from other States admit that the quality of Melbourne beer almost makes up for the influence of the teetotallers, who for many years ensured that it could not be legally purchased after 6 p.m. This curious compromise between the teetotal and brewing interests, with its background of political parsons and liquor lobbyists, has a private history of its own which need not concern us here. We may, however, examine the way in which the land boom and the ensuing depression laid the foundations for today's near-monopoly in the brewing trade. Immediately we do so, the dichotomy of the teetotal movement of those days springs into relief. For James Munro, in public a leader of the prohibitionists, was secretly financing one of Melbourne's biggest brewers through his Federal Bank.

The brewer's name was Edward Latham, major shareholder and director of the Carlton Brewery. Latham's background was obscure. He was orphaned in Lancashire at an early age, and according to his authorised biography, spent his early years from five to fifteen at 'a boarding school'—obviously an orphanage—with two older brothers. Each of the Lathams was sent to work in Lancashire's 'dark Satanic mills,' places of almost indescribable horror in the England of the 1840s. Edward's fate was to toil in a boiling-down works, where only the strongest survived. One of his brothers fell victim to the White Plague, tuberculosis; and Edward determined to rescue him. How he found the money, how he escaped from the soap-boiling works, are unfortunately not matters on record. The two brothers, one a pale ghost spitting bright red blood, the other bursting with rude health, the two of them living examples of natural selection in the industrial jungle, embarked in 1864 for the legendary colony of Victoria. The day after they stepped ashore in Melbourne, Edward's brother died—twenty-five years of age.

After spending some months in Tasmania, where he married early in 1865, Latham returned to the mainland with money and an introduction to G. M. Milne, brother of Sir William Milne of Adelaide. Together they looked around for a profitable enterprise. One promising idea was to go into business as brewers. People seemed to keep on drinking, despite the exhortations of the prohibitionists. Latham and Milne bought the Carlton Brewery, at that time a tiny enterprise which was producing fifty hogsheads of beer a week. Latham rolled up his sleeves and got to work. The head brewer, Alfred Terry, was instructed to double, treble, then quadruple production. Latham himself got out among the hotels and persuaded many publicans to stock and recommend the Carlton product instead of the bewildering array of brands available in those days. Before long the brewery was selling not fifty hogsheads a week, but 1,200.

As early as 1870, Latham was prospering so greatly that he started building 'Raheen', an enormous red brick mansion on extensive grounds in Studley Park Road, Kew. For some unknown reason Latham did not complete the building, but sold the structure to Sir Henry Wrixon, M.L.C. ('Raheen'survives as the property of the Roman Catholic Church and residence for many years of the late Archbishop, Dr Daniel Mannix, although much of its land has been subdivided over the years). The Lathams shifted to 'Knowsley' in another part of Kew.

Shortly afterwards, Latham started one of Australia's first private fire brigades—consisting of horse-drawn water wagons which dashed with great jangling of harness and clanging of bells to the scene of any conflagration, later claiming a reward from the presumably grateful owner of the premises which had been saved from destruction. Other private brigades were started in emulation, and soon teams all over Australia were claiming records in getting to a fire after the alarm was given. A contest called the Britannia Cup was arranged to test the claims. Latham's fire brigade won the trophy for four years in succession—1878 to 1881.

Now began a significant connection between the wealthy Latham family of Kew and the poverty-stricken Baillieu family of Queenscliff. Was there already an attraction between the lusty young boatman, Willie Baillieu, and Latham's only daughter, the 13-year-old Bertha? We may pose the question but cannot answer it. All that is known is that when the Lathams were holidaying at Queenscliff in 1878, Latham asked Baillieu to join the crew of his yacht, the *Hygeia*. We can imagine, however, that all members of the family were attracted by the tall young man's wonderful exuberance and vitality. The Lancashire mills with their emaciated toilers seemed far distant from the sun-drenched shores of Queenscliff.

By 1882 Latham's brewery was so prosperous that he was able to float it on the stock market. A company called the Melbourne Brewing & Malting Co. Ltd was formed, Latham retaining the largest interest but making a tidy fortune from the sale of the balance of the shares. Some of the money went on a large donation towards the building of St Paul's Cathedral; some to buy a sylvan retreat at Queenscliff in 1883, where Anglican clergymen 'suffering from exhaustion, or broken down by age or illness, may find a pleasant and comfortable convalescent home.' We may add that whatever strains broke down the Anglican clergymen of Melbourne, opposition to the brewery interests was not foremost among them.

Edward Latham, who developed the Carlton Brewery into a major enterprise.

Carlton Brewery advertising changed quickly to meet the new century.

As previously noted, W. L. Baillieu married Bertha Latham in 1887. After that, Edward Latham appears to have relied largely on the young auctioneer for advice and management of his investments. The house 'Ainslie' in Studley Park Road was bought in Baillieu's name, but Latham moved into it. Together they took over the West End Brewery and re-floated Latham's Melbourne Brewing Co. into the Carlton & West End Brewery Co. Ltd. Then Baillieu persuaded Latham to put his spare cash into some of his land ventures.

It was a fatal move. When the land companies crashed, Latham was found to be involved to the extent of £112,000 in debts he was unable to meet. He owed Mrs J. T. Peacock £25,000 on the purchase of a building in Flinders Lane. He owed David Syme, Samuel Gillott, and J. F. Levien £11,000 for his share in the purchase of Scotts Hotel. He owed the Commercial Bank £15,000 for his guarantee of the overdrafts of W. L. Baillieu and J. G. Baillieu. He had borrowed £8,000 from the E.S. & A. Bank and £7,000 from the A.M.P. Society. Calls on his shares in the Camberwell Estate Co. and the Real Estate Bank totalled nearly £15,000. In another claim, E. L. Baillieu and W. J. Malpas, the sharebroking partnership, revealed that they had been buying up and 'bulling' shares in the Carlton Brewery for Latham, but had been left with the liability on the shares registered in their name.

In common with several other speculators, Latham did not disclose in his secret composition the large loans he had been given by the Federal Bank, of which he was a director. These included:–

Edward Latham	£35,000
Latham and Ashton	£21,000
Latham and Baillieu	£10,000
TOTAL:	£66,000

Early poster advertising the Carlton Brewery.

Among his assets, Latham valued his carriage at £100, a wagonette at £60, and his two horses at £40 the pair. His creditors agreed in May 1892 to accept 1s. in the £1 in satisfaction of their claims.

Less than eight months later, Latham was back in the company flotation business again. On 23 December 1892, he floated Edward Latham & Co. Ltd with £50,000 nominal capital. The purpose of this company was to acquire from J. R. Fryer 'the buildings, plant and erections known as the Southern Brewery,' situated in Richmond. The other subscribers to the new company were Bertha Latham, T. R. Latham, W. L. Baillieu, and Bertha Martha Baillieu.

In this way Latham proceeded to rebuild his fortunes on the more dependable basis of beer. As one of his fellow brewers, Nicholas FitzGerald, M.L.C., said during the depression, 'The consumption of a light, nutritious and wholesome beer in this country is an absolute necessity to working men.' Latham was the first to agree that investment in brewing and tied houses was better than investment in land company shares.

Many breweries, however, had been ruined by the simple fact that workless men could not afford to buy much beer. Others struggled on against heavy odds. A few years later, Latham, Baillieu and others combined several of the survivors into a new company called Carlton & United Breweries Ltd. One by one, over subsequent years, the C.U.B. swallowed its competitors with apparent relish. By 1965, exactly one hundred years after the Lancashire lad Edward Latham first found fortune in competitive enterprise, his empire had developed into a total monopoly which up to then had succeeded in preventing other Lancashire lads from starting their own breweries.

37

Keeping the Federal Bank in the Family

In preceding chapters we have caught glimpses of that unusual institution, the Federal Bank, which its founder James Munro ran as a convenient method of diverting huge amounts of the public's money into the pockets of himself, his family, and their associates. As we have seen, the truth about these activities was partially revealed by *Table Talk* in June 1893. The full story did not come out until nearly a year later, when various accountants and liquidators had completed their investigations. A series of court cases then took place, mostly based on the question of whether Alfred Priestley, manager of the Federal Bank, should be allowed to continue in his position as liquidator. During these hearings, the accuracy of *Table Talk's* mysterious source of information was confirmed over and over again. Many additional and extraordinary facts were brought into the light of day.

The Federal Bank commenced business in 1881 with six directors: James Munro, J. B. Watson, John Robb, John Whittingham, William McLean, and J. J. Casey. Casey resigned in 1884, J. B. Watson died in 1889, and W. L. Baillieu's father-in-law, Edward Latham, was appointed to the board in the same year. Manager of the institution, and liquidator until dismissed by the court, was Alfred Priestley.

The bank suspended payment and closed its doors in January 1893, beginning the process of private voluntary liquidation under Priestley's direction. The English depositors appointed William Riggall, of the Melbourne legal firm, Blake & Riggall, as local representative to watch their interests. On request, Priestley supplied Riggall with an overdraft list which purported to be accurate. Riggall at first accepted Priestley's list as complete. Then, said Isaac Isaacs (briefed by Blake & Riggall to appear in court): 'It was pointed out by *Table Talk* that this list was not a correct statement. Had it not been for the announcement in *Table Talk*, Mr. Riggall would never have suspected that the figures supplied to him were not exact.' Riggall deposed that 'After reading the article [in *Table Talk*] I saw Mr. Priestley and showed him the newspaper, and asked him if the figures quoted were correct. He replied that substantially they were correct.' What scurryings there had been behind the scenes to try and minimize the extent of the scandal! Riggall immediately forced Priestley to supply him with a complete overdraft list, and took court action to remove him as liquidator. The following liabilities were then confirmed, among others:

James Munro (various accounts)	£202,000
Munro & Baillieu	123,000
W. L. Baillieu	44,000
W. L. Baillieu & Theodore Fink	10,000
William McLean (a director)	97,000
E. Latham (a director)	66,000
Whittingham Bros. (directors)	25,000
Alex. Munro (son of James Munro)	28,000
G. M. Munro (son of James Munro)	8,000
R. L. Balding (son-in-law of James Munro)	5,000
J. G. Baillieu	5,000
R. F. Baillieu	2,000
E. L. Baillieu	2,000

To the astonishment of the court and the public, it was ultimately disclosed that through the Federal Bank, James Munro had lent himself, his family and his friends nearly three-quarters of a million pounds of the public's money. Munro and his immediate family had taken more than £270,000. Four other directors of the bank—McLean, Whittingham, Robb, and Latham—had taken nearly £240,000. W. L. Baillieu and the Munro-Baillieu partnership had taken £230,000. Addressing the court, Isaac Isaacs described 'the farce of advancing to A on B's guarantee, and to B on A's guarantee. For instance, W. L. Baillieu obtained an advance and got Munro's guarantee, and then Munro got an advance and Baillieu went security.' Regarding the advances to Munro & Baillieu, Priestley told the court that they had mostly been made by the assistant manager, a Mr Pinnock. 'I complained to the directors of the irregularity of Mr. Pinnock's proceedings', said Priestley with virtuous indignation. He claimed that in 1892 he had given an ultimatum to the directors that either he or Pinnock would have to leave the bank. Pinnock had been dismissed and had left the country for South Africa.

Referring to advances made to James Munro's other bank, the Real Estate Bank, Priestley said the arrangement was that the Federal Bank, the Commercial Bank, and the City of Melbourne Bank had each lent £30,000 in an endeavour to prop up the Real Estate Bank when it was near collapse. Mr Justice Holroyd described this particular arrangement as 'a job'. Priestley also admitted that the directors had decided to buy the bank's shares with its own funds, in order to prevent further market depreciation. A. T. Robb, a son of John Robb, was engaged for this purpose, and bought £11,000 worth. The shares were then transferred to employees of the bank's directors.

Mr Justice Holroyd: 'My view of the transaction is, I may candidly say, that it is illegal, and the question is whether it is not fraudulent.'

Attempting to defend the various transactions, Mr Higgins (for Priestley) said: 'Of course it is now well known that no profits were made by the directors, and that they came out of it very badly.'

Mr Justice Holroyd: 'The mischief of it is that the people whose money they

When the Federal Bank's walking-stick marked 'Credit' snapped in half, the remainder of the Associated Banks shunned their fellow-member.

took came out of it worse. They speculated with other people's money, and caused an enormous amount of misery. That is the real truth of it.'

In November 1894 the affairs of the Federal Bank were referred to Judge Molesworth for investigation in the Insolvency Court. William McLean, a director, told in evidence how the directors' accounts were juggled to appear as though they were in credit on balancing date, 30 September. By arrangement with the City of Melbourne Bank, he drew a cheque on that bank for £25,000 and paid it into the Federal Bank. To the auditors, this made him appear as a creditor on that day, not a debtor. The following day, he paid the £25,000 back to the City of Melbourne Bank.

After sale of its assets, the Federal Bank wound up by paying 9s. 6d. in the £1 to depositors and other creditors. One prominent creditor was the Melbourne Savings Bank, from which the Federal had also borrowed £25,000 in its desperate struggles to stay afloat. The Federal's premises at 307 Collins Street were sold up and rebuilt as the M.L.C. Building, which in turn was demolished in 1971 for construction of the new M.L.C. Building of today.

38

Theodore Fink, a Solicitor of the Rialto

Older residents of Melbourne remember him as an energetic little Pickwickian figure, wearing one of his extraordinary hats and a perpetually pleasant but enigmatic smile. Theodore Fink was one of the most powerful men in Melbourne, a close associate of the Collins House group, a director and controller of the *Herald* newspaper organization for nearly half a century, a dedicated Christian Scientist, and a philosopher who had a disconcerting habit of disappearing for days at a time on long country rambles where only the sun and the stars shared his lonely secrets.

Did he follow the right road in becoming a businessman—one of those tortured souls called 'a press baron'—or should he have devoted his considerable talents and energies to literature? The question never ceased to torment him. Theodore Fink, the newspaper chief, disappeared long ago beneath a torrent of newsprint covered with ephemera. Theodore Fink, the youthful poet, wears better. Listen to the young man, a busy solicitor writing in 1893, when the banks were crashing all around him:

> Once I had faith in the years that Time
>   Held in his hand to be showered on me,
> With gifts of heroes and deeds sublime,
>   And fame thereof rumoured o'er land and sea;
> And a name that was honoured and yet was mine.
>   Those were things that youth held could be,
> With other bright visions that would not stay,
>   But grew dim—as this outer light grows grey.

A name that was honoured and yet was Theodore Fink's? Unfortunately, rude ambition had already snatched him up and set him down in a den of land speculators. His fame was the dubious notoriety of finding a legal escape hatch for himself and all the other bankrupt financiers who had helped to bring Melbourne to its knees. Doomed all his life to search for honour, Theodore Fink ended it with his Orwellian attempt to rewrite history, in the form of the expurgated edition of Meudell's *Pleasant Career*.

Theodore Fink, born in the Channel Islands in 1855, was one of a family of five boys and five girls, children of Moses and Gertrude Fink. In 1860 the family emigrated to Geelong, Victoria, where Theodore was educated at Geelong College. Later he attended Melbourne Grammar, where he won the poetry

Theodore Fink, as seen by *Melbourne Punch* after he took the journal over.

Fink's partner Robert Best, who finally repaid his land boom debts in full.

prize with topical verses on 'The War Around Paris'. Fink was a schoolmate and lifelong intimate of Alfred Deakin. Both became solicitors, both burnt their fingers in the land boom, and both rose to national fame.

Fink served his articles to H. J. Farmer, Melbourne's leading mercantile lawyer of the day, and was admitted to practice as a solicitor in 1877. Only twenty-two, he rapidly established a reputation of his own for expertise in handling financial and constitutional cases. During these busy years, too, he flung himself into the activities of the literary and artistic world which was the nearest thing to Bohemia that Melbourne ever produced. He contributed constantly in prose and verse, both in light and serious mood, to Melbourne newspapers, the *Melbourne Review, Melbourne Punch*, and possibly *Table Talk*. He argued sociology at the Eclectic Society with H. G. Turner, Marcus Clarke, and Alfred Deakin; read omnivorously; and found time to marry Kate, daughter of George Isaacs, in 1881. They lived at 'Broceliande' in Walsh Street, South Yarra, shifting later to 'Weemala' in Lansell Road, Toorak.

In 1886 Fink was taken into partnership by R. W. Best, M.L.A. for Fitzroy, and P. D. Phillips, a famous barrister of the day. The firm became legal advisers to the Board of Works, several municipalities, and many of the new building societies and land banks. They set up their offices, appropriately enough, in the new Rialto Building, itself a creation of the boom period, at the western end of Collins Street. Readers may still see the Rialto standing today between William and King Street, and ponder on the deals consummated within its neo-Gothic walls and curious galleries.

With so many booming land companies among the firm's clients, Fink apparently could not resist the prevailing mania, and was soon speculating heavily on his own account. By 1891 he had involved himself in debts exceeding £70,000—although like everyone else he thought he was amply covered by the value of the property he was buying. When he left on an eight months' trip to Europe in March 1891 to buy art treasures, no hint of the disasters to come troubled his speech at a farewell banquet:

> I am an honest laborer in the legal vineyard, and the fact that so many of you are in the full enjoyment of three meals a day, and able to walk about—out of gaol (laughter)—shows that I need a change (laughter) . . . My physician, one of our most accomplished veterinary surgeons—(loud laughter)—warned me that I might carry my habit of working two hours a day too far—(laughter) . . .

When Fink hastily returned towards the end of 1891, there were more tears than laughter in the colony of Victoria. The land banks and building societies had started to tumble. Now it was every man for himself. Fink realized that if his land and share holdings continued to lose their market value, and his creditors started pressing him for payment, the inevitable end was the Insolvency Court and ruin of his legal reputation. Was there any lawful solution?

Early in 1892, when the need was greatest, Fink came across a little-used provision of the insolvency law called 'Composition by Arrangement'. The original purpose of this statute was to enable certain debtors whose livelihood would be jeopardized by adverse publicity to meet their creditors privately and arrange to pay them so-much-in-the-£1, thus avoiding the odium of public bankruptcy proceedings. Only a very small circle need ever hear of the arrangement, and by this means an honest trader's credit, or a professional man's position, could be preserved. Composition by Arrangement was never intended to shield reckless speculators from the results of their folly. It might reasonably apply to perhaps two or three bankrupts in the course of one year. The results of such secrecy were found to be so pernicious that the system was drastically changed in England by Act of Parliament in 1883, and in Victoria in 1897. Even today it remains a complex and controversial area of the law.

From the date of Theodore Fink's first composition with his creditors in January 1892, to the end of that year, no less than eighty-five private compositions were approved in Victoria. They included most of the prominent land boomers, along with Theodore Fink's brothers Benjamin and Wolfe, and his father-in-law George Isaacs. The following year, another fifty-two private compositions were completed, cleaning up most of the stragglers. Practically all the compositions were arranged by Theodore Fink's legal firm, Fink, Best & Phillips; and another well-known firm of insolvency experts, Braham & Pirani. A list of those involved is given in Appendices A and B.

On 19 January Fink called together a meeting of his creditors at George Meudell's office at 59 Queen Street, Melbourne. Meudell agreed to act as trustee for the creditors. They were presented with Fink's balance sheet, which on the face of it did not look too hopeless:

Debts	£73,557
Assets	59,425
Deficiency	£14,132

The debts were real enough, being largely amounts which Fink had contracted to pay on mortgage. The assets were more open to question. £46,000 was represented as 'Value of real property'. But what was the 'value' of property at the beginning of 1892? Almost nothing, and decreasing all the time.

A list of Fink's debts was read out to the meeting. His major debt was an overdraft to the Federal Bank for £10,000. His connections with Messrs Munro & Baillieu had cost him £7,000 for calls on shares in the Bourke Street Freehold Co. Ltd; and another £2,000 in promissory notes. He had borrowed £10,000 from his wife and her father. Another £5,000 had come from the Commercial Bank and the Bank of South Australia. The creditors present at Fink's meeting included W. L. Baillieu, C. M. Davies, A. G. Hall, Wolfe Fink, E. L. Baillieu, Maurice Aron, W. J. Malpas, and Alfred Priestley. They were informed that the amount available for payout was £3,317, and agreed to accept a composition of 3s. in the £1 in settlement of their claims. The composition was duly submitted to the Chief Clerk in Insolvency, H. W. Macleod, and approved by him. Theodore Fink was legally free of his debts, and as solvent as the next man.

He did not stay that way for long. On 19 July Fink called a *second* creditors' meeting. This time he presented them with a balance sheet showing a further £16,000 in debts and practically nil assets. At this meeting, a number of debts which should have been disclosed at the first meeting were now set down.

The biggest was a sum of nearly £7,000 claimed by A. G. Hall, an employee of Fink's legal firm. Hall claimed that he made a promissory note for £7,000 in April 1891 'at the request of Fink & Best and Munro & Baillieu for their accommodation and as their trustee.' The promissory note was cashed by the Federal Bank, then dishonoured. In Fink's second insolvency, we find the Federal Bank advancing £178 to him on another promissory note, five weeks after being told they would get 3s. in the £1 on the original £10,000 he owed them. Few speculators could wish for more accommodating bankers.

Fink's other debts included £2,500 for calls on Chaffey Bros shares; another £2,000 to B. J. Fink; and another £1,000 to his wife Kate. Even George Meudell had lent him £150 after the first composition, for which Theodore Fink had signed a promissory note. Fink had also borrowed £500 from the Melbourne Trust Finance Co. Ltd on no security. This firm was managed by Salis Fischer, who acted as trustee in the matter of Fink's second composition, and was closely associated with him in many ways for another four years. (In 1896 Fischer, forty-one years of age, bought a phial of prussic acid from the dispensary at the Mutual Store, took it home, and poisoned himself. 'Financial troubles' were given as the reason.)

Whatever their various thoughts and motives, the creditors this time accepted Fink's proposal to pay 6d. in the £1, thus giving him the distinction of being the only debtor in Victoria, and probably in Australia, who ever compounded with his creditors twice in the one year. At thirty-eight, Theodore Fink had left an indelible mark on British legal practice.

For many years, even after Fink's death, the story persisted that Fink had offered his creditors his Herald shares in part payment of his debts, but that they had refused them, considering them a liability. The facts were that under a takeover agreement dated 17 May 1889, Theodore Fink and W. L. Baillieu each took up three £1,000 shares (out of a total of thirty such shares issued) in the Herald & Sportsman Newspapers Co. Ltd. Each had paid only £400 on their shares, leaving a balance of £2,600 to be paid by instalments. Fink did not include his interest in these Herald shares as an asset in either of his private compositions, and there is no evidence that the matter was raised by his creditors. The official returns of shareholders showed that both Fink and Baillieu retained their shares during and after their secret compositions. (By 1894 Fink had actually increased his holding to six shares of £1,000 each.) There are several possible explanations of the matter, and the reader must form his own opinion. There is, however, no question that had it not been for the existence of the process of secret insolvency, both Fink and Baillieu would have lost their Herald shares, with incalculable consequences for the future.

Theodore Fink's partner, P. D. Phillips, did not take a cheerful view of all these events. At the end of 1892 he retired from the partnership and went into business at 453 Collins Street as P. D. Phillips & Son. To replace Phillips, the partners took in the aforesaid A. G. Hall, who according to Fink's composition of 19 July had received 6d. in the £1 on his debt of £7,000. An understanding, nay, a generous partner! The firm continued as Fink, Best & Hall for many

A NEW VERB – TO 'FINK' IT.

Smith.– Hullo, Brown! I saw that you were to have a meeting of your creditors the other day. You didn't funk it?
Brown.– No; I *fink'd* it. A halfpenny in the pound.

years. Of the trio, R. W. Best was the only man who repaid his land boom debts in full, although it took him thirty years to do so.

When the Federal Bank scandal erupted in 1893, it was discovered that the Federal had lent A. G. Hall £20,000 on overdraft. Hall was not pushed into bankruptcy over the debt. The Federal Bank kindly 'wrote off' the debt for him just before closing its doors—as it did with most of the other Munro, Fink, and Baillieu connections.

When his time of troubles was over, Theodore Fink bounced back with enviable vigour. In February 1893 he gravely told a meeting of the Bankers' Institute of Australasia: 'The administration of the State finances has been deplorable . . . The fool's paradise in which we dwelt has been rudely terminated . . . Nothing is more misleading than the cant about the boundless resources of a young country'—and so on. The audience listened just as solemnly, and if anyone gave the banker's equivalent of an ironic cheer, the fact was not recorded.

During 1893 Fink consolidated his reputation as Melbourne's leading barrister dealing with commercial cases. He defended Sir Matthew Davies against every onslaught, his brilliant interpretations of complex financial transactions throwing sufficient light to convince the most obtuse juries of his client's injured innocence. Fink's defence of Dow and Ferguson similarly won acquittals for these two directors of the Premier Building Association.

In the 1894 elections which swept most of the land boomers out of Parliament, Fink was elected to the Legislative Assembly as member for Jolimont. The voters were of course unaware of his speculative activities or his secret insolvencies. Fink's early parliamentary career was most notable for his vehement opposition to the Turner government's attempts to strengthen the Companies Act, the Banking Act, and the Insolvency Act. Fink emerged as little more than a mouthpiece for ultra-conservative policies, albeit a brilliant one.

As the great reform movement of the middle 1890s lost its impetus and faded away, Fink came more into public prominence. In 1899 Allan McLean, a stock and station agent who had been a Minister in James Munro's Cabinet, succeeded in ousting Turner as Premier. McLean appointed Fink a Minister without Portfolio, and then President of Royal Commissions on Technical Education and the University of Melbourne. Fink's enormous energies at last found a socially worthy outlet. For five years he laboured on these subjects. His recommendations, adopted almost in full, set a new and progressive course for Victorian education.

In 1901 Fink stood for the Kooyong seat in Federal Parliament, but was defeated by the Hon. William Knox, one of the early controllers of the Broken Hill Proprietary Co. Ltd. Fink then channelled most of his abundant energies into building up the Melbourne *Herald* from an insignificant and struggling newspaper into one of the world's most powerful press organizations. He continued to study educational problems, concentrating first on questions of apprenticeship, then joining the Melbourne University Council in 1906 and giving seventeen years' invaluable service.

39

Benjamin Fink, the Greatest of Them All

Theodore Fink was significant in the land boom largely because of his legal stratagems. His elder brother, Benjamin Josman Fink, was the real epitome of the era. Nobody else, with the possible exception of Sir Matthew Davies, started so many billowing companies, borrowed so heavily, speculated so widely, failed so disastrously, or left such a swathe of ruin and despair. By the time he filed his composition, B. J. Fink had piled up debts of more than £1,500,000, on which he paid ½d. in the £1. Multiply his debts to represent present-day money values, and it may be seen how deeply this one man alone had eaten into the financial structure of the comparatively small community.

In 1863, at the age of sixteen, Benjamin was already feeling his way as an entrepreneur. He left the family home in Geelong, where the eight-year-old Theodore and his eight other brothers and sisters were eating up the victuals faster than they could be replaced. Benjamin sailed to New Zealand to start his own business as an importer and produce dealer. For three years he made modest profits, in his spare time touring both islands to visit the gold diggings which fascinated him as an open door to wealth. In 1865 he returned to Melbourne and took the first job that offered: as a clerk in Wallach's, Maurice Aron's furniture store in Elizabeth Street. Wallach's had begun business in 1850 in a tent pitched on a vacant block opposite the present G.P.O. A substantial shop and warehouse was built on the site in 1862. Fink's job in this establishment was to demonstrate and sell the pianos, and sell pianos he did, better than anyone before him or after.

This was the real start of B. J. Fink's meteoric business career. By 1874 he was joint owner with Aron of the prosperous emporium, which supplied the villas of Melbourne with their ornamental hall-stands, ormolu tables, and other ornate Victorian furnishings. By 1880 Fink was looking for wider fields to conquer, and the booming 1880s came looking for men like him. His first move was to buy out his partner. Francis Grey Smith, Chief Manager of the National Bank, lent him £60,000 for the purpose. Three years later Fink was able to open branches of Wallach's in Wynyard Square and Clarence Street, Sydney. Shortly after that he rebuilt the entire Wallach's establishment in Elizabeth Street, Melbourne, at a cost of £120,000, allowing for 2½ acres of floor space to cater for Melbourne's eager shoppers.

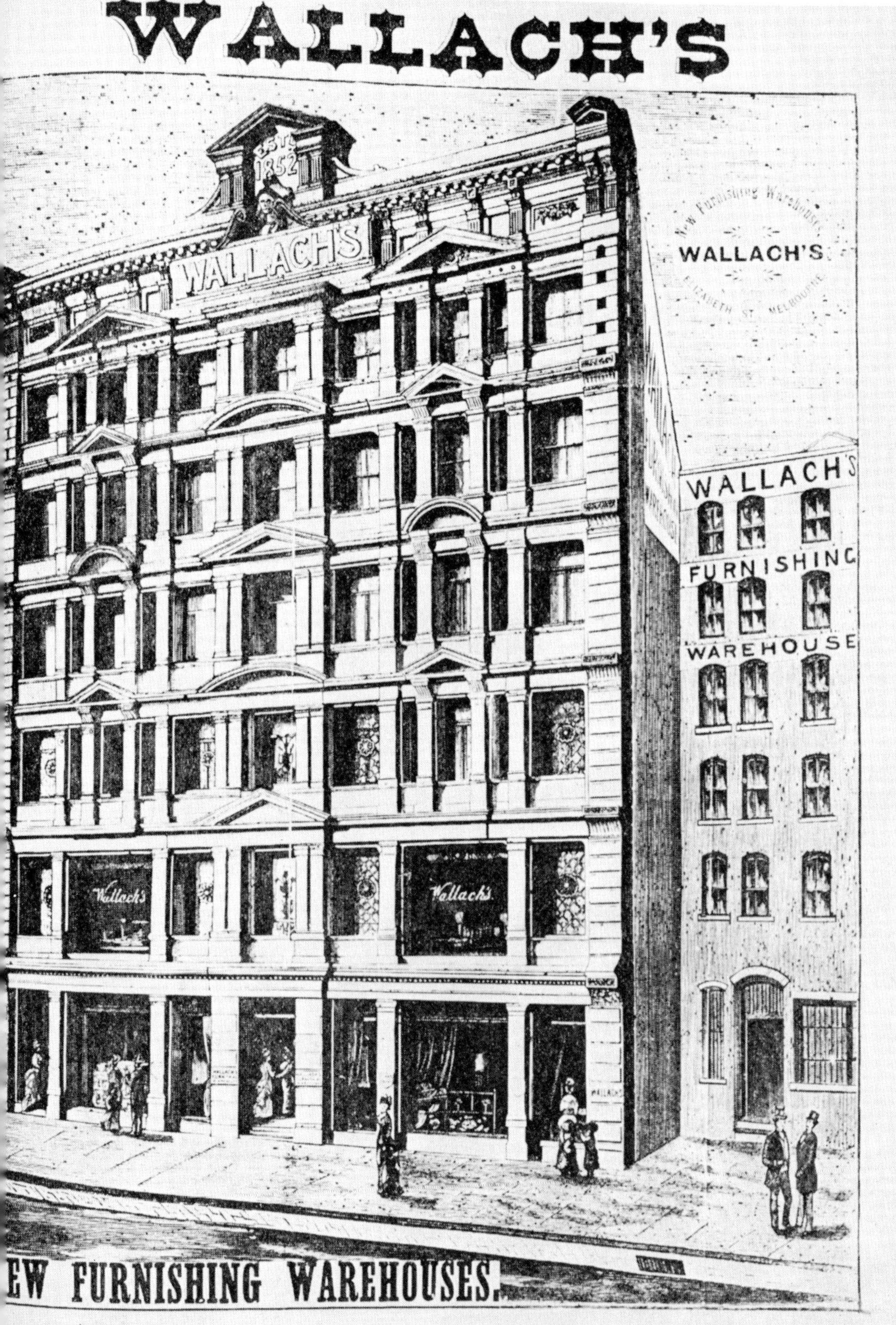

Wallach's, the Melbourne emporium which Benjamin Fink took over with the National Bank's help.

Fink's next coups were made in the mining field. He paid the Australian Coal Company £9,000 for its run-down mine at Newcastle, sold the machinery for more than the purchase price, and held the mine itself for further development. Returning to Victoria, the thirty-three-year-old financier bought for a song a gold mine near Maryborough which was about to be abandoned, and kept it in successful production. Fink stood for Parliament, and was elected as an Independent M.L.A. for the district. His policy as announced to the voters was that businessmen should be elected to run the country on sound business lines, a principle which even then found support among sturdy traditionalists. In Parliament Fink never made a speech worth remembering. His authorized biographer in a book of puffs called *Australian Representative Men* (charges: 10 gns per biography; 3 gns per copy of the book) got around this difficulty rather neatly:

> Although known as 'the silent member', he is by no means looked upon with a 'curling lip' or a 'cold eye', but, on the contrary, respected for his independence, truthfulness, and utter incorruptibleness . . . The mere mention of his name in connection with any company is considered ample guarantee of its *bona-fides*.

As Parliament became more a businessman's club and less a State legislature, many 'good openings' and 'quick killings' were passed on to the silent member. Fink reacted gratefully, introducing many M.P.s into his own schemes.

Fink next proceeded to amalgamate his own private bank, the Joint Stock Bank of Ballarat, with the City of Melbourne Bank. Fink's bank had been established in Ballarat in 1880, the miners over-subscribing its £100,000 capital within a few hours. The amalgamation made the City Bank the colony's biggest buyer of gold. After that Fink was able to call on the City Bank for modest loans, which exceeded £300,000 by the time he met his creditors. In 1885 Fink briefly returned to his old stamping ground at Maryborough to save the famous Duke Mine from closure. Armed with thousands of shareholders' proxies, and backed by demonstrations of angry miners, he ousted the entire board of directors. Three years later the mine, with Fink as its golden boy and chairman

B. J. Fink and the famous Duke mine which he saved from closure.

Demolition of Fink's Buildings in 1967.

of directors, was still yielding 1,500 oz. of gold a week. The miners kept their jobs and voted solidly for Benjamin Fink, M.L.A.

Fink now began his extraordinary plunge into the land boom which was to establish him as Melbourne's prince of speculators. Several volumes would not encompass the full range of his activities, and only some of the most outstanding can be mentioned. In 1888 Fink paid £50,000 to C. J. Ham and David Elder for the leasehold of a block of land, 60 ft x 66 ft, on the corner of Flinders and Elizabeth Streets. The original owner of the site was Daniel McArthur, but Thomas Budd had won the title by 'adverse possession'—that is, by paying the rates for the statutory period of sixteen years. The old shops on the site had been occupied by the Mutual Store while its own premises were being rebuilt. Fink spent £40,000 on a massive office block named Fink's Buildings, which returned him £6,000 a year in rent until the crash. The same year Fink bought the rear portion of the old Cole's Book Arcade, running through to Little Collins Street, for £40,000 (equivalent to £710 a foot). The Trustees, Executors & Agency Co. Ltd lent Fink the money. He went to the wall still owing them £33,000. In rapid succession Fink bought the Gresham Buildings, in Elizabeth Street near Flinders Street, for £52,000 (£1,000 a foot); then Altson & Brown's premises in Collins Street. These were redesigned as offices and grandiloquently renamed Rothschild Chambers. Annual rents totalled about £6,000 in each building until the crash, when they fell away almost to nothing.

Benjamin Fink entered the hotel business through his furniture companies, which equipped many of the biggest hotels and coffee palaces. First he furnished James Munro's new Federal Coffee Palace, buying a large block of its shares and becoming its chairman for a period. Then, as though to prove that his vision was not circumscribed by temperance principles, Fink leased the Ballarat Star Hotel at the corner of Swanston and Little Bourke Streets, spending £10,000 on its redecoration. In 1885 he took over the lease of the Albion Hotel in Bourke Street. The Trustees, Executors & Agency Co. Ltd lent him £14,000 to spend on improvements. In 1888 he bought the Saracen's Head Hotel in Bourke Street from J. S. Johnston, a former owner of the *Argus*, for £30,000. Fink demolished the hotel, reconstructed it, and went bankrupt still owing Johnston £23,000.

One of Fink's greatest triumphs was the public flotation of McCracken's Brewery in 1888. Fink undertook to pay the McCracken family £250,000 for the right to float the old family firm, founded in 1851, into a £2 million company on the stock market. He retained 130,000 shares for himself, selling them for an enormous profit, all of which immediately went into other ventures. Buyers of McCracken's shares were guaranteed a dividend of 8 per cent for at least three years, and with Fink's reputation behind them the shares sold at high prices. Well they might, for the system of 'tied houses' was now being introduced into the hotel trade by this and other breweries. When he filed his composition, Fink still owed Peter McCracken £113,000—much of it without security. The honest brewer hadn't been able to keep pace with the swift financier: in fact he died not knowing whether his family had been left rich or poor. A brother, Colier McCracken, had used much of his cash from the flotation to build a huge mansion in Leslie Road, Essendon, completed in 1890. After the crash he was forced to sell it to Edward William Cole, proprietor of the famous Book Arcade, who lived there for some years. In 1920 the mansion was bought by the Church of England for conversion into a girls' grammar school, Lowther Hall, and it still stands today although its demolition is being considered.

In April 1890 B. J. Fink and his former partner, Maurice Aron, set about the formation of a monopoly in the retail furniture trade. They formed three public companies from their existing furniture interests and took equal shares in each. Wallach & Co. Ltd, W. H. Rocke Ltd, and Maurice Aron & Co. Ltd were incorporated with a total capital of £700,000, of which £350,000 in shares was left in the names of Fink, Aron, and their nominees. Their bold venture might have succeeded, but the depression caught up with them, hitting the furnishing trade before all others. All three companies were finally wound up by the banks

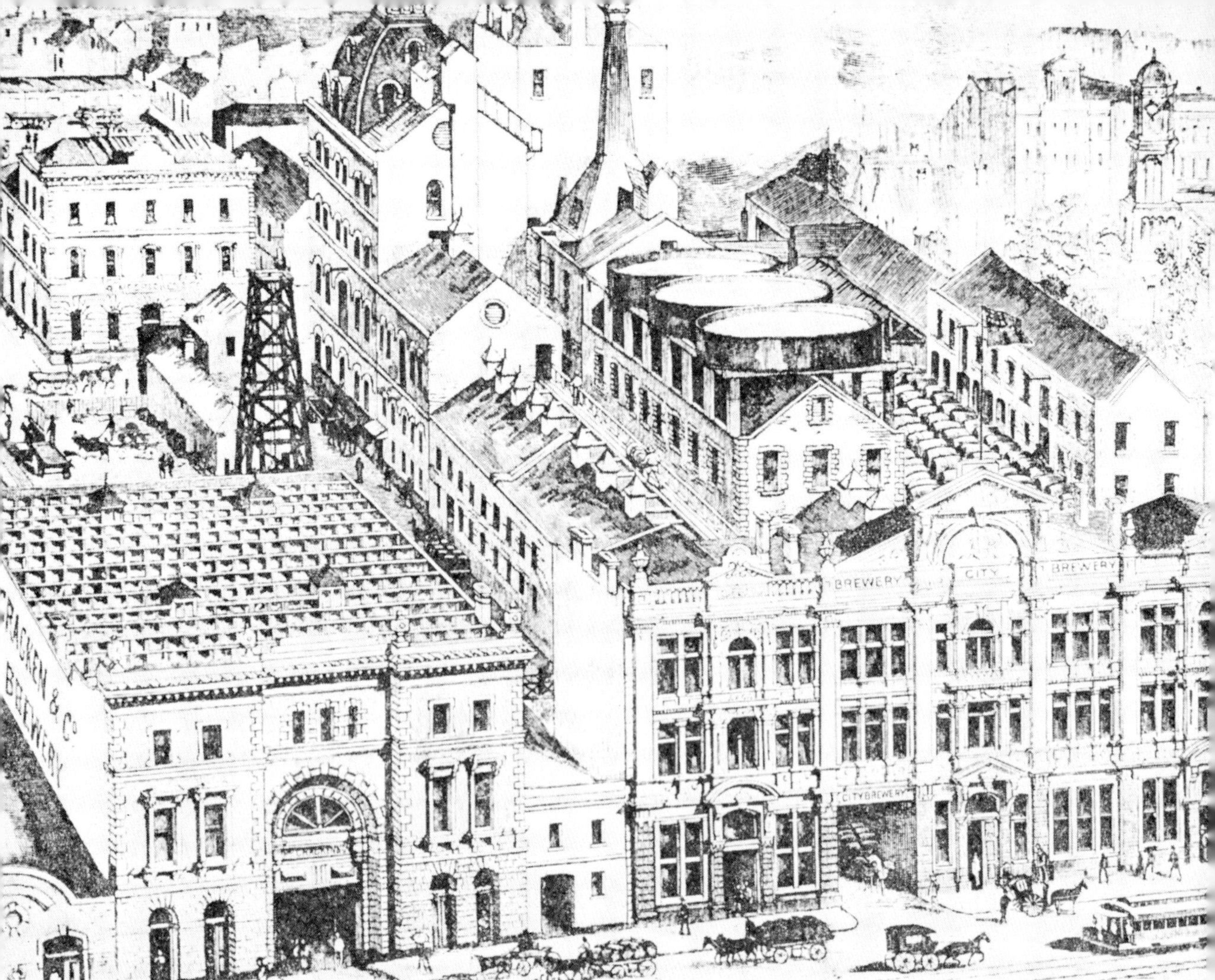

McCracken's City Brewery in Collins Street, Melbourne, floated as a public company by B. J. Fink.

in 1893. The following year, Maurice Aron attempted to resuscitate Wallach's. The company was reconstituted with Aron and J. C. Alford as the directors, but with practically all the shares in the hands of two employees who were 'men of straw'. Aron and Fink held one hundred shares each. This attempt failed, the company was again reconstructed, and struggled on for some years before finally succumbing.

Fink's biggest speculative enterprise was called the Mercantile Finance Co. Ltd. He formed the company in 1885 by taking over the accountancy business of Andrew Lyell and J. M. Howden, and floating it on the Stock Exchange. The investing public did not show much interest until dividends of 40 and 50 per cent were declared, and shares were being issued at £7 premiums. Then they poured millions into the business. The money in turn was used to buy land, to finance Fink's other interests, and to re-lend at high interest rates to other speculators.

George Meudell, who replaced Andrew Lyell as assistant manager of the Mercantile Finance Co. Ltd, described Fink's 'black bag in which were mining scrip, bank shares, Crown grants, promissory notes . . . He would say, "Here you are, George, take this title round to the Savings Bank and get them to prepare a mortgage for ten thousand pounds, and I will call in tomorrow and sign it." ' Meudell did so more than once. When Fink went bankrupt he owed the Melbourne Savings Bank more than £50,000, all of it money belonging to small depositors. The Mercantile Finance Co. Ltd altogether succeeded in losing just on one million pounds. What sleight of hand could make so much public money disappear without suspicion being raised? It was not until years later, when liquidators had sorted out the complexities, that the answers were known.

In the first place, reported the liquidators, the profits were always largely imaginary, and the huge dividends were actually paid out of capital or the moneys of depositors. In order to keep up the excitement the share market was manipulated. The liquidators reported:

> In examining the transfer register we find that large numbers of shares had been bought about this time in the names of officers and clerks in the company's office, and have received evidence to show that Mr Fink personally, and Messrs Fink and Howden in their capacity of directors of the company, had been directing large purchases of shares at this time. The knowledge on the Stock Exchange that these gentlemen were buying largely had no doubt a great effect in bringing forward other buyers, and so creating an abnormal demand for the company's shares . . .

The published balance sheets did not show more than a book value of about £2. 12s. each for the company's shares. The dealings in the market were therefore pure gambling on the future prospects of the company, and the directors had, in the liquidators' opinion, no justification for their action in demanding £7. 10s. per share for a new issue of 100,000 shares to existing shareholders. Commented the *Age*: 'Our pity for the victims of the land boom must always be tempered by the consideration that no sensible person could expect 50 per cent dividends from any legitimate business. To the sober mind the figure itself is suggestive of fraud.'

On 21 September 1892 B. J. Fink met his creditors and presented his forlorn balance sheet, showing debts of £1,520,000. To this figure should be added another £310,000 owed to the City of Melbourne Bank, but secretly written off

Colier McCracken's great mansion in Essendon still stands today as a girls' school.

by the directors of that institution (see chapter 31). Thus Fink's debts really totalled at least £1,830,000.

Although filed as a secret composition, Fink's schedule did not remain secret for very long. The details were widely publicized, and all Melbourne was able to see how Fink had cross-financed and cross-guaranteed his multifarious enterprises, building an empire on the shifting sands of unsecured credit. To take but one example, Fink poured money into Maurice Aron & Co. Ltd to buy shares, and then got back far more in the form of personal loans. Fifteen months before the composition, Wallach & Co. Ltd borrowed heavily from the Australian Joint Stock Bank of Sydney Ltd. The only security taken by the bank was B. J. Fink's personal guarantee. Since Fink was borrowing heavily from Wallach's at the same time, the money in effect finished up in Fink's own account.

An extraordinary feature demonstrated in the list of debts was the willingness of even conservative bankers to lend large sums to speculative land companies on Fink's personal guarantee. On close examination, most of these land companies turned out to be creations of Fink and his associates. In effect, he was guaranteeing himself, a practice which would surely surprise even the most broadminded banker today. The National Bank, for instance, made unsecured advances of £46,000 to B. J. Fink's companies in 1891—again relying on Fink's personal guarantee—and had to be content with its repayment at ½d. in the £1.

As though to round off this financier's nightmare, there was an account from George & George Ltd for £205, being for household groceries supplied. Fink, chairman of Georges a year previously, regretted that he could not see his way clear to paying more than ½d. in the £1 on that account. Nor on an invoice from McCracken's Brewery for £260, being for beer consumed. Roared the *Age*:

> It is a disgrace to the law of the colony that men charged in trust with the custody of other people's money should have unlimited power of squandering it on their personal speculations, satisfying all requirements when the smash comes by paying a farthing or a halfpenny in the pound.

So it was all over. The brightest comet in the universe of land boomers fell spent to the earth. No more could he walk along The Block flinging an arm right and left and saying, 'I own that . . . and that . . . and that . . . ' Fink and his wife Catherine (his first cousin) were forced to quit their mansion in St Kilda Road. Fortunately, everything was in Mrs Fink's name. When auctioned early in 1894, her possessions were found to include many thousands of pounds worth of 'the most sumptuous carpets'; specially built suites of furniture, including one made by Pfaff, the German Emperor's cabinet-maker; and many valuable paintings, bronzes, and antiques. There were also several ponies, a prize cow, and a phaeton. Fink's house, 'The Grange', on the corner of St Kilda Road and Domain Road, next to the old Botanical Museum, had originally been built by the government for General Chute. After the Finks' departure, it was occupied by Mrs Jane Robertson, in return for her dishonoured loan of £17,000 to Kate Fink. The house was later demolished to make way for the wide sweep of the Shrine lawns down to St Kilda Road.

The Block Arcade was continued through to Elizabeth Street, giving it the largest area of floor mosaic in Australia. The extension was designed by D. C. Askew and built for £34,000.

In 1892, the year of his insolvency, Benjamin transferred to his wife several large tracts of land in Melbourne's western suburbs. As late as 1909 Catherine was still subdividing and selling this land in partnership with Sir Thomas Bent, who by then had become Premier of Victoria. In 1895, the Eighth Union Building Society sold Catherine a fifty-year lease on the Ballarat Star Hotel, on which Benjamin Fink had defaulted. In 1899 the Caledonian & Australian Mortgage & Agency Co. Ltd sold her back the freehold of Fink's Buildings, on which Benjamin had also defaulted. This huge pile was demolished in 1967 and replaced by a Commonwealth Bank building.

Late in 1893, David Finlayson, manager of the Union Bank, issued a writ in the Supreme Court seeking the cancellation of B. J. Fink's composition, on the ground that 'registration of the composition was obtained by fraud'. In the case of the Commercial Bank's debt, claimed Finlayson, the schedule 'did not show the full and complete account of the finances between the bank and Fink'. It was a serious allegation against the ethics of the Commercial Bank as well as against Fink. The case was hastily settled out of court before it could come to a hearing.

George Meudell, who knew Fink better than most people, claimed that he was threatened with assassination, and had to flee to London with his family. There is no other contemporary record to verify this claim, but it is true that Fink departed hurriedly with his family. He died of diabetes in London in 1909, apparently intestate but in reality supported in comparative luxury by the wife to whom he had transferred all his remaining assets, worth at least £250,000.

40

Georges of Collins Street

One of Melbourne's leading universal outfitters in the days before Sidney Myer appeared on the scene was the old Federal Emporium operated by Messrs George & George. Occupying a large building in Collins Street where Block Arcade now stands, the George family supplied everything from knickerbocker suits for daring cyclists to dresses for milady's social occasions and unmentionables for her nether limbs. In those days the business bore little similarity to its present suave and dignified status. The partners, William Henry Harrison George and Alfred Harley George, joined later by John Marshall and James Gordon Haggart, described themselves as 'drapers, outfitters and general furnishers,' and took pride in the extent of their middle-class trade.

Unfortunately the partners became attracted by the notion of making quick profits from the land boom in addition to their regular income from drapery. They were drawn into the wide net cast by B. J. Fink, were raised high for a fleeting glimpse of glory, then dumped into a rather noisome bargain basement labelled 'Secret Insolvencies.'

In March 1888, Fink made a three-cornered deal based on the Georges' drapery business. No. 1 phase was to purchase for £70,000 the freehold site on which their Federal Emporium stood. No. 2 phase was to purchase the bankrupt Equitable Co-operative Society (then trading on the present site of Georges Ltd). No. 3 phase was to take over the Georges' business and shift it to the Equitable site. A fourth development was to find a use for Georges' former site. Let us examine these moves in greater detail.

The Equitable Co-operative Society had leased a large block of land on the Collins Street hill from Scots' Church, paying £800 a year rent. On this site the Society erected its warehouse and shop front in 1882—then succeeded in losing its entire paid-up capital of £30,000 over the following seven years. 'The collapse of the Equitable was attributable to the grossest mismanagement,' commented the *Illustrated Australian News*. 'A number of school boys could not have shown themselves more unfit for the position of directors.'

The opportunity for a cheap takeover seemed too good to miss. Fink talked to the Georges, and persuaded them to float their business into a £150,000 public company called George & George Ltd. The original subscribers were B. J. Fink (chairman); A. H. George and John Marshall (joint managing directors); Henry

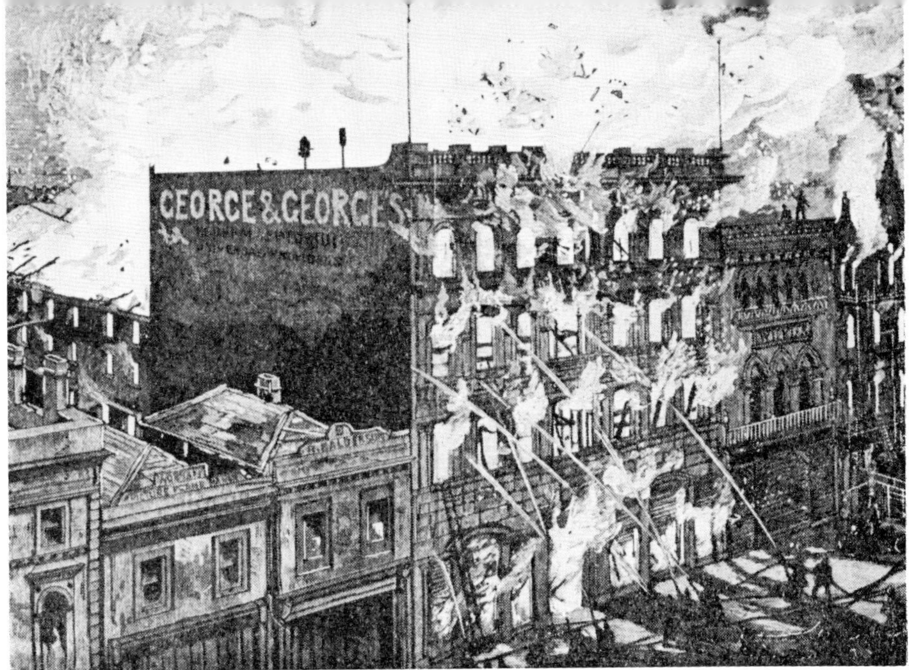

Conflagration which burned down George & George's Federal Emporium in 1889, as seen from the roof of the Bohemian Club opposite.

Meeks (a Melbourne merchant); George Pilley (gentleman); and J. M. Howden (Fink's nominee). J. G. Haggart was appointed secretary and head accountant.

With the money gained from the flotation, George & George Ltd bought the Co-operative Society's shares for 16s. each, thus securing ownership of the building, the stock, and the remainder of the 50-year lease of the site. A further £25,000 was spent on extensions to the building to take it right through to Little Collins Street, providing nearly two acres of floor space. The Collins Street frontage was turned into 'one vast shop' (a layout which is still retained), a 'handsome tea-room and telephone room' was provided on the first floor, and a great deal of new stock was purchased.

Georges held a gala opening as soon as the extensions were complete. In proposing the toast of 'Success,' J. M. Bruce, director of Paterson, Laing & Bruce Ltd (and father of S. M. Bruce, a future Prime Minister), said that enterprise of this kind should 'inspire confidence in those who had given themselves up to grumbling and a belief that the city of Melbourne was just about "done".' Replying to the toast, B. J. Fink said that Georges would become 'the Bon Marche of Australia.' The new premises were the best answer that could be given to 'the pessimism and croakings of the last few years as to the indebtedness of the colony.' (Exactly one year later, Fink filed his schedule for £1½ million and paid ½d. in the £1).

Much of the Federal Emporium's old stock was left in the former premises further down Collins Street. On the night of 13 September 1889, a fierce conflagration completely destroyed the building, spreading to Allan & Co. and Glen & Co. on either side. Three firemen lost their lives while trying to halt the blaze. The Federal Emporium's stock was insured for £28,000. The building was valued at £30,000 but part of this insurance had lapsed. Allan & Co's. losses of £22,000 were fully covered, and Glen & Co's. losses of £30,000 were partly covered.

W. H. H. George, the draper who left Melbourne after paying 3d. in the £1 on his land boom debts.

J. M. Bruce: an answer to the grumblers.

John Turner, the minister's son who became a leading land boomer.

Surveying the guttering ruins, Fink immediately decided to capitalise on this apparent misfortune by building an arcade of smaller shops, thus utilising the Collins Street frontage to the best advantage. Together with C. J. & T. Ham, he formed the City Property Co. Ltd for this purpose. Enormous sums were spent on buying the adjoining land at £1,500 a foot. With the expenditure of another £40,000 on construction, 'The Block' and Block Arcade arose to entice and delight boom-time shoppers.

Meanwhile, further up Collins Street, the Georges were delving into land speculation in conjunction with a colorful auctioneer named John Turner. Turner was the son of a Baptist minister of Fitzroy. He had been postmaster at South Yarra, simultaneously holding the office of Mayor of Prahran, until retiring from the postal job in 1884. At the age of forty-five he began a glittering new career as land boomer, and within three years had become one of Victoria's leading *rentiers.*

Turner and the Georges formed 'The John Turner Land Company,' secured large loans from various financial institutions, and bought up blocks of land from other speculators. Unfortunately for the Turner-George combination, the other speculators were already starting to unload their holdings. The three men were unable to meet the commitments they had undertaken, and were forced to make secret compositions early in 1894, each paying only 3d. in the £1 on their debts.

Alfred Harley George had amassed nearly £45,000 in debts. Most of the money came from the Union Finance Co. and the Victorian Permanent Building Society. Nearly £7,000 came from Fink's Mercantile Finance Co. and Davies' Mercantile Bank. W. H. George Snr. had loaned him another £5,000. W. H. H. George had accumulated more than £30,000 in debts which he was unable to meet. The money came from identical sources to those which had financed A. H. George.

The Georges were in low water indeed. Their schedules showed that in 1893, A. H. George borrowed £30 and W. H. H. George borrowed £40 from the Rev. Samuel Chapman of the Baptist Church in Collins Street. No doubt the minister comforted himself with the thought that it was more blessed to give £70 than to receive 3d. in the £1.

Their protege, the auctioneer John Turner, had run up an account of more than £70,000. About one-third of this money came from the City of Melbourne Bank. Nearly £20,000 came from banks controlled by James Munro. Another £10,000 was loaned to him by George Isaacs, the father-in-law of Theodore Fink.

Meanwhile, John Marshall, the manager of Georges' store, had also involved himself hopelessly in separate land transactions. In one instance alone, he owed the Dominion Bank (of which he was a director) more than £20,000 on a land purchase. Altogether, the gambling draper accumulated the startling total of £225,000 indebtedness on land and share dealings. He proceeded to sue C. H. James, founder of the Dominion Bank, for £200,000 damages for alleged breaches of internal agreements. When his case was laughed out of court, Marshall had no alternative but to go bankrupt. His estate showed a final deficiency of £185,000.

After the smash, B. J. Fink disappeared from George & George Ltd's board, from Collins Street, and from Australia. A. H. George resigned as a director, but was permitted to carry on as general manager for another fifteen years. W. H. H. George, having paid his 3d. in the £1, left Melbourne in despair, but finally opened another drapery business known as George & Kersley in Wellington, New Zealand.

The Melbourne company made great efforts to survive under a new directorate. It cancelled Fink's shares and others which had been forfeited, wrote down its capital, and by 1897 was able to show a modest trading profit of £1,327. In the early 1900s there was another series of annual losses due to 'disastrous conditions of trade.' In 1905 the directors reported that 'heavy losses had been sustained in realising the entire Bicycle Stock.' In 1907, the grocery, wine and spirit departments were closed down. Shareholders agreed at last to voluntary liquidation, and George & George Ltd was finally wound up in 1911. It began a new phase as 'Georges Ltd', and under this title gradually developed into Australia's most exclusive department store.

A relative of the original George family, Arthur John George, returned from Wellington to become the company's secretary in 1936, executive director in 1938 and managing director in 1943. In 1961 the company was taken over by Cox Bros. Ltd, the other directors resigning but A. J. George remaining temporarily as governing director. The takeover method used was an elaborate technique of share-booming involving several prominent Melbourne men and attracting an official investigation under section 178 of the Companies Act 1961, but no further government action.

In 1963 A. J. George retired as governing director. In 1966 the Cox Bros. Ltd group crashed and piecemeal liquidation of its units began. Georges Holdings Ltd was separated, and in 1967 re-floated as Georges Australia Ltd, under which style it still trades successfully. Georges, in fact, having survived fire, bankruptcy, successive takeovers, government investigation, liquidation and further reconstruction, seems indestructible.

41

G. W. Taylor, Another Land-Booming Mayor of Prahran

A Welshman named George William Taylor was one of the first to exploit the rising value of Melbourne's vacant paddocks and hillsides. He rose from obscurity to the point of dealing in millions, won municipal honours, built himself a beautiful mansion, fell like so many others with a resounding crash, and sank back into obscurity.

Taylor was born at Rhos, North Wales, in 1840, into a stern and austere household where the doctrines of the Welsh Calvinistic Methodist Church were rigidly followed. Taylor's father wanted him to become a minister, but according to his authorised biography 'his mother objected vehemently.' George himself, at the tender age of thirteen, had already expressed a distinct preference for the earthly glories of a commercial career. He became an assistant to a local storekeeper, then at the age of nineteen made his way to London.

Three years later, Taylor emigrated to Australia on the *Annie Archbell*, and found a position in Melbourne as a draper's assistant. On his meagre income from that trade, he married Victoria Isabella Cook. They had a total of eight children, of whom four lived.

George was still a long way from his dream of commercial success. In 1874, when thirty-four years old, he took the plunge, setting up a small business in Prahran as an auctioneer. Fate was kind to the young adventurer. He quickly won success, 'being recognised by those who are authorities on the matter, as a man of fertile resource and a ready tongue,' in the words of his friendly biographer. 'Added to these are his keenness, unerring judgment, lucidity of expression, and honesty of purpose . . . ' According to George Meudell, who knew him well, Taylor was 'a weak, excitable man with unbounded confidence in himself.'

Whatever his virtues and failings, Taylor was soon successful enough as an auctioneer to expand into the estate agency field as well. Prahran in those days was comparatively sparsely settled in the areas away from Chapel Street, and Taylor bought several vacant paddocks on its northern outskirts at low prices. During the 'Berry Blight' and the accompanying economic crisis the value of

G. W. Taylor, the Welsh emigrant who tried to sell the paddocks of Prahran for £5 million.

Taylor's mansion 'Wynnstay' was set in the middle of rolling acres now thickly covered with houses.

Alfred Deakin was appointed chairman of G. W. Taylor's biggest land boom company. When everything crashed, his friend David 'Gamaliel' Syme advised Alfred 'Saul' Deakin: 'You've put your foot in it, my son.–Begone to India.–Talk wheat and irrigation.'

land fell almost to nothing, but Taylor determinedly held on to his paddocks. His holdings began to soar in value as the 'Era of Extravagance' began.

Part of the pattern of success for a young man on the way up was to enter local politics. Taylor stood as a candidate for Prahran Council, described accurately enough as 'in those days a graduation college for land boomers.' He was defeated in 1875, then again in 1876, but was finally rewarded for his persistence by being elected in 1877. Seven years later Taylor was selected as mayor. With the enthusiastic co-operation of his aldermen, he demolished the modest Town Hall which had cost £15,000 to build in 1860, and erected substantial new chambers at a cost of £75,000.

Next step, in the lexicon of the day, was a seat in Parliament. To bring himself to the notice of a wider public, Taylor announced a public tribute to the Berry-Service Government, for the 'bold and patriotic manner' in which it had provided effective defences for Victoria against the 'probable invasion by Russia.' Members of the Government and 300 other leading citizens were entertained at a sumptuous banquet in the new Town Hall, where the fervour of patriotic emotion grew as the level in the champagne bottles diminished. The following year Taylor 'bethought himself of future generations,' and persuaded a somewhat more reluctant council to spend £30,000 on parklands in Prahran. These were opened in 1885 by the Governor, Sir Henry Loch, after which there was a modest luncheon for 200 guests at the Town Hall. In the afternoon, Taylor held a garden party for 1,000 people at his rambling mansion, 'Wynnstay,' set in a large estate at the corner of High Street and Orrong Road, Armadale. In a neighbouring paddock, no less than 7,000 shouting, fighting children were provided with 'games and delicacies in abundance.' Nothing quite like it had been seen before. Naturally there had to be a return ball, at which the grateful citizenry presented Taylor with an illuminated address and Mrs Taylor with a diamond bracelet.

Obviously there could not be found a fitter candidate to represent the people in Parliament. Taylor stood for the seat of St. Kilda—and was soundly trounced. 'The evanescence of popularity is immemorial,' commented his biographer sadly. Swallowing his chagrin, Taylor returned to business.

Taylor had started subdividing his own suburban blocks, and buying more to replace them, about 1880. 'In a few weeks he was reputed to have made a clear profit of thousands of pounds,' said *Table Talk*. 'His judgment of values of suburban paddocks was supposed to be unerring, and lots of *gobe-mouche* investors would gleefully "go one higher" at auction sales than Taylor's bids, confident that somehow the land could be sold again at a profit. Taylor maintained the illusion by sometimes buying despite all competition.'

With his profits, Taylor kept on buying more and more land on low deposits, until he eventually controlled more than 35,000 acres of suburban land. He owned large strips of the bayside from Brighton to Mordialloc; vast tracts of Caulfield, Glen Iris, Oakleigh, Preston, and Pascoe Vale; and broad acres in Lilydale, Dandenong, Berwick and Bacchus Marsh. He conducted a veritable orgy of buying, making part payments, refinancing, and buying again.

In his far-flung speculations, Taylor usually worked hand-in-glove with B. J. Fink, who gave him ready access to the funds of the Mercantile Finance Co. Ltd. Their most spectacular enterprise was the flotation of the Australian Assets Purchase Company, with nominal capital of £5½ million—say, $160 million today. The company's purpose was to buy most of Taylor's interests at inflated prices, to repay Taylor and Fink in cash for their assets, and resell the land as building allotments. George Meudell, who was working for Fink at the time, was given the job of writing the prospectus. 'It was a rare farrago of high-priced rubbish,' Meudell said unrepenitently, 'and every title or option had been mortgaged to a bank, a building society, or to a life assurance company.'

Taylor was paid £463,000 in cash for his properties, in addition to being given a large parcel of shares. The name of the company was soon changed to the Australian City & Suburban Investment Co. Ltd and refloated with £5 million capital. Alfred Deakin, M.L.A., was enticed on to the board and agreed to act as chairman. His fellow directors were G. W. Taylor, James Bell, Orlando Fenwick, and J. M. Howden. Theodore Fink was the company's solicitor, and the Commercial and the National were its bankers.

A prospectus was issued under Deakin's aegis inviting investors to buy the 2½ million £2 shares, paid up to £1. This document, issued at the height of the boom, claimed that 'Any institution based upon landed property . . . must participate in the steady advancement which necessarily follows the increase of population and growth of the nation.' The company's investments 'must always command an adequate return.'

Thousands of investors rose to the bait and snapped up most of the shares. During the next two years, Taylor quietly and cleverly liquidated most of his remaining holdings and disappeared from the colony, taking all his cash with him. His land companies rapidly 'slithered to oblivion,' and calls were made on the unfortunate shareholders. In August 1891, the Sheriff sold up what little property of Taylor's remained in Melbourne. It was sufficient to pay the merest scraping of a farthing in the £1 towards the calls on many thousands of shares still registered in his name.

The bewildered shareholders were furious but apparently helpless. At one meeting of the bankrupt Mercantile Finance Co. Ltd, a shareholder asked the chairman of the liquidators, Colonel Templeton, whether Taylor had been paid by the company to remain in London. Colonel Templeton replied that 'it would not be advisable to answer the question.' (Cries of 'Shame!'). Shortly afterwards, B. J. Fink also made his hasty departure for London, never to return.

Meudell ran across Taylor in Cornhill, London, in 1895. 'Had a hearty laugh,' said Meudell, 'when he unfolded a scheme for securing emigrants in the United Kingdom to send in here to settle on orchards and bee farms in the suburbs of Melbourne.' Taylor never dared to return to Australia, and died in London in 1913.

42

Mark Moss, Temporary King of Norwood Castle

Up to 1957, the seeker after land boom curiosities might walk along the Esplanade at the Melbourne bayside suburb of Brighton and view an extraordinary red and yellow stucco castle known as 'Norwood.' Set in extensive grounds, the mansion contained thirty-four rooms, including four main bedrooms and six children's rooms. Through the massive front doors, the visitor entered a 'Noble Baronial Entrance Hall,' itself thirty feet high, and dimly lit by rays of sunlight filtering through thirty-four stained glass windows depicting famous characters from Shakespeare's plays. Further on, the lavish ballroom was also fitted with a series of stained glass windows, this time depicting various sporting scenes.

On the ground floor of this remarkable mansion were also a breakfast room, smoking room, Roman bathroom, kitchens and pantries. On the first floor, up a grand staircase, were the main bedrooms and bathrooms. Up another flight was a billiards and smoking room. Maids' quarters were situated in a separate wing. Suits of medieval armour, majolica fireplaces, and colossal candelabra decorated the huge, gloomy house. In its heyday, peacocks roamed freely around the 10-acre grounds, which were dotted with orchid houses, marble statues, stables and other outbuildings.

The builder and owner of this extravagant palace was a Jewish financier named Mark Moss, who arrived in Victoria during the gold rush decade of the 1850s. Moss had soon established a thriving money-lending business. In those erratic days when people borrowed freely, and when money-lenders' interest rates were not limited by law to forty or fifty per cent, he prospered remarkably well.

During those years of acquisition and accumulation, Moss lived at 'Rosebank', situated on the corner of Albert and Clarendon Streets, East Melbourne. So popular and prosperous a figure was the money-lender that when Sir Hercules Robinson, Governor of N.S.W., made an extended visit to Melbourne in 1877, His Excellency preferred the hospitality of Mr and Mrs Moss to that of Government House. 'Rosebank' was 'really charming, and Sir Hercules thought that all the arrangements about it were simply perfect,' gushed the *Melbourne Bulletin.*

Mark Moss, the money-lender who built the extraordinary castle 'Norwood' at Brighton (Vic.)

Entrance porch to 'Norwood' was decorated with griffins and other mythical beasts. Philip E. Treeby was the architect.

On his return to Sydney, the Governor sent Moss two large framed photographs of himself and Lady Robinson, and asked that they be given a place in his study.

Now that he was in effect under vice-regal patronage, it hardly seemed necessary for the money-lender to burnish his shining public image further. Nevertheless, Moss proceeded to donate several trophies to the Brighton Yacht Club, where he was able to hob-nob with other notable non-sailing members like Thomas Bent and W. K. Thomson. The two speculators convinced Moss that Brighton was the coming place, and he began looking around for a suitable estate in the suburb.

Apart from his yachting exertions, Moss was anxious to encourage the sport of bowls. He became president of the Fitzroy Bowling Club, then president of the Victorian Bowling Association. In 1881, he donated a gorgeous silver trophy for the Intercolonial Bowling Tournament. The prize was five feet long and three feet high, and contained 100 ounces of silver. It depicted a miniature bowling green, on which three-inch players, all modelled in solid silver, struck frozen attitudes to study the finer points of the game.

Now came the glittering days of the land boom. With men all around him conjuring vast fortunes out of the air, Moss could not ignore the opportunity. Sometimes alone, sometimes in partnership with a public notary named Henry Penketh Fergie, he entered into a series of speculations which were to increase his apparent assets to about half a million pounds, entice him into the building of 'Norwood,' and finally bring him to a secret composition with his creditors.

One of Moss' boom-time transactions was to buy the Victoria Hotel in Bourke Street with the help of a £15,000 mortgage from the A.M.P. Society. Then he bought the Swan Hotel in Fitzroy for £8,000; and the Freemason's Hotel for the same figure. Many other valuable properties—shops, land, and office blocks—were bought in the city, inner suburbs, and at Rob Roy.

Meanwhile, Moss continued his money-lending activities. These were not so fruitful during the years of easy finance; but after the banks tightened their lending policies again in 1888, Moss found increasing demands for loans at high interest rates. In scores of schedules filed by insolvent land boomers, the name of Mark Moss appeared as a creditor for short-term loans of £300, £400, or £500. Many such loans had to be compounded at 1d., 6d., or 1s. in the £1.

While conditions were still bouyant, Moss bought the large block on the beachfront at Brighton where 'Norwood' was to be built. It was then the site of a substantial 17-roomed house. Moss obtained a mortgage of £15,000 from the Bank of Victoria on the property, demolished the old house, and sent an architect overseas to bring back ideas for his dream castle. 'Norwood' arose, and was ready for occupation in 1891.

Already, however, Moss was starting to feel the pinch. By the time he moved into 'Norwood', he had already lost many thousands of pounds through the insolvencies of other speculators. Financial institutions in which he held large parcels of shares were beginning to crumble. It was quite obvious to the experienced financier that heavy calls would be made on many of these shares. In 1891, therefore, he transferred his holdings in the Mercantile Finance Co. Ltd to an infant named George Scott (an 'infant' in law being anyone under twenty-one years of age, who could not be legally sued for calls on shares). The liquidators of the Mercantile Finance Co. uncovered the arrangement, and the Supreme Court ordered the shares to be transferred back to Moss, along with the liability for calls.

Shortly after his attempt to transfer the shares, Moss made over to his wife (in March 1892) the title deeds to the East Melbourne house 'Rosebank', and other properties valued at about £15,000. Eighteen months later, Moss assigned his estate to a public accountant, Andrew Lyell, 'for the benefit of his creditors.' At this time Moss was nearly a quarter of a million pounds on the wrong side of the ledger, his main debts being:–

Liabilities of partnership, Fergie & Moss	£95,000	Various speculations
Bank of Victoria	£58,000	Mortgage of 'Norwood,' etc.
Federal Bank	£32,000	
A.M.P. Society	£15,000	
Commercial Bank	£11,000	
Calls on shares	£11,000	
Real Estate Bank	£ 4,500	

Fireplace in the hall of 'Norwood' was 9 feet wide and 14 feet in total height, bearing a carved inscription: 'Come when you mind / And a welcome find.'

A preliminary meeting of creditors held on 27 November 1893 refused to accept a proffered composition of 5s. in the £1. Three months later, the creditors discovered the earlier transfers of properties to Mrs Moss. These transfers had nearly run for the two years legally necessary to secure the assets from Moss's creditors. The delays involved in compulsory sequestration of his estate would have taken the matter beyond the two-year limit. Therefore, on 2 March 1894, the creditors decided to accept the 5s. composition previously offered. They agreed to sell 'Rosebank' back to Mrs Moss for £4,000, on five-year terms, but the remaining assets were to be liquidated and the proceeds distributed to the creditors.

The estate of Henry Fergie, erstwhile partner of Mark Moss, was sequestrated after his death in 1896, A. S. Baillieu acting as trustee. Fergie's debts were found to total £24,000. Sale of his assets enabled a payment to creditors of 1s. 9d. in the £1. As with Moss, Fergie was heavily indebted for calls on shares in suspended companies like Goldsbrough Mort, the Commercial Bank, and Real Estate Bank.

After only three years' occupation of 'Norwood', Mark Moss and his family were forced to shift back to 'Rosebank'. Later on, when times improved, they bought another block of land on the Brighton Esplanade, very close to 'Norwood'. Here they built a much less pretentious attic villa which they also called 'Rosebank.' The East Melbourne house was demolished to make way for the Freemasons' Hospital.

'Norwood' was repossessed by the Bank of Victoria, being occupied by Richard White from 1894 to 1916. In 1918 its grounds were subdivided and auctioned, twelve blocks fetching £50,000. The great house was left standing on less than two acres of land. 'Norwood' was finally demolished in 1957 after an auction sale of its contents, and the remaining land subdivided again. Today, where one man's ambitions once found their fantastic expression, featureless suburbia holds sway.

Less than half a mile down the Esplanade, Mark Moss and his wife dreamed their life away in their new 'Rosebank'. They left this house, and a considerable legacy, to their son Harry Lyon Moss, born in 1874. Harry Moss used the money to buy low-priced shares in Myer's and B.H.P. when the bottom dropped out of the stock market again in 1929. By this simple method, he accumulated a fortune as the shares recovered over the next thirty years.

As he grew older, Harry Moss began to lead the life of a recluse. Fearful that people would do anything to get control of his money, he refused to speak to neighbours or old friends. The ghosts of the past grew to menacing proportions in his mind. Occasionally he could be seen shambling down the Esplanade, leaning heavily on a stick, and later being wheeled around in an invalid chair by a hired nurse. Moss refused to spend a penny on 'Rosebank', and the dark, eerie house fell into complete decay. In 1960, just three years after the demolition of his father's fantasy, 'Norwood', Harry Moss died in a private hospital. He left most of his fortune of nearly £1 million to the Children's Hospital.

VI THE MATTHEW

DAVIES GROUP

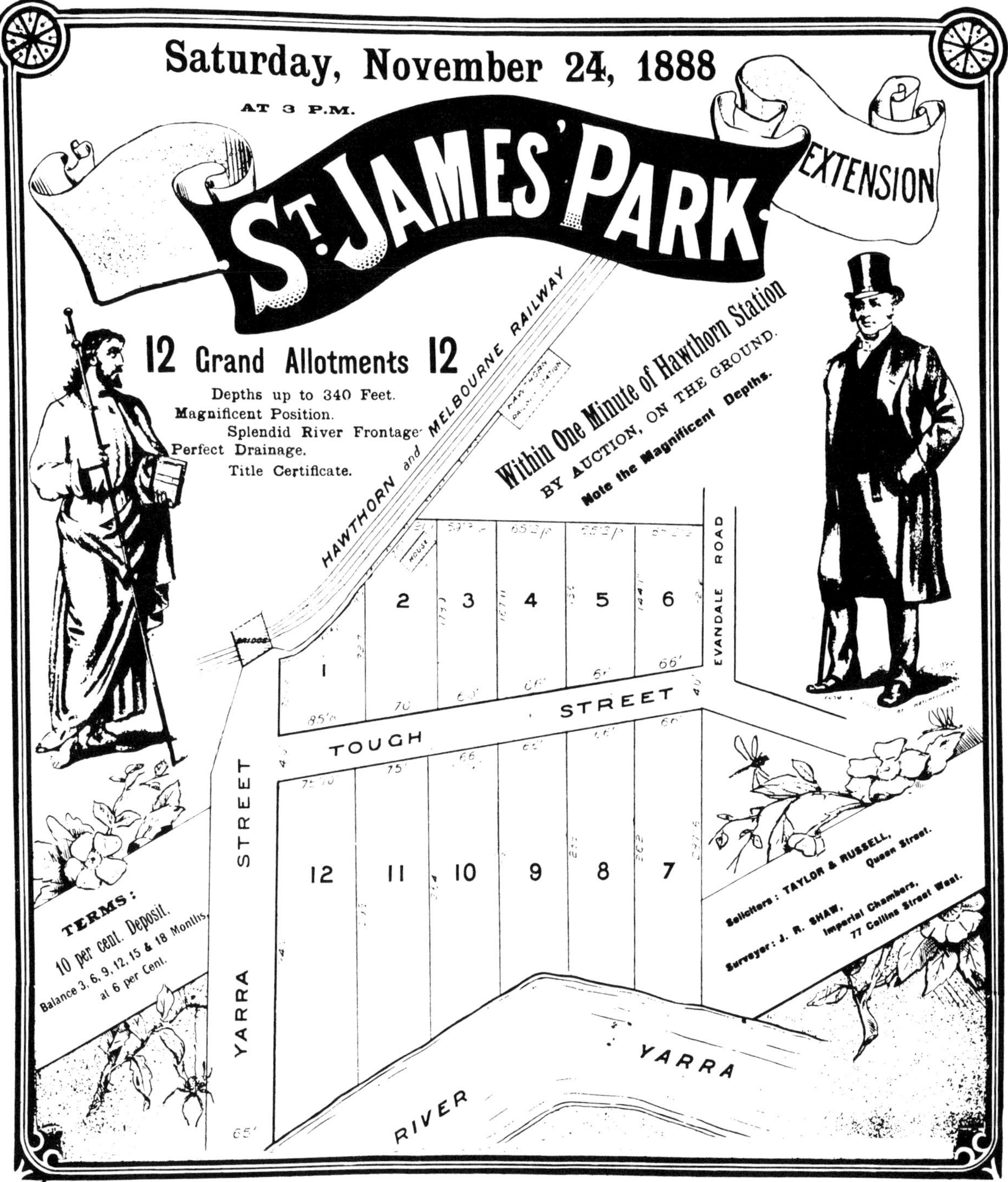

43

The Rise and Fall of Sir Matthew Davies

Like a dazzling rocket, a Geelong lad named Matthew Henry Davies rose to the pinnacle of business and political leadership during the boom years. Like a spent rocket, he fell just as swiftly to the ground, amid general obloquy, a flurry of criminal charges, and ultimate ruin.

Matthew Davies was born at Geelong in 1850, the son of Ebenezer and Ruth Davies, who had emigrated to the colony from Berkshire, England. There were five boys and three girls in the family. Three of the five boys became solicitors, and all five were associated in land speculation. The eldest son was J. M. Davies, later to be a Minister of Justice. The second was G. S. Davies, manager of the Australian Deposit & Mortgage Bank Ltd. The third was J. B. Davies, managing director of the Freehold Investment Co. Ltd. The fourth son was Matthew Davies. The fifth was Walter Davies, LL.B. Matthew was educated at Geelong Grammar and Geelong College, and articled to his eldest brother in 1870. Five years later he was admitted to practice as a solicitor. In the same year he married Elizabeth, daughter of the Rev. Peter Mercer, D.D., of Melbourne.

One of Matthew Davies's earliest clients in his legal business was C. H. James. Constant attention to James's transactions showed Davies how to buy suburban land cheaply and sell it dearly. By 1877 the young solicitor had already made enough money to take a leading part in floating the Australian Economic Bank, successor to the moribund Australian-European Bank. In 1885 the bank's name was changed once again to the Mercantile Bank, and under this guise became one of the most notorious of the financial institutions of the boom era.

In 1880 the thirty-year-old Matthew Davies made his first entry into public life. He stood as candidate for the Prahran Council, and was elected at the top of the poll. Only one year later he was unanimously elected mayor. While Matthew Davies was still an alderman of Prahran, he formed the Colonial Investment Co. Ltd, whose function was simply to borrow money, buy land, and resell it at a profit. Thirteen years later, an official liquidator was to describe this company as 'helping to ruin and bringing misery to hundreds of persons and many families'.

In 1882 Matthew Davies formed his third major company, the Freehold Investment & Banking Co. Ltd, and put his brother Joseph in charge. When

Sir Matthew Davies, M.L.A., founder of a vast network of speculative companies.

John Mark Davies, M.L.C., who became Minister of Justice and bank director.

this enterprise collapsed, the *Age* was to comment that 'No magician could have a more happy potency for converting paper profits into solid cash, and distributing them in dividends', and the directors were to be prosecuted through the courts.

Davies, it appeared, radiated a peculiar charm which persuaded many of his relatives and business associates to fall in with his plausible schemes. Of medium height and build, with a full, light brown beard, he had 'a cheerful, good-natured expression of countenance', and a 'polite and affable demeanour', according to *Table Talk*. 'He is an active and industrious man, possessing far greater energy than his quiet manner would suggest.' Said Meudell: 'He was an able man of singularly fine presence and charming manners.' In the business world, Davies's name had become 'synonymous with good nature and good fortune, and he found an eager crowd of investors always ready to take shares in his companies, with never a question as to their *bona fide* nature.'

Davies's attractive personality and abundant energy took him into Parliament in 1883, when he was elected on his first attempt as member for St Kilda. Davies stood as an Independent, putting forward a policy of high tariffs and removal of the railways from political control. The same year, he went into partnership in Chancery Lane with two other solicitors, C. S. Price and J. Wighton, both of whom were to be dragged down with Davies when he fell.

In 1884 Davies formed yet another financial institution, Henry Arnold & Co. Ltd. The main purpose of this company was ultimately shown to be the borrow-

Sir Matthew Davies's mansion, which once occupied the corner of Lansell and St Georges Roads, Toorak.

ing of money from the public to provide new finance for other Davies institutions. In 1888, when local deposits started to dry up, the company's name was changed to the English & Australian Mortgage Bank Ltd, and a branch was opened in London to tap the overseas money market. By the time it collapsed in 1892, this company alone had managed to lose £1 million. A. G. V. Peel, referring to this company in his report to the British Treasury, wrote caustically: 'It was the Empire that made Sir Matthew Davies a knight, it was his colony that made him Speaker of its Assembly, it was the folly of his fellows that made a trusted financier of Sir Matthew Davies.'

The 'folly of his fellows' provided enough spare cash for Matthew Davies to build a huge mansion on the corner of St Georges Road and Lansell Road, Toorak. The house was mortgaged to one of the banks for £80,000. The furniture alone cost £10,000—and went for £3,000 at the auction after Davies's bankruptcy. 'All Melbourne was dazzled by the splendour of his residence, and the magnificence of his entertainments', said *Table Talk*.

The year 1887 saw further expansion of Davies's prolific interests. He was appointed Minister without portfolio while Alfred Deakin was absent in England, and chairman of the Royal Commission on Banking which recommended that all banks should be able to participate in the buying and selling of property. In October 1887 Matthew Davies was elected Speaker of the Legislative Assembly in succession to Peter Lalor, narrowly defeating Thomas Bent and Thomas Cooper for the position. Curiously enough, Davies was the first native-born Speaker, and the first one who was not an Irishman. In 1889 the electorate of St Kilda was divided into four constituencies, and Davies was returned unopposed for Toorak. He donated £10,000 to the Imperial Institute and other public bodies, being rewarded with a knighthood in 1890. Davies also helped to start the Young Men's Christian Association in Melbourne, acting as its honorary secretary for a period, and opening charity bazaars for various churches. To the *Bulletin* he was simply a 'miserable, lucre-loving trafficker in the temple', but at this distance there seems little reason to deny Davies his measure of genuine religious feeling.

It would be a futile task to trace all of Davies's financial interests during the boom. The liquidator of one Davies institution listed no less than thirty-four major companies in which Sir Matthew was the key figure. Some of these were so hopelessly insolvent that the creditors simply let them wither away without the formality of liquidation. Some of them came into court by indirect means, such as the Country Estates Co. Ltd, whose affairs were fully exposed by medium of an unsuccessful libel action against the Age.

The last important company formed by Davies was the Victorian Mortgage & Deposit Bank Ltd, which was incorporated in 1889 to take over the assets of his own Victorian Land Co. Ltd. This institution was managed by his wife's brother, James Stewart Mercer. It succeeded in losing some £300,000 in shareholders' funds and deposits before closing down three years later.

The great crisis in Matthew Davies's affairs came at last, as it came to most Victorians, in 1892. In October 1891 his Freehold Investment Co. Ltd paid an 8 per cent dividend—yet three months later was forced to close its doors. Within six months of the passing of the Voluntary Liquidation Act in December 1891, practically every company in the Davies ring had been liquidated by its own directors. In February 1892 Davies's English & Australian Mortgage Bank Ltd and Victorian Mortgage & Deposit Bank Ltd were forced to suspend payment. The same month his Mercantile Bank declared an 8 per cent dividend, and, in passing, cashed a £20,000 promissory note for James Munro as the ex-Premier hurriedly left for England. Then the Mercantile Bank suspended payment too. Davies went abroad in an attempt to raise new finance. On the way to London he was shipwrecked in the S.S. *City of Chicago*, losing all his baggage in the wreck. The *Bulletin* commented:

Poor Matthew, this is shocking!
  You lost everything, you say
(Save a trifle in a stocking,
  Which the wife has put away).
But a little while before, sir,
  Men lost everything they had
In financial wrecks ashore, sir—
  That was also very sad.

He arrived in London in July 1892, but failed entirely in his endeavours to raise new finance. He hotly defended his companies before a committee of angry English shareholders, then quickly returned to Australia to find the pack in full cry. The public, which had admired and trusted him, was in turn bewildered and furious at the disappearance of millions of pounds in savings and investments. Heads had to roll. Davies was forced to resign from Parliament and to give up all his public positions. Once again the *Bulletin* was ready with a grim jest: 'Why is the Melbourne Mercantile Bank like the New Testament? Because it begins with Matthew and ends with Revelations.'

The contents of Davies's mansion were auctioned, giving the *Bulletin* paragraph writers new opportunities:

> Even the auction sale of that fallen Australian magnate's furniture was a 'cronk' affair. Many vanloads of the deposed potentate's stuff had been removed weeks before the event, and other van-loads from a local furniture warehouse were brought up to fill the vacuum. This will send a cold shudder through many ladies who gave fancy prices for items of Blank & Co.'s old stock in the belief that they were getting souvenirs of a once great and rich man.

After the sale of furniture, the huge house was offered for rent at £10 a week, but there were no takers. It remained vacant for most of 1893, then for some years was occupied by a caretaker. In 1898 it was occupied by the Oldham family.

Davies himself was subjected to an extraordinary series of criminal charges, counter-charges, committals, and acquittals. After a brilliant defence by Theodore Fink and Frank Gavan Duffy, Davies was finally found 'not guilty' of criminal conduct as a director. Nevertheless, he was forced to file his schedule in insolvency in 1894, his address then being 'Emo House', Grange Road, East Malvern. His balance sheet showed debts of £280,000. The sole remaining mortgage was one for £28,000 given in 1891 by the Bank of New South Wales. This proved, claimed Davies, that he had never borrowed personally from his own companies. The balance of his indebtedness was due to calls on shares which he held in his own institutions—the Mercantile Bank (£15,000) and Freehold Investment Co. Ltd (£226,000). This proved, said Davies, that he had never speculated personally in other people's shares or property.

In 1890, Davies continued, his personal assets amounted to £650,000 clear of debts. Since then, his assets had been turned into liabilities. Davies's schedule and examination went through smoothly enough, and four months later he applied for a discharge from insolvency. Judge Molesworth refused to grant it until he paid his creditors 7s. in the £1. Davies appealed to the Full Court and won an unconditional discharge—as did his brother, J. B. Davies. The Chief Justice, granting Sir Matthew's application, said, 'By reason of entirely external circumstances, a plague and pestilence which fell upon this country, the insolvent's means were taken from him.' Charity had at least not vanished from the law courts.

After his sequestration, Davies resumed business with his old partner, C. S. Price, at 430 Chancery Lane, and according to one affidavit made about £500 a year as barrister and solicitor. In 1898, after Price went bankrupt, Davies continued in business by himself, and lived quietly at 254 Albert Street, East Melbourne. As the events of the great depression faded into bitter memory, Davies again began building up a modest position in community life. He became a Deputy Grand Master of the Grand Lodge of Freemasons, and President of the Philharmonic Society. When he died, he owned 'Ariston', a house in Armadale; and 'Lockwood', a farm at Narre Warren.

Joseph Davies, the Freehold Investment Co. Ltd's managing director, filed his schedule in April 1894, with an enormous list of debts totalling £594,000. It was disclosed that in 1887 the Mercantile Bank (run by brother Matthew) had given him an overdraft for £10,000. In turn, Joseph had given a guarantee to the Mercantile Bank for £25,000 lent to various Davies companies. It was a travesty of accepted banking procedure.

In 1888 Joseph Davies had borrowed £20,000 from the Melbourne Savings Bank. He was lent another £12,000 by the Bank of South Australia. Jointly with B. J. Fink, he borrowed £24,000 from the Caledonian & Australian Mortgage Co. Ltd. Most of this money he used to buy up shares in his own company, the Freehold Investment Co. Ltd, and thus prop up their price in the stock market.

After his bankruptcy, Davies's art collection and furniture in the Malvern house were sold up. They included Wilton carpets and plush silk hangings, some of the curtains being hand-embroidered, also some unique Japanese cabinets and screens. His collection of pictures, including examples of Rolando, Portal, Peele, Taschaggeny, Catani, Corcos, Koek-Koek, and other artists, was sold together with 'a fine collection' of bronze and china ornaments, a Bluthner upright grand piano, and a full-sized billiard-table by Alcock.

In 1895, when events had quietened down, J. B. Davies applied to the Insolvency Court for his discharge. His estate had paid about ¼d. in the £1 on his enormous debts, and his total income as an accountant was now about £4 a week. The application found Judge Molesworth in a particularly liverish mood. When J. M. Davies presented the schedule on his brother's behalf, His Honour asked him whether it would not be better to go to a Supreme Court judge, who would be 'thoroughly independent in dealing with an insolvency of this character', instead of coming to him as a judge of the County Court, who was 'to a great extent dependent on the goodwill of members of Parliament, and whose salary was liable to reductions.'

This was a case, the judge continued angrily, which involved £600,000 worth of debts, and practically no dividends had been paid. The insolvent was supported in his application by a prominent member of the Upper House, and the person making the application (J. M. Davies) was once head of His Honour's department. There was a well-founded fear that, if he offended politicians or the friends of politicians, the consequences might be 'very serious indeed'. He considered this 'a case of reckless speculation,' and was not prepared to grant a release. Changing from anger to irony, Judge Molesworth asked why the applicant did not withdraw the application and 'get the necessary number of creditors to accept a dividend of a peppercorn in the pound'.

An immediate storm burst in Parliament and press. The judge was reprimanded by the Attorney-General. In a public reply, Molesworth disclosed that the Crown Law Department was attempting to remove him from the Insolvency Court and send him to the country. He also disclosed that on 14 August 1894, the County Court judges had asked the government for freedom from political interference, and had received no answer. 'In the public interest we should be, not only free from all political interference, but even from the suspicion of it', the judge wrote to A. P. Akehurst, secretary of the Crown Law Department. Press, public, and his brother judges stood firmly behind Molesworth, and the attempt to remove him was abandoned.

J. B. Davies appealed to the Supreme Court, and here the strict letter of the insolvency law was upheld. Mr Justice Hood, delivering judgment for the Full Court, said:

> The intention of the Legislature clearly was that an insolvent who has complied with the provisions of the Act, and who has not committed any of the offences therein specified, should get a discharge from his debts and be allowed to make a fresh start in life . . . The court cannot see in . . . [Davies's] conduct any reckless speculation, or gambling, or anything but misfortune.

Thus J. B. Davies was given an unconditional discharge.

While his younger brothers, Matthew and Joseph, were building up their great land companies, the eldest brother, John Mark Davies, was busily making a reputation as one of Melbourne's leading solicitors. J. M. Davies was first admitted to practice as a solicitor in 1863, very soon going into partnership with another young solicitor, J. M. Campbell. By the time the land boom commenced, the two men had built up a prosperous legal business at 44 Elizabeth Street, Melbourne. Soon the younger brothers were making such apparent fortunes from land speculation that Davies and Campbell decided to join in too.

In 1886 they formed an institution known as the General Land & Savings Co. Ltd, with £1 million capital divided into £10 shares, paid up to £5 per share. This company immediately entered the busy land market. It bought a block of buildings near the City Bank in Elizabeth Street for £200,000; half an acre of land in Flinders Street for £100,000; 300 acres at Glenroy for £100,000; and 180 acres at Coburg for £50,000. Subdivision and reselling went on at a hectic pace, and for some years the company paid high dividends.

By 1889 the company was to all appearances so well established that J. M. Davies decided to join brother Matthew in the political arena. As a member of the Conservative group he had little difficulty in winning the Legislative Council seat of South Yarra. The following year, James Munro made his bid for supreme political power, and succeeded in toppling Duncan Gillies from the Premiership. Casting around for supporters, Munro persuaded J. M. Davies to accept a seat in Cabinet as Minister of Justice. They were an ill-matched combination. Munro bought radical support by following a one-man one-vote policy; Davies abhorred the notion that a poor man's vote should count as much as a property-owner's vote. Davies resigned from Cabinet on the issue, and consented to return only when Munro promised to abandon the policy which had put him into power.

J. M. Davies appeared to be riding the crest of the wave. His legal business was sound and profitable, his land company was declaring large dividends, and he occupied the State's top politico-legal position. He was appointed solicitor to, and then a director of, the Commercial Bank. No one seemed to question the

Part of J. M. Davies's huge mansion in East Malvern, still standing today as Malvern Grammar School.

propriety of a Minister of Justice receiving substantial fees from a bank which was deeply involved in speculative activities.

Davies began building an enormous mansion in Willoby Avenue, East Malvern, estimated to cost about £70,000. Situated on several acres of level parkland opposite the convent, the huge two-storey grey stucco building was lavishly appointed and decorated. The largest parquet floor in the southern hemisphere was laid in the main ballroom, where the visitor could look up fifty feet to a great central lantern. A noble staircase led visitors up to a rectangular gallery, which gave access to bedrooms situated on the upper floor.

No sooner was the huge house completed than Davies's time of troubles began. His political leader, James Munro, bolted to England as Agent-General; and when William Shiels reconstructed the government he pointedly omitted J. M. Davies from the Cabinet. Outside Parliament, during those breathless summer days, Davies had to face the gathering thunderstorm of the financial crisis, the serious allegations being openly made against all companies in the Davies network, and the sense of impending doom in the air. In 1892, when his own insolvency seemed imminent, J. M. Davies resigned as a director of the Commercial Bank and the Trustees, Executors & Agency Co. Ltd. He resumed private practice as a solicitor, and began to wind up his companies.

A meeting of the main institution, the General Land Co. Ltd, was called in February 1893. J. M. Davies, as chairman, put forward an ingenious proposal. The company's debts, he disclosed, amounted to £450,000. The directors had gone carefully through the share register, and even if the full amount of £5 per share was called up, they could not see more than £16,000 forthcoming from the hard-pressed shareholders. They therefore proposed that the calls should be contributed only by those shareholders able to pay, and the resulting sum offered to creditors in full settlement of their claims. It was the first and only known application of Marxist principles to the liquidation of a private company. Shareholders who could not pay the call would not be forced into insolvency, but 'should make an effort to borrow from their friends, or contribute out of their future earnings, to pay a portion of their liability'. Since Davies himself held about 10,000 shares, liable to a call of £50,000, his proposal would save him from almost certain insolvency. Incredibly enough, the motion was approved by the meeting, the company's creditors eventually being paid about 2s. in the £1.

This unprecedented method of winding up a company appeared to be going smoothly. Then suddenly Davies, the practised solicitor, was faced with a Supreme Court action. One of the shareholders, Richard Lloyd Gurden, a city surveyor, applied for a full investigation of events under court supervision. In his petition, Gurden claimed that the General Land Co. Ltd had merely been formed to take over land already owned by the directors, which they could not profitably sell on the open market. Gurden also alleged that the company had bought hundreds of thousands of shares in other Davies companies, to make it appear as though there was a huge demand for the shares. Finally, he claimed, the directors had paid themselves large dividends out of shareholders' funds in 1890, when the company had not made a trading profit. These serious allegations were published and never refuted. On the day that his application was due to be heard by the Supreme Court, Gurden's solicitor appeared and withdrew the petition. His only explanation was that Gurden had been promised that a 'competent committee' would be appointed to supervise the gradual calling-up of all amounts owing on shares. No further enquiry, government or private, was made on the allegation of a fraudulent balance sheet. The General Land Co. Ltd disappeared from public view without a ripple.

Davies locked up most of his mansion in East Malvern, and lived in one wing. It became known as 'Davies' Folly'. Large sections of the grounds were subdivided and sold up gradually to help pay his debts. The magnificent house later became the scene of receptions for a new generation of debutantes, and other important social occasions. Then it was converted into Malvern Grammar School, and countless thousands of heedless schoolboy feet trampled the ornate inlaid floor of the main ballroom, converted into an assembly hall. Davies himself shifted to 'Valentines' in Burke Road, Malvern.

J. M. Davies stood again for the South Yarra seat in Parliament in 1895, but was soundly trounced by George Godfrey, a leader of the investigators and liquidators of boom companies. Davies later fought his way back into Parliament and respectability, becoming Attorney-General in the Irvine and Bent Ministries from 1903 onwards, and President of the Legislative Council from 1910 to 1919. It was also the period of W. L. Baillieu's greatest power in State politics. They made an impressive pair in the solemn red plush surroundings of the Victorian Upper House.

44

The Network of Davies Companies

(i) The Colonial Investment & Agency Co. Ltd

From the enormous tangle of companies formed or taken over by Sir Matthew Davies, it is possible to select half a dozen major enterprises which in themselves illuminate the murky financial background of the boom. The 'subscribed capital' of all his companies amounted to nearly £10 million, but much of this was represented by inflated share exchanges for land purchases, comparatively little being subscribed in actual cash.

Davies's first major undertaking on his own account was the formation of the Colonial Investment & Agency Co. Ltd, floated in 1879 when he was a youthful member of Prahran Council. With a 'subscribed capital' of £200,000, this fledgling company did very well out of land deals for many years. This early success encouraged Davies to start many similar enterprises. It also encouraged the public to place £250,000 on deposit with the company—most of which was ultimately lost along with the capital.

In 1883 Davies amalgamated the company with the Mutual Trust & Investment Society by means of a share exchange. In 1884 he took over and amalgamated the Victorian Land & Agency Co. Ltd, and in 1885 the Melbourne Trust Estate Co. Ltd. During these happy years all the transactions were highly profitable, and good dividends were being paid. A head office was established at 87 Queen Street (now a branch of the National Bank). Directors of the company were Sir Matthew Davies, Francis Joseph Smart, Dr T. H. Steel, and Templeton Bunnett. As his other interests expanded, Davies ceased to handle the daily running of the company, and Smart, an architect, was elected chairman.

A few examples of the company's transactions show the changes in its fortunes. In 1885 the directors paid £3,000 for 1,000 shares in the Union Mortgage & Agency Co. In 1892, three weeks before going into liquidation, they unloaded them for £300—a tenth of their former value. In 1887, the company bought a tract of land in the Bullarook district from another Davies enterprise for £20,000. In 1892 the liquidators looked at the land and decided that it was not even worth the £6,000 still owing on it. They surrendered the equity and the entire amount already paid was lost. In 1888, the company bought Brunton's Mills in Spencer Street for £56,000. When the payments were suspended, the mortgagor fore-

F. J. Smart, the architect who was appointed director of the Colonial Investment & Agency Co. Ltd.

Sir Edward Braddon, Agent-General and later Premier of Tasmania, who became a London director of the disastrous Freehold Investment Co. Ltd.

closed and put the property up for auction. There were no bids, the Colonial losing £40,000 on this one deal.

Other large amounts were spent on buying shares in other Davies companies—the Mercantile Bank, Mentone Land Company, Victorian Mortgage Bank, and the English & Australian Mortgage Bank. As these companies collapsed, calls on their shares became due and had to be paid out of shareholders' funds.

As a result of such transactions and the general fall in values, the company lost more than £200,000 from 1888 to 1892. During this period, it showed satisfactory results to the world by a novel system of 'assumed profits' based on the constant inflation of land values. Dividends of £70,000 were paid out in the four years. In April 1891, it was claimed that the profits of the company amounted to £50,000 for the year, which was included in the non-existent reserve fund of £130,000. In fact the company had earned only £61. 12s. 6d. in the twelve months!

Later in 1891, when things were getting desperate, the directors borrowed £110,000 from the National Bank, and continued to pay dividends from these funds. But, said the liquidators' report, 'The company had systematically arranged matters so that no overdraft appeared in their balance sheets as due to the bank . . . The sums were expressed as due on contract, as if on some property transaction.' In return for the overdraft, the Colonial's directors secretly gave the National Bank a general lien on practically all its properties and other assets. 'There was not a line in the minutes referring to it,' reported the liquidators, 'either authorising it or in any way acknowledging it to have been done.'

On 14 December 1891, ten days after the passing of the Voluntary Liquidation Act, Sir Matthew Davies called a meeting of shareholders and depositors and revealed a little of the true situation. He said that the whole of the so-called reserve fund of £130,000 had been absorbed by losses, as well as the 'hidden reserve' of £25,000, and another £100,000 had been written off the value of the company's properties. Despite all this, he still had hopes of the company's future prosperity, and asked depositors to show their confidence by renewing their deposits for a further three years.

But the situation was too desperate. Early in 1892 another meeting was called, and the shareholders were asked to agree to the process of secret voluntary liquidation. At this stage they were still unaware of the revelations to come, although one depositor, the Rev. Dr Chapman, made a fiery speech about 'the miserable imposture called the reserve fund,' which was 'a snare and a delusion,' and 'never had any existence.' As liquidator the shareholders first elected J. M. Pratt, M.L.C. Pratt declined to have anything to do with the liquidation, so C. Balderson, a large depositor, and R.T. Blackwell were elected.

Just before their report was completed, the directors made a last-minute attempt to forestall them. Circulars were mailed to all shareholders asking them to give their proxy votes to the directors. A meeting was quickly summoned, and F. J. Smart took the chair amid 'a storm of dissent.' Smart told the shareholders that Sir Matthew Davies had resigned, and that the manager, George Cornell, had 'broken down.' The new manager, C. Cameron, said that if the company were to be wound up there and then, there would still be a small credit balance, 'taking matters at their worst.' By this time the shareholders were too suspicious to agree to an immediate and secret liquidation. They decided to wait for their own representatives' report.

Within a month, Balderson and Blackwell were ready to move. In July 1892, another meeting was called to hear their report, for which a milling crowd of several hundreds gathered at the Olderfleet Building in Collins Street. 'The ordinary city man was in a decided minority,' reported *Table Talk*. 'The majority of those present were of mature years, grey-headed and spectacled, who had evidently lost largely by the concern. Many women with anxious faces were present.'

The liquidators' report was appalling. The manner in which the company was conducted had 'brought ruin and misery to hundreds of persons and many families.' The investigators had received hundreds of letters, 'some very heart-rending, others insulting, reproachful and vengeful.' The affairs of the company 'could not have been in a much worse position.' The reserve fund, which was never more than a book entry, had totally disappeared.

'We have no hesitation,' the liquidators reported scathingly, 'in stating that the directors must have known two or three years ago that the company was drifting towards insolvency.' The assets, shown as £520,000, were to a large extent merely a book entry. 'What a farce to ask the depositors to sign agreeing to renew their deposits for three years to enable the company to tide over their difficulty!'

Of the cash losses of more than £200,000 in four years, about £100,000 had been invested in and lost by other companies in the Davies group. 'Those in charge must have had some qualms of conscience in going on paying dividends,' said the liquidators. 'We cannot understand how business men could let the company drift into the hopeless position in which it now stands.'

It was the finish. Even F. J. Smart had nothing to say. Less than three months later, the former architect, an Icarus whose wings had melted, made a secret composition with his creditors, paying them 4d. in the £1. His main creditor was the Commercial Bank. He also owed £35,000 for calls on shares he had bought in the Davies companies.

George Cornell, manager of the company throughout the boom, filed his schedule in May 1892, showing more than £12,000 in debts on various land purchases. Where had he got the money from? Why, from Sir Matthew Davies' own bank, the Mercantile.

(ii) The Freehold Investment Co. Ltd

The second of the major Davies companies, formed in 1882, was the Freehold Investment & Banking Company of Australia Ltd. Matthew Davies appointed his older brother, Joseph Bartlett Davies, as managing director. Apart from the Davies brothers, the foundation directors were James Balfour, M.L.C., John Moodie, and C. H. James, the latter retiring shortly after the company's formation. The enterprise had a nominal capital of £1½ million, but erected a vast tissue-paper structure on the basis of its £260,000 paid-up capital. 'It was this large unpaid capital which attracted depositors by its promise of security,' said the *Age* after the crash, 'and we learn accordingly that a credulous public poured their coin into the bank to the extent of £1,381,000.'

The company was formed specifically 'to invest in landed property, both freehold and leashold,' and to retain most of the properties situated in areas where values were likely to increase. By buying such lands on mortgage, the company became extremely vulnerable to fluctuations in economic conditions. Hence, perhaps, the worried optimism of an article on the company published in *The History of Victoria and Melbourne* in 1888: 'When the directors . . . commenced to deal in land, many persons who considered themselves authorities, condemned this "out of the ordinary" way of doing business, but the directors, who had thoroughly considered the practicability of their scheme, ignored the opinion of these wiseacres . . . The company is now recognised as one of the most prosperous and stable financial institutions in the colony.'

We may hasten over most of the land deals conducted by the Freehold Investment Co. Ltd, which was able to show good profits while land values were increasing rapidly. In 1884 the directors leased a site opposite the Town Hall, on the south-western corner of Collins and Swanston Streets, and erected the block of offices and shops known as Nicholson's Corner. These began to return good rentals.

In 1886 the directors arranged a 50-year lease of the south-eastern corner of

The Victoria Buildings and Queens Arcade, Melbourne, erected by the Davies interests on the site of today's City Square.

Collins and Swanston Streets. Owner of the land was Dr Thomas Black of St Kilda, to whom the company paid £3,000 a year in ground rent. They erected a huge office block called Victoria Buildings, put a large statue of Britannia on the facade, and gathered £10,000 a year in rentals for the shops in Queens Walk and offices above. After the crash the property fell into the hands of the banks. In 1963, the A.N.Z. Bank sold the old building to the Hammerson group of companies. Finally it was taken over by the City Council and demolished in 1966, the space becoming part of today's city square.

Probably the Freehold Investment Company's biggest suburban transaction was the 'opening up' of Surrey Hills by the purchase and subdivision of the Windsor Park Estate. After that the company bought a large area at Blackburn for nearly a quarter of a million pounds, then 3,500 acres of land at Doutta Galla, Truganini, and Wookurkook.

By 1886 property values had soared so high that the company's assets were revalued by C. J. & T. Ham. A bonus of 35s. a share was paid in addition to the usual 8 per cent dividend. A further revaluation was made by the Messrs Ham in 1888, when it was claimed that the company's properties had increased in value by another £700,000. This optimistic announcement, made as the boom passed its zenith, had the effect of increasing deposits with the company by nearly £600,000 in the following two years.

In 1888 the company also opened a London branch to tap English deposits. An impressive London board was appointed, consisting of Sir Graham Berry, Victorian Agent-General; John Badcock, former London manager of the Bank of N.S.W.; C. G. Miller, formerly of the Commercial Bank; and Sir Edward Braddon, Tasmanian Agent-General.

The same year, Joseph Davies bought a large mansion in Glenferrie Road, Malvern, next door to John Grice's superb 'Stonnington'. The purchase price was £36,000, on which Davies paid £10,000 deposit and the first few instalments to the owners, Robert Harper and Mary Officer. The property was later repossessed, the mansion demolished, and the site subdivided. Davies also built himself a more modest weekend retreat at Mentone, opposite the Mentone Coffee Palace, on steeply rising ground overlooking the bay. Today the old structure forms part of St Bede's Roman Catholic College for boys; while the coffee palace has become an hotel.

By the end of 1888, the best days of the boom were over and the reaction set in. The directors found it almost impossible to sell land, office rents began falling off, and smaller companies went out of business. The Freehold's directors thereupon evolved a number of ingenious schemes, on the very borderline of legality, to maintain the company in a state of apparent prosperity. All their efforts to keep afloat were in vain. In February 1892, the company suspended business 'pending readjustment,' and asked depositors to renew for a further three years.

At the shareholders' and depositors' meeting which followed, Joseph Davies attempted to defend the company's policies on the ground that C. J. & T. Ham's valuations had shown an enormous surplus of assets over book values.

'I have done my best for the company,' he said. 'I cannot see why this irritation on the part of the depositors should exist.' (Laughter and groans). *Table Talk* commented: 'It is well-known that valuators during the land boom departed altogether from the sound principles of capitalising the actual earning power of a property, and estimated to suit their clients . . . "Expert opinions" looked so much better in the minutes of companies recording advances, and in advertisements, that high fees were paid for them.'

Another director, James Balfour, M.L.C., told the meeting that he had known J. B. Davies since boyhood, and had 'perfect confidence' in his integrity. He felt his own position very keenly, charged as he was with using depositors' funds to pay shareholders' dividends. 'I trust I would scorn to be guilty of such an act, and I only regret that the liquidators before issuing their report did not first intimate to me their views,' he said angrily.

James Mason, a colonist of forty-four years' standing, refused to accept the directors' explanations. 'We did not know that our money was being used for visionary speculations,' he complained. 'I deposited £8,000 in the institution for the benefit of charitable societies, and the money has been lost.' The meeting agreed with Mason that the liquidation would be best supervised by the courts.

In September 1892, the official liquidators presented a preliminary report estimating the company's deficiency at £90,000, after allowing for the repayment of £1,300,000 held on deposit. 'The choice of investments by the company has been particularly unfortunate,' said the liquidators with considerable restraint. The 'investments', in fact, consisted largely of shares bought in other Davies companies, now practically worthless.

By the time of winding-up, the company's properties had been written down to £1,380,000, mainly consisting of city and suburban lands. What were they really worth? Said the liquidators: 'In the depressed state of the land market we have found it to be almost impossible to realise the assets, unless at unwarrantable sacrifice.'

The liquidators—C. G. Miller, T. R. B. Morton, and J. M. Gillespie (later chairman of Robertson & Mullens)—tried to gather in the uncalled capital of £1,381,000. They received only £18,000. 'The great weakness of the share register is that so many shares are held by cognate companies,' they complained. 'There is no reasonable hope that the balance will be received.'

After further investigation, the liquidators were startled to discover that over the previous three years, the sum of £370,000 had been paid out in dividends, interest, etc., but the company's income had amounted to little more than £200,000. Yet four months before the liquidation, Joseph Davies had declared a £22,000 profit and 8 per cent dividend! During the three years, the directors had taken £67,000 dividends for themselves and paid the remainder to other shareholders. There was only one source for these payments: the company's reserves and deposits.

In order to justify these dividends, several large sales were made on or about the last day of each financial half-year. For instance,

Demolition of Queens Walk and Victoria Buildings in 1966.

(1) The Albion Park Estate was sold to John Munro in 1889 for £160,000, on only £2,500 deposit. The deposit itself was paid 'by a relation of one of the directors.' No further instalments were paid, but the 'sale' was counted as profit.

(2) The Freehold's directors formed a satellite company called the Blackburn & Tunstall Property Co. Ltd. This new company 'bought' the Blackburn Park Estate for £225,000, on £7,500 deposit. Only the deposit and first instalment were ever paid, but the 'sale' was counted as profit.

(3) A tract of land at Malvern was sold to John Turner in 1891 for £30,000, on £1,000 deposit. Once again no payments were made, but the 'sale' was counted as profit.

(4) The Freehold Investment Co. Ltd formed another 'company within itself', the Melbourne Property Co., to which £145,000 worth of properties were 'sold,' and added to the Freehold's 'profit' figures.

(5) Another Davies company, Henry Arnold & Co. Ltd, 'bought' Phair's Hotel in Collins Street from the Freehold Investment Co. Ltd for £38,000. The alleged profits from the 'sale' were added to the Freehold's balance sheet.

As these and other internal 'sales' were made, the amounts were transferred in the balance sheet to 'Loans and Balances Owing'. This, said the liquidators, was used as 'evidence of great vitality in the company's business.'

What was Henry Brock, the company's auditor, doing while all these complex and illegitimate transactions were being put through the books? Henry had liquidated himself, after costing the Commercial Bank several thousands for various land deals. His address: 'Of parts unknown.' Mrs Brock told the Insolvency Court that she had received a letter from her husband, saying he was leaving the colony because of the pressure of his debts, and that 'she would not see him again for a long time.'

The liquidators now disagreed on the question of prosecuting the directors. One of their number, T. R. B. Morton, who had been secretary of the Freehold Investment Co. Ltd, resigned. The remaining two liquidators applied to the Supreme Court for 'advice and direction' on the commencement of civil or criminal proceedings against the directors. Mr Justice Hood sanctioned immediate civil action, ruling that the question of criminal action should wait upon the result of the civil case.

But the liquidators soon found that it was useless to proceed even with a civil case against the directors for recovery of the money wrongly paid out in dividends. The directors had either gone bankrupt or were teetering on the edge of insolvency. Soon most of them were involved directly or indirectly in the criminal prosecutions of 1893 against Sir Matthew Davies.

An uproarious meeting of the Freehold's creditors and depositors took place at the Athenaeum in February 1893. J. M. Davies and James Balfour demanded that the liquidators read out counsel's opinion on whether criminal prosecutions against the directors should be undertaken. J. M. Gillespie, acting as chairman of the meeting, refused to do so, but added: 'For my own part I do not believe that the directors had any criminal intention. (Applause). My own opinion is that, given a fair trial, criminal proceedings would not lie. (Applause).' James Mason, the depositor whose earlier motion had resulted in official liquidation, protested that the meeting was being taken advantage of to whitewash the directors. (Scenes of wild uproar). After half an hour of shouting, charges, and counter-charges, the meeting concluded in complete disorder.

The liquidators did their best to realise on the various properties and pay a small dividend. The company's name was changed to the Freehold Assets Realisation Co. Ltd (managing director, J. M. Gillespie), and later became Argo Investments Ltd.

(iii) The English & Australian Mortgage Bank Ltd

In 1884, when his other enterprises were thriving, Matthew Davies started yet another major financial institution. This was first registered as Henry Arnold & Co. Ltd, 'Henry Arnold' being the name of one of Davies's sons. It followed the same general policy as the Freehold Investment Co. Ltd, but with some extraordinary elaborations.

An office was set up at 89 Queen Street, next door to the Colonial Investment Co. Ltd. Directors of Henry Arnold & Co. Ltd were Matthew Davies, James Bell, George Jenkyn, and James Wighton (Davies's legal partner); the manager being Edward Nicholls. The history of some of Henry Arnold's transactions was examined by A. G. V. Peel in his scathing report to the British Treasury in 1893.

At each issue of Henry Arnold shares between 1884 and 1888 the premiums rose until, in May 1888, 10,000 shares were issued at the enormous premium of

£7. 10s. 0. The total capital was now 55,000 shares, of which 50,000 were paid up to £5, and 5,000 fully paid up to £10. The total premiums received on the shares issued between 1886 and 1888 amounted to £116,000. Everyone thought, said Peel, that Henry Arnold & Co. Ltd was as safe as the Bank of England. This prosperity however was only a reflection of the boom.

What was the character of the business? Firstly, shares were continually bought from, and interchanged with, similar companies. Hence, loss was certain as soon as these began a downward course. All would inevitably stand or fall together. Secondly, large cash profits were made during 1887 and 1888 on the purchase and resale of land. On one sale of city property bought at £38,000 there was a cash profit of £21,000. Thirdly, the land boom was ending, but the directors continued to purchase and finance largely.

In 1889 an expedient commonly used in Australian finance was resorted to. In order to make out that they were richer than they really were, the directors had the whole of their freehold properties revalued. Thus, the book value of £313,000 was revalued as £371,000. This was done at a time when freehold values were falling every day!

The company dealt largely in its own shares. For instance, it would advance money to its directors, taking their shares as sole security. When they closed their doors they had more than 10,000 of their own shares held as security for their own advances.

That they might appear at balance time to have more cash than was really the case, they made such arrangements as these: 'On 30th March, 1889, the City of Melbourne Building Society deposited £3,000; repaid 2nd April, 1889.' 'On the same date Gascoigne & Co. deposited £10,000; repaid 1st April and 30th April.'

In 1888, Henry Arnold & Co. Ltd advanced £53,000 to a land agent. A condition was that the latter was to buy some land at Footscray, and that the profits were to go in part to the company. The agent bought the land for much less than £53,000, and bolted with the balance, so that the land was left on the hands of the company. A mysterious organisation known as the Cut-paw-paw Company now arose; it bought the land in question from Henry Arnold, and when the transaction was effected coolly offered the Cut-paw-paw shares in payment. But before the matter could be settled the Cut-paw-paw had in turn disposed of the land to the Footscray Land Company Ltd, which retaliated by itself presenting its own shares in payment instead of cash.

Thus the position was that the Footscray owed cash to the Cut-paw-paw, and the Cut-paw-paw owed cash to Henry Arnold, and all about the same piece of land which was originally owned by Henry Arnold, and was now owned by the Footscray. Eventually, by an absurd denouément, the unfortunate Henry Arnold Company advanced £46,000 to the Footscray in order that the Footscray might pay cash to the Cut-paw-paw in order that the Cut-paw-paw might pay cash to Henry Arnold. Thus the latter actually advanced money to its debtors in order to get them to pay their debts to itself.

In 1889, when the company found money getting tighter in Australia, it followed the usual expedient of opening an office in London to attract fresh deposits. As one of their London directors, the company engaged Sir George Baden Powell, M.P. The other London director was John Paterson, a principal of the Melbourne softgoods firm of Paterson, Laing & Bruce. The name was changed to the English & Australian Mortgage Bank.

In 1891, the bank purchased the Royal Permanent Building Society, which was controlled by James Wighton (Davies's partner) and James Mercer (brother-in-law). The bank gave the building society a loan of £300,000 on the sole security of the society's almost worthless shares. This wild transaction finally broke the bank, forcing it to suspend payment early in 1892.

At the meeting of shareholders, Sir Matthew Davies claimed that the company had earned good interest on its £800,000 deposits, and was still showing a profit of £10,000 a year. In actual fact, as was to be revealed within twelve months, the company had lost more than £1 million of its assets. The directors proposed that the company should reconstruct and reopen for business, but the shareholders could not be rallied, and voted the company into liquidation. The first liquidators appointed were Edward Nicholls, the manager; George Jenkyn, one of the directors; and G. A. Kay, London manager. All three liquidators were summarily dismissed by a later and more disillusioned shareholders' meeting.

But Davies continued his last-ditch efforts. In July he arrived in England, and told a meeting of British depositors (who had put £500,000 into the company) that most of the Melbourne depositors had signed an agreement to take preferences shares in exchange for their deposits. With few exceptions, he claimed, the whole of the company's assets were 'absolutely free of encumbrances.'

Both London and Melbourne shareholders were growing increasingly suspicious, largely as a result of *Table Talk's* investigations into the Davies companies, which were cabled to England. In August 1892, the shareholders appointed a committee of investigation, headed by Dr W. H. Embling, M.L.C. Dr Embling presented the results to an astonished meeting in Melbourne in January 1893.

The company's total losses, he said, amounted to £1,054,068. All the paid capital, all the uncalled capital, all the reserve funds, and most of the depositors' funds had gone. 'It is impossible not to come to the conclusion,' commented *Table Talk*, 'that the company was intended to enable Sir Matthew Davies and individuals associated with him to unload on to the public . . . [The creditors' duty] plainly is to let a jury decide whether fraud has been perpetrated.'

How were the Davies companies able to get their balance sheets approved by the auditors? The answer in the case of the E. & A. Mortgage Bank was most instructive. The chief auditor was Charles Thorpe, another useful brother-in-law of Sir Matthew Davies. Thorpe had been charged in 1881 with defrauding the Bank of Victoria of large sums. Defended by Matthew Davies at that trial, Thorpe contended that he was not morally guilty of theft, as he had refunded the money. The judge did not agree, and sentenced him to two years'

imprisonment. After his release from gaol, Davies gave him the job as auditor.
The other auditor of the E. & A. Mortgage Bank's accounts was Hugh William Sinclair, who made a private composition with his creditors in 1894, and paid 2d. in the £1 on his debts. Sinclair, it transpired, had been doing quite a bit of speculating in land shares on his own account. And where had he borrowed the money from to use for speculation? Where else but the Mercantile Bank, through a generous overdraft dating back four years!

(iv) The Victorian Mortgage & Deposit Bank

As we have already seen in the introductory chapter on Sir Matthew Davies, the last big institution he formed was called the Victorian Mortgage & Deposit Bank. This company was incorporated in 1889 to take over the remnants of Davies's own Victorian Land Company. In effect, it merely put unsaleable blocks of land behind a more grandiloquent title, in a last attempt to raise more cash from investors. The paid-up capital of the old company was £160,000. Investors were impressed by the new flotation to the extent of another £140,000.

Davies appointed his wife's brother, J. S. Mercer, to manage the new bank. The other directors were G. N. Turner, John Moodie, James Johnstone, W. Bowen, and J. Warnock. Once again the old device was tried of opening an office in Lombard Street, London, to attract deposits from English investors. George Feathers, who had been secretary of the old company, became London manager of the new company. Lieut-Colonel Bosanquet added the lustre of his name to the London board, for a consideration.

The manager, J. S. Mercer, had originally conducted an estate agency at 98 Elizabeth Street, Melbourne, under the style 'J. S. Mercer & Co.' His major function now was to subdivide tracts of land bought by the Davies group, and resell the blocks on £5 deposit. One of his biggest transactions was the selling of the extensive Gascoigne Estate, adjoining Caulfield Station, where daily auctions were held to dispose of the land. Another major subdivision was the East Brighton Park, between Centre and Tucker Roads, which Mercer advertised enthusiastically as 'Lands Unlocked for the People.'

By the end of 1891, the directors of the Victorian Mortgage Bank were faced with plain indications that many depositors would refuse to renew their fixed deposits when the time fell due. A run on the bank reduced cash deposits by about £60,000. On 1 February 1892, the directors issued a circular stating that unless depositors renewed for a further three years, the company would have to go into liquidation, with probable loss of all its assets. The bluff was called, depositors and shareholders refusing to allow the business to be carried on any longer.

However, the directors still had enough voting power to ensure that their own men carried out the liquidation, and few details of the bank's inner workings ever came to light. The two liquidators appointed were the bank's manager, J. S. Mercer; and another close associate of Sir Matthew Davies and B. J. Fink, J. M. Howden. A shareholder objected to Howden's appointment, on the ground

J. S. Mercer, acting for Sir Matthew Davies, showed land buyers 'running to a fortune'.

Pedestrianism Extraordinary!

HE WHO RUNS MAY READ.

Where is this man running to?
Why cert.
He is running to a fortune,
Or in other words a home.

Monopoly and High Prices no longer supreme.

Lands Unlocked for the People.

SCHOOLS AND CHURCHES CLOSE BY.

EAST BRIGHTON PARK,

Between CENTRE, TUCKER, and MANCHESTER ROADS.

About 60 Splendid Villa Sites,

WITH LARGE DEPTHS, AT AN UPSET PRICE OF 9s. PER FOOT FOR THIS SALE.

Close to Train Accommodation, being between East Brighton and M'Kinnon Road Stations, from either of which it is only about a quarter of a mile distant. Ingress from stations on two sides of the Estate. Best Garden and Orchard Soil. High Land, with Good Drainage.

Terms, £5 Deposit, Balance Quarterly.

that he allegedly held nearly 80,000 shares 'which he had never paid for.' The accusation went unanswered.

One curious episode did reach the light of day through the law courts. It involved a well-known Melbourne solicitor, William Bruce, who had once been an articled clerk to Sir Matthew Davies, and had gone in for extensive land-booming activities on his own account. Various Davies institutions loaned him many thousands of pounds which he used for speculation. Among his investments, William Bruce bought 4,000 partly-paid shares in the Victorian Mortgage & Deposit Bank. When the boom began to collapse, and it appeared likely that calls would be made on the shares, Bruce transferred them to a juvenile named W. H. Lucas, an office boy.

The bank failed, made its calls on the shares, and found that it could not legally collect from Lucas because he was under age. The matter was taken to court, where Mr Justice Hood described the scheme as a 'contemptible and dishonest practice', and 'a fraudulent device'. What even the judge did not know was that Bruce had made a secret composition the previous September, paying 7d. in the £1 on nearly £70,000 debts. His comments might have been even more caustic if he had known that practically all the money came in the first place from depositors in the various Davies institutions.

The Victorian Mortgage Bank itself died without a murmur. In a city where millions were being lost every week, what was another £300,000?

45

The Mercantile Bank Cases

None of the Davies companies so far examined were 'real' banks. Although they accepted deposits, discounted bills, and conducted general business in a very similar manner to that of the established banks, they were formed primarily for the purpose of speculating in land. They would never have been accepted into the august circle of the Associated Banks. Matthew Davies decided to emulate his friend James Munro and start a more conventional bank.

His instrument in achieving this purpose was a humble institution called the Australian Economic Bank, which had started business in 1877 with capital of £30,000. In 1885 Davies and his friends took it over and floated it into a £1 million company, of which £400,000 was paid up. The name was changed to the Mercantile Bank, directors being Matthew Davies, David Beath, John Moodie, George Shaw, and William Anderson. Later, Beath, Moodie and Shaw resigned without stating their reasons. New directors appointed were T. B. Muntz, James Oddie, and James Bell, M.L.C. General manager was Frederic Millidge.

Apart from Davies, therefore, the directors during the critical years of the boom were Anderson, Muntz, Oddie, and Bell, all of whom were to face criminal charges. William Anderson was a Scottish-born farmer from Port Fairy (Vic.), an elder of the Presbyterian Church, President of the Royal Horticultural Society, and Minister of Public Works in the Gillies government. Thomas Bingham Muntz was a civil engineer by profession but a financier by preference. After the crash he made a secret composition with his creditors and paid 2s. in the £1. James Oddie was a Ballarat businessman who had started his own institution called the Freehold Bank, and taken deposits amounting to £70,000. He was attracted by the idea of riding to higher things on the Davies rocket, and amalgamated his bank with the Mercantile in exchange for a parcel of shares and a seat on the board. James Bell, M.L.C., was a Melbourne businessman who became Minister of Defence in the Gillies-Deakin government.

Under Davies's masterful control, the business of the Mercantile Bank increased enormously. Its head office was established at 333 Collins Street (now Mercantile Options Pty Ltd, rebuilt in 1911). The bank issued its own notes, and branches were established in suburbs and country. A London branch was opened in 1886, with agencies throughout Scotland and Ireland to accept

AFTER THE CRASH

Mercantile Bank manager (*after climbing out from under the ruins*).– I proclaim a dividend of fifteen per cent and move that £50,000 be carried to the reserve fund!

long-term deposits, which by 1891 totalled nearly £2 million. Depositors were encouraged by Davies's pronouncement that it was the aim of the directors 'to do a safe business rather than to strive to make large profits.'

At the beginning of 1892, with dozens of other land companies both inside and outside the Davies group being forced to close their doors, the fate of the Mercantile Bank hung in the balance. Its shares see-sawed up and down as the date of its annual meeting drew closer and doleful rumours swept the city. The Australian deposits, being mainly short-term, were being rapidly withdrawn. The British depositors, who had nearly £1 million in the bank, were alarmed but could do nothing, since their deposits were on long fixed terms. Davies made a desperate bid to stabilize the situation. In January 1892 the Mercantile arranged to borrow £100,000 from the Commercial Bank, repayable at call. The following month, at the last annual meeting ever held by the bank, he declared a profit of £22,000 and a dividend of 8 per cent. Was this dividend paid out of the Commercial Bank's loan? That question was to plague half a dozen judges and juries in the years to come.

Two directors, James Bell and Sir Graham Berry (who had recently returned from London and joined the Melbourne board), made rallying speeches to this last meeting in February 1892. 'The rumours about the bank that have been circulated are entirely unfounded', said Bell. 'A good institution has been established', said Berry, 'and it is for the shareholders to act like men and not run away like children.' What nonsense it all was! The directors already had before them a private document, later produced in the court actions, which showed the Mercantile's losses to that date:

Loss on shares and companies controlled by Sir M. H. Davies	£300,000
Loss on accounts introduced by Sir M. H. Davies	£240,000
Loss by depreciation of property	£140,000
Loss on general business	£150,000
TOTAL LOSSES	£830,000

By the end of February the shares had fallen from £3 to 18s., and the run on local deposits intensified. Davies appealed to the Associated Banks for assistance. The banks replied that they were willing to assist the Mercantile 'through any crisis', provided that (1) it could offer reasonable security; and (2) the directors would allow three outside bank officers to examine the books. Davies accepted the first condition, but refused to allow access to the books. The banks then withdrew their offer, and the Commercial Bank took back its £100,000 lent on call. On 4 March 1892 the Mercantile was forced to close its doors.

Where, now, could Davies turn? Only to the refuge of the Voluntary Liquidation Act, which would allow him to appoint his own liquidators and wind up in comparative secrecy. A crowded shareholders' meeting called to approve this move was held on 21 March under the chairmanship of T. B. Muntz, who suppressed attempts at discussion or cross-examination of directors. Three liquidators were appointed at £1,000 a year remuneration each: the general manager, Frederic Millidge; the manager, J. B. Ainslie; and one director, Sir Graham Berry, who had just become Treasurer of Victoria.

The liquidation would have proceeded normally and quietly, had not *Table Talk* been given some inside information about the bank's affairs. On 1 April the journal published a partial overdraft list showing that twenty-six land companies and speculators had been given advances totalling £440,000. Most of them were members of the Davies group. James Munro, the former Premier, had discounted £20,000 in bills the morning before the bank closed, according to Maurice Brodzky's journal. *Table Talk* also disclosed that: (1) in February the Mercantile had been able to show a large cash balance only because of the secret advance of £100,000 from the Commercial Bank; (2) the Mercantile had made £80,000 in loans on the security of its own shares; (3) the directors were paid fees two days after the bank closed; and (4) the custom of directors was to pay in large cheques to bring their accounts into credit just before each half-yearly meeting, and withdraw the amounts immediately afterwards. Even after these sensational allegations, all remained quiet for some time. There was no reply to the *Table Talk* article, but after it was reprinted in the *Financial Times* the London depositors applied for compulsory winding-up of the Bank's English activities under court supervision.

In July 1892 the liquidators called a meeting in the bank's small boardroom to present their report. As soon as Sir Graham Berry took the chair, there were 'loud cries' for him to vacate it, and allow the shareholders to elect their own chairman. Theodore Fink asked whether it was in order for anyone other than the chairman of liquidators to preside. His objection was shouted down, and James C. Park was elected. Meanwhile, shareholders were still arriving and jostling in an excited group outside the boardroom. The meeting was adjourned until the next day at the Athenaeum Hall.

At the resumed meeting, Sir Graham Berry presented an optimistic liquidators' report, showing an estimated debit balance of only £4,000 when the bank's affairs were finally settled. In actual fact, the loss of depositors' money reached nearly one million pounds, apart from loss of the entire paid-up capital, the reserve fund, and the undistributed profits. In answer to questions, Frederic Millidge, general manager, said that the £20,000 in bills discounted for James Munro just before the bank closed had been drawn by Donald Munro (of Munro & Baillieu) six months previously, on condition they could be renewed for a further six months if required. Then Millidge said he had been appointed to another position in London and was leaving the colony almost immediately. (Uproar.)

The most important result of the meeting was the appointment of a committee of investigation, consisting of William Simpson, George Godfrey, J. C. Park and W. F. Ducker. This expert committee made a thorough probe into the bank's affairs, but could not agree on whether to publish names of individuals involved. Simpson therefore called his own meeting in August 1892, attended by about one hundred shareholders. Once again Melbourne was to be shaken by

The seven directors and officers of the Mercantile Bank finally prosecuted by the Shiels Government: James Bell, M.L.C.; T. B. Muntz; William Anderson, M.L.A.; Sir Matthew Davies, M.L.A.; Frederic Millidge; C. W. Ellis; and C. J. Richardson.

revelations of financial chicanery. Even the conservative *Argus* headlined its report 'STARTLING DISCLOSURES'.

Opening the meeting, Simpson said his report contained 'nothing but what he was prepared to substantiate in a court of law'. Before he could proceed, there was a determined attempt to stop him.

> Rev. W. H. Fitchett (whose paper, the *Daily Telegraph*, was being financed by the Mercantile Bank): 'Are you not breaking faith with the shareholders and depositors in not leaving this report till tomorrow's meeting?'
>
> Simpson: 'If you don't wish to hear it you can leave the room.' (Uproar.)
>
> Fitchett: 'Did you give a pledge not to divulge the information? . . . '
>
> Simpson: 'Mr. Fitchett is either my guest or he is not. I shall not be interrupted further, but shall call assistance and remove him if he is not quiet.' (Uproar.)
>
> Fitchett: 'You will not put me out.'

Eventually Simpson was permitted to read his report in comparative silence. He recalled that Sir Matthew Davies had told the last annual meeting that:

> With the exception of one small advance to one director . . . no director has personally obtained an advance from the bank. I, myself, who am a large depositor and shareholder, have never had a single shilling of the bank's money, a bill discounted, or an overdrawn account for many years.

Simpson read out to the meeting a long list of individuals associated with and companies controlled by Sir Matthew Davies. Altogether they had borrowed £660,000 from the Mercantile Bank. The *Table Talk* revelations were more than justified. J. B. Davies (Matthew's brother) owed £66,000. Messrs Price and Wighton (Matthew Davies's partners) and their employees had borrowed £40,000. The 'manager's special account' of £10,000 was used by Millidge for operations on the Stock Exchange, to prop up the price of the bank's shares.

'Looking over the list of Davies companies,' said Simpson, 'where Sir M. H. Davies is not himself, there you will find his dummy. By dummy I mean a clerk or relative not worth a brass farthing, carrying the liability of thousands.' The following relatives by marriage of Sir Matthew Davies had been given large overdrafts: John Moodie, a director, owed £60,000. Charles Fartiere, a youthful relative, received nearly £12,000. A. J. Fuller, a brother-in-law employed by Davies as his private secretary, received nearly £3,000. J. S. Mercer, another brother-in-law, received £2,300 on overdraft, and discounted £8,000 in bills a few days before the bank failed. Charles Thorpe, the bank's auditor, received £8,000. Robert Kingston, the umbrella manufacturer who committed suicide, received £6,000, and when he died left a note recommending his family to the care of Sir Matthew Davies.

'As the details of various transactions were laid bare there was a good deal of ironical laughter and ejaculations of surprise and indignation', reported the *Argus*. A 'plentiful crop of writs' for libel was promised by the individuals named in Simpson's report, but not a single one ever came to light. 'Nevertheless', said the *Bulletin*, 'many people expect Simpson to be touched with something hard, one of these dark nights. An awful idea, which is quite freely suggested in the city of financial stink.'

On the following day the remaining liquidators presented their report to another shareholders' meeting at the Athenaeum Hall. They completely confirmed the facts of Simpson's revelations, but omitted most of the personalities involved. However, they added,

> We regret to report that the names of the auditors, the accountant, and solicitors to the bank appear among the list of debtors thereto for considerable amounts . . . a most objectionable practice . . . The last balance sheet was false, and all back to 1890 were faulty and false also . . . Suspending payment legally meant the stoppage of every payment, . . . [but] your committee find that four of your directors have set this moral and legal aspect at defiance, by taking from the coffers of the bank on March 7 last the sum of £300 in payment of their hard earned fees.

Thomas Bent, the new Speaker of the Legislative Assembly, who held exactly ten shares in the bank, rose towards the end of the meeting and made an impassioned speech. 'So far as Mr. Godfrey is concerned I regard him as a professional wrecker', said Bent, to the accompaniment of loud groans and hoots. 'I am surprised at the deliberate way in which you all combine together to injure your public and private reputations and prosperity.'

Chairman: 'I am astonished at Mr. Bent, who ought to know better.'

Bent (after a long reply): 'We should make a fresh start. Let us keep as clear as we can of these lawyers.' (Cheers and laughter.)

After a good deal of commotion and abuse, the meeting adjourned.

The *Bulletin* smacked its lips in the following issue. 'Speaker Bent has publicly stated that "Victorians are honourable men" incapable of doing anything that English creditors can find fault with. *That* settles it. We have long waited for a reliable opinion on the character of Smellboom, and Bent was the man to give it.'

During these months Sir Matthew Davies was overseas trying to raise fresh capital, but the newspaper cables completed the ruin of his mission. A London representative of the *Australian Mail* interviewed Davies at the end of July. 'I cannot for a moment believe that any such depreciation as three-quarters of a million has occurred', said Sir Matthew. 'The liquidators are representing things in their gloomiest light in order to bring the liquidation to a successful issue and so gain the kudos for themselves.' The press, now hot on the scent, also caught up with the late manager, Frederic Millidge, in London. Talk of criminal prosecutions was absurd, said Millidge. 'The committee should carefully consider whether by doing so they would not involve other large institutions and firms in bankruptcy.'

The adjourned meeting of shareholders was resumed late in September 1892, when William Simpson explained his reasons for imputing fraud to the people he had named. In fact, he claimed, Matthew Davies had originated the bank with fraudulent motives. The *Age* reported:

> The remark caused a profound sensation. Sir Matthew Davies, who was sitting in the front row, rose to his feet amidst great excitement, and advanced towards the platform. His friends interposed and dragged him back . . . Meanwhile Mr. Simpson again and again essayed to speak. Every time, however, that he did so a tornado of cat calls, hoots and other substitutes for articulate speech was launched at him, and at last he took a seat and waited for calm.

Later, when Simpson rose again he was greeted with 'mingled cheers, groans and hisses'. He said he had been in business for thirty years as a legal accountant, and 'had never made a proposition he had not been able to establish in the courts'. When the shareholders found out how things had been done they 'would be amazed at their folly in trusting such men, and would think all the lunatic asylums in the colony were hardly large enough to hold them.' (Cheers and laughter.)

Thomas Bent staged another extraordinary performance in reply to Simpson.

> Bent: 'I have watched him too long, and let me tell that gentleman I am quite as honest as he is, and perhaps more so (Laughter) . . . I have lost more money . . . '
> J. G. Thomson: 'Where did you get it?'
> Bent: 'What I got, I got honestly (Cries of 'Land boomer'). I am not one of the land boomers. ('Oh, oh,' and laughter).'

Once again the meeting concluded in wild disorder.

Simpson made his full accusations in the following issue of *Table Talk*, occupying several pages of closely packed type in which he said:

> The fraud of the century has been perpetrated, and the ultimate loss to the depositors must be over one million pounds . . . The character of Victoria for commercial morality will be blasted for ever unless the Government insists on a full and searching investigation. Are we to say to the people of England, 'A few families out here have pocketed £6 million or £7 million, but we are all tarred with the same brush?'

At yet another shareholders' meeting, held in October 1892, Davies rose to make his defence. He was heard quietly, but with growing impatience, for the great financier blamed all the bank's troubles on the fact that the companies to which it had loaned money had all closed their doors. Next morning the *Argus* said:

> The statement was lamentably weak and insufficient. The main issues are mostly ignored; the attempted rebuttal of the allegations of the committee is a failure . . . The question of questions is whether the balance sheet of last February correctly presented the affairs of the bank. If it did not it was false, perhaps fraudulent.

That question was to bring Sir Matthew Davies and his fellow directors into court many times in 1893—after one of the most sensational political battles ever fought between two Cabinet Ministers.

It was now the cheerless Christmas of 1893. Shopkeepers waited in vain for customers to come in to buy Christmas delicacies and presents. There was widespread destitution. And there was one question on everyone's lips: Would the government issue instructions for the arrest of its former Speaker, the great financier Sir Matthew Davies?

On 15 December 1892 officers of the Crown Law Department privately advised the Attorney-General, William Shiels, that in their opinion it was justifiable to initiate criminal proceedings against the directors of the Mercantile Bank for issuing 'a false and fraudulent balance sheet' the previous February. There followed a tortuous series of Cabinet meetings on the question, and what

W. F. Ducker, liquidator of the Mercantile Bank and chief witness for the prosecution of its directors and officers.

David Gaunson, who defended Frederic Millidge, manager of the Mercantile Bank.

the *Age* described as 'a legal coma'. Finally, on 4 January 1893, after another long Cabinet meeting, Shiels issued instructions for the prosecution under section 159 of the Crimes Act of Sir Matthew Davies, James Bell, William Anderson, and T. B. Muntz, directors; Frederic Millidge, manager; and C. Ellis and C. J. Richardson, auditors. Sir Graham Berry and James Oddie, the remaining two directors, were not included in the indictment, on the ground that they were not implicated in the publication of the balance sheet. Summonses were issued against the others still in Melbourne. Millidge, the late manager, was arrested at Ravenscourt Park, near London, and spent the night in the cells at Bow Street before being shipped back to Melbourne to stand trial.

Before committal proceedings could begin, however, there was a sudden change of government. James Patterson became the new Premier, and named as his Attorney-General Sir Bryan O'Loghlen, whose connection with land boomers has already been noted. One of O'Loghlen's first official acts was to alter the indictment against the Mercantile Bank directors from 'issuing a false balance sheet' to that of 'conspiring to issue a false balance sheet'—demonstrably a more difficult charge to prove. One member of Parliament, H. R. Williams, obtained enough supporters to move the adjournment of the House to debate O'Loghlen's action, but the new Speaker—none other than O'Loghlen's close associate, Thomas Bent—ruled that the motion was not 'urgent public business' and hence could not be discussed.

Committal proceedings on the new charge began before Mr Panton, police magistrate, and a bench of J.P.s, on 8 March 1893. Sir Matthew Davies was defended by Theodore Fink; James Bell by Alfred Deakin; Frederic Millidge by David Gaunson; and the others by lesser-known barristers. A good deal of highly complex and technical evidence was presented during the next few weeks. The highlight of the prosecution's case was the evidence of William Francis Ducker, liquidator of the Mercantile Bank, who had had access to all surviving documents. Ducker gave evidence of such misleading practices as the borrowing of £40,000 from the Alliance Bank of London, which was entered as deposits in the Mercantile's balance sheet. The emergency loan of £100,000 from the Commercial Bank had also been entered as deposits. This, too, said Ducker, had given investors a misleading idea of the Mercantile's strength. Ducker told the court that the overdraft account of Robert Kingston had been transferred from his estate after his suicide. Sir Matthew Davies was one of his executors. The debit on this account in 1891 was £390,000.

In a long statement to the court, Sir Matthew Davies claimed that the affairs of the bank had been left almost entirely in the hands of the managers. The directors had no part in the issue of the balance sheet, except to authorize it formally after the auditors had checked it. The matter of borrowing £100,000 from the Commercial Bank to strengthen their funds 'might have been imprudent, but it was honestly done'. Millidge also made a long statement, stating that if the Commercial Bank had not reclaimed the £100,000, the Mercantile Bank would have been able to continue in business.

The weeks of charges and counter-charges, accusations and excuses, came to a close on 1 May. The following day, Mr Panton and the bench of seven J.P.s took their places in a tense court to announce their decision. Mr Panton stated

John McDonald, J.P., the only magistrate who would commit Davies.

Mr Panton, police magistrate, refused to commit Sir Matthew Davies and others for trial.

that he and the bench, with one exception, were agreed that the charge of conspiracy should be dismissed. The exception was John McDonald, an elderly J.P., who maintained that there was a prima facie case of conspiracy against Davies and Millidge. An extraordinary scene followed. One of the J.P.s, George Craib (a brother-in-law of Sir Graham Berry), exclaimed that he would never speak to McDonald again if that gentleman persisted in committing the accused for trial. Henry Berry, another J.P., deplored the fate of the accused 'at the hands of a jury without status as regards business education'. Another J.P., Mr Gardiner, said that 'a verdict of committal would not tend to improve the present calamitous state of things.'

McDonald sat there silently during these impassioned outbursts from the bench, then calmly answered: 'When the names of the magistrates who have addressed the court are published, the public will probably arrive at their own conclusions. To me, as a very old magistrate, the case is very clear.' The other magistrates then left the bench, and McDonald continued the hearing alone.

When the case resumed the following week, however, Thomas Bent claimed his right as a J.P. He sat on the bench and spoke to McDonald

> with such animated gestures that those in the Police Court were impressed with the dumb show, as much as if they had heard him remonstrating at the perversity of sending boom finance issues for the decision of a jury uneducated in its mysteries.

Commented the *Age*:

> Not the least remarkable of the many remarkable phases of this remarkable trial is the mysterious and unusual appearance of Mr. Thomas Bent, Speaker of the Legislative Assembly, on the bench, beside the justice whose position . . . is a very delicate one. This is the same Mr. Bent who spoke in support of the directors and managers at one of the meetings of shareholders of the Mercantile Bank, and whose eccentric and partisan utterances would, perhaps, have been forgotten but for his singular action in taking a seat on the bench at the trial of the chairman and manager.

After further delays, on 12 May Mr McDonald formally committed Davies and Millidge for trial. Davies was released on a £1,000 bond provided by C. J. Ham and James Balfour. Millidge was released on sureties provided by Henry Francis, the well-known city chemist, and E. H. Cameron, the Government Whip. The remaining five defendants were discharged, the news of James Bell's acquittal being received joyfully in his home town of Dunolly. The mayor invited his friends to a glass of wine in the council chambers, where Bell's health 'was drunk with effusion'.

A few days after the committal of Davies and Millidge, when public interest had temporarily subsided, an astonishing announcement came from the Attorney-General's office. On the night of 17 May Sir Bryan O'Loghlen summoned press representatives and gave them the news that he had decided to abandon the prosecution. 'For the last six days I have fed and slept on the details of the matter, and having arrived at a determination am prepared to accept the consequences, even if they tear me to pieces', he told the reporters.

Next day, as public emotion reached a new height, there was an unexpected reaction from within the government. The Solicitor-General, an earnest and rather humourless man named Isaac Isaacs, summoned his own press conference and told the reporters that he had equal constitutional powers with the Attorney-General to decide whether a case, once committed, should go to trial. He said, in effect, that if Sir Bryan O'Loghlen would not send Davies and Millidge for trial, then he would. (In those days the Solicitor-General was an elected member of Parliament, and a member of Cabinet.)

An anguished meeting of Cabinet followed. The Premier, J. B. Patterson, called the position 'simply preposterous', and claimed that the Attorney-General's powers overruled the Solicitor-General's. Isaacs retorted that unless the Solicitor-General's powers were upheld, he would resign from the government. After a private three-hour conference with O'Loghlen, ending in a deadlock, Isaacs returned to his office and ordered his staff to file the presentments against Davies and Millidge. But, he discovered, O'Loghlen had got there first, and had ordered the law officers not to carry out any of Isaacs' instructions on the matter. Isaacs stormed back to see O'Loghlen. He pointed out forcibly, as he later told the *Age*, that 'There was not one individual in the whole department, from the secretary down to the doorkeeper, that would be permitted to obey me, a responsible Minister of the Crown, administering the Department of Justice.' In the early hours of 24 May, Isaacs called at the newspaper offices and told the editors that he would conduct the case against Davies and Millidge as a private citizen. Later the same day, the Premier wrote to Isaacs calling on him to resign, in view of his 'entirely disloyal attitude' to his colleagues, the effect of which was 'plainly to expose the Government to ridicule'. Isaacs resigned that night, saying that 'The only regret I feel at laying down my office is that there will now fall upon our country a degradation which might have been averted . . . Under existing circumstances it is more honorable to relinquish than to hold.' Feeling throughout the colony ran high. Sir Archibald Michie, Q.C., applauded the 'noble stand' taken by Isaacs. Protest meetings against the government's attitude were held in scores of suburbs and country centres. In London the *Financial Times* called O'Loghlen's actions 'astounding', and 'a mere burlesque of legal procedure'.

Isaacs resigned his parliamentary seat of Bogong, in order to force a by-election on the issue and test public opinion. His first major speech was delivered at Beechworth. As his train drew in, a band played 'See the Conquering Hero Comes', and the ladies of the town presented him with 'a pretty floral device' as a symbol of appreciation and sympathy. Enthusiastic meetings and crowded banquets marked his every move. At Chiltern Isaacs told the electors that the government had 'created what is new to this country—an aristocracy of criminals'. (Cheers and applause.) No-one dared to oppose him in the election, and Isaacs was returned to Parliament by universal acclamation.

Isaacs' moves to fight the Mercantile case himself were withdrawn when a stockbroker, James Wilson Reid, claimed the honour of applying to the Full Court for appointment of a Grand Jury to investigate the case, 'in order that the course of justice might not be thwarted'. Affidavits from William Simpson and W. F. Ducker were read, giving details of their investigations into the Mercantile Bank. After some discussion, the Full Court granted the rare application and instructed the sheriff to summon a Grand Jury.

In the midst of this political and legal battle, Sir Matthew and Lady Davies suddenly disappeared from Melbourne. It was discovered that they had sailed for Colombo by the German steamer *Salier* on 27 May. The previous day, a stranger had applied for two berths in the second saloon. They could not be granted because that section was full. The following day the stranger returned one hour before the ship sailed and booked two first-class passages for Sir Matthew and Lady Davies. No one saw them slip aboard, and for some time there was considerable doubt as to whether they had actually sailed.

As soon as he read the news in his morning paper, the Premier summoned Sir Matthew's brother J. M. Davies, a former Attorney-General, and told him that Sir Matthew must return to Melbourne immediately, if not voluntarily, then by force. J. M. Davies promised to telegraph his brother when the ship reached Adelaide. When no reply was received, the Premier instructed the Crown Law Department to obtain a warrant for Sir Matthew's arrest, and to telegraph it to Adelaide for immediate execution. The telegram was lodged at 11 a.m. (10.30 a.m. in Adelaide). Half-way through the transmission, a thunderstorm raging near the South Australian border brought the lines down. The resourceful telegraphists, realizing the importance of the message, sent it to Sydney with a request to re-transmit it on a direct wire from Sydney to Adelaide.

In Adelaide, meanwhile, Sub-Inspector Doyle and another detective were waiting on board the *Salier* in anticipation of instructions from Melbourne. None arrived by sailing time at noon, so they left the boat. A few minutes later, a signal was received by the harbour's semaphore station instructing Sir Matthew Davies to disembark at Adelaide. At 12.30 p.m. a constable, armed with a warrant of detention, set off in a steam launch to chase the *Salier*. He caught up and steamed alongside, but the captain of the *Salier* refused to heave to. Thus Sir Matthew and Lady Davies steamed away peacefully to Colombo. There another telegraphed warrant awaited them. To make doubly sure, Detective-Sergeant Whitney caught the steamer *Australian* from Melbourne five days later to bring Sir Matthew back in custody.

Meanwhile, the Grand Jury had been summoned from the ranks of 'special jurors'—men whose properties were rated at more than £60 a year, and whose income from real estate exceeded £60 a year. Despite these rather unusual property qualifications, the jury found a true bill against Davies and Millidge after six days' closed enquiry. Sir Matthew Davies returned voluntarily from Colombo. On 11 July Sir Matthew and Lady Davies arrived at Spencer Street station, looking 'somewhat worried' but otherwise 'enjoying good health'. Sir Matthew was warmly welcomed by his friends, and Lady Davies was presented with a bunch of violets. The same day, Mr Nicholson, police magistrate, committed Davies and Millidge for trial, releasing them on £100 bail.

More sensations were due before the trial itself commenced. The *Evening Standard*, a Melbourne newspaper of the day, had somehow obtained and

IKE IMPERATOR!

Melbourne Punch takes a cynical and somewhat anti-Semitic view of Isaac Isaac's appeal to the electors of Bogong.

published the Grand Jury proceedings, which were supposed to be held in camera. David Gaunson, on behalf of Millidge, moved to attach the publisher, James Thomson, for contempt of court. The Chief Justice, Sir John Madden, called it 'a most cynical contempt', sent the publisher to gaol for seven days, and fined him £100. Commented the Adelaide *Register*: 'It does seem a most peculiar fact that the whole of the revelations connected with the Mercantile Bank should have had no other effect up to the present date than that of indirectly being the means of sending an editor to gaol.' Then one of the grand jurors, Martin Farkas, told Joseph Symes (who published the statement in his paper the *Liberator*) that he was 'repeatedly felt, sounded and urged by Davies' friends not to find a true bill'.

Early in August 1893 the case against Davies and Millidge came before the Chief Justice. Theodore Fink immediately moved to dismiss the Grand Jury presentment, on the ground that an alien, a Mr Rousseau, was a member of that jury. Sir John Madden agreed with Fink, quashed the presentment, and discharged Davies and Millidge. The whole case was back where it started. Said the Sydney *Daily Telegraph*: 'If this is the end, it is a lamentable and disgraceful one, which will leave a stigma on the administration of justice in Victoria and on the names of the men who, by a trivial technicality, have escaped being sent to trial.'

But it was not the end, or even nearly the end. On 15 August 1893 another depositor, Charles Cox, secretary of the 'Liberty & Property Defence League', undertook a fresh charge against all directors except Sir Graham Berry. The following day, Mr Panton, S.M., refused to issue a summons, on the extraordinary and quite illegal ground that the defendants 'had been harassed, and the country put to much expense'. Nor was he willing to hear legal argument on the matter. *Table Talk's* next issue called Mr Panton's action 'The most serious of the long list of grave scandals in connection with the failure of the Mercantile Bank.'

New summonses were prepared. These were immediately signed without question on 19 August by W. J. Lormer, J.P., and served on Sir Matthew at his brother's home in Malvern, and on the other six original defendants—Anderson, Bell, Muntz, Millidge, Ellis and Richardson. Now the committal proceedings had to begin all over again. This time they were heard at the District Court before Mr Nicholson, P.M., and seven J.P.s. When the new proceedings started on 18 September 1893, only Sir Matthew Davies appeared. The remainder were represented by counsel, who claimed that the court had no jurisdiction because the alleged offences were committed more than twelve months previously. Mr Nicholson was 'thunderstruck'. He issued warrants for their immediate arrest, and they were brought into court under police custody.

All the old ground was ploughed over once more, and a certain amount of new evidence introduced. The main sensation of the hearings was introduced by Sir Matthew Davies, who claimed he could prove that the late John McDonald, the J.P. who had first committed him (and had died on August 9), 'had determined to commit him for trial . . . before a word of evidence was heard.'

George Davies, J.P.: 'The man is dead . . . It is an act of cruelty to bring forward an allegation such as that.'

W. J. Lormer, J.P., then disclosed that 'From the very first day I took my seat on the bench as a justice in this case, there has been a systematic attempt at intimidation and coercion so far as I am concerned.' During the currency of the case he had been attacked by *Melbourne Punch*, and investigations were made into his private life and business affairs in an endeavour to discredit him. Lormer read a letter to the court which said in part, 'If you commit these men for trial you are a doomed man; nothing will save you; we will hang for you. As sure as God is in heaven you shall go to join McDonald.'

The prosecution closed after twenty-eight days of hearings, and Sir Matthew Davies and other barristers followed with ten days of defence submissions. They claimed it had been clearly established that there had been no wrongdoing, within the meaning of the existing Companies Act. William Simpson (chief prosecution witness) was described as a 'bloodhound book-keeper' who should be prosecuted for 'indecently exposing his figures'. (Laughter). But a majority of the bench committed Davies, Muntz, and Millidge for trial. The auditors (Ellis and Richardson) and other directors (Bell and Anderson) were acquitted.

Now at last the final act could be played. In February 1894—two years after the alleged offences—Davies, Millidge and Muntz appeared in the Criminal Court before Mr Justice Hood. The whole wearisome rigmarole was started once again. Lady Davies attended the court every day, except when ill, and listened patiently to the tedious list of figures, dates, and complicated transactions. After thirteen sitting days, the evidence was completed and Mr Justice Hood addressed the jury. He said he was 'utterly unable to unravel' the question of the £100,000 loan from the Commercial Bank, and had not been helped by the fact that neither side this time had called H. G. Turner, the general manager, as a witness. If the jury was not satisfied that there was anything wrong with the balance sheet, said the judge, and could on that ground acquit the prisoners, 'every man who was not vindictive, ignorant or prejudiced would rejoice'. Finally, he said, there was nothing which would ever degrade trial by jury so much as 'a jury giving way to the passion of the people on points that ought to be decided entirely by the evidence'.

With these words ringing in their ears, the members of the jury retired for an hour and a quarter, and returned to announce that they found all the defendants not guilty. Did they decide on the evidence? Did they feel sympathy at last towards Sir Matthew Davies in his long agony? We shall never know.

One thing was certain. In those wonderful days of untrammelled banking, it was no crime to borrow £100,000, use it to declare an 8 per cent dividend one month, and close down for lack of cash the following month.

46

How Thomas Bent Escaped the Net

'Tommy' Bent. 'Honest Tom' Bent. The man who carved up Brighton's broad acres and converted it into a closely settled suburb. The man whose name behind a boom company was a certain guarantee of its financial success. Even after all these years, the name is still remembered, loved, and hated. And deservedly so. Even though he and his enterprises crashed along with those of nearly every other land boomer, Thomas Bent fought his way back to become Premier of Victoria—and not the worst one, by any means.

Bent was born in Penrith, New South Wales, in 1838, the son of a contractor who took his family to Melbourne in 1849. The Bents lived at Fitzroy for two years, where Tommy attended St Mark's Anglican School and brawled with the local larrikins; then the family shifted to East Bentleigh to become market gardeners. Bent helped his father on the land for some years, then started his own market garden near McKinnon at the age of twenty-one. 'I had no childhood', he said in after years. In 1861 Bent shook the clay from his boots and became rate collector for the Brighton Council. In this position, his rude health and natural ebullience made him hundreds of friends and admirers among the very people he was dunning for rate payments. Soon everyone knew the bluff, hearty rate collector—and remembered him when the time came to vote. After a year of collecting rates, Bent stood for Moorabbin Shire Council, being elected with ease. He was just twenty-four years old. With his down-to-earth approach, and his automatic assumption that his primary duty as councillor was to get as many benefits as possible for his own electors, it was not surprising that the voters, in H. G. Turner's words, 'regarded Mr Bent as a sort of patron saint'.

In 1871, at the age of thirty-three, Bent coolly decided to stand for the State seat of Brighton against the great George Higinbotham, who was later to become Chief Justice. No one expected Bent to win. But he enjoyed extraordinary support among the mass of the voters. Besides that, many of Brighton's wealthy conservatives were alarmed by Higinbotham's advanced ideas, and Bent picked up more votes among them. 'A rough diamond', they said. Higinbotham did not help his own cause by displaying little interest in Brighton affairs. At one election meeting, Bent's brother got up and asked him a loaded question about

George Higinbotham, defeated by Thomas Bent at the 1871 elections.

"Brighton's Beau Idéal."

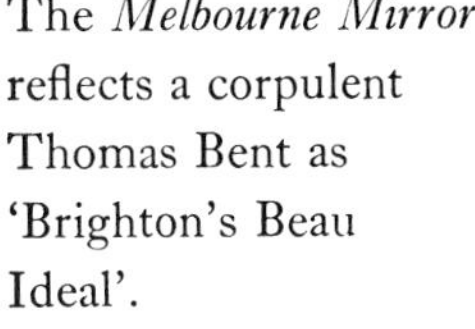

The *Melbourne Mirror* reflects a corpulent Thomas Bent as 'Brighton's Beau Ideal'.

local problems. The question had to be explained to Higinbotham before he could attempt to answer.

Bent fought a clean enough campaign in public against Higinbotham, although the *Southern Cross* alleged that he stacked the voting rolls with his supporters 'in a very questionable manner'. His 'grass-roots' campaigning and extravagant promises of local benefits for Brighton won him the election by a slender margin of fourteen votes. The legend went that one of his supporters, George Coates, rounded up his employees and took them to vote for Bent at the last minute, making up his majority.

As a coming man, Bent M.L.A. had little difficulty in subsequently being elected to Brighton Council in 1873. His capacity for work in those early days was phenomenal. Although a member of Parliament and two councils, it was said that he never once missed a council or committee meeting. In 1874 he was elected mayor of Brighton—the first of nine such occasions during his lifetime. He also sat on Moorabbin Council continuously for twenty years, except for a three months' break when he resigned to help his father and brother in the construction of Mordialloc Road—a contract which had been arranged for them by Bent himself.

Contemporary descriptions and portraits of Bent give us a composite picture of a bluff-spoken, bullet-headed, burly figure, usually genial but irascible when crossed. Abstemious in his youth, he soon became a man of great if not gross appetites; his rolling, corpulent frame looming over many a laden banquet table. He had a large, aquiline nose, and a full dark beard, which turned grey during the financial crisis. To *Table Talk*, Bent 'always sustained that hearty good humour and irrepressible love of fun and banter which agreeably seasoned even the most unpleasant things that he has done and said.' One of Bent's favourite stories concerned his experiences as a member of the Royal Commission on Local Government in 1873. The commissioners visited Camperdown, a wealthy town in the Western District. One of the commissioners was seen chipping pieces from the bluestone buildings, and Bent slyly let it be known that he had discovered gold in the stone. Camperdown's buildings suffered severely from the onslaught of amateur miners before the jape was revealed.

Bent, Brighton, and the land boom grew together. He bought up great areas of market gardens for subdivision, so that for some time Bent was the largest landowner in Brighton. His biggest windfall was a decision by Nicholas Were in 1873 to sell his holdings in the Brighton Estate, amounting to no less than one-eighth of the entire municipal area. Bent bought these acres, situated between New Street and Hampton Street, for £80,000. Within a few years they were worth many times more. On paper, Bent could almost reckon himself a millionaire. Where did the former market gardener's son get the capital for such transactions? His first humble savings undoubtedly came from hard physical labour. But as Bent became more prominent in municipal and then State political affairs, financial institutions became more interested in him.

He was financed for huge sums by the Commercial Bank and the Bank of Victoria, among others.

Bent carried out his first subdivision in 1873, making enough profit to pay back most of the money he had borrowed. He cut up forty acres of land in Church Street, building and reselling several houses, each with their own extensive grounds. His next coup was to buy the Elmshurst Estate, more centrally situated in Church Street, and subdivide that too. Land which had been bought in the original Dendy Special Survey for £1 an acre, and taken over by Were when Dendy went bankrupt, was soon selling for £1,000 an acre and more. To provide services for the expanding suburb, and incidentally to boost the value of his blocks of land, Bent urged the Melbourne Gas Company to extend its mains, which by 1871 had reached as far as Caulfield. When the company procrastinated, Bent himself organized the Brighton Gas Co. Ltd in 1877 to bring the service to his clients and voters. A fellow director of the gasworks was W. K. Thomson, half-owner of McEwan's hardware store, who had bought the land in North Road, Brighton, on which he was to build the great mansion 'Kamesburgh' before going bankrupt. In 1885 Bent clashed seriously with his fellow directors in the gas company, which was making excellent profits from the supply of gas to a restricted area. Bent wanted the supply extended to his other subdivisions further out. When the directors refused, Bent formed another enterprise called the Central Brighton and Moorabbin Gas Co. Ltd. David Munro, a partner in many of Bent's speculations, and owners of other large tracts of Brighton land, formed the board of the new company. Mains of greater capacity were laid, a price war followed, and Bent brought the opposition company to its knees. They amalgamated, and for many years enjoyed a monopoly in the supply of gas to the Brighton-Sandringham area.

Pushed along by Bent's unbounded vigour, Brighton expanded enormously during the 1880s. In 1880 the suburb had 870 houses and nearly 5,000 residents. By 1890 it had 2,110 houses and nearly 10,000 residents. Valuations rose from £440,000 to nearly £3 million over the ten years. During the thrilling decade, Bent was always mayor of Brighton or very much the guiding hand of the municipality's affairs. A constant stream of loan money arranged by Bent was put into street construction and lighting. A new town hall was built for £10,000. (It still stands in Wilson Street, Brighton, bearing the foundation stone laid by Bent.) In the State sphere, Bent became vice-president of the Department of Works, and used the position to reorganize Brighton's water supply. The first roads on the subdivisions were built wholly at council expense. This piece of log-rolling was a little too much even for the boom era, and a new arrangement had to be made whereby council and property owners shared the cost.

Bent's State political career began in earnest in 1880, when he was appointed Minister of Public Works in a short-lived government headed by James Service. After Service was defeated and Sir Bryan O'Loghlen came into power, few people expected Bent to join the new government. However, according to *Table Talk*, he had 'no inconvenient political integrity, giving his vote for

Thomas Bent, Gustave Lachal and F. E. Selman subdivide Maribyrnong Park.

Conservative or Liberal just as the local interests of Brighton might be best served.'

The plum with which the new Premier bought Bent's support was the Railways Department. As Minister of Railways in the O'Loghlen government, Bent saw one of his favourite dreams come true. The railway was extended in 1882 from Bay Street, Brighton (now North Brighton Station), through to Sandringham. In addition, the line was duplicated to provide fast two-way traffic. The value of Bent's and all other land in the area soared to new heights. Bent's extraordinary subsequent record as Minister of Railways has already been reviewed in the chapter on the railway and tramway boom. But however bitter the attacks made on his commercial and political morality, Brighton had its railway, and the electors loved him. The newspapers on the other hand unanimously hated Bent, attacking him at every opportunity. Part of the enmity was said to stem from Bent's action as Railways Minister of introducing a charge for the carriage of newspapers, and making reporters pay half-price for fares instead of merely showing a press pass. There were also deeper reasons. Bent was the outstanding example of a man using his political position blatantly for personal profit, and degrading the standards of public life. 'Honest Tom' must have been genuinely surprised by the continual charges of jobbery laid against him. In his ethos, what was good for Bent was good for Brighton, what was good for Brighton was good for the whole colony, and what was good for the colony was good for Thomas Bent. It was a perfect circle, neatly completed to the eternal personal and political profit of himself.

Typical of the tone of newspaper attacks on Bent was the *Illustrated Australian News*'s comment on his election as leader of the Opposition in 1886. 'This move is not popular with members', the journal claimed, 'for the reason that Mr. Bent is a very undesirable individual personally, and politically he is, if possible, less so.' Bent heartily reciprocated the newspapers' enmity, leading the *Bulletin* to observe: 'Bent doesn't believe in them noospaper fellers a bit, 'e don't, and his opinions on the h'indecency of h'any sort of public inkwiry . . . are exceedingly strong.'

As his Brighton subdivisions tapered off, Bent invested his considerable fortune from about 1883 onwards in speculative deals throughout the colony, and even in other colonies. His name appeared again and again in land transfers, company prospectuses, and all types of financial transactions. To give but a few examples, he bought the Yarra Grange Estate—2,200 acres on the Yarra—for £40,000. He was allied with that champion land boomer, B. J. Fink, in such enterprises as the Melbourne Central Property Co. Ltd. In yet another venture, Bent went into partnership with Gustave Lachal and F. E. Selman. They bought C. B. Fisher's Maribyrnong Park Estate, one mile from Ascot Vale station, and subdivided it in 1888. Colourful advertisements by the auctioneers, Baylee, Shevill & Co., called the sale 'A Red Letter Day in Melbourne'. The land was 'the Fairest and Most Picturesque Spot' in Victoria. Buyers were invited to enjoy the 'exquisite pleasure of the view from Maribyrnong Bridge'. Since it was 'impossible for any pen to do justice to its varied beauties', visitors were given free railway passes and driven to the estate by horse cabs which met every train. W. J. Archer, a wealthy Tasmanian landowner and magistrate, sold his grazing property 'Saundridge' for £38,000, sank most of the proceeds into the Heights of Maribyrnong Estate Co. Ltd at the suggestion of Thomas Bent (who he said got him drunk first), lost everything he owned, sued Bent, lost the case on technical grounds, and wrote a bitter pamphlet called *Euchred* (Melbourne, c. 1889) to warn others of his experience.

In 1888 Bent immortalized his name in the annals of land speculation by floating a company known as the Thomas Bent Land Co. Ltd. The purpose of this company was to buy from Bent himself some 95 acres of land at Ringwood. Attracted by the magic of the Bent name, many people, including bank managers and members of Parliament, rushed to buy the shares, which were paid up to 8s. Bent got the cash for his land. But the subdivided blocks could not be sold, and the company collapsed ignominiously.

'Honest Tom' was not downhearted. The following year, he saved the Gillies-Deakin government from collapse by crossing the floor of the House during an equal division on the question of increasing the Railways Commissioners' salaries. A few weeks later, the government paid Bent £27,000 for 500 acres of land alongside the Yan Yean Reservoir. An official government valuation had priced the land at £10 an acre, but the government's payment to Bent was shown to be £54 an acre. The newspapers howled for his blood, and even people who had trusted Bent began to regard him with suspicion.

More of his land companies failed for want of buyers, and Bent's fortune began trickling away. His own explanation of his difficulties was given when he appeared as a defence witness in the prosecution against the directors of the Premier Building Association:

Bent: I have never lost in consequence of my valuations.

Purves, Q.C.: Then it was not in consequence of your land valuations that you became insolvent, or nearly?—No; before that I had half a million of money. It was through other people failing that I lost it . . .

How did you lose it?—Because in June last I met with an accident, and while I was ill my good friends let me in for £750,000 of property.

How much did you owe before that?—Not much.

The your good friends were thieves?—Yes.

Land boomers, perhaps?—Yes.

Then land booming is thievery sometimes?—Yes.

Then all your friends were thieves?—I didn't say all of them.

And you say that your friends put you in for £750,000 of property. Were you mad?—I was ill and not aware of what I was doing.

Out of your mind?—I was for a while.

And your friends took advantage of your condition to get you to sign these contracts?—Yes, they did.

Did you ever attempt to repudiate your contracts on the ground of lunacy?—I did not.

Why not?—Because I did not.

Yet you lost £750,000?—Oh, I'll make it all up again.

Further entertainments were yet in store for readers of the Melbourne press.

Thomas Bent, M.L.A., as Speaker of the Victorian Legislative Assembly.

In 1892 Bent succeeded in defeating Sir Henry Wrixon and John Gavan Duffy for the position of Speaker of Parliament. Quipped the *Leader*: 'Why is Speaker Bent the First Commoner in the land? Because no one commoner than Speaker Bent can be found.' The *Age* was even more cynical: 'Mr Bent became Speaker because Sir Bryan O'Loghlen had some old political scores to repay.'

Now the clouds of general financial disaster began to gather, and Bent's conduct seemed to deteriorate in proportion to the blackness of the clouds. Quite against the rules of the House, he attempted to suppress discussion of the government's actions in connection with Sir Matthew Davies and the Mercantile Bank. He appeared in person at shareholders' meetings, and abused in scurrilous fashion those who called for investigations. At a Lord Mayor's dinner, he said that Davies and others like him had merely 'over-reached themselves', leading the *Australasian* to comment:

Why make hysterical remarks,
  And talk of shame and sin,
Just because a few lone widows
  Have been badly taken in?
For women will be women, spite
  Of all the sermons preached,
And they'd still have had their money,
  Had the banks not over-reached.

Then mope no more—the cabbage grows
  By each Moorabbin rill;
There's golden grain from Pascoevale
  And rich Kensington Hill,
While deep in Brighton's gravel-pits
  The sturdy miner delves.
Why mope because the sanguine few
  Have over-reached themselves?

Exactly, Mr Speaker, Sir.
  You are our pride, our joy,
Our best colonial product,
  And our bouncing Brighton boy.
We know that in your bosom lies,
  No poor regard for pelf,
So merely say, 'Dear Mr Bent,
  Don't over-reach yourself.'

The *Australasian*'s warning was in vain. Bent *had* overreached himself, and was in serious danger of losing everything he owned as company after company suspended payment and made calls on his shares. The end came with the closing of the Commercial Bank, which was still financing Bent for large amounts. The bank foreclosed on its mortgages and wrote off the balance. A similar position arose in the case of Bent's debt of £80,000 to B. J. Fink's Mercantile Finance Co. Ltd. In this case, at least, the full facts became known, for the company was officially liquidated and a public report issued. In the liquidators' words, 'Mr Bent was released from his obligations on July 8, 1889, the securities he handed over in exchange being now valueless, and a heavy loss has therefore been made.'

A favourite legend about 'Honest Tom' Bent was that he paid every penny of his debts. It would be nearer the truth to say that Bent paid every debt necessary to keep his affairs out of the Insolvency Court. This was nowhere better proved than in the notable case *McMahon* v. *Bent*. One of Bent's investments was a parcel of 36,000 shares in the Australian City & Suburban Investment & Banking Co. Ltd, a creation of the ex-mayor of Prahran, G. W. Taylor. With unpaid calls, there was a liability of more than £40,000 due on these shares. An extraordinary transaction whereby Bent purported to sell the shares for the total sum of 10s. was investigated by Mr Justice à Beckett in the Supreme Court in 1894. The matter was brought before the court in an application by William McMahon, the professed transferee of the shares, for an order directing Bent's name to be substituted for his on the list of contributors. McMahon's affidavit said that in August 1892 he was asked by Bent to sign his name to a document, which he did without reading the contents or having them explained to him. At that time he was a labourer in the employment of the Brighton Council, and received a daily wage of 7s. He subsequently discovered that the document was a transfer to him of 36,000 shares in the company, and as a claim of £40,300 had been made on him in respect of the shares, he repudiated the contract. In evidence, McMahon told the court that out of his savings he had been able to buy a block of land at Brighton for £250, where he and his family of six now lived and worked as market gardeners. If the order for payment was enforced, his property would be sold up and his family rendered penniless.

Bent was cross-examined on his version of the affair, and went into a complicated history of his transactions with the Mercantile Finance Co. Ltd, which held these shares as security. The company refused to take a transfer of these particular shares, and he was then advised by his solicitors to transfer them to a man of straw, in pursuance of which advice he induced McMahon to enter into the contract now under challenge. He repeated over and over again that he denied any liability on account of the shares, as he had understood that the responsibility rested with the Mercantile Finance Co. Ltd, but he could not give any satisfactory explanation of why he was so anxious to get rid of them if the possession involved no responsibility. His Honour, without calling any further evidence, gave judgment in favour of McMahon. He said that to think a man who took over these shares would incur no legal liability on them was 'manifestly absurd and incredible'. McMahon was not conversant with business affairs, and was induced to sign on the representation that it was a mere formality. McMahon's summons for placing Bent on the list of contributors was granted, with costs against Bent.

The *Age* described the affair as 'a shady transaction' and added that

> Mr Bent's ideas of honesty are certainly peculiar . . . Surely a man who has officiated for some 30 years as a law giver, has been a Minister of the Crown and Speaker of the Assembly, should have some idea of the nature and purpose of law.

Then again:

> Mr Bent has been, as Speaker, the right man in the wrong place. As Treasurer, he would have disposed of the deficit in the twinkling of an eye, and might even have given us some valuable hints as to an easy method of extinguishing the national debt.

HIS TURN.

BUSTED BOOMER BENT: "I'm starving and homeless and out of collar. What shall I do?"
UNEMPLOYED PERSON: "Back to the land, old man, and grow cabbages. You never should have left it."

Bent was now faced with a choice between going bankrupt or paying the calls and legal costs. How and where he got the money to stay beyond the reach of the Insolvency Court remains a well-buried mystery. But he was, temporarily, a broken man. Even his erstwhile admirers, the electors of Brighton, had humiliated him at the 1894 State elections. At one of his election meetings, held in North Brighton drill hall on 8 September 1894, two local clergymen, the Rev. J. Rickard and the Rev. J. Hay, stood up to denounce Bent's private character. An extract from the *Age* report serves to set the scene:

> Mr. Bent said he appeared once more before them—(A Voice: 'For the last time'; cheers, and cries of 'No, no')—to thank the people of Brighton for the kind consideration they had always extended to him. (Cheers, groans; a voice: 'Soft soap', and laughter).

Later in the proceedings, the two clergymen 'advanced to the platform amidst indescribable disorder caused by cheers, groans and boohoos'. The Rev. Rickard moved a motion that Bent was unfit to represent the constituency, for reasons which he specified but which were omitted by the newspaper reports because of their extremely defamatory nature. The 'wildest uproar' followed, the atmosphere being filled with 'piercing shrieks, groans and cheers'.

Mr Bent: 'If they will submit something about my moral character, and I can get at them, I will let them see about it. (Cheers and groans).'

The meeting terminated in extraordinary uproar. On the Sunday night, at the Brighton Congregational Church, the Rev. Rickard announced from the pulpit that he believed he had done his duty.

The following Saturday, the *Age* disgustedly referred to Bent as 'issuing into public life, the spawn of Conservative rancor . . . In the [land boom] transactions which have just come to light, his best defence is "peaching" on his old pals, and declaring that "the other fellows should be on the roads, not me." ' Two days later, the *Age* printed across four columns a facsimile of a handwritten letter drafted by Bent in 1881 when Minister of Railways. The letter proved beyond doubt that Bent had agreed to build a railway siding at Bloomfield (Gippsland) provided that the local member, F. C. Mason, voted in support of the government in a crucial division. Publication of the letter sealed Bent's fate in Brighton. At the election four days later, W. H. Moule, a local solicitor (later a judge), had no difficulty in beating Bent by 1,579 votes to 925.

Charles Llewellyn Rees, proprietor and editor of the *Southern Cross*, on 28 September 1894 wrote the electoral obsequies:

> I'm a poor 'ard wuckin' female, but I try to pay my way,
> I mangles on the premises, I washes by the day,
> But I 'old my own opinions, and I mean to give 'em vent,
> On the city shampain lunching, and the views of Mr. Bent—
> Of Mr. Thomas Bent,
> The Speaker, Mr. Bent—
> Which I gives yer 'Stinkin' Fishes,' coupled with the name of Bent.

Bent retired in deep gloom to his dairy farm, 'Korongah', near Port Fairy, and milked cows for six years, paying occasional visits to Brighton to attend council meetings. The task of financial reconstruction in Melbourne largely passed him by. As the years passed, the bitter memories of depression hardships, blamed by the public on the land boomers, were slowly healed by time. Bent himself found a measure of prosperity returning to his affairs. In later life he made a great show of raising his hat to every cow he saw, in thanks for the money he had made by dairy farming. It also seems likely that Mrs Bent had come to the rescue. Some of his assets had been put in her name and she was liable for the rates on the property involved. In November 1895 a fellow member of Brighton Council, Richard Cheeseman, a florist by profession, raised the question of Mrs Bent's liability to pay the rates. Bent called him 'a liar' and 'a perjurer' in open council. Cheeseman sued for slander and won modest damages.

With unfailing optimism, Bent stood again for State Parliament in 1896 for the Melbourne South electorate, but polled only forty-nine votes. At his election meetings, interjectors shouted 'Who stole the mace?' and advised Bent to 'mount his bike', 'go home', and 'pay his rates'. The *Age* commented that 'Somehow communities seem to have long memories at times, and fond ones.'

During the crash Bent had lost his mansion 'Landcox', whose enormous grounds originally ran from North Road through to Union Street, North Brighton (parts of the mansion still stand, but today it is a Roman Catholic orphanage, still overlooking the artificial lake and avenue of great pines which Bent constructed in Landcox Park). In 1896 Bent shifted his family to a large single-storey brick house which still stands at the corner of Bay and Warriston Streets, Brighton. The new house was only a few yards from that part of the highway where the statue of Bent, erected in 1913, may still be seen gazing dramatically down Point Nepean Road.

In 1897 dairy-farmer Bent stood for the State Parliamentary seat of Port Fairy, but was again ignominiously defeated, polling so few votes that he lost his deposit. In 1900 he made an extraordinary comeback in Brighton, campaigning with huge posters across the main streets: BENT NEVER BEATEN. And so it came to pass. Not only was he elected, but later he also became Premier, and Minister of Railways and Public Works. An older and wiser Bent introduced many progressive measures. Perhaps his greatest claim to fame was the completion of the Mildura railway, seventeen years after that town of battlers had been promised its lifeline. The ageing Premier visited Mildura, where a concert was given in his honour. He imbibed freely, walked on the stage to recite 'The Gambler's Wife' to the cheering audience, but broke down in happy tears instead.

Bent could never quite foresake his old methods. He bought 'St Ninian's' and 'Ripponlea', two famous Brighton properties—and immediately, in his capacity as Minister of Railways, built a railway tram-line from St Kilda Station to Brighton, officially opened by himself in 1905. Large estates along the route were soon subdivided and sold, among them being most of the historic 24-acre 'St Ninian's' property.

The old warhorse was knighted in 1908, a year before his death. His wayward life was aptly summarized by Paddy Reynolds, licensee of the Cathedral Hotel, Melbourne:

> Say what you like about Tommy Bent, but he was a man. He mightn't have much honesty if there was big money to be got, and he liked his gin and tonic strong and fraquint, an' had a rovin' eye for wimmen, but outside them matters he was as pure as the drivellin' snow.

47

The Cautionary Tale of David Munro

Life was grim but life was also full of extraordinary possibilities for poor immigrants to Australia in the 1850s. When John Munro, the village blacksmith of Kirkintilloch, Dumbartonshire, Scotland, decided to emigrate with his seven children and three other relatives, he could easily dream of a better life for them all, but had no way of knowing that one son would rise to the top of the engineering profession, destined to build marvellous bridges across the Yarra river which still serve their purpose while later bridges crumble and fall into the mud. Nor that the same son would be sucked into the land boom, lose his business and a large fortune, and die as a mumbling alcoholic whose estate did not even justify filing a will.

The Munro family emigrated on the *Tudor* in 1854, Mary Munro dying during the voyage of cholera. The remaining adults indentured themselves to A. Ross of Geelong for a total income of £90 a year plus rations for the whole family. When their contract was complete, John Munro set up shop as a blacksmith and contractor in King Street, Melbourne, where each of his sons joined him as they became old enough.

In 1858 they won a contract to build the Moorabool railway viaduct in Geelong, and after successfully completing it, shared in many other government contracts. But the father drove his sons too hard: by 1869 most of them had left the business to follow their own pursuits. Only young Daniel remained in the firm, which was now styled John Munro & Son. In September 1869 the firm went bankrupt, with a deficiency of £1,419 due to bad debts and other business losses. In the Insolvency Court it was shown that the father had kept every penny under his own control. The son owned only the £3 worth of clothes he wore in court: 'a very unsatisfactory Estate', thought the official assignee.

After release from sequestration, Daniel Munro changed his name to David, and started his own engineering and machinery supply business. Finally it occupied large blocks of land in Queen Street, a'Beckett Street and Elizabeth Street, Melbourne. As his trademark and proud boast, Munro adopted a phoenix arising from the flames, and the motto *Resurgam*. Builders, farmers and miners could buy from him every type of sawmilling, threshing and mining plant, either for cash or on his 'New Purchasing Lease System'.

Munro patented or improved several machines widely used by selectors, including a posthole-boring machine, a 'Victory Self-adjusting Windmill', portable engines of all kinds, and so on. Like many self-made men of the day, Munro was fairly harsh on his employees. During a slump in business in 1887 he cut their wages from 7s. to 6s. 6d. a day. The men's protest left him unmoved: he told them that he regarded their union leaders as 'vermin to be squelched'.

In those days the main exit from Swanston Street, Melbourne, was plagued by a narrow toll bridge. Men driving sheep and pigs across it had to pay a farthing toll for each beast. Bullock wagon drivers paid 18d. to cross. Gentlefolk in their carriages had to pay 18d. or 2s. according to the number of horses harnessed up. The rapidly expanding city was choking at its narrow egress over the Yarra. So the government decided to build a much wider bridge, paid for out of the public revenue, to cost about £140,000. David Munro's tender was accepted, and with the completion of the fine new bridge in 1888 his name became a byword in modern engineering. Huge bluestone piers were sunk deep into the Yarra mud, supporting three 100 ft steel spans with ornate decorations. The roadway, 99 ft wide, enabled the new cable trams to cross the river for the first time and travel down St Kilda road.

The government also awarded Munro the contract to rebuild the old Falls Bridge for £45,000, renaming it Queens Bridge. It still stands. He built the railway from Fitzroy to Whittlesea for £100,000, and from Frankston to Crib Point for £53,000; and undertook dozens of other major enterprises. All this hard work, tendered for at competitive rates, yielded him a clear profit averaging £10,000, free of income tax. What more could any reasonable man want?

Unfortunately Munro developed close links with Thomas Bent after sharing the construction of the Nepean Road tramway with him. Bent was mayor of the suburbs through which the tramway ran, and thus gained in two ways; profit from the actual construction of the tramway along the public road, and increased value of his local land holdings along the tram route. Munro also became a fellow director with Bent in the company which supplied gas to their new housing developments.

Bent and a staunch Presbyterian merchant named John Blyth next suggested to Munro that he should convert his engineering business into a public company and offer shares on the stock exchanges. In 1888, the firm was floated and became known as David Munro & Co. Ltd. In return for the business, Munro received 40,000 shares with a face value of £5, paid up to £2. 10s. each, and 80,000 shares paid up to £1—but no cash. Bent and Blyth took up 10,000 shares, and persuaded William Kiddle to take up several thousand more. (One of Blyth's seventeen living children had married this prominent grazier, so the flotation was partly a family affair).

Munro then plunged into the land market with gay abandon. How exhilarating it was, to be a real part of the throbbing mercantile community, directly concerned in the grand upsurge of suburban expansion, instead of fiddling about with steam engines and steel bridges! On the strength of his half ownership in David Munro & Co. Ltd., he borrowed great swags of money from the Bank of South Australia, the Bank of Australasia, and other generous financial houses. His wife Sarah borrowed large sums from B. J. Fink's Mercantile Finance Co. Ltd., which promptly discounted the bills to the Land Mortgage Bank.

With the cash, Munro bought up rolling tracts of land at Somerton, formed a syndicate to 'develop' it, then borrowed more money from the syndicate for other ventures. This piggy-back financing was a wonderful if dangerous way of living. In association with Thomas Bent and John Blyth, Munro also spent large sums buying up and 'developing' the Powers Court Estate and other subdivisions.

Paper profits rolled in. Munro proceeded to buy several acres of land in Glenferrie Road, Kooyong, alongside the railway line, and built a large, rambling mansion where his friends could be entertained in proper fashion, for a short time.

While all these glamorous things were going on, what was happening back at the engineering works? There was (Munro testified later, in the Insolvency Court) something like £500,000 worth of contracts in hand. Munro was still the managing director, for a minimum term of five years, and the major responsibility was his. But things began to go wrong. Could it be because he was not there to watch them?

When extra cash was required to finance the contracts held, Munro agreed with a suggestion by Bent and Blyth that he should negotiate a large overdraft with the City of Melbourne Bank. A little while later, to his astonishment, he was summoned to the bank and informed by Colin Longmuir that he must resign as managing director, as the only alternative to cancellation of the overdraft!

This cynical plot forced Munro out of his own business, and put it in the

'If you want a bridge built, ask for Davy Munro' advised this cartoonist.

John Blyth, one of the speculators who helped to mislead David Munro.

hands of bank nominees who were, in Munro's opinion as given to the Insolvency Court, 'totally incompetent'. Many of the contracts were delayed, some running up to twelve months behind schedule, and the company incurred large losses. The market value of its shares dropped to nil, a call of 5s. per share was made, and Munro was virtually a ruined man. Finally he was forced to forfeit all of his 120,000 shares in David Munro & Co. Ltd. Even that was not the final humiliation. The new controllers changed the company's name to the Melbourne Locomotive & Engineering Works Ltd, so that even the name of its brilliant founder disappeared from public view.

Meanwhile, Munro was desperately trying to salvage something from his land holdings. In 1888 he had floated the Caledonian Land Bank Ltd, the purpose of which was to acquire Munro's own real estate properties at Brighton and Canterbury. Meetings of shareholders in 1889 and 1890 claimed that Munro had sold the properties to the company at grossly inflated valuations. Munro angrily offered to make good any loss, produced a large bag stuffed full of bank notes which he apparently had ready for the purpose, and purchased the shares of several dissatisfied shareholders on the spot. Eleven days later a shareholders' committee of investigation asked Munro to buy all the remaining shares. He refused, writing a scornful letter to the newspapers criticising shareholders who sought to 'relieve themselves of their personal liability'. Just nineteen days later, Munro relieved himself of his liabilities by filing a voluntary petition in insolvency.

And so the bitter day of his second bankruptcy arrived, in April 1890. Including the calls on his shares, Munro had managed to accumulate the enormous indebtedness of nearly £380,000. Large sums were still owing on tracts of land he had bought but only partly paid for. His current overdrafts included £36,000 with the Bank of South Australia, £13,000 with the General Finance Co. Ltd, £12,000 with the Bank of Australasia, £12,000 with the Somerton Park Syndicate, and £4,500 with J. S. Vickery.

Later on, Munro's wife Sarah was also forced through the indignity of examination in bankruptcy. She had accumulated the sum of £45,000 in debts undertaken on her husband's behalf, mainly with the Land Mortgage Bank (£31,000) and J. S. Vickery (£8,000).

The Munros were forced to shift from their new mansion to a humble workman's cottage in Gatehouse Street, Parkville, where David no longer spoke about unionists as 'vermin to be squelched'. The creditors carved up their land and later a raggle-taggle of maisonettes was built on the Kooyong site.

It did not help much to learn, later on, that grave irregularities and criminal practices had taken place within the City of Melbourne Bank, nor that its manager had disappeared at sea while on his way to face the investigators in London. By that time Munro was steadily drinking himself into insensibility, sorrowfully watched by his wife, three sons and two daughters. He died of haemorrhage and alcoholism in 1898, aged fifty-four, with the same assets his father had allowed him so many years before: one suit of clothes. *Nil resurgam.*

VII FINALE

SINGLE TAX
LET THE LAND BEAR TAXES
HURRAH FOR GEORGE
GEORGE
DAVIES
JAMES

HENRY GEORGE AND HIS DISCIPLES: 'Sell all thou hast and give to the poor' was the sardonic advice offered by *Life*.

48

Church, Society and State

As we have seen in earlier chapters, a surprising number of the fraudulent, the near-fraudulent, and the nearly honest financiers of the late Victorian period were regarded as upstanding Christian gentlemen. There was James Munro, the discredited Premier who was a leading member of the Toorak Presbyterian Church. There was James Mirams, deacon of the Collingwood Congregational Church before his imprisonment. There was Joseph Johnson, the prominent Methodist who spent two years in Pentridge Gaol. A glance through the list of members of the Y.M.C.A. committee of 1888 gives the names of Sir Matthew Davies, William McLean, John Kitchen, James Balfour, and other acolytes of the boom. All these and many others professed a high Christian morality, while at the same time, consciously or unconsciously, carrying out policies which helped to wreak havoc on their fellow citizens.

The simplest explanation of this paradox was that the community demanded that its leaders should be regular churchgoers and religious workers. Even in the ferment caused by new theories of science and evolution, exceptions were comparatively rare. No investor, for instance, would dream of putting his money into a company run by a professed atheist. In general, to be accepted by society, a financier had to be known as 'a pillar of the church', and a frequent contributor to worthy charities. Some entrepreneurs undoubtedly took advantage of this public sentiment, and hypocritically donned a cloak of religion to cover their activities. But most Victorian financiers, particularly men of the stamp of James Munro and Matthew Davies, were obviously possessed of deep and genuine religious feeling. What, then, was the explanation of this deeper paradox? The *Bulletin* had an entertaining but oversimplified explanation:

> The land banks . . . were nearly all run by shining lights of the Church—by Christians of high repute and good standing—and 19 Christians out of every 20 proved to be unmitigated swindlers, without one human sentiment in their callous souls and unfeeling hearts. Among all the deceased offices hardly one ever made a serious effort to retrieve its position; they existed only to get in deposits, and as the deposits came in they were scrambled for by everybody from the managing-director down to the office-boy, and when they ceased to come in the establishments closed up in peace. The balance-sheets were bogus from first to last. The auditors, who, like the directors, were mostly men of religious tendencies, attested these balance-sheets unanimously, and either it was that not one among them all had intelligence

DOINGS IN THE PRESBYTERIAN ASSEMBLY.

"That the ministers of this church be requested to draw the attention of the congregations, at such time as may be advisable, to their discountenancing the practice of horse-racing; that His Excellency Sir Henry B. Loch, Governor of this colony, and Lady Loch, be hereby earnestly petitioned no longer to lend their countenance to the demoralising practice of horse-racing by attendance in person upon the course; that both Houses of Parliament be petitioned to no longer sanction, by suspending the public business of this country, a pursuit at once demoralising, anti-social and fraught with much danger both to the spiritual and temporal interests of the community."

"BROTHER, LET US HAVE ANOTHER SHAKE FOR SOME SUBURBAN PROPERTY."

DEANERY PARK, COBURG

Coburg.

Coburg.

Tram

Terminus.

Railway Station

ON THE ESTATE.

Patterson

and Sons,

WILL SELL

100

ALLOTMENTS.

BUSINESS

AND

Mansion Sites

ON

SATURDAY, OCTOBER 27,

1888.

THE DEAN.

COBURG.

Saturday Oct. 27,

ON THE GROUND.

Railway Sta

ON THE GROUND.

COBUR

Special Train

Free Pa

Saturday, Octob

TERMS – EXCEPT

SURE PROF

Must be the Outcome of

chase in This Esta

Remember

Deanery P

DEANERY PARK, COBURG, WILL BE SOLD B

Messrs. Patterson and Sons

> enough to discover that the office he represented was utterly insolvent, or else they were all willing to perjure themselves for a small consideration.

According to the *Bulletin* and all who thought like it (and who could blame them in the agony of the times?), to be a Christian was almost automatic proof of being an 'unmitigated swindler'. It made good reading for Darwinians and atheists. But the full truth probably lay more in the peculiar brand of Christianity being practised.

The Scottish immigrants who by and large commanded the commercial activities of Victoria had brought with them an attenuated but still virulent strain of the Calvinist doctrines on which their Presbyterianism was based. John Calvin's theocracy, which in the 16th century supervised the moral, social and commercial life of Geneva through a reign of terror, was partially reproduced wherever the Scots settled in large numbers. To be sure, opponents of Calvinism were no longer beheaded or burnt alive. But the basic beliefs survived. These included the idea that God had chosen certain men (i.e., Calvinists) to carry out his will on earth. These elect few would do no wrong, and were predestined to enter heaven. The rest of mankind was inflicted with original sin, doomed to total depravity, and predestined to spend eternity in hell. In Britain, this monstrous philosophy was expounded in the Westminster Confession of Faith, and was the belief officially held by the Presbyterian Church, although never reaching the extremes of cruelty practised in Geneva.

As the rule of landed aristocracy was gradually supplanted by the new industrial and commercial class, a significant change took place in Calvinist Presbyterianism. Since God had chosen certain men to govern the world's affairs, it was quite obvious that the newly successful commercial leaders must have been chosen by him. God guided them in methods of making money; and in turn, the fact that they made fortunes was a sign that they were among the Elect.

Now a fatal corruption entered this wonderfully logical scheme. Since God was guiding these financiers, and helping them to make fortunes so they could assume their rightful place as social leaders, it followed that whatever methods were used to make money must be justified. God could do no wrong, and neither could his chosen servants. Thus in financial scandal after scandal during the late Victorian era—not only in Australia but also in Britain and the U.S.A.—the public was astonished to learn that the frauds had been committed by God-fearing businessmen of the Calvinist stamp.

Although tens of millions of pounds of the public's savings disappeared, and enormous suffering was caused, to the true believer the frauds were not frauds at all. Huge sums had been loaned to friends and relations, but only because they were more trustworthy than strangers. Misleading balance sheets had been presented 'in order to maintain public confidence and prevent further losses'. In other words, it was the right thing to do. In other words, God had told them to do it.

It made little difference that other people's money was involved. One of God's mandatory instructions to the Elect, as the natural leaders of mankind, was to

deawake Dean advertises land sale at Coburg.

Most Rev. Dr T. J. Carr, Roman Catholic Archbishop of Melbourne, thought the depression was due to 'imaginary causes'.

make the earth multiply and be fruitful. To achieve this divine purpose, it was necessary to accumulate capital. To get the capital, the device of the joint stock company was used to take the money from those who did not deserve to have control of its use, and transfer it to those who had been 'chosen' to develop the new way of life. Where there walked a capitalist, there walked a man of God. When times grew hard, the shareholders and depositors (the real owners of the money) were often the last whose interests were considered. The important thing was to keep God's great work going. Anything was justified to achieve this end, even a little bit of temporary swindling, which would soon be put right when conditions improved. So the justification went, round and round in vicious circles.

In Melbourne, there were many expressions of the Calvinist philosophy, the division of the world into the shining angels of God and the doomed people of the gutter, and not all of these expressions came from Presbyterians. In April 1893, when employment was almost impossible to get, and people were literally starving to death in Melbourne, the Most Rev. Dr T. J. Carr, Roman Catholic Archbishop of Melbourne, said he thought that 'Much of the existing depression is due to imaginary causes, and sentiment largely predominates in the prevailing scare.' Speaking thus, he proceeded to declare open a bazaar whose profits were devoted to reduction of the debt on the Church of the Immaculate Conception, Hawthorn.

In South Melbourne, after hungry men and women had collected their handouts of bread and mutton from the Town Hall relief centre, the local Presbyterian minister, the Rev. Charles Bell, summoned them to a meeting on a vacant block opposite. In a violent harangue, he said that the workmen of Victoria were to a great extent responsible for their present condition. Their troubles were, he believed, directly traceable to the protectionist policy followed by the colony.

The Wesleyan Conference of 1893, for its part, resolved to try to discover why the working-men of Victoria no longer bothered to attend church. The *Age* promptly replied on their behalf that the reason was that the church was averting its eyes from urgent social questions. 'The liquor question, the land question, the wages question, and the question of the more equal distribution of wealth, the reformation of the criminal, the evils and the cure of the sweating system, the social evil [i.e., venereal diseases], infanticide and other kindred topics, are among the problems which they are just as well qualified to deal with as the professional politicians, and which they may assuredly help to solve if they bestow on them a tithe of the ingenuity which they have expended upon the number of the Beast, the Seven Vials, the Horn that had eyes, and other similar charades.'

The great contribution of the Presbyterian Assembly of 1893 was to declare that charity work was not its concern, but was the responsibility of individual congregations. The Assembly did, however, issue a powerful call for a 'Day of Humiliation and Prayer' throughout the State. The Rev. D. Gordon pointed out that the crisis was obviously a visitation from God. The people of Brighton, among whom he worked, talked only about making money, and the depression was God's way of punishing them. He felt certain that if they had a day of humiliation and prayer, they would probably witness the end of the present calamitous condition.

The Rev. J. K. McMillan said that the people should humble themselves before God and ask him to restore such times of prosperity as experienced in the past (i.e., during the land boom). The following day, the Assembly prayed for a solid hour, pleading for an end to the financial crisis. The crisis obstinately remained, and even got worse.

The year after that (May 1894), the Presbyterian Assembly was the scene of a shameful controversy on the question of children left destitute by the depression. The previous November, a Presbyterian Society for Neglected and Destitute Children had begun work under Miss Selina Sutherland, a cottage at the rear of the Assembly Hall being used as a temporary receiving home. Within six months, Miss Sutherland had plucked ninety-one youngsters out of their life of begging, thievery and child prostitution on the streets of Melbourne, and found suitable homes for them under approved foster-mothers.

Unfortunately, Miss Sutherland had not asked the miserable children whether they were Presbyterians. Nor had she made sure that they would receive a formal Presbyterian upbringing in their new homes. Most ministers at the Assembly were aghast. The Rev. Dr Rentoul said that Miss Sutherland was 'very fractious under authority, self willed, and careless about acting in the interests of the church.' She had placed sixty children in homes at Kilmore who were described as 'doing splendidly', yet the Presbyterian clergymen at Kilmore had no knowledge whatever of these children. Professor Harper said that it was not advisable for Miss Sutherland to give this 'indiscriminate relief', and it was not good for the church that children should be taken in this wholesale manner. As Jesus wept, the Rev. P. J. Murdoch (later Moderator-General; and

'Wharf rats' and 'mudlarks', society's contemptuous names for children abandoned by their parents, lived by begging, odd jobs and petty crime. Above, the police turn one group out of their boiler home.

father of Sir Keith Murdoch), proposed the motion that Miss Sutherland should be instructed to give preference to Presbyterian children, who should be sent only to approved Presbyterian homes.

There was a significant contrast a month later when Bishop Goe opened a Home for Neglected Children near 'Norwood' in Beach Road, Brighton. 'No denominational distinction will be made in the children taken into the home', said the Bishop. 'We will not inquire whether the children are branded with a big P. for Presbyterian or a great M. for Methodist.' Miss Sutherland left the Presbyterian Church and conducted the new home with outstanding success for many years.

Miss Selina Sutherland fed and clothed starving children without asking them which church they belonged to.

Rev. P. J. Murdoch moved in the Presbyterian Assembly that Miss Sutherland should be instructed to feed Presbyterian children first.

One or two church leaders were courageous enough to speak out on the true causes of the depression. We have already seen how two Brighton clergymen campaigned against Thomas Bent and broke up one of his election meetings. The Rev. Dr Bevan, of the Collins Street Independent Church, told the 21st anniversary meeting of the Y.M.C.A.:

> In that time of wild and mad speculation, when everything seemed to be prosperous, I grew to be very anxious for the moral condition of the people, especially of the young men. I gave up some of the old men altogether, as they were past hoping for. (Laughter). They were either so confirmed in gambling or in speculating, or in financial improprieties, that their cases were quite hopeless; many of them had, however, cleared out, and perhaps it was just as well. (Laughter). But in that time there was great peril for the young men of the city, who began to think that money was to be made, not by honest labour, but by financing; that positions were to be gained not by quiet, steady, persevering work, but by some sudden leap. I knew men who jumped from humble positions into 'financial agents' and 'land speculators,' who built for themselves big houses; and, perhaps naturally, the young people argued that they could do the same.

A few months later, Dr Bevan said that he would rather be 'a bookmaker or a tout on a racecourse than a master of such finance' as had been exhibited by the land boomers. 'Many a man,' he said, 'has taken part within the last few years in shady financial manipulations who would have been shocked to make a bet, take part in a sweepstake, or venture his money on a horse; yet, all the while, he has been engaged in transactions, perhaps carrying on an institution, on lines very little different, if at all, to those which control the betting ring . . . Today we walk down our streets, and see closed doors, which, a year or two ago, shone in all the glory of brass plates; now, with an air of desolation and diminished lustre, reminding us of ruined reputations and the widespread misery caused to the unfortunate people who deposited their hard-earned savings therein.'

The Prahran Independent Church inaugurated the 'Pleasant Sunday Afternoon' addresses in April 1893, and invited Mr Justice Hodges to make the opening speech. His Honor was delighted to have the opportunity of philosophising about some of the examples of commercial morality he had dealt with in court:

> When you come here, you will be taken away from considering whether by buying this piece of land at one figure and selling it at another you will make money, even though it be to take it out of your brother's pocket and put it into your own . . . Unfortunately the desire for gain is not a greed to make money by ordinary hard work, but arises out of a desire to make it by a single stroke of the pen or by a single act. (Applause). If a spirit [of righteousness] had existed, the calm and steady life of the people would have rendered impossible such wild proposals as those that stalked over the colony in 1888, and we would not have had the depression of 1893. (Applause). The exaltation of 1888 and the depression of 1893 are the outcome of the unrestful and excitable nature which we have for many years been cultivating.

Mr Justice Hodges later took up the new craze of bicycling, and was seriously injured in a collision at St Kilda Junction in 1896. Obviously *he* wasn't among the Elect.

49

Feeding the Hungry

The collective efforts of land boomers, politicians and bankers had driven Victoria into the vale of despair. But working against these anti-social elements, attempting to ameliorate the immediate suffering caused by the depression, were the scattered efforts of charity workers, sensitive individuals in Parliament, and persons of tender feelings at all levels of society. Some of their efforts to drain the social cesspool seemed pathetic or merely misdirected. The invisible factor against which they were unwittingly struggling was a sinister aftermath of Victorian *laissez-faire* economics—the idea that governments should not intervene to relieve the sufferings of the unemployed, but should leave the economy alone to adapt itself to its own new level. In practice, that policy meant death and disaster to thousands of people.

To the present-day Australian, accustomed to an elaborate and humanely administered system of 'social services' covering most of his physical disabilities occurring from cradle to grave, it is startling to realize that at a time still within living memory there were no such things as the dole to keep him alive when he lost his job, or a pension when he got too old to work. In the 1890s, there was simply no official system of coping with mass unemployment and actual starvation. If a person lost his job for any reason, and could not get another, he and his family either lived on the charity of friends, turned to thieving or begging or just starved. Economics in those days literally dealt with questions of life and death.

The idea that the State should care for the unemployed and their families was so contrary to accepted beliefs that when the Melbourne Ladies' Benevolent Society spent £7,000 in 1893 on the relief of distress, many members complained that assistance to unemployed people was 'foreign to the design of the society'. Then, too, the general depression cut charity contributions just at the time when they were most needed. On Hospital Sunday, 1892, the sum of £200 was collected at Toorak Presbyterian Church, as against £287 the previous year. St John's, Toorak, gave £40 as against £130 the previous year.

Individual efforts to feed the hungry had little effect on the real causes of their predicament, but undoubtedly helped to keep many people alive. Mrs Harrison Lee, president of the Women's Christian Temperance Union, arranged that 'every deserving person who could pass a means test' could pick up a free loaf

Mrs Harrison Lee, leading temperance worker, arranged bread distribution to the unemployed.

Rev. H. F. Tucker, whose efforts to settle workless men on the land were successful in a few areas.

of bread every day. The Federal Butchering Co., of Richmond, gave away twenty joints of meat a day. A Mr Robertson, who owned a farm thirty-five miles from Melbourne, advertised that unemployed men could take whatever timber they wanted from his land, provided they grubbed out the stumps as well. In April 1893 the Toorak Ladies' Benevolent Society held an open air festival in aid of the unemployed. The Victoria Gardens in Prahran were hung with lanterns, three brass bands played popular airs, and the Victorian Society of Bellringers performed. There was no record kept of the reactions of homeless men trying to sleep on benches or under bushes in the gardens.

The mayor of South Melbourne, T. A. Thistlethwaite, handed out hundreds of orders for loaves of bread and legs of mutton. In some cases the relief was refused, as the applicants were found to be substantial property owners. In another part of South Melbourne, the Presbyterian Church in Clarendon Street opened a food depot. Applicants handed in their sugar-bags on Tuesdays and Fridays, and got them back on Wednesdays and Saturdays filled with old bread, meat and vegetables, supplied by the local tradesmen. Said Mr Briggs, executive officer of the depot: 'The distress is really very great. Amongst the sufferers, too, are people well brought up, but who refuse absolutely to come here. They would rather starve than accept charity. I have known people eat orange peel rather than ask for bread.'

On the other side of the city, many penniless women and their children found a refuge at Dr Singleton's Night Shelter for Women, situated in Islington Street, Collingwood. John Singleton, a Dublin-born doctor, was perhaps the greatest single charity worker in Melbourne. He had sworn off liquor for life after a paralytic drinking bout in Ireland in his youth. He came to Victoria, and in 1869 opened the colony's first free medical dispensary in Collingwood. Over the next twenty years he treated about 140,000 people free of charge, doing most of the work himself. He built a 'Model Lodging House' in King Street, accommodating 400 destitute men each night. Then he established a 'Home for Fallen Women', which gave temporary shelter to 3000 prostitutes in the 1880s and 1890s. 'Guests' at his homes received a piece of bread and cup of tea as their dinner, then attended compulsory Divine Service. They were given a clean bed, tidied up the dormitories in the morning, and were given another piece of bread and cup of tea before facing the streets for the day.

Other 'refuges' for men were opened by the Salvation Army. An *Australasian Sketcher* reporter who visited one such refuge found

> A great bare barrack-room with about 70 beds. They are all occupied, and the place is badly ventilated and the air is full of sound and smell. You would judge the men to be dirty, fit for nothing better, perhaps. And, from glimpses one gets of their faces, they seem, generally, mature or middle-aged men, who ought to be established in life.

In the more enlightened surroundings of the Gordon Institute for Boys in Bowen Street:

> You might see, like enough, one little fellow with only a single boot to his name, but it is polished to an extra brilliancy as if to atone for the other foot's shortcomings. The rags and terribly evident poverty of some of these lads would have a saddening influence on the visitor not accustomed to meeting want at close quarters, were it not for the jolly smiling faces . . . The boys are employed in many capacities—as newspaper boys, others as street cleaners under the Corporation, and some are employed on farms up country; these latter are corresponded with regularly once a month, instructive papers being sent to them . . . The Gordon Institute is still devoid of adequate sleeping accommodation for homeless lads, who otherwise have to sleep out in the gutters, or go to some cheap lodging-house, where the moral influence is frequently very bad.

In case the lads should be softened by all this good living, Parliament passed a Juvenile Offenders Act, under which youthful offenders of less than sixteen years could be ordered a birching in lieu of imprisonment when they ran foul of the law. 'As to young fellows of the larrikin class' who were over sixteen years, they were rendered liable to imprisonment and solitary confinement on a diet of bread and water.

Another example of the child welfare methods of the day was the report of an Education Department committee, issued in 1891, on the subject of neglected children who were wandering the streets at all hours of the day and night, trying to earn their bread by selling papers, race cards, matches, and so on. It was estimated that 10,000 children in Melbourne between the ages of six and fifteen were not attending any school at all. The Education Department committee felt strongly that they should be going to school instead of trying to earn a living. It recommended that street vendors' licences should be issued bearing the name of each child's school; that truant officers should be empowered to arrest any child found in the streets and not able to give a satisfactory account of himself; and that lads charged with breaches of the regulations should be

Dr John Singleton, the reformed alcoholic who treated 140,000 poor people free of charge.

Prostitutes and other destitute women and children were given shelter for the night at Dr Singleton's Home for Fallen Women in Collingwood (Vic.), where attendance at religious service was compulsory.

J. Macfarlane

birched upon conviction. It is difficult to estimate how many children were converted from paupers into criminals by the application of these rules.

The State government's only important contribution towards alleviating the distress was the passing of the Village Settlements Act of 1892, with the aim of settling the 'deserving poor' on the land. After a difficult start, and several scandals, some of the villages became self-supporting. The idea for the settlements did not even originate with the politicians. That honour belonged to the Rev. H. F. Tucker, whose scheme was based on co-operative enterprise evolving into eventual private ownership. Directors of the scheme bought land in large areas at a low figure—£3 to £10 per acre—on long terms of six to ten years, and subdivided the areas into blocks of ten acres and a commonage. Intending settlers were carefully selected for fitness, and sent with their families to the settlements. Tents were used for shelter until huts could be erected, and food and implements supplied on credit at the settlement store. Settlers sold their produce to the store and were paid a quarter of its value in cash, the balance being applied to the reduction of his debt. Members who would not live amicably with their fellows were required to withdraw, and intoxicating beverages were completely prohibited.

Some of the settlements were complete failures. By 1896 the government had found it necessary to remove 500 people from 'the wretchedly poor land where they had been dumped down'. Many at Lyonsville were near death due to starvation, and were existing on the charity of local storekeepers. Their removal cost the State nearly £2,000, and they had to abandon £3,000 worth of improvements. Another notorious failure was an attempt to establish a fishing village on Flinders Island. The *Lady Loch* took eighteen unemployed men with fishing tackle and small boats to the island, but only a few pilchards were ever caught and the camp had to be abandoned. On the other hand, successful settlements (now thriving communities) were established at Red Hill, Croydon, Horsham, and other areas. Acting independently, the Salvation Army bought 630 acres of land at Pakenham, settled eighty unemployed men on it, and 'treated saint and sinner with equal consideration'.

The government decided to compile a register of unemployed, in a somewhat optimistic attempt to assess the extent of the problem. On 10 June 1892 the Public Works Department opened the register in the Olympia Hall, Flinders Street. By the end of November some 15,000 men had registered for work. But, said one man to the *Age*: 'What's the use o' the Government registering our names like a lot of sheep, if they ain't got work to give us when we've registered?'

While it was the fashion to decry the work of the Labour Bureau, it did succeed in finding temporary work in country areas for about 5,000 men. Only 1,000 men could be placed in city jobs—a striking commentary on the stagnation of secondary industry. Even these 1,000 were largely employed on the construction of Dudley Street through the West Melbourne swamp, and on the repainting of government buildings. Of 1,100 carpenters who had registered for work, only 126 were placed. Terms offered by the Labour Bureau could hardly be called handsome. Prospective employers told the Bureau how much they were willing to pay, and the men could 'take it or leave it'. A dozen men were offered work at 10s. a week for clearing scrub at Yea. They were given railway passes, but had to sign an agreement to refund the cost of the tickets out of their first month's pay. Men who refused such 'jobs' were permanently struck off the register. The Trades Hall Council protested vigorously against the harshness of the system, but without effect.

The government's action in providing relief work, however reluctantly and inadequately, had some curious results. In 1893 Captain Evans, Inspector-General of Penal Establishments, reported that he could not find enough hard labour for his prisoners to perform. When he asked the Railways Commissioners if they could take a large quantity of broken metal, they replied that the unemployed had already broken up enough rock to last them for many years. Nevertheless, when J. B. Patterson became Premier, he could not be accused of lack of sympathy with the unemployed. In the presence of one deputation of men asking for work, he completely broke down and wept. 'It is heartrending for Ministers to be waited upon day after day by numbers of men with the cry: "Give us some work! Our wives and children are starving!" ' he said. 'My colleagues are doing nothing else from morning to night but trying to find work for men who want it.'

In August 1893 the Legislative Council appointed a select committee to consider the problem. Donald Melville, M.L.C., said that never since 1853 had he seen the condition of the working class so bad. Simon Fraser, M.L.C. for South Yarra, replied that he did not think men were actually starving, because he 'never yet knew a family in Australia not prepared to give food to the wayfarer.'

J. L. Dow, the *Age* journalist, started a crusade to prevent the banks from foreclosing on farmers who could not meet their overdrafts during the crash. As he told the 1895 Royal Commission:

> I go to men upon the land, to men up the country, and I see them being thrown out on the road . . . I know of cases where a storekeeper offered to pay the interest, and the banks have refused it. They wanted the principal, and the man is sold up simply because of his debt of, say, £2 an acre . . . Wherever the land will bring the amount of the debt they want the coin.
>
> The Chairman (Joseph Winter): You said a total of 30,000 souls had been sold off farms averaging 225 acres, and aggregating 1,500,000 acres?
>
> Dow: These figures are carefully taken out of statistics, compiled from *Hayter's*, that is, reckoning five souls to a family.

While the existing institutions struggled, and mostly failed, to cope with the flood of hopeless, helpless humanity, attempts were made to find new solutions, but in the usual well-meaning, sporadic and disorganized fashion. The *Age* started a 'Snowball', enlisting the aid of several prominent people to control the fund. The Rev. Dr Watkin accepted the post of secretary, and outlined some of the problems involved to the first meeting. The government's Labour Bureau, he said, was 'worse than useless', because it merely attracted needy people from country areas. A squatter had written to him stating that the Bureau had relieved him of all the 'worthless sundowners and loafers' with whom he had previously been pestered. A second problem, said Dr Watkin, was that many poor women who were formerly able to earn money by washing were prevented from doing so by the number of cut-price Chinese laundries which had opened in Melbourne. Another member of the *Age* committee, Mr Graham, president of the Trades Hall Council, said he was trying to open a co-operative laundry to provide work for widows. Miss S. Sutherland, invited to address the meeting, said their object should be to provide for the women and children, and not for the men, 'who for the greater part preferred idleness and loafing'. Despite these contrary views, the *Age* fund raised several thousand pounds.

Matthew Lang, Mayor of Melbourne, formed the first central organization which later became known as the Lord Mayor's Fund. By July 1892 £6,000 had been subscribed to the Mayor's Fund; another £5,000 had been voted from the Flood Relief Fund; and £1,300 was raised by a benefit race meeting at Caulfield.

The following year, interested people tried to centralize all private charitable work under the banner of a 'Charity Organization Society'. Its committee members included Professor Morris, Sir Henry Wrixon, the Rev. Drs Bevan, Watkin, and Strong, Judge Molesworth, James Service, Alfred Deakin, R. W. Best, David Syme, Sam Winter, Henry Byron Moore, and Sir Frederick Sargood. The secretary of the society, Jacob Goldstein, laid down a strict rule to be applied to every applicant who claimed that he was starving and homeless:

> The work should not be made attractive, and should not be at the disposal of new-comers. It should not be under Government control, and should only be given to the really necessitous. Every effort should be made to induce the unemployed families to leave Melbourne and settle in the country, but departures for other colonies should not be at the expense of the charitable.

In his report issued on 20 March 1893, just before the great bank smash, Goldstein claimed that the number of unemployed was being exaggerated 'for political reasons'. Apart from that, 'the poor of Melbourne were found to live under much more wholesome and sanitary conditions than is generally asserted.' Of the really needy cases, 'some 200 souls were maintained at Werribee Sewage Farm for 10 weeks at an average cost of 7½d. per head per week.' All in all, his report was a great comfort.

50

Reforms and Remedies

By the beginning of 1894 the worst fury of the economic tornado had spent itself, and men began looking to the task of repair. They were faced with the immediate necessity of restarting the social engine in order to provide even the common necessities of life. Beyond that, there was a grim and grave determination to ensure that never again would the State and its people be brazenly plundered by groups of politicians and financiers. Such moods do not last for long; nor do they need to. This one lasted long enough to put a few sharp teeth into those Acts of Parliament which purported to regulate the activities of private enterprise.

We have seen in preceding chapters how the State was finally forced to admit some responsibility towards those who were actually starving in the streets. While this sentient social wreckage was being cleaned up, patched up, or buried, the work of reconstructing the soundest of the remaining financial institutions proceeded apace. One by one the suspended banks reopened for business. Slowly, ever so cautiously, they began lending money again. Factories opened their doors. People were given employment, and wept when they brought home their first week's wages. Farmers bought seed and planted wheat. With many a setback, the community at last regained a measure of its earlier vigour.

Statistics showed the degree of recovery. In 1893 there were 14,000 vacant houses in Melbourne. Two years later, this figure had dropped to 10,000 houses vacant. The population of the metropolitan area in 1893 was 437,000. It dropped by 15,000 during the next twelve months; then recovered to 433,000 by 1895. Nevertheless, the value of property remained incredibly low for many years. Thousands of title deeds were held by mortgagors, for the land and houses were hardly worth the expense of advertising them for sale.

Many ingenious schemes were propounded for settling the complex debts and transactions left over from the boom. Early in 1893 *Table Talk* seriously suggested 'a gigantic lottery', in which the assets of land boom companies would be the prizes, and the proceeds would be distributed among the creditors. The following year the suggestion was taken up by the liquidators of the Bank of Van Diemen's Land. The Tasmanian Parliament passed a special Act to allow the bank's trustees to hold 'A Grand Lottery' to dispose of properties on which it had foreclosed. First prize, valued at £26,000, was a large corner property in the centre of Hobart, together with wholesale drug stocks—a somewhat novel bonus for any lottery winner. Second prize was Hadley's Orient Hotel, valued then at £22,500.

Lotteries were not permitted in Rechabite Victoria. Instead, a variety of 'assets realization schemes' were propounded. In general they were based on the idea that the liquidators should hold on to the properties until values started to recover, then sell them slowly so as to avoid flooding the market, making small payouts at intervals to the creditors. In practice, it was found that the expenses of liquidation over a period of several years often ate up a large share of the proceeds.

In 1893 the *Statist* suggested that 'a great Assets Realization Company' should take over from all bankrupt institutions their remaining properties which could not be sold easily. This would rationalize the process greatly and reduce the costs of liquidation. Nothing was done along these lines until 1897. In that year the creditors of four insolvent banks (the Federal, Mercantile, City of Melbourne, and English & Australian Mortgage banks), pooled their efforts and halved the cost of finalizing their affairs.

While these multifarious private arrangements were being made, George Turner's new government was grappling with the wider implications of the smash. This government had been elected with an overwhelming popular mandate to pass laws dealing with the glaring abuses of the finance and investment system, which had led to such widespread suffering. The general form of the remedies needed was clear enough, in the light of the astonishing revelations made by liquidators and dozens of court enquiries. But at every point the Turner government was burked by a sullen and vindictive Upper House. The draft bills of the new Attorney-General, Isaac Isaacs, were models of enlightened company legislation. By the time they had been mauled by the Legislative Council, a chamber consisting largely of company directors and landowners, the bills contained little of their visionary aspects. Rather than achieve nothing at all, or be forced into a premature dissolution and election, the Turner Cabinet accepted many of the Council's amendments. It may be fairly said that if Isaacs's original ideas had been passed into law, many of the financial scandals of the following century would not have affected Victoria. But that is another story.

The Turner government's first task was to reform the old system of Commissioners' Savings Banks. These banks, and the Victorian Post Office Savings Banks, had previously acted almost as independent enterprises, with very little central direction or supervision. The little people paid in, and the big people took out. Too often the Savings Banks' funds were foolishly lent to speculators with a glib enough story. The Savings Banks lost nearly a quarter of a million pounds through insolvencies of such speculators.

The Savings Banks dated from an Act of Parliament in 1853, later amended by the Savings Bank Statute 1865. They enjoyed remarkably wide freedom, being empowered to advance on land or property to any amount they wished, in contrast to the Savings Banks of New South Wales, which were restricted to a

Depositors in the Melbourne Savings Bank on Saturday night. Some of their money was lost to speculators, and the savings bank system had to be reformed.

maximum of £8,000 on any one mortgage. The only real limitation on the powers of the Victorian Commissioners was that they could lend only on the security of first mortgages, up to half the current valuation.

A board of honorary Commissioners was appointed by the Governor-in-Council, meaning in effect by Premier and Cabinet, to exercise sole control of the investment of the funds. This combination of political patronage, absence of paid, professional Commissioners, and almost unlimited powers, was to prove extremely damaging to the interests of depositors. During most of the land boom period, the Commissioners were Sir Caleb Joshua Jenner (chairman), William McLean, David Elder, Alfred Shaw, and James Grice. In 1890 there was a run on the bank, and Jenner, Elder, and Shaw resigned. They were replaced by Captain Archibald Currie (chairman), F. Race Godfrey and George Meares. Being honorary Commissioners, all these men naturally had other interests. Being appointed during a period of universal speculation, naturally some of their interests were speculative. Being solid and respectable businessmen, they were of the teetotal party almost to a man. Let us see what happened.

The cash which these respected businessmen were charged with supervising and investing amounted to about £4 million in the case of the Commissioners' Savings Banks. Another £2 million deposited in the Post Office Savings Bank

Sir Caleb Joshua Jenner, chairman of the Savings Bank Commissioners, helped to involve the bank in land boom losses.

Captain Archibald Currie took over from Jenner during the breaking of the boom.

was largely out of their reach—although not beyond the reach of the politicians. The £4 million in the Commissioners' Banks was split up as follows: about £2¼ million was lent out on mortgage; another £1¼ million was deposited on long terms in various private banks to earn interest at fixed rates; some £300,000 was put into government debentures. The balance was spent on bank premises and other capital items.

Now let us examine the £2¼ million lent on mortgage. John Robb received £70,000 of it to build Robb's Buildings at the western end of Collins Street. He went bankrupt, and the bank had to foreclose on the empty echoing granite pile. The coffee palaces, those havens for thirsty teetotallers, were especially favoured by the Savings Banks, and got at least £150,000 between them. The Grand Coffee Palace was lent £70,000 when it agreed to surrender its liquor licence, and took years to repay the debt. The Federal Coffee Palace Co. Ltd was lent £70,000 to build its soaring archways and towers opposite Robb's Buildings. The *Daily Telegraph*, unofficial and unsuccessful organ of the teetotal interests, was lent an undisclosed amount to erect its building in Collins Street (later the site of the Regent Theatre).

Apart from these unfortunate investments, the Savings Banks had more than a million pounds locked up in the suspended banks. Some of the amounts involved were:

English, Scottish & Australian Chartered Bank	£132,000
London Chartered Bank of Australia	£106,000
Commercial Bank	£89,000
Federal Bank	£84,000

Some of these deposits were in turn used by the private banks to finance their own favourite speculators, particularly in the case of the Commercial and Federal Banks. Under the various bank reconstruction schemes, most of this money was compulsorily converted into preference shares. The amount on deposit with the Federal Bank had to be written down to show a final loss of £36,350. Thus the supposed guarantee of 'first mortgage protection' for depositors turned out to be not so certain after all.

With this emphasis on metropolitan land booming schemes, it was no wonder that farmers throughout the countryside complained of the difficulty of getting overdrafts at reasonable rates. The Savings Banks rarely advanced money to farmers against their assets—indeed they seemed to regard the idea as usurping the private banks' prerogative—so that it was the usual thing for farmers to be forced to pay overdraft interest rates of 8, 10, and 12 per cent.

The public got an early inkling of the Savings Banks' troubles, and made two serious runs on their funds. In May 1890 the *Evening Standard* disclosed that the Melbourne Savings Bank had lent £70,000 to one coffee palace. That in itself was not serious, in the context of the time. But the depositors, with that curious telepathic sense that seems to operate in small communities, universally believed the worst. Within three days nearly £300,000 had been withdrawn, and 3,500 accounts were closed.

In April 1893, when disaster loomed in every direction, another run took place on the Melbourne Savings Bank. Just a few months before, John Alsop, the bank's Actuary, had advertised it as 'The Largest Body of Depositors in the British Empire'. Now the body started to disintegrate. Another 5,000 depositors closed their accounts, drawing out £500,000 in gold.

By 30 June the Commissioners were forced to report to the government that the Savings Bank could not make enough money to pay the interest due to remaining depositors and the expenses of management. Beset by a multitude of other troubles, the Patterson government took no action. The Commissioners began eating into the banks' £200,000 cash reserve. Soon the funds were practically all gone, and interest rates had to be cut.

When the Turner government swept the polls in 1894, one of its first actions was to attempt to restore the position of the Savings Banks. A Credit Foncier Bill (popularly called the Cheap Money Bill) was introduced into Parliament. It provided for the amalgamation of the Commissioners' Savings Banks with the Post Office Savings Bank. The combined deposits, by then reduced to about £5½ million, were to be used as capital for the new bank. Directors, committee members, and officers of private banks, building societies, etc., were prohibited from becoming Commissioners. Individual loans were limited to £1,000. Commissioners were forbidden to lend money to companies of which they were directors. Loans were to be given to farmers at cheap rates. And so on.

The Bill was held up by the Legislative Council, whereupon the Turner government appointed a Royal Commission on State Banking to gather more evidence on the question. The Commission consisted of nine members, both liberal and conservative, with Joseph Winter, M.L.A., as chairman. Its stated purpose was to enquire into the question of establishing a State Bank, and to try and arrive at recommendations which would satisfy both Houses of Parliament. The Royal Commission reported in 1895 that the Commissioners' Savings Banks had followed 'an unsafe policy' of investment. More than £2 million had been advanced to a select group of 130 speculators—an average of £15,400 each. On one property alone, the sum of £125,000 had been advanced. As far as the Post Office Savings Bank was concerned, it had handed all its depositors' money to successive State Treasurers, who had blithely used most of it on current government expenditure, resulting in 'a large accumulated deficit.'

One witness, John Langlands, a Horsham storekeeper, gave damning evidence against the old Savings Banks' lending policies. Langlands happened to be a local trustee for the Savings Banks. He deposed that Horsham residents had paid £14,000 into the local branch of the Melbourne Savings Bank, but 'not one penny' had been re-lent in the district. Time and time again the trustees had asked the Commissioners in Melbourne to lend money to the farmers, but without success. The farmers' income from wheat sales just covered the interest on their mortgages to the private banks. In order to buy groceries, they had to exchange butter and eggs with local storekeepers.

The facts emerging from the Royal Commission were indisputable, but its recommendations were not so unanimous. The conservative members regarded the idea of a State Bank with horror. 'It would be disastrous', wrote Nathaniel Levi, M.L.C., in a dissenting minority report. 'A State Credit Foncier might result in great and widespread disaster', agreed Robert Murray Smith, M.L.A. The private banks took up the chorus. At the half-yearly meeting of the National Bank in November 1896, the vice-chairman, John Grice, said that a State Bank 'would materially damage the credit of the colony'. As though forecasting the bank nationalization battle of many decades later, Grice warned ominously that 'Directors, managers, and employees of banks have so far refrained from using their immense political power', but now the time had gone by for 'folding their arms' and waiting. In Parliament another veteran of the land boom, Theodore Fink, M.L.A., pronounced the final malediction on the idea of a State Bank. It was, he said, 'revolutionary and dangerous in the highest degree'.

None of their direful predictions came true. The Bill was greatly watered down by the Legislative Council, but even in its mutilated form, had much the long-term effect desired by its sponsors. Today the State Savings Bank of Victoria stands as one of the world's great credit institutions, whose techniques have largely been copied by the private banks.

The tribulations encountered by the Turner government in trying to introduce a State savings and lending system were trifling in comparison with the difficulties it encountered in tightening up the Companies Act.

As we have seen, the existing Companies Act was based on the *laissez-faire* belief that if the actions of entrepreneurs and financiers were governed largely by the complex interaction of free competition, everything would turn out for the best. This fond illusion persisted for many years, even to the present day, in the face of compelling and even horrifying evidence to the contrary.

The Companies Act of the day did prohibit obvious dishonesty, such as the publication of false balance sheets with intent to defraud. The difficulty lay in initiating and proving such charges, particularly in the context of the sudden fall in the value of assets after the boom. Whether or not a director was a criminal often resolved itself into a mere matter of opinion. Thus it was possible to find magistrates and judges who honestly believed that Sir Matthew Davies was a cunning rogue, and others who were just as firmly convinced that he was an innocent victim of events. There could be no final answer, although we may be certain that today Davies and others would have been imprisoned for a long period. Somewhat different circumstances existed in the case of James Munro, who lent most of his banks' money to his friends and relatives in the knowledge that it would be used for speculation. Few could be found to defend his actions. But he could not be charged in the criminal courts, for such offences were not recognized by the Companies Act of the day. Munro, and others like him, simply extended the common practice of nepotism to a remarkable degree where millions of pounds of other people's money was involved.

George Turner, Premier of Victoria, whose government had the thankless task of cleaning up after the land boom and bust.

These were only some of the loopholes for the cunning, the unscrupulous, or the hypocritical; for the general state of the law almost begged company promoters to defraud the public. Under the Victorian Companies Act of 1864 (consolidated with amendments in 1890), companies were not compelled to keep what we would regard as proper books and accounts, nor even to have their records independently audited. It was possible for a company secretly to lend its shareholders' and depositors' money to directors; to lend it on the non-existent 'security' of the company's own shares; to pay dividends not made out of current profits; to call itself a 'bank' or 'savings bank'; secretly to mortgage its uncalled capital; and to make statements in prospectuses which today would be regarded as criminally misleading.

In addition to the 'Limited Liability' companies, a large number of 'No Liability' companies had also been formed, mainly for the purpose of encouraging mining ventures. Under this system, whenever new calls were made, shareholders had the option of paying the calls or forfeiting their shares. But so loose was the 1864 Act that no-liability companies were also allowed to receive money on deposit, to buy shares in other companies, and to conduct their business in a way which made fraud a comparatively easy matter. All these things were done under the banner of the divine right of the capitalist. The scandals became so blatant that the *Age* was compelled to comment in a leading article: 'Company law is foully encrusted with the hoary rogueries of [the last] three decades.'

The struggle to strengthen the Companies Act began as early as 1891, during the brief period when James Munro was Premier. Ephraim Zox, M.L.A., asked him in Parliament whether he was prepared to introduce a bill to protect the funds of depositors in the land banks. Munro's reply, not unexpectedly, was a decided negative. Later the same year, the company directors who largely comprised the membership of the Legislative Council tried to amend the Companies Act in the reverse direction—to enable speculators to escape the results of their actions. This bill, drafted by Agar Wynne, introduced a novel idea even for Victoria—that shareholders should not be liable to pay the uncalled capital on their shares. The Upper House passed the bill with hardly a dissenting voice, but after a shocked public outcry it was hastily buried by the Legislative Assembly.

Two rather more valuable bills were passed by the Council in 1893, while the Patterson government was in power. Sir Frederick Sargood introduced the first, which was intended to prevent the 'spec. selling' of bank shares in the stock market. For the first time, it was made a criminal offence to offer bank shares at less than the market price, in cases where the seller did not actually possess the shares but relied on buying from panicky holders before they were due to deliver the scrip. Towards the end of 1893 an even more valuable measure prohibited any company from lending money on the security of its own shares, or from secretly lending money to its own directors. C. J. Ham, M.L.C., thought this 'very harsh and unfair'. J. M. Davies, M.L.C., also protested; but both these measures were passed.

Still there had been no comprehensive amendment of the old Companies Act. More was needed than mere 'patching and darning'. Fortunately, during the period of depression through which the colony was now passing, only a few new companies were being floated under the provisions of the old Act. Little real harm was done by the legislative delays. The horses had already bolted, and it did not matter very much if it took another year or two to shut the stable door.

In 1894, when the Turner government came into power, it set about drafting a comprehensive amending bill, with no fewer than 173 clauses. All the flagrant abuses of commercial morality which had shocked the world were to be abolished by Act of Parliament. As Isaac Isaacs outlined each stringent new clause to the Assembly in 1895, he found members cheering him until the House echoed. Any director who lent company funds to himself, or misled shareholders in any way, was to be gaoled, fined heavily, and sued for damages from his private assets. A new era of legally enforced honesty was about to begin. At least, that was how it seemed when the bill was quickly passed and sent on to the Upper House.

Now began a great battle between the two chambers which held up the bill for nearly two years. Bitterly, clause by clause, the Legislative Council altered the bill's definitions of criminal behaviour, watered down its punishments, and emasculated its intentions. Speaker after speaker complained that the government was treating all company directors as thieves and criminals, potential or actual.

By March 1896 the *Age* declared in exasperation:

> The Council's action in the Companies Bill is one dictated by the most direct of personal interests. It is a House of company directors, and it is determined to minimize the responsibility of directors towards shareholders . . . It has insisted on the Companies Bill doing nothing to compel directors to do their duty.

Each time the bill was returned to the Assembly with further amendments, Isaacs had to face insistent new attacks from the conservative faction in that House. G. D. Carter succeeded in persuading him to water down a clause providing that at least one-half of the nominal capital of a new company must be paid up in cash. Theodore Fink expressed the fear that the bill would seriously hamper amalgamations, reconstructions, and new flotations.

In August 1896 the Upper House played its last card by referring the bill to a select committee. Just 'an excuse for destroying the measure which the Assembly has adopted', snapped the *Age*. 'The Council . . . seems determined to emasculate it and then send it down to the Assembly just as Parliament is rising.' In the event, that was precisely what happened. The select committee took three months to reach its conclusions, and finally reported back to the Upper House on lines which could have easily been predicted. Late on Christmas Eve, 1896, the Council sent the bill back to the Assembly with a message that it would make no further compromise on five vital clauses. These clauses would have required all banks to state their balance on a particular day (to prevent the old 'balancing trick'); would have facilitated company investigations; prohibited advances to directors; prevented directors from sharing commissions with employees; and abolished dummying of shares.

But it was Christmas Eve. The House was due to rise. Isaac Isaacs sadly told the members that he had been 'much exercised in his mind' as to the proper course to take. He thought the House would be wrong to abandon the bill even in its mutilated form, as it contained provisions of undoubted value to the community. The public 'would insist on giving quick effect to the provisions rejected by the Council.'

So the new Companies Act came into being. It did contain many useful provisions, and helped to regularize company affairs. In one respect Isaacs was wrong. As the radical phase died away, the public did not 'insist' on more drastic measures. Many more financial scandals were to occur in the twentieth century before any further serious attempts were made to perfect the Companies Act.

The amendments to the Companies Act were a desperate and somewhat unsatisfactory compromise. The Turner government was faced with a much simpler and less controversial task in tightening up the insolvency laws. The business community and the conservative party might disagree with the government's notions of what constituted a fraud-proof Companies Act. But the processes of insolvency were such a noisome scandal that there could be little argument. Every trader in the community needed to know whether his clients were solvent or not. The iniquitous process of secret composition had sapped confidence to such an extent that every man's credit was at the whim of rumour and malice.

In earlier days of capitalist enterprise, bankruptcy had been regarded almost as a criminal offence. Debtors might rot in prison for years until their debts were paid in full. In the early nineteenth century, a more lenient view of insolvency began to prevail. The English Parliament established a Court of Bankruptcy in 1831, and most debtors were released when they surrendered all their property. Later they were given a chance to make a fresh start in business life, provided their estate paid at least 7s. in the £1. This provision was meant to ensure that traders did not run their business down below the point where it would realize that figure. However, the Court could dispense with even that provision in a case where an honest debtor had met with misfortune beyond his control.

In Britain two Acts were passed, in 1883 and 1890, under which all 'private arrangements' had to be registered, accounts rendered to the Board of Trade, and the facts published in trade circulars. Court examination of the debtor had to precede submission of his offer to the creditors. The Official Receiver had to be satisfied that the offer was a fair one, and that the insolvent had not been guilty of any misconduct, before granting a release from sequestration.

The existing Victorian Insolvency Act was largely based on the earlier English statutes. After a succession of frauds, English legislators had realized that bankruptcy had to be completely under the control of the courts and open to the public, but the Victorian Parliament had not seen fit to alter its approach. The English reformers set out to destroy all private methods of settlement between an insolvent and his creditors, holding that it was a vital matter of public knowledge when a trader went bankrupt. In Victoria, by contrast, the Insolvency Court was 'a maimed and restricted tribunal'. The *Age* could comment that: 'It has been for years a standing jest in the community that a royal road to riches in this colony is through the Insolvency Court. The mere existence of any widespread feeling as this acts as a laxative to the public conscience, lowering the moral tone of the community.'

Under Victorian law three-fourths of the creditors (in number and value) present at a meeting could force a composition of any amount upon all the creditors, no matter what the conduct of the insolvent had been. Many such meetings were 'packed' with the insolvent's friends and supporters, in order to gain the required three-fourths majority. Sometimes their wives were put down for fictitious loans in order to swell the voting. Provided that the debtor complied with the letter of the law, the court had no power to prevent the composition from being registered, and the debtor being freed forthwith from all his obligations.

The court could not enquire into the insolvent's conduct, nor the amount in the pound he proposed to pay. It could not order a compulsory sequestration to replace a composition, nor set aside fraudulent dealings after registration. Such matters had to be made the subject of a special motion before the Supreme Court—an expensive and thankless task for the average creditor. The Supreme Court even ruled that once the composition had been duly entered, the Insolvency Court lost its few original powers for investigating the application.

Sometimes the small compositions offered by debtors were never paid. George Meudell, who attended many creditors' meetings, wrote:

> Half of the 'compotes' offered to pay from one farthing to threepence in the pound, most of them never paid a bean, a peppercorn, or a mustard seed! . . . The insolvencies were all smothered in bank parlours and lawyers' offices; smothered, stifled, strangled and buried with extreme unction.

According to *Table Talk*, some of

> these high souled debtors used to drive up to the Insolvency Court in well-appointed carriages, and none had 'paid what they owed' to the extent of parting with gold watches and rings, or were without sufficient petty cash to pay for a cab to drive from their solicitors to the court, and 'shout' for the assembled creditors when the composition was duly effected.

Why did so many creditors allow their debtors to make secret compositions? In many cases, public exposure of their involvement for huge amounts in speculative transactions would have shaken their own credit. Sometimes they even purchased the interest of a number of smaller creditors in the estate, and in this manner arranged the three-fourths majority. 'Creditors . . . are sometimes not disinclined to hush up a nasty business', said the *Age*, with justifiable cynicism.

The appointment of 'friendly' trustees was another festering scandal in Victoria. British law prohibited the appointment of trustees 'who are conjunct or confident with the bankrupt, or who hold an interest opposed to the general interest of the creditors.' But in Victoria, any person who could get a sufficient number of votes from the creditors was allowed to act as trustee. The court had no power to object, and no audit was ever made of the quarterly returns submitted to the court as the trustee wound up the estate. Under these conditions, a class of men arose who made a profession of trusteeship, getting their income from the 5 per cent commission allowed on the gross assets realized. Many trustees acted for their friends and business associates (as Salis Fischer, for instance, acted for Theodore Fink in the latter's secret compositions). Other trustees canvassed for votes, or employed touts to do it for them, and made all sorts of private deals on the side which detrimentally affected the general body of the creditors. These professional touts 'scent out possible insolvencies beforehand', said the *Age*, 'just as carrion birds are said to fleck the sky the instant a camel stumbles in the desert . . . Tens of thousands of pounds are known to have reached the pockets of these "trustees", and never to have been traced beyond them.'

Various protests were made against the scandalous state of the law. The Chamber of Commerce and the Associated Banks prepared a list of suggestions in 1886, and a bill was drafted by G. B. Kerferd, the Attorney-General. Before it could be presented to Parliament, Kerferd was elevated to the Supreme Court bench. Henry Wrixon became Attorney-General, and dropped the bill as though it were a live bomb.

In 1892 *Table Talk* reported that it had asked the secretary of the Crown Law Department for statistical details of the number of private compositions registered, without revealing the names of the people involved. The official refused, whereupon *Table Talk* tried to get the information from William Shiels, the Minister in charge of the department. Shiels refused, on the ground of 'adverse reports from officers of the department'. *Table Talk* warned: 'If these compositions are allowed to remain secret, it will not be many months before a commercial panic will eventuate which will shake the credit of Victoria to its foundations.'

It was one of the most mordantly accurate prophecies ever made, for within the year, practically every financial institution in Melbourne had closed down. After the government refused to give any information, *Table Talk* set about interviewing every creditor, solicitor and trustee it could find. By September 1892 the journal had compiled an accurate list of forty-seven secret compositions, which it published without giving the names of the insolvents.

The following month, Judge Molesworth joined in the battle. An application came before him for the release from sequestration of James W. Wallace, a civil servant who had speculated in land and shipping shares. The trustee of his estate had disappeared with £220 he had collected, and the creditors had subsequently agreed to accept a composition of ¼d. in the £1. When Wallace failed to pay even the humble farthing, the judge leaped at the chance of rejecting the composition and delivering a forthright lecture:

> I am sorry to say that in this community it is not considered a disgraceful thing for a man to enter into contracts which he cannot pay when called upon; and it is not considered a thing to be ashamed of for a man to offer his creditors one farthing in the pound, even when those creditors include tradesmen from whom he obtained goods such as groceries, meat, clothing and the like. I believe that the morality of the Insolvency Court is in some respects worse than that of the racecourse. If a gambler at the races who contracted to pay £1,000 in the event of a certain horse winning were, on being called to pay, to offer 1,000 farthings, his conduct would be described in language more forcible than elegant.

Judge Molesworth now determined to stop every composition where he could find a legitimate reason. He rejected an application by a land agent, Howard Tapley Clarton, for approval of a farthing-in-the-pound composition on his £38,000 debts, on the ground that the composition 'was not for the benefit of the creditors'. Then he rejected an application by William Hay Dickson, an accountant who had handled some of Joseph Clarke's affairs. Dickson had offered to repay his creditors 3d. in the £1 every six months, up to a total of 1s. in the £1. A few months later, Molesworth gaoled two insolvents for filing false schedules—A. E. Sampson, a tea merchant; and J. S. Sundercombe, a boot dealer.

In this way, some of the abuses of the insolvency system were overcome. But all the really scandalous compositions had already been approved, registered, and filed away to gather dust for the next seventy years until disinterred by the present writer. Where new compositions were presented according to law, the court was powerless to refuse them.

Towards the end of 1893 the former Chief Clerk of the Insolvency Court, C. H. Williams, publicly drew attention to the scandal of secret compositions in an address to the Bankers' Institute of Australasia:

> One does not know which man has put his composition papers through the court the day or the week before, and that same man might be asking for credit shortly after. Moreover, the opportunities of what is known as 'cooking a majority' are so many as almost to amount to temptation.

Williams disclosed the existence of a special fund consisting of unclaimed dividends, which according to the Act should be used to finance investigations into fraudulent bankruptcies. However, when he asked the Crown Law Department for information on the fund and how it had been used, the officials refused to supply it. Williams tried to do something about one insolvency—'one of the grossest frauds I ever met with'—but found that he and the court were legally powerless to act.

Meanwhile, in the political arena, Isaac Isaacs had sent on his Companies Bill to a hostile Upper House. He now began drafting his proposals for insolvency reform, described by the *Age* as 'A legislative broom for sweeping clean the commercial life of the people'.

The new Bill, introduced in July 1896, attempted to grapple with all the scandals which had arisen. Private compositions in future were to be registered and open to the public. Settlements on wife and children, made by an insolvent divesting himself of his assets, were void unless previously registered. All insolvents were to be examined, and reports sent to the Attorney-General every month on cases of suspected fraud. Trustees were to be registered by the court and required to put up a substantial bond. Their activities were to be supervised by an official accountant. The Insolvency Court was given greatly increased functions, including the power to imprison offenders for any breach of the Act. The Bill was debated strenuously by both Houses, but in this case the Upper House was not able to impose the same delays and mutilations which emasculated the Companies Act. The new Insolvency Act passed into law with comparative ease, and did much to restore confidence and credit.

The last note of opposition came from the well-known insolvency expert, P. D. Phillips, a former partner of Theodore Fink. In 1897 Phillips told the Institute of Accountants:

> One would suppose that the Premier believes traders, merchants, solicitors and all their associates are a bad lot—(Laughter)—that require to be specially watched . . . [The new Act] discountenances any effort between a trader and his creditors to settle their business without the interference of the court . . . [It is] unsuited to the needs of a free and self-reliant people.

Through the eyes of a later and more fortunate generation, the land boom era may be regarded as a watershed in the development of a free yet regulated private enterprise system in Australia. On one side of this watershed, the scene is a gloomy and awful desert, littered with the wrecks of bold caravans which had set out aimlessly on their varied undertakings with a buoyant disregard for their effect on the balanced progress of the land. The disasters of the 1890s made it apparent to most people that while uncontrolled capitalism might be a marvellous way of unleashing human energy and ambition, it could also be a devilish force capable of recoiling indiscriminately on the just and the unjust and causing enormous suffering. Thus the other side of the watershed, indeed the entire topography of the Australian economy since the great crash of the 1890s, may be viewed as a series of attempts to reconcile the rugged virtues of independent enterprise with the necessity for protecting society from its frequent excesses. The emphasis has varied according to the temper of the times, but as industry and commerce have become ever more complex, infinitely more productive, and tending to amalgamate into larger units, the need for careful social planning of each sector of the economy has come to be accepted by even the most conservative of politicians. The present and future state of the economy has become the paramount question of government, economic indicators being watched constantly and anxiously for signs of weakness, and the accelerator or the brake being applied instantly the economy shows signs of drifting back into its old 'boom and bust' pattern. It is all very different from the brash, happy-go-lucky attitude of the 1880s. Yet twentieth-century Australia owes some sort of debt to those who boomed and those who suffered, for they provide one of the most striking examples in history of the interdependence of all parts of the social order.

Appendix A

THE SECRET COMPOSITIONS OF 1892

Name	*Occupation*	*Date of creditors' meeting*	*Deficiency (Difference between claimed debts and assets)*	*Composition in the £*
Baillieu, William Lawrence	Auctioneer	26 July	£38,432	6d.
Barker, George Dexter	Broker	12 May	£2,444	¼d.
Beard, Charles	Auctioneer	27 June	£12,262	1s.
Beattie, Robert	Accountant	1 July	£9,548	3d.
Bechtold, F.	Florist	10 October	£878	6d.
Benjamin, Maurice Edward	Solicitor	1 June	£9,040	1d.
Biccard, Louis Thalman	Stockbroker	8 August	£5,391	½d.
Brisbane, William	Auctioneer	27 July	£4,755	¼d.
Bruce, William	Solicitor	7 September	£52,476	7d.
Butters, James Stewart	Broker	7 October	£19,310	Set aside
Campbell, Archibald Henry	Journalist	21 September	£2,290	1d.
Clark, Thomas William	Hatter	10 May	£2,019	2s. 6d.
Cromie, John	Unemployed	1 September	£2,586	2s.
Cudden, William James	Accountant	20 September	£12,782	¼d.
Derham, Charles Walter	Grain broker	26 April	£12,758	1s.
Derham, Frederick Thomas	Merchant	24 October	£450,727	1d.
Derrick, William	Gentleman	26 September	£11,446	1d.
Dickson, Raynes Waite	Solicitor	28 October	£92,560	3s.
Drysdale, Henry Henderson	Gentleman	22 August	£11,861	3d.
Dunn, Alfred	Architect	9 August	£28,912	6d.
Earl, Robert	Produce merchant	8 February	£1,268	5s.
England, McHenry	Merchant	24 September	£19,913	1s.
Evans, James	Grocer	19 September	£15,137	1d.
Evered, Henry George	Broker	29 August	£10,237	1d.
Fiedler, Henry Moritz	Legal manager	1 September	£3,853	3d.
Fink, Benjamin Josman	Merchant	21 September	£1,019,275	½d.
Fink, Theodore	Solicitor	19 January	£14,132	3s.
		19 July	£21,900	6d.
Fink, Wolfe	Barrister	2 July	£17,612	1d.
Fuller, Arthur John	Accountant	12 August	£28,271	3d.
Gill, Walter Tyrell	Solicitor	28 October	£1,401	19s. 11d.

*The information contained in Appendices A–D has been extracted from insolvency records filed in the Archives Division, La Trobe Library, Melbourne.

Name	*Occupation*	*Date of creditors' meeting*	*Deficiency (Difference between claimed debts and assets)*	*Composition in the £*
Gillman, Francis	Barrister	25 October	£4,043	6d.
Gladstones, Robert	Accountant	14 September	£2,181	3d.
Grant, Andrew Robertson	Doctor	22 September	£784	3s. 6d.
Hammill, Herbert	Broker	5 December	£7,835	9d.
Hammond, Joseph Jackson	Gentleman	20 September	£4,729	3d.
Hart & Benjamin	Solicitors	12 May	£11,058	3s.
Hart, Edward	Solicitor	20 July	£1,367	2s. 6d.
Hart, Lionel Maurice	Cigar manufacturer	4 July	£2,858	1d.
Hearle, Arthur Herbert	Clerk	8 November	£469	1d.
Henderson, William Philp	School-master	9 November	£6,052	1d.
Hind, Henry Dalzell	Dentist	1 August	£1,850	7s.
Isaacs, George	Gentleman	13 September	£14,098	1s. 6d.
Johnson, James Isaac	——	——	£7,552	1d.
Kitchen, John Ambrose	Merchant	21 July	£163,557	1d.
Kitchen, John Hambleton	Manager of soap factory	4 August	£8,661	1s.
Kitchen, Theophilus	Manufacturer	29 July	£37,105	1d.
Kozminsky, Abraham	Commission agent	18 July	£92,266	1d.
Latham, Edward	Brewer	26 May	£32,795	1s.
Lemon, Robert Hans	Broker	19 July	£34,037	¼d.
Leslie, Donald	Unemployed	23 September	£9,631	3d.
Levy, Alfred Lazarus	Licensed victualler	24 October	£2,888	3d.
Levy, Montague	Licensed victualler	6 October	£2,242	2s. 6d.
Lightfoot, Edward William	Grain merchant	17 August	£19,625	¼d.
McIntosh, William Atkin	Grazier	22 April	£17,551	1s. 1d.
McMahon, Peter Louis	Importer	13 September	£6,121	3d.
Macmeikan & Co.	Estate agents	17 September	£3,469	1d.
Macmeikan, John	,,	,,	£7,733	1d.
Macmeikan, Percy Alexander	,,	,,	£17,223	1d.
Max, Sina	Sharebroker	24 November	£2,439	1s.
Meader, William	Licensed victualler	29 June	£8,040	¼d.
Munro & Baillieu	Auctioneers	26 July	£55,627	6d.
Munro, Donald	,,	,,	£26,203	6d.
Muntz, Thomas Bingham	Engineer	16 December	£10,575	2s.
Park, Leslie John	Insurance secretary	16 June	£2,607	19s. 11d.
Paterson, James	Landowner	2 November	£11,690	1s.
Pope, John	Butcher	6 December	£7,850	6d.
Purves, James Drysdale	Accountant	20 September	£9,458	2d.
Richards, George Thomas	Clerk	26 October	£369	1d.
Richardson, Charles	Estate agent	9 September	£148	1d.
Rylah, Josephus Marshall	Accountant	26 August	£961	2s.

Name	*Occupation*	*Date of creditors' meeting*	*Deficiency (Difference between claimed debts and assets)*	*Composition in the £*
Serle, Walter Henry	Secretary	29 August	£10,541	6d.
Smart, Edward Andrew	Solicitor	15 September	£3,626	3d.
Smart, Francis Joseph	Architect	5 October	£24,960	4d.
Stamp, Richard Bulmer	Finance agent	18 July	£11,616	6d.
Stillman, Wilfred L.	Clerk	15 September	£18,673	¼d.
Street, William Parker	Accountant	28 July	£3,405	1d.
Taylor, Charles Frederick	Barrister	4 April	£18,030	2s. 6d.
Turner, William	Bank inspector	6 September	£18,155	3d.
Ward, Alfred	Manager	6 December	£1,316	¼d.
Wilks, Roland W. M.	Estate agent	27 August	£5,045	1d.
Williams, Frederick Augustus	Chemist	28 December	£3,135	1s.
Woolf, Joseph	Solicitor	11 August	£328,845	1d.
Wylie, Robert	Chemist	21 December	£7,586	1s.
Youngman, Henry	Gentleman	22 December	£30,306	1d.

Appendix B

THE SECRET COMPOSITIONS OF 1893

Bailey, William Valentine	Contractor
Burnip, William	Importer
Burns, Andrew	Accountant
Burton, Frederick Andrew	Publican
Butler, Richard Harding	Accountant
Chegwidden, Francis Peter	Dentist
Clarton, Howard Tapley (Application refused)	Land Agent
Coburn, Charles Wheeler	Accountant
Colley, William	Lithographer
Crockett, William George	Salesman
Dempster, Andrew	Engineer
Derham, Thomas Plumley	Solicitor
Derrick, Sidney Thomas	Storekeeper
Dickson, William Hay (Application refused)	Accountant
Donaldson, Thomas Robert	Commission agent
Eagar, Arthur Geoffrey	Accountant
Evans, Margaret Ann	Licensed victualler
Fenner, George Ogilvy	Accountant
Fishbourne, William Yorke	Doctor
Ford, William Henry	Solicitor
Gillespie, James Magregor	Manager
Gillespie, Robert Winton	Clerk
Goldberg, Abraham	Financier

Greenlaw, William	Bank Manager
Groube, George	Civil servant
Harber, Alfred	Shot manufacturer
Harris, John	Dealer
Head, John	Clerk
Herman, Marks	Financier
Hunt, James William	Accountant
Jessup & Clark	Stockbrokers
Kenny, William	Baths proprietor
King, Samuel Grey	Merchant
Kingston, Edward	Unemployed
Laidlaw, William	Clerk
McRorie, Daniel (trading as Taylor & Co.)	Importer
Martin, Joseph Charles	Architect
Morris, John	Stationmaster
Morrison, Philip Alexander	Stockbroker
Paterson, Charles Stewart	Gentleman
Pottinger, John Gale	Advertising agent
Radams Microbe Killer Company	Chemists
Raphael, Julius	Merchant
Ross, George Gordon	Timber merchant
Schofield, James	Woolbroker
Scott, John	Engineer
Shann, Richard	Gentleman
Stevens, John	Manager of Mutual Store
Stewart, Andrew	Printer
Turri, Guiseppe Garibaldi	Patent agent
Vincent, Joseph	Accountant
Woolf, Louis Sydney	Barrister

Appendix C

OCCUPATIONS OF THOSE WHO MADE SECRET COMPOSITIONS IN 1892 AND 1893

Occupation	*1892*	*1893*
Solicitors and barristers	13	3
Stockbrokers and financiers	10	8
Auctioneers and estate agents	8	1
Merchants and produce brokers	8	5
Accountants	7	8
Manufacturers	4	1
Licensed victuallers	3	2
Architects and builders	2	3
Others	30	21
TOTAL	85	52

Appendix D

INSOLVENT STOCKBROKERS OF THE 1890s

Broker	*Liabilities*	*Dividend in the £ (where known)*	*Remarks*
Barker, G. D.	£18,321	¼d.	Heavy loser on Southern Cross Land Co. Ltd
Beckwith, T. W.	9,800	—	Losses on mining shares
Biccard, L. T.	7,806	½d.	
Brock, Henry	5,406	Nil	Left Australia secretly, owing £5,400 to Commercial Bank
Brown, G. G.	10,367	—	Lent £3,000 by South Melbourne Building Society
Butters, J. S.	27,035	½d.	Private composition set aside by Supreme Court
Clarke, C. E.	27,291	6d.	Gaoled for four years on Land Credit Bank frauds
Cosgrave, J. T.	14,754	1s.	Was a shipping manager; borrowed £3,600 from Dalgety & Co. Ltd
Dean, A. F.	31,165	1s.	Borrowed £18,700 from the Bank of Victoria
Dean, J. B.	4,347	1s.	Borrowed £3,000 from Union Bank; heavy loss on mining shares
Evered, H. G.	10,292	1d.	Borrowed £2,600 from Federal Bank; had £4,000 deficiency on Geo. Godfrey's shares
Fiedler, H. M.	3,873	3d.	
Fink, B. J.	1,520,175	½d.	See chapter 39
Greenway, Davenham	17,380	Nil	Lost £27,000 on Commercial Bank shares
Hammill, H.	8,572	9d.	
Henriques, A. A. & F. A.	7,654	5s.	A. A. Henriques went bankrupt again in 1897 and paid 6d. in £1
Hickling, E. R.	£2,560	—	
Jessup & Clark	11,951	2d.	Borrowed heavily from Mercantile Bank
Keane, M. J.	3,843	—	Secretary of Stock Exchange
Lemon, R. H.	58,770	¼d.	Borrowed £12,000 from Land Mortgage Bank
MacLeod, M.	2,410	3d.	Left Australia
Max, S.	4,213	1s.	

Broker	*Liabilities*	*Dividend in the £ (where known)*	*Remarks*
Meadows & Fry	15,526	—	Meadows operated many land schemes through Fry; was held responsible by court
Moore, H. B.	66,183	3d.	Borrowed £22,000 from London Chartered Bank of Australia
Palmer, F. G.	5,310	1d.	Losses on mining
Palmer, W. C.	11,142	—	
Penglase, W.	3,907	—	
Rumball, R. A.	16,472	—	
Russell, M.	13,946	¼d.	Went bankrupt in 1874, 1890, and 1892
Russell, T. C.	31,514	—	Owner of Wirths Hotel; director of Colonial Bank; borrowed £20,000 from Royal Bank; went bankrupt in 1880 and 1892
Walton, J. N.	63,511	—	Borrowed £50,000 from City of Melbourne Bank
Webb, W.	8,246	5s.	Borrowed from Federal Bank
Wilson, H.	8,051	6d.	Borrowed from Colonial Bank; lost on land at Caulfield and Mordialloc

Sources

Most of the original documents concerned with company affairs, private compositions and public insolvencies during the land boom period have been preserved in the Public Record Office of Victoria. This work may have been written, but could never have been officially authenticated, without the use of those documents and the untiring assistance of the Archives staff in locating them.

The author also wishes to acknowledge the assistance of the La Trobe Library staff in locating illustrations for this edition.

On questions of fact, newspaper statements have not been used unless corroborated by official investigations and/or court hearings. Where court evidence was uncontested or borne out by the final judgment, it has been taken as the final authority; but in other circumstances an attempt has been made to indicate both sides of the matter in dispute.

Where newspaper sources are the only ones available, the *Age* has generally been quoted because of its reliability, its practice of printing company reports and court actions almost verbatim, and its freedom from the ultra-conservative bias which afflicted the remainder of the daily press at the time.

In addition, a great deal of reliance may be placed on *Table Talk's* various exposures and comments, which were almost universally borne out by official investigations, court actions, and archival material which has now become available.

The first edition of G.D. Meudell's book *The Pleasant Career of a Spendthrift* is another useful source, trustworthy in most respects, even though Meudell did not have access to official documents when he wrote it. The expurgated edition must be treated with the greatest reserve as an accurate source of historical fact.

H. G. Turner's *History of the Colony of Victoria*, vol. II, is a useful contemporary account of major political events of the day, so long as the reader makes due allowance for Turner's hatred of the radical movement and his own involvement in the land boom.

Bibliography

Adams, Francis, *The Australians*. London, 1893.

Barrett, Bernard, *The Inner Suburbs*. Melbourne, MUP, 1971.

Bate, Weston, *A History of Brighton*. Melbourne, MUP, 1962.

Beever, E.A. and Freeman, R.D., 'Directors of Disaster?' in *Economic Record*, March 1967.

Blainey, Geoffrey, *A History of Camberwell*. Melbourne, 1964.

——, *Gold and Paper, a History of the National Bank of Australasia Limited*. Melbourne, Georgian House, 1958.

Book of Matthias, The. South Melbourne, 1892.

Brodzky, Maurice, *Historical Sketch of the Two Melbourne Synagogues*. Melbourne, 1877.

Butlin, N.G., *Investment in Australian Economic Development 1861–1900*. London, CUP, 1964.

Butlin, S.J., *Australia and New Zealand Bank*. London, Longmans Green, 1961.

Casey, M., et al, *Early Melbourne Architecture 1840 to 1888*. Melbourne, OUP, 1953.

Coghlan, T.A., *Labour and Industry in Australia*. 4 vols. London, 1918.

Cooper, J.B. *The History of Malvern*. Melbourne, 1935.

Davies, Sir Matthew H., *The Mercantile Bank of Australia Limited (in liquidation), Statements by Sir M.H. Davies regarding the report of the Committee of Investigation*. Melbourne, 1892.

Deakin, Alfred, *The Federal Story*. Melbourne, MUP, 1944.

De Hugard, N., *A History of Anzac Hostel*. Melbourne, 1963.

Dibbs, G.R., *The Imperial State Paper on 'The Australian Crisis of 1893'*. Sydney, 1894.

Doyle, E.A., *The Story of the Century*. Melbourne, 1951.

Duffy, F.G., and Higgins, H.B., *The Insolvency Statute, 1871*. Melbourne, 1882.

Dyer, E.J., *Victoria and Its Resources*. Ballarat, 1893.

Eggleston, Sir Frederic, *Life of George Swinburne*. Sydney, 1931.

Fitzpatrick, Brian, *The British Empire in Australia: An Economic History, 1834–1939*. Melbourne, MUP, 1941.

Flanagan, Joseph, *A Sample of the Commercial and Financial Morality (?) of Melbourne*. Melbourne, 1898.

Freeland, J.M., *Architecture in Australia*. Melbourne, Cheshire, 1968.

Grant, J., and Serle, G., *The Melbourne Scene 1803–1956*. Melbourne, MUP, 1957.

Gresswell, D.A., *Report on the Sanitary Condition of Melbourne*. Melbourne, 1890.

Hall, A.R., *The Stock Exchange of Melbourne and the Victorian Economy 1852–1900*. Canberra, ANU Press, 1968.

Harper, Rev. A., *Life of James Balfour*. Melbourne, 1918.

Herman, Morton, *The Architecture of Victorian Sydney*. Sydney, Angus & Robertson, 1956.

Hill, Ernestine, *Water Into Gold*. Melbourne, 1937.

House of Were, The. Melbourne, 1954.

Insolvency Reform. Melbourne, 1895.

Leavitt, T.W.H. (ed.), *Australian Representative Men*. Melbourne, 1887.

——, and Lilburn, W.D. (eds.), *The Jubilee History of Victoria and Melbourne*. Melbourne, 1888.

McIntyre, A.J., *Sunraysia. A Social Survey of a Dried Fruits Area*. Melbourne, MUP, 1948.

Mennell, Philip (ed.), *The Australian Crisis of 1893: Full Text of the Banking Reconstruction Schemes*. London, 1894.

Meudell, George, *The Pleasant Career of a Spendthrift*. London, 1929.

——, *The Pleasant Career of a Spendthrift and His Later Reflections*. Melbourne, 1935.

——, *The Romance of Australian Banking*. Melbourne, 1927.

——, '*The Unofficial History of Victoria*'. (Unpublished MS. in La Trobe Library, Melbourne.)

Mirams, James, *The Present Depression: Its Cause and Cure*. Melbourne, 1892.

——, *A Generation of Victorian Politics*. Melbourne, 1900.

Morris, E.E., *Newer Methods of Charity*. Melbourne, 1895.

Palmer, Vance, *The Legend of the Nineties*. Melbourne, MUP, 1954.

Peel, A.G.V., *The Australian Crisis of 1893*. London, 1894.

Phillips, P.D., *A Treatise on the Insolvency Law in Force in the Colony of Victoria; with an Historical Review of English Bankruptcy Legislation*. Melbourne, 1899.

Proceedings of the Second Australasian Conference on Charity. Melbourne, 1891.

Report of the Royal Commission on Banking Laws. Melbourne, 1887.

Report of the Royal Commission on State Banking. Melbourne, 1895.

Report of the Select Committee on the Companies Act. Melbourne, 1896.

Robb, Emily, *Early Toorak and District*. Melbourne, 1934.

Robertson, E.G., *Ornamental Cast Iron in Melbourne*. Melbourne, Georgian House, 1967.

Rogers, Dorothy, *Lovely Old Homes of Kew*. Melbourne, 1961.

Rosa, S.A., *The Truth About the Unemployed Agitation of 1890*. Melbourne, 1890.

Saunders, David (ed.), *Historic Buildings of Victoria*. Melbourne, Jacaranda, 1966.

Serle, Geoffrey, *The Rush to be Rich*. Melbourne, MUP, 1971.

Shann, Edward, *An Economic History of Australia*. London, 1930.

——, *The Boom of 1890 – And Now*. Sydney, 1927.

Shiels, William, *The World's Depression*. Melbourne, 1894.
Sinclair, W.A., *Economic Recovery in Victoria 1894–1899*. Canberra, 1956.
Sketches of the Poor. Benevolent Society of N.S.W. Sydney, 1892.
Staples, C.R., *Laverton, the New and Model Suburb*. Melbourne, 1886.
Sutherland, Alexander, *Victoria and Its Metropolis,* vol. 1. Melbourne, 1888.
Turner, H.G., *A History of the Colony of Victoria, 1797–1900*. 2 vols. London, 1904.
——, *Insolvency – a Lecture to the Bankers' Institute of Australasia*. Melbourne, 1898.
Victorian Adelaide. Libraries Board of South Australia, 1968.
Vincent, J.E.M., *The Australian Irrigated Colonies*. London, 1887.
Wettenhall, R.L., *Railway Management and Politics in Victoria 1856–1906*. Canberra, 1961.
Women's Work during Fifty Years in connection with the Melbourne Ladies' Benevolent Society, 1845–1895. Melbourne, n.d.
Worthless! The Story of a Melbourne Waif. Melbourne, Try Excelsior Class, 1890.
Yelland, Rev. Charles, *Mission Work in Collingwood*. Melbourne, 1891.

Sources of Illustrations

Title page: Demolition of 'Illoura' in St. Kilda Road, Melbourne, 1964

2–3 *Life*, 6 December 1888.

5 *Australasian Sketcher*, 22 March 1888.

9 *Australasian Builder & Contractors' News*, 21 September 1889. *Melbourne Punch*, 28 June 1888. *Building & Engineering Journal*, 27 May 1893.

10 *Melbourne Views* (Nan Kivell Collection).

11 Leavitt & Lilburn (eds.), *The Jubilee History of Victoria and Melbourne*, vol. 1 (Melbourne, 1888). *Australian Engineering & Building Journal*, 9 March 1889.

13 *Illustrated Australian News*, 29 December 1875.

15 *Building & Engineering Journal*, 7 June 1890. Ibid, 30 May 1891.

19 *Melbourne Punch*, 1888.

20 *Illustrated Sydney News*, 25 January 1879.

22 *Melbourne Bulletin*, 28 August 1885. Troedel Collection, La Trobe Library, vol. 24.

23 Troedel Collection, vol. 24.

25 *Melbourne Punch*, 2 October 1890.

26 *Melbourne Punch*, 10 November 1892.

29 *Bulletin*, 13 August 1892.

30 *Illustrated Australian News*, 1 June 1893.

31 La Trobe Library Historical Collection. *Bulletin*, 14 January 1893.

33 *Australasian Sketcher*, 12 July 1873. Ludwig Becker: *Men of Victoria* (Melbourne, 1856).

38 *Melbourne Punch*, 13 April 1893. *The Blade*, 12 December 1890.

41 *Illustrated Australian News*, 1 July 1892.

42 *The Ant*, 17 March 1892.

47 *Melbourne Punch*, 6 April 1893.

51 *Melbourne Punch*, 4 February 1892.

52 *Melbourne Punch*, 27 September 1888.

54 *Daily Telegraph*, Melbourne, 20 February 1886.

57 *Life*, 29 September 1887.

58 *Melbourne Punch*, 19 July 1888.

60 *Melbourne Punch*, 21 February 1878.

63 *Illustrated Australian News*, 1 March 1892. Ibid, 1 February 1893.

65 *Melbourne Punch*, 1855.

67 *Table Talk Annual*, 1904. *Commercial Album of Victoria* (Melbourne, n.d.). *Melbourne Punch*, 1886.

68 *Illustrated Sydney News*, 27 May 1893.

71 *Australasian Sketcher*, 11 February 1882.

74 *Australasian Sketcher*, 13 March 1880. *The Traveller*, 1 December 1904.

76 *Australasian Sketcher*, 24 March 1887. *Melbourne Punch*, 1888.

79 *Free Lance*, 30 July 1896.

80 *Free Lance*, 7 May 1896.

84 *Melbourne Punch*, 25 December 1890.

85 *Melbourne Punch*, 21 July 1892.

87 *Melbourne Bulletin*, 22 December 1882. *Victoria and Its Metropolis* (Melbourne, 1888). *People's Weekly*, 28 September 1889.

88 *Bulletin*, 18 June 1892.

91 *Melbourne Punch*, 1882.

94 *Melbourne Punch*, 29 October 1874.

95 *Weekly Times*, 31 August 1895. *Leader*, 18 March 1899. Ibid, 18 March 1899.

98–99 *Melbourne Punch*, 12 August 1869.

100 *Australasian Sketcher*, 22 May 1880. *Illustrated Australian News*, 1 August 1891.

102 La Trobe Library Historical Collection. *Melbourne Bulletin*, 1881.

103 *The Jubilee History of Victoria and Melbourne*. *Table Talk*, 17 January 1901.

104 *Illustrated Australian News*, 31 March 1888.

106 *Bulletin*, 1 April 1893.

108 *The Jubilee History of Victoria and Melbourne*.

109 *Illustrated Australian News*, 1 February 1894.

113 J. Thompson: *Illustrated Handbook of Victoria* (Melbourne, 1886).

115 *Melbourne Bulletin*, 6 October 1882. *Table Talk*, 25 April 1901. *Weekly Times*, 11 June 1904.

116 *Illustrated Handbook of Victoria*.

120 *Illustrated Sydney News*, 25 January 1879. *Australasian Builder and Contractors' News*, 24 August 1889.

122 La Trobe Library Historical Collection. *Australian Storekeepers' Journal*, May 1895.

125 *Weekly Times*, 5 November 1892.

127 *Life*, 14 May 1891.

129 *Free Lance*, 2 July 1896.

131 *Bulletin*, 26 August 1893.

135 Brodzky: from a family group taken about 1895. Molesworth: *Leader*, 3 September 1898.

138 Smith (ed.): *Cyclopedia of Victoria* (Melbourne, 1903). *Scientific Australian*, 20 June 1901.

142–3 *Australasian Sketcher*, 12 July 1873.

145 Troedel Collection, vol. 25.

149 *Jubilee History of Victoria and Melbourne*. *Australian Representative Men*.

151 *Illustrated Australian News*, 24 July 1886.
152 *Melbourne Punch*, 27 March 1890.
155 *The Blade*, 12 December 1890.
156 *Melbourne Punch*, 13 February 1890. Ibid, 15 May 1890.
159 *The Book of Matthias* (South Melbourne, 1892). *Jubilee History of Victoria and Melbourne.*
164 *Melbourne Bulletin*, 1881.
165 La Trobe Library Historical Collection.
167 *Australasian Sketcher*, 5 September 1889.
169 *Pictorial Australian*, November 1889.
170 *Melbourne Punch*, 5 June 1890.
172–3 Ibid, 27 April 1893.
175 *Melbourne Bulletin*, 24 July 1885.
176 *Jubilee History of Victoria and Melbourne. Melbourne Bulletin*, 20 March 1890.
178 *Jubilee History. Melbourne Punch*, 27 March 1890.
181 *Building & Engineering Journal*, 7 February 1891.
183 *Melbourne Truth*, 18 July 1903.
184 *Melbourne Punch*, 25 February 1892.
188 *Sands & MacDougalls' Directory. People's Weekly*, 14 September 1889.
191 *Australian Engineering & Building News*, 1 May 1880.
192 *Illustrated Australian News*, 5 March 1887. *Australasian Sketcher*, 13 May 1876.
195 *Illustrated Australian News*, 31 October 1878.
196 *Australasian*, 26 January 1895. *Weekly Times*, 22 October 1892.
197 *Bulletin*, 7 May 1892.
201 *Bulletin*, 2 July 1892.
204 *Melbourne Punch*, 1887.
207 La Trobe Library Historical Collection. *Scientific Australian*, 20 March 1900. *Jubilee History.*
208 *Melbourne Punch*, 28 July 1892.
210 *Australasian Builder & Contractors' News*, 9 August 1890. *Leader*, 24 June 1899.
213 *Australasian*, 29 April 1893. *Melbourne Punch*, 16 September 1886.
217 *Melbourne Punch*, 2 December 1886.
218 *Bulletin*, 10 June 1893.
223 *Australasian Sketcher*, 5 July 1879.
224 *Illustrated Australian News*, 2 July 1894. *Weekly Times*, 2 March 1901. *Melbourne Truth*, 18 July 1903.
225 Troedel Collection, vol. 23.
226 *Melbourne Punch*, 17 December 1903. *Australasian Builder & Contractors' News*, 9 April 1892.
229 La Trobe Library Historical Collection. *Leader*, 19 February 1881. Ibid, 15 April 1899.
230 *Australasian Builder & Contractors' News*, 29 March 1890.
235 *Australasian*, 15 April 1893.
236 *Bulletin*, 22 April 1893.
239 *Weekly Times*, 5 May 1900. *Scientific Australian*, 20 December 1898.
240–1 *Melbourne Punch*, 8 March 1894.
243 *Australian Representative Men.* La Trobe Library Historical Collection.
245 *Victoria and Its Metropolis.*
246 *Weekly Times*, 1 March 1902.
249 Troedel Collection, vol. 24.
250 *Illustrated Australian News*, 2 May 1892. *Jubilee History.*
258 *Illustrated Australian News*, 3 March 1886.
264 *Bulletin*, 8 October 1892.
269 *Victoria and Its Metropolis. Melbourne Punch*, 21 July 1904.
270 Troedel Collection.
273 *Melbourne Punch*, 2 February 1893.
275 *Melbourne Punch*, 10 December 1925. *Life*, 20 August 1891.
279 *Melbourne Punch*, 10 November 1892.
282 *Melbourne Punch*, 26 July 1888.
283 *Australian Representative Men. Australasian Sketcher*, 5 November 1881.
287 *Australasian Builder & Contractors' News*, 20 September 1890.
289 *Building & Engineering Journal*, 18 March 1893.
291 *Australasian Sketcher*, 3 October 1889.
292 *Draper of Australasia*, 27 February 1904. *Cyclopedia of Victoria*, vol. 1. *Melbourne Bulletin*, 8 February 1884.
295 *Australian Representative Men. Jubilee History.*
296 *The Blade*, 28 November 1890.
300 *Melbourne Bulletin*, 6 January 1882. *Building & Engineering Journal*, 12 December 1891.
302 *Building & Engineering Journal*, 3 October 1891.
304 *Melbourne Punch*, 9 June 1887.
305 Troedel Collection, vol. 25.
307 *Australian Representative Men. Table Talk*, 12 June 1902.
308 *Jubilee History.*
316 *RVIA Journal*, May 1907. *London Graphic*, 28 June 1897.
319 *Victoria and Its Metropolis*, vol. 2.
327 *Melbourne Bulletin*, 24 July 1885.
329 *The Ant*, 10 March 1892.
332 *Illustrated Australian News*, 1 February 1893.
336 *Illustrated Australian News*, May 1893. *Leader*, 22 May 1880.
337 *Bulletin*, 20 May 1893. *Melbourne Punch.*
341 *Melbourne Punch*, 1 June 1893.
345 *Melbourne Mirror*, 1 March 1889. *Australasian Sketcher*, 31 July 1880.
348 *Melbourne Punch*, 27 September 1888.
350 *Australasian*, 1 July 1893.
353 *Boomerang*, 26 September 1894.
358 *Melbourne Punch*, 1887. *Cyclopedia of Victoria*, vol. 1.
360–1 *Life*, 3 April 1890.
363 *Melbourne Punch.*
364 Ibid, 11 October 1888.
366 La Trobe Library Historical Collection.
368 *Australasian Sketcher*, 23 April 1881. *Weekly Times*, 9 October 1909. Ibid, 10 December 1898.
371 *Australasian*, 4 July 1896. *Weekly Times*, 27 August 1904.
373 *Jubilee History*, vol. 1. *Illustrated Australian News*, 1 June 1891.
379 *Australasian Sketcher*, 8 October 1881.
380 *Leader*, 5 July 1890. *Cyclopedia of Victoria*, vol. 1.
383 *London Graphic*, 28 June 1897.

All other illustrations from the author's collection.

Index